THE METAMORPHOSES OF THE CIRCLE

THE METAMORPHOSES OF THE CIRCLE

BY GEORGES POULET

TRANSLATED FROM THE FRENCH
BY CARLEY DAWSON AND ELLIOTT COLEMAN
IN COLLABORATION WITH THE AUTHOR

THE JOHNS HOPKINS PRESS
BALTIMORE, MARYLAND

TO ELSA

AUTHOR'S PREFACE

THERE IS NO MORE "accomplished" form than the circle. No form more lasting, either. The circle that Euclid describes and the one which modern mathematics traces, not only resemble one another but merge with one another. The dial of the clock, the wheel of fortune, traverse time intact, without being modified by the variations which they register or determine. Each time the mind wants to picture space, it sets in motion a selfsame curve around a selfsame center. No matter what the degree of angle may be, men of all epochs have used only one compass.

The form of the circle is thus the most constant of those forms thanks to which we are able to figure for ourselves the place, either mental or real, in which we find ourselves, and to locate within it, what surrounds us, or that with which we surround ourselves. Its simplicity, its perfection, its ceaseless universal application, makes it the foremost of those recurring and chosen forms which we discover at the base of all beliefs; and which serve, too, as a structural principle for all types of consciousness. The art historian Focillon wrote about them as follows: "These forms, shaped with a powerful precision and as though stamped in some very hard substance, traverse time without being affected by it," and he added: "What can be altered, is the manner in which they are interpreted by the generations which pour into them diverse varieties of content."

By "Metamorphoses of the Circle" one must therefore understand, not the metamorphosis of a form by definition non-metamorphosable, but the changes of meaning to which it has never ceased to adapt itself in the human mind. These changes of meaning coincide with corresponding changes in the manner by which human beings represent to themselves that which is deepest in themselves, that is to say, the awareness of their relationship with the inner and the outer worlds; their consciousness of space and duration. To retrace a certain number of these parallel metamorphoses is the object of this book. A book written *more geometrico* no doubt, but with a geometry that is altogether subjective.

*　*　*　*

TRANSLATORS' NOTE

With its publication of *The Metamorphoses of the Circle,* The Johns Hopkins Press presents for the first time in English the third volume of the critical thought of Georges Poulet, a man pre-eminent in Europe for the illumination he has brought to the work and action of literature, and the profundity with which he has gauged its effect on man.

In *Studies in Human Time* and its sequel *The Interior Distance* Georges Poulet has added new dimensions to art. In *The Metamorphoses of the Circle* he has encompassed life with a transparency which draws vision both ways, outward and inward, and has given an enduring motion and tone to the highest human endeavors which, still, need their prophets.

Since the completion of the *Metamorphoses,* the author has published in France *L'espace proustien, Le point de départ, Trois essais de mythologie romantique,* and he is now at work on a further volume in the series *Studies in Human Time,* and on a study of modern critical thought. Doctor Poulet is Professor of French at the University of Zurich.

The translators thank the author for his suggestions and revisions, all of which give the text an authenticity and clarity which otherwise would not have been possible.

Because of the nature of the material, it has been decided to collect the notes at the end of the book and to reproduce them as they appeared in the original French edition. For the convenience of English-speaking readers, English quotation marks have been substituted for the French style of the original.

CARLEY DAWSON

October, 1966　　　　　　　　　　ELLIOTT COLEMAN

CONTENTS

INTRODUCTION

THERE is a famous definition of God which, during the centuries, has played an important part, not only in the thought of theologians and philosophers but also in the imagination of poets: *Deus est sphaera cujus centrum ubique.* God is a sphere of which the center is everywhere and the circumference is nowhere.

It is in a pseudohermetic manuscript of the twelfth century, *The Book of the Twenty-four Philosophers,* that this phrase appears for the first time.[1] It is one of the twenty-four definitions of God set forth by an equal number of masters in theology. They themselves, as well as the author of the book, remain anonymous. The twenty-four definitions follow one another in an order whose coherence one must grasp. In particular, the three first definitions are linked with one another in the closest possible manner. Here is the first: *Deus est monas monadem gignens et in se reflectens suum ardorem;* God is a monad which engenders a monad and reflects in Himself His own ardor. The second definition is that of God being a sphere, of which the center is everywhere, and the circumference nowhere. The third presents itself as follows: *Deus est totus in quolibet sui;* God is entirely complete in every part of Himself.

One sees the tie that unites these three propositions. If God as the Father begets an image of Himself, who is the Son, the love that has made Him create this image of Himself, returns it to Him identical. The Father reflects Himself in the Son, the Son reflects Himself in the Father, and this reciprocity of love is nothing more nor less than the third person of the Trinity, the Holy Ghost. The cycle is complete. The infinite activity that binds the three Persons constitutes an immense sphere, at every point of which the same plenitude can be found. In the divine sphere, which has no circumference, every point is identical with every other point, every moment is identical with every other moment. God is wholly Himself in whatever part of His Being or His existence that one may consider; or more precisely, there is in God no division of parts, no succession of moments in time, but an absolute simplicity and an absolute simultaneity. One can therefore say that in God the immensity of the circumference can be found again in the unity of the central point, or that the totality of His Being is present in whatsoever fraction of time or space one may, arbitrarily, distinguish in Him.

In other terms, the infinite sphere can be interpreted as a figuration of the divine immensity, but it can also be interpreted as a figuration of that other divine attribute, eternity. From this point of view, it is nothing else but a metaphoric transposition of another celebrated definition of eternity, that of Boethius: *Aeternitas est interminabilis vitae tota simul et perfecta possessio;* Eternity is a perfect and simultaneous possession of a limitless existence.[2]

In defining eternity in this way, Boethius was doing nothing more than to repeat the words of a long succession of philosophers; from Parmenides, who affirms that the Absolute Being (represented by him in the form of a sphere) is "altogether present in the Now;"[3] to Plotinus, for whom eternity is "a life that persists in its identity always present to itself in its totality . . . like a point in which all lines meet."[4] Invariably the definitions of eternity conjoin with two terms and two notions which are contradictory, and that only the divine life can reconcile: *omou pan, totum simul, trestout ensemble, insieme tutto, allemittenander, altogether at once,* one of these terms expressing the totality of time, the other, on the contrary, the absence of time or instantaneousness. Eternity is a *nunc stans,* an eternal moment, a simple point of duration, but in which all the points of the circle of this duration find themselves present and conjoined.

This double quality of eternity is clearly explained by Saint Bonaventure in a text that has equal reference to the definitions of Boethius as to *The Book of the Twenty-four Philosophers:*

> If one says that eternity signifies a measureless existence, one must reply that one does not thereby exhaust the meaning of the word "eternity"; because this means not only interminability, but also simultaneousness; and if, on the one hand, by the mode of interminability one must understand an intelligible circumference, without beginning and without end, on the other hand by the mode of simultaneousness one must understand simplicity and indivisibility that are the modes of the center; and these two things are affirmed concerning the Divine Being at one and the same time, because He is at once simple and infinite; and so it is that one must understand the circularity in eternity.[5]

As an infinite circumference, eternity, therefore, is the vastest possible circle of duration; as the center of this circumference it is the fixed point, and unique moment, which is simultaneously in harmony with all the circumferential points of this duration.

Therefore, he who wishes to hold in mind these two contradictory properties of divine eternity must in some manner project his own mind in two opposite directions. He must expand his imagination beyond measure. He must also contract it in the extreme. He must identify himself with the immense circumference that embraces all duration, but also with the central point that excludes all duration. He must transport himself simultaneously both toward the circumference and toward the center.

It is this double movement of the mind that we see represented in Dante's *Divine Comedy.*

In Canto 14 of *Paradise* Dante makes use of the following image:

> From the center to the circumference, and likewise from the circumference to the center, the water moves in a round vase, according as it is smitten from without or from within.[6]

As the water in a receptacle flows indifferently either toward the periphery or toward the center, the soul of the poet moves toward a God Who encompasses everything, as well as toward a God Who is at the center of all things. This dual character of an absolute centrality and an absolute circularity, which the Dantean Godhead possesses, manifests itself in a series of passages that culminate in the beatific vision of God in the form of both a circle and a point. God, says Dante, is *il punto, A cui tutti li tempi son presenti,* a point at which all times are present;[7] *Ove s'appunta ogni Ubi ed ogni Quando,* to which all When and all Where are focussed.[8] An evident rapport links these two passages of the *Paradise* to a chapter of the *Vita Nova,* where the god of Love appears to Dante and says to him: "I am the center of a circle to which all points of the circumference are equidistant; you are not;"[9] probably signifying by these words that differing from Dante, whose thought is limited to the present moment, the divine thought, center of all moments, comprises the future as well as the past. This is the identical doctrine of Saint Thomas Aquinas:

> Eternity is always present to whatever time or moment of time it may be. One can see an example of it in the circle: a given point of the circumference, even though indivisible, nevertheless cannot coexist with all the other points, because the order of succession constitutes the circumference; but the center that

is outside the circumference, is immediately connected with any given point of the circumference whatever.[10]

> Eternity resembles the center of the circle; even though simple and indivisible, it comprehends the whole course of time, and every part of it is equally present.[11]

It is, without doubt, to these two passages that another schoolman of the period, Pierre Auriol, refers, when he writes:

> There are those who use the image of the center of the circle, in its relation to all points of the circumference; and they affirm that this is similar to the *Nunc* of eternity in its connection with all the parts of time. By which they mean that eternity actually coexists with the whole of time.[12]

From these texts it follows that for Dante, as for most of the thinkers of his time (Duns Scotus is the only exception), the position occupied by the central point of the circle represents not only the unity and fixity of divine duration but the multiplicity of simultaneous rapports that it holds with the peripheral and mobile duration of creatures. Eternity is not simply the pivot around which time turns; it is also that point where, like the rays of the circle, the events of the past and the future converge and unite in the consciousness of God. This is what the Neo-Platonist Proclus was one of the first to explain in a passage with which the Middle Ages were familiar:

> If the center could have a knowledge of the circle, this knowledge would be central and essential. Thus simple knowledge, which is that of Providence, indivisibly perceives all the parts, small or great.[13]

This passage may well have been in the mind of Gerson, when he wrote:

> Let us imagine a center endowed with a cognitive force similar to that of the angels, and each ray endowed with the same power. It will follow that every ray comprehends all the points in its course, not only in so far as they are successive stages of the latter, but also as definite objects of knowledge.[14]

Eternity is therefore the cognitive center, where, in the unity of divine omniscience, the entire succession of times coexists. "At the center," says Denys the Areopagite, "all the lines from the same circle make only one; this point possesses in itself all these lines not only merged one with another, but also with this unique starting point from which they emanate."[15]

But if all things coexist in God, it is not only because they are thought by Him and merged in Him. God is not uniquely a center of knowledge; He is also a center of force. When Dante describes the divine point to which all times are present, he adds that from this point "light radiates" and on this point "heaven and all nature, depend."[16] This dependence is specifically ontological. Heaven, all nature, the whole of creation in its spatial and temporal unfolding, have existence only because everywhere and always the action from a creative center causes them to exist. Doubtless this creative action is, essentially, spatial, since every place in the universe is at the receiving end of its action. But it is also temporal, since every new moment is also the effect of this continuous creation. God possesses time not solely by His omniscience, but also by His omnipotence. He is present in all times by the double exercise of His cognitive power and His creative power. In one way as in the other, His radiating action immediately and simultaneously attains to all the points of duration as to all those of space. In Dante's poetry, exactly as in Neo-Platonic thought, God is a point that infinitely enlarges Itself, a radiating seat of energy, which diffuses Itself excentrically, universally:

> *E si distende in circular figura*
> *In tanto, che la sua circonferenza*
> *Sarebbe al sol troppo larga cintura.*[17]

(And it spreads forth in a circular figure
So far that its circumference
Would be too wide a girdle for the sun.)

But of all the significations that Dante attributes to the divine Point, perhaps there is none more profound than that by which he assimilates it to the Trinity. God is a unique center of activity, but this activity is the same one which brings about the generation of the Word, and the procession of the Holy Ghost. Twice, in his final stanzas of the *Paradise,* Dante makes allusion to the mystery of the Trinity; the first time under the form of a triple arrow shot from a bow of three cords; and in the final lines of the poem, precisely under the form of the divine Point which dilates, and which, in dilating, produces three circles. This image has behind it a long tradition. One of the masters of Saint Augustine, the rhetor Marius Victorinus, made use of it in a writing designed to refute the heresy of Arius. In order to describe the Logos, identical to the One and yet distinct from it, Marius Victorinus imagined a sphere of which the diameter was so small that the circumference coincided with the center. "In this case," he wrote, "the extremities and the center are one within the other; . . . what exists simultaneously, without distance, constitutes the first sphere, perfect, unique of its kind; all the other spheres merely attempt to approach it."[18] Likewise, in certain schiastic passages of Saint Augustine, one can see a verbal representation of the circular movement by which the Son is found in the Father, and the Father in the Son: *"In pricipio erat verbum, et verbum erat apud Deum, et Deus erat verbum."*[19] These variations on the famous passage of the Gospel according to Saint John, have no other purpose than to form a circle of words equivalent to the spiritual circle constituted by the Trinity. Besides, it is in no other way that Christoforo Landino, in the fifteenth century, explains the episode of the third circle in the final passage of the *Divine Comedy:* "The poet," he says, "expresses here a unique essence in the three Persons by means of the circular figure. Many centuries before, Mercure Trismégiste had so defined God as a perfect sphere, in as much as the knowledge of God is the knowledge of Himself. Consequently, this knowledge proceeds from self to self, like the circle, without beginning and without end."[20]

But the best illustration of the triple circle of the Trinity is found in the writings of the German mystic Heinrich Suso:

> It is said by a wise teacher that God, as regards to His Godhead, is like a very wide ring in which the center is everywhere and the circumference nowhere. Now imagine the following image: If a heavy stone is thrown with great force into a sheet of still water, a ring is formed in the water. And of itself this ring makes another, and this other, a third. . . . The three circles represent the Father, the Son, and the Holy Ghost. In this deep abyss, the divine nature in the Father speaks forth and begets the Son. . . . This spiritual and superessential begetting is the plenary cause of all things, and of all souls that come into existence.[21]

In the center and divine circle one must therefore see in the first place the representation of the internal action of the Trinity; but one must also see a prefiguration of the external movement, no less circular, by which this divine activity spreads Itself outward, in order to surround Itself with a new series of circles, which are those of creation. Creation is the common work of the three Persons; the mystery of their operations perpetuates itself everlastingly. From this point of view, every point in space, every moment of time, becomes the eternal place and moment where the Father begins once again to engender the Son, and the Son lovingly to reflect Himself in the Father. Any place and moment of time form the seat and center of the Divinity. Such is the constant doctrine of the Middle Ages: "Everywhere is the center of thy power," Saint Bonaventure says to God.[22] No one affirms this doctrine with greater insistence than Master Eckhart, in the works in which the two celebrated definitions of God, as a monad and a sphere, are ceaselessly interwoven one with another, to signify that in every moment and in every place, God constitutes Himself the center of all moments and all places. To the first two definitions of God, taken from *The Book of the Twenty-four Philosophers,* Eckhart is fond of adding the third, the one according to which *"Deus est totus in quolibet sui,"* "God is fully in every part of Himself." Already, in his *Itinerarium Mentis,* Saint Bonaventure said something approaching it:

> *Quia aeternum et presentissimum, ideo omnes durationes ambit et intrat, quasi simul existens earum centrum et circumferentia. Quia simplicissimum et maximum, ideo totum intra omnia, et totum extra omnia, ac per hoc est sphaera intelligibilis, cujus centrum est ubique, et circumferentia nusquam.*[23]

(Because God is eternal and absolutely actual, He enfolds all durations and exists simultaneously in all their moments as their center and circumference. And because He is infinitely simple and infinitely great, He is wholly within all and without all; and it is for this reason that He is an intelligible sphere of which the center is everywhere and the circumference nowhere.)

But in Eckhart these two formulas: *"Deus est totus in quolibet sui," "Deus est simplicissimus et maximus, ideo totus intra omnia et totus extra omnia,"* are fused together and take on a more radical significance. *"In Divinis,"* says Eckhart, *"quodlibet est in quolibet et maximus in minimo."*[24] "In divine things, everything is in everything else and the maximum is in the minimum." This formula was to become the basis of the philosophy of Nicolas de Cusa. It was to have an immense influence on Leonardo da Vinci and Giordano Bruno. But one can already see an application or a prefiguration in the poetry of Dante. At the very end of the *Divine Comedy,* when he is describing the moment when he fixes his look upon the divine Point, Dante adds:

Un punto solo m'è maggior letargo
Che venticinque secoli alla impresa
Che fe'Nettuno ammirar l'ombra d'Argo.[25]

(One moment only is for me a longer lethargy
Than twenty-five centuries were to the undertaking
That made Neptune admire the share of Argos.)

No doubt the extraordinary beauty of these lines is owing, in the first place, to the force of the metaphor. Even when distended beyond measure in its duration, the most glorious undertaking of which mankind had the remembrance is nothing by comparison to the instant where, in spite of time and forgetfulness, one remembers having seen God. But by a most bold and unusual play of words, Dante, in this passage, deliberately confounds two points and two instants. *Un punto solo* is evidently, here, the Italian expression *un punto di momento,* an instant of duration. But it is in this point of human duration that it has been given precisely to Dante to apprehend the divine Point, the point of eternity. Consequently, when he arrives at the end of his long periplus, Dante arrives at a point that is at once divine, and the point at which he apprehends the divine. The final object of the poem is no longer an object around which one can turn and toward which one tends; it is an object one possesses, a point with which one coincides. And if one coincides with it, that is because it is no longer now an exterior and remote object. The divine Point is the very center of the soul, it is God interiorly possessed in a human moment.

One can therefore see here in Dante the veiled but striking expression of a doctrine that, precisely in the same era of time, acquires in the mystic writers its whole force. God is a point, because He is a center, not only of the universe, but of the soul. The synderesis, *l'apex mentis,* the *Seelengrund,* the *Fünkelein,* all these expressions profusely employed by the mystics, signify that the maximum is in the minimum, the infinity of the divine sphere is in the infinite minuteness of the center, and that this center is indeed that of the soul. Because God is an immense sphere of which the plenitude is contained in a center everywhere present, the soul is a center that contains this sphere. Such is the unanimous tradition of mystics from Eckhart to Madame Guyon.

For example, Harphius, the great intermediary between German mysticism and Spanish mysticism, writes as follows:

The soul is called spirit with regard to what there is most intimate and most elevated in its powers; for the powers of the soul are united in the mind as in their sources, and it is from this source that they expand outward, as sun rays do beyond the circle of the sun, just as it is into this source that they flow back. This center is situated in the soul, and in it shines the true image of the Trinity; and it is so noble that no suitable name may properly be found for it; and one cannot speak of it except by circumlocutions.[26]

Thus the movement by which the soul approaches God is centered motion that takes place in the interior of the soul itself. This is explained by another mystical writer, this time of the seventeenth century, the Englishman Peter Sterry, in terms that irresistibly make one think of the movement—at first excentric, and then concentric—followed by Dante in his poem:

There is a Fountain of Life, where endlessly springs up in an unconfined Circle, in a bottomless depth, forms of glory innumerable, one within another. . . . The Soul circles round this Deep of the Divine mind, but as one Spirit encompasses another without circumscription, extension or distance. Yet the soul, without confinement or adequation, contains in its Unity and Center this glorious Deep of the Divine Mind . . . as the Unity of its Unity, the Center of its Center.[27]

So it appears that Dante's journey, like all mystical journeys, is an inward one. Its final goal is a God in which the soul sinks itself because it sinks into itself: "O divine eternity," exclaims the French mystic Pierre Poiret, "call us back from our dispersion amidst passing temporal vanities, and gather us into the still center of the heart where we can give place and attention to the all-powerful and ineffable operations of thy manifestation, of which one moment is worth more than all the duration of time."[28]

This still center of the heart is reached by Dante in a moment which is at the same time the final moment of his journey, and of his poem. All his voyage, all his poem, constitute only the succession of movements by which the mind finally accedes to a place and to a moment where there is no longer either movement, succession, or dimension. Then the extreme of grandeur coincides with the extreme of smallness. "The eternal center," says Jokob Boehme, "and the Birth of Life, and Substantiality, are everywhere. Trace a circle no larger than a dot, the whole birth of Eternal Nature is therein contained."[29]

Moreover, this final coincidence of eternity with the moment of vision, and the immense sphere of God with the narrow sphere of the creature, is foreshadowed in the final lines of the *Divine Comedy,* in the passages which celebrate the most striking example of this conjunction of the immense infinite with the infinitely small. Just before the final vision of the poem, Dante makes Saint Bernard pronounce the eulogy on the Mother of God. *"Nel ventre tuo si raccese l'Amore."*[30] Love, rekindled in the Virgin's womb, is the immense sphere of the divinity mysteriously reappearing in the narrow sphere of a human body. The Incarnation, also, is a manifestation of the maximum in the minimum, and the infinite in the finite. It is of this geometrical paradox that one of Dante's inspirers, Alain de Lille, sings, in a hymn that dates from the end of the twelfth century:

> *Sphaeram claudit curvatura*
> *Et sub ipsa clauditur.*
> *In hac Verbi copula*
> *Stupet omnis regula.*[31]

One of the most beautiful examples of this inscription of the divine sphere in the sphere of humanity is found in the *Roman de la Rose.* Just after having defined eternity, in the same terms as Boethius, as

> Possession of life that by the end cannot be seized,
> Altogether at once, without division,

Jean de Meung introduces in his poem an episode of primary importance. Profoundly different from divine eternity that possesses at once all the elements that constitute it, human existence moves from moment to moment, without any of them ever attaining plenitude. Everything changes, everything perishes, nothing endures. Alone, in creation, forms remain. But, again, what will guarantee their permanency? To answer this question, Jean de Meung recalls first a famous passage of the Timeus: that where the demiurge, addressing the interior divinities, whose mission is precisely that of maintaining the permanence of forms, reminds them that they themselves have no permanence, and that it is from Him alone that they obtain their stability:

> Par nature mourir pourreiz
> Mais mon vueil ja ne mourreiz.

(By nature die could you
But by my will never will you.)

The only fixity that there is in the universe, therefore, finally hangs on divine good will. Human reason cannot go further. Vainly it tries to find in itself some grounds for belief that God's benevolence toward His creation will always endure. Consequently, to escape the anguish into which he is thrown by the thought that a new divine decree could hand over the world to the most radical vicissitude, one must lift oneself up to the contemplation of revealed truths and remind oneself that the good will of God was manifested once and for all, in the most extraordinary manner, in the mystery of the Incarnation. This reveals to man that he is firmly tied to the eternal will. For eternity has incarnated itself in time and the infinite sphere within the boundaries of the human sphere. Such is the assurance the Virgin possesses:

> Car el sot des qu'el le portait,
> Dont au porter se confortait,
> Qu'il iert l'espere merveillable
> Qui ne peut estre terminable,
> Qui par touz leus son centre lance,
> Ne leu n'a la circonference . . .

> (For she knew as soon as she carried him,
> Whose carrying was comforting,
> That he was the marvelous sphere
> That can never be terminated,
> That midst all places its center throws,
> Whose circumference is in no place . . .)

Then, linking to the mystery of the Incarnation the mystery of the Trinity that precedes and announces it, Jean de Meung sets, as it were, within the symbol of the circle, the symbol of the triangle, in a way typical of all emblematists of the Middle Ages:

> Qu'il iert li merveilleus triangles
> Dont l'unite fait les treis angles.

> (There are the marvelous triangles
> Whose oneness equals three angles.)

Finally the two symbols appear, completely merged one within the other:

> C'est le cercles trianguliers,
> C'est li triangles circuliers
> Qui en la vierge s'ostela.[32]

(This is the triangular circle,
This is the circular triangle
That within the Virgin found its home.)

This recalls a Latin hymn attributed to Philippe de Greves:

Centrum capit circulus
Quod est majus circulo,
In centro triangulus
Omni rectus angulo,
Sed fit minor angulus
Unus de triangulo,
Dum se mundi figulus
Inclusit in vasculo.[33]

What is striking in these two poems is the metaphysical paradox that situates the infinite in the finite; but there is also the ethical paradox that places the ultimate of grandeur in the ultimate of humiliation. From this point of view, the spectacle of the incarnated Christ is no different from that of the Christ descended into the lowest part of creation, that is to say, Hell. In one case as in the other, the mind finds itself in the presence of grandeur reduced to the most exiguous dimensions. When, in the first part of his *Divine Comedy*, Dante was describing his own descent into Hell, he could not but have thought of that other descent at the narrowest and most foul place in the universe. "It is not only on the surface of the earth," writes Saint Bonaventure, "that the Christ came, it is in its profoundest center, 'in the entrails of the center and in the heart of the earth' that He worked for our salvation; for, after His crucifixion, his soul descended into Hell and restored the voided celestial thrones. It is in this profound center that salvation lies, for he who draws away from the center of humility is lost." [34]

Descended into the womb of a virgin, or into the womb of the world, the Christ is that Immensity that renounces Its celestial expanse, the sphere reduced to a "center of humility."

Perhaps the most beautiful passages on this center of humility and the incarnation of the circle are to be found in the seventeenth century, in the writers of the Counter-Reformation:

"We adore," writes Bérulle, "an infinite God, but One Who has made Himself finite, and is bound, Himself, in the circumference of human nature."[35]

Johann Scheffler similarly says:

Als Gott verborgen lag in eines Mädgleins Schoss,
Da war es, da der Punct den Kreiss in sich beschloss.[36]

(When God lay hidden in the womb of a Virgin
Then the Point contained the Circle.)

One of the most impassioned poems on the incarnation of the circle is that of the English Jesuit Richard Crashaw, *In the Glorious Epiphanie of Our Lord God.* It is a hymn sung by the three Magii who, from differing regions of the earth, have converged toward that central place where the Saviour of the universe was born:

> To Thee, thou Day of night! thou East of West!
> Lo, we at last have found the way
> To Thee, the world's great universal East.
> The Generall and indifferent Day.
> All circling point. All centring sphear . . .
> O little All! in thy embrace
> The world lyes warm, and likes its place.
> Nor does his full Globe fail to be
> Kist on Both his cheeks by Thee.[37]

There is no trait more characteristic of the baroque imagination than this interesting movement by which the immensity of the universe becomes a toy in the hands of a child, while the smallness of the child becomes the immensity of a God Who embraces the world.

But the image of the God Who embraces the world should recall to us also another aspect, and perhaps the most important, of our theme. For the doctrine of the Incarnation, as that of the Trinity, implies a God Who is not content with being the center and the circumference of the universe, but Who, from His center, animates and peoples, in the most fecund way, the space that His circumference contains.

This aspect of the theme is admirably described in a Spanish poem dating from the beginning of the seventeenth century. The author is the conceptist Alonso de Bonilla:

> God is the original circumference
> Of all spherical figures,
> Since rings, orbs, circles and altitudes
> Are included at the center of His essence.
> From this infinite center of knowledge,
> Issue immense lines of creatures,
> Living sparks of the pure light
> Of this inaccessible omnipotence.
> Virgin, if God is the center and the abyss
> From which emerge such exterior lines
> And if Thy womb includes God in it,

> Thou art the center of God's own center
> So much so, that at the issuance of Thy womb
> God is a line issued from out of Thy center.[38]

Center that is prolonged in the line, circle begot from the radiating center. Long before, the Pythagoreans had insisted on the generating force of the point. For Plotinus the center is "the father of the circle."[39] For Scot Erigène it is "the initial universal point."[40] So also, the Jewish Cabbala and Arabian thought make of the central point the starting point from which the world has developed. All medieval philosophy of light is a long commentary on the spherical diffusion of every luminous point. *"Omne agens multiplicat suam virtutem sphaerice."* [41] This phrase of Grosseteste is applicable to all activity, but, first of all, to God. God is a light propagating Itself, a force that multiplies and diffuses Itself. None has better described this phenomenon of Divine expanding creation than Master Eckhart:

> There is a reflection and a conversion
> of God within and upon Himself, and an
> installation and a fixation of God in God.
> But there is also a seething up and an overflowing
> of God out of Himself. . . .[42]

Therefore, it is easy to perceive that from Eckhart, precisely, this is no longer a static God, settled in Himself, Who fascinates all intellects; this is, on the contrary, a dynamic God, seething and overflowing. In other terms, what—about the time of, and throughout the Renaissance—increasingly absorbs the attention of theologians and philosophers, is less the spectacle of a Divinity considered in Itself, than that of His action on the world. Following Nicolas de Cusa, Ficino, Pico, Patrizzi, Campanella, and above all, Bruno in Italy, Charles of Bouelles, Pelletier of Mans, Ramus, La Boderie, Yves of Paris in France, Paracelsus, Kepler, Boehme, Kircher, Leibniz in Germany, the Platonists of the Cambridge School, and the poets called "metaphysical" in England, all return, no less indefatigably than the scholastics of the Middle Ages, to the emblem of the circle and the center; but what strikes them in this image is the circle perceived as a dilation of the center. The divine reality is no longer situated at two extremes, in an invisible circumference and within an ineffable central point; it is everywhere present and moving in the cluster of activities that It projects in every direction around Itself. As Robert Fludd later writes:

So that from God all things did flow and spring, namely out of a secret and hidden nature to a revealed and manifest condition, from an unknown estate into an evident and known existence; from a pure Archetypal simplicity into a real type or similitude; from a radical fountain into a Sea, and from a mere point into a circle of circumference; verifying that saying of the wise Philosopher: God is the centre of everything, whose circumference is nowhere to be found.[43]

This universal explication and manifestation of the divine in nature haunts the imagination of the men of the Renaissance: "God overflows everywhere"[44] said Pontus de Tyard. And Ronsard:

> Dieu est partout, partout se mêle Dieu . . .
> Car Dieu partout en tout se communique . . .[45]
>
> (God is everywhere, everywhere God mingles . . .
> For God everywhere, in all things, communicates Himself . . .)

Finally, Ramus:

God fills everything with His perpetual power, and nowhere and never is He filled up. Thus a certain philosopher has rightly said of Him: God is a sphere of which the center is everywhere, and the periphery nowhere.[46]

After all these texts one can see what a profound transformation the symbol of the infinite sphere underwent at the time of the Renaissance. This is no longer transcendence, but divine immanence which is placed in strong relief. God being the center everywhere, is everywhere a diffusive and repletive force. To employ Henry More's expression, every place and every moment appear as "a reiteration of the divine center."[47] "The divine center is in every place," says Marsile Ficin, "as the virtue of God, distributed in His creatures, is in every minute particle of the universe."[48]

God, infinite center, is not a contracted God, limited to the center; it is a God Who diffuses Himself from this center: "Wherefore although some novelists," writes the English philosopher Cudworth, "make a contracted idea of God, consisting of nothing else but will and power, yet His nature is better expressed by some in this mystical or enigmatic representation of an infinite circle, whose inmost centre is simple goodness, the radii and expanded area thereof all comprehending and immutable wisdom, the exterior periphery of interminate circumference, omnipotent will or activity, by which every thing without God is brought forth into existence."[49]

Father Mersenne says the same: "God is an indivisible center whose irradiation expands up to the periphery of all things."[50]

But if every point of the universe thus reveals itself as a center from which God irradiates Himself, there follows that man can also place himself in every one of these points to contemplate from around about himself the magical spectacle of this divine irradiation. "The soul is a kind of center," says Giordano Bruno.[51] It is a center, not alone, as the mystics believe, because in it God has His favorite dwelling-place, but because this divine place of residence is also the converging place for all cosmic phenomena. "The whole universe surrounds man," says Paracelsus, "as the circle surrounds the point."[52]

This new central position occupied by man has nothing in common with the median position occupied by the earth in ancient cosmology, now disappearing. There is no longer any question of a fixed point, the lowest of all, placed at the center of the finite and finished world. What is now in question is any point, since it is in any point that thought can place itself to contemplate the cosmic spectacle and operations that God accomplishes in creation. In whatever situation man may place himself, in whatever moment that he thinks, he is always able to discover himself in the center of an infinite universe, that God develops around him so that he shall be conscious of this very universality. "I have placed thee at the center of the world," says God to man in a celebrated discourse by Pic de la Mirandole, "so that thou shalt more conveniently consider everything that is in the world."[53] "The soul is the center of nature,"[54] says Marsile Ficin. And Charles de Bouelles: "Man is a nothing facing the all . . . , so that he shall become the eye of everything, the mirror of nature, detached and separated from the order of things, placed far from everything to be the center of everything."[55]

The soul, like God, is therefore a center of infinite information. But it is also, like God, a center of force. The mystical doctrine of the synderesis transforms itself into a doctrine of psychic diffusion: "From the depths of thy being," says the Spanish mystic Juan de Los Angeles, "from the center or the point of thy soul thy powers proceed in a manner no different from that by which the rays come from the sun."[56] Cudworth was to say the same: "This is an ever bubbling fountain in the centre of the soul, an elater, or spring of motion . . ."[57] There is in the soul a "secret centrality" that manifests and develops itself by a "free dilation."[58]

But how to imagine this "free dilation," unless as the movement by which man profits by every moment and every place to enfold in his gaze the universe that the divine force has precisely disposed around this moment and this place? Everywhere is the center of the divine activity. Everywhere too is the center of the activity inherent to the soul. Neither one nor the other has limits. "The soul will become an immense sphere"[59] exclaims Campanella. "My soul is an infinite sphere in a center,"[60] proclaims Thomas Traherne. The infinite sphere has now become the symbol, not only of God, but of man. The infinite sphere is nothing now but the field encompassed by human consciousness.

At this point we can stop and consider the road traversed. In passing through the ages, the great emblem of the center and the sphere has singularly changed in meaning. Now it no longer is exclusively applicable to God, but also to man. It is man who, equally with God, discovers himself to be center and infinite sphere. Even more, it is every moment, every place where man finds himself, that constitutes itself as the ever renewed center of this infinite sphericity; for every place and every moment offers to man a new point of view. As he places himself therein, he perceives around him, a universe no less infinite than the universe glimpsed in the next place or in the preceding moment. So much so, that the world being composed of an infinity of places and of moments, is an infinity of worlds, all infinite, that the human consciousness apprehends everywhere and always. Such is the richness that relativist thought discovers in the cosmos. This richness appears to him as a manifestation of the divine Being. But let the figure of God, as will happen a century later, withdraw itself to the horizon of thought, let the variety of the world appear in itself, stripped of all theological signification, then the symbol of the center and the sphere will reduce itself to a simple perspective diagram. Man in the eighteenth century will no longer embrace within his gaze the sphere of God, but the sphere of scientific knowledge. The divine encyclic will become a simple encyclopedia.

THE METAMORPHOSES OF THE CIRCLE

I

THE RENAISSANCE

WHEN DANTE describes the divinity as it appears to him at the end of his celestial journey, he represents it under the form of a point around which concentric circles are disposed. This is the *nunc stans,* the immobile point of eternity, which the flowing points of time surround, and to which they are related, as the points of a circumference are related to the center. It is also the absolute minimum, the monad that in the simplicity of its principle contains the totality of numbers and the absolute maximum of extent.

If the divine point appears at the end of the *Divine Comedy* as the terminal point of this great poem (given that God is the end term of all spiritual life), it is striking that it should appear as the initial point of a poem no less ambitious, but whose design is the exact reverse of that of Dante's, the *Microcosm* of Maurice Scève. In fact, Dante wished to describe the movement by which, finally, everything ends in God. Scève's objective, on the contrary, is to describe the means by which, originally, all comes from God. Scève's God is no longer, like that of Dante, the God of the final cause; He is that of the efficient cause. As, later, in the *Semaines* of Du Bartas, the *Microcosm* of Scève proceeds to unfold the more and more vast effects of a first causative act, which, primarily, is seized and apprehended in its initial and central reality. So it would seem that it is in this sense that one must understand the first lines of the *Microcosm.* They describe a God Who has not yet created the world, Whose creative force has not yet been deployed, a God enclosed and condensed within Himself, a God-point:

> The First in His nothingness enclosed, was hidden in His All,
> Beginning of Self without principle, and without end,
> Unknown, excepting to Himself, knowing all things

1

> As of Himself, by Himself, in Himself all encompassed
> Mass of Deity, in Itself amassed,
> Without place, and without space's measured limits,
> Which nowhere else could stay than in Its own . . .

The meaning of these lines is clear if one compares them to Pythagorean and Neo-Platonic texts, certain of which have already been cited, on the generative force of the point. One should remember Plotinus saying of the center that it is "the father of the circle." By the same token, for Hierocles, commenting on the Golden Verses, the center is "the starting point of the circle."[1] Proclus was to say: "The circle is everywhere centrally present in the center; for the center is the cause, and the circle is what has been caused by it."[2] Lastly, according to Damascius, another Neo-Platonist, "the center contains at one and the same time all its rays, but anteriorly to their separation."[3] In a famous passage, already referred to and on which the whole of the Middle Ages had commented, Denis the Areopagite takes up this comparison. In Chapter V of the *Divine Names,* God is successively identified by him with the unity in which all numbers pre-exist, and with the central point of the circle, where "all the rays, reassembled by one and the same union, simultaneously exist."[4] The "First in His nothingness enclosed," of Maurice Scève, the "mass of Deity, in Itself amassed," is the Pythagorean or Plotinian monad; it is also the central point through a processus of disimplication, there will unfold itself the cosmic circle which was coiled up within it: *Essence in itself replete with latent infinity.*

God is therefore for Scève the point from which swells and blossoms the sphere of the universe. This is the very doctrine held by his friend Jacques Pelletier of Mans in a whole series of poetic and theoretical writing.

For example in Sonnet 42 of *l'Amour des amours:*

> O All enclosed in thy roundness!
> O clear height! O black depth!
> O one! O two! from which the entire deed starts up action . . .[5]

"Unity, which represents the Point in Geometry," Pelletier writes in his *Arithmétique,*[6] "is not Number, but only the origin of Number." And in *l'Usage de géométrie:* [7] ". . . the Center of the Circle is to be considered a wonder of its kind. Which center, though it sits in the true midst and, as do points, seems to be bereft of parts, for all that, potentially, has the greatest capacity. For the innumerable lines which find their termination in the Circumference are equally drawn from the Center, and these likewise that are led from the Circumference all terminate in the Center: which renders it infinite in posse, as is the Circumference."

But the passage by Pelletier, where in the most striking manner the poetry of centrality and circularity is expressed, is found in the poem *La science,* in Folio 59 of his *Oeuvres poétiques intitulées louanges:*

> The Point, which is everywhere, and stands up in the now
> The One, that is in all Number, and beyond it subsisting,
> This great polished Circle, and this Center from which spring
> All the lines to the Ring and to it are connected,
> Infinite in effect, finite in appearance,
> Of which the Center is everywhere, and the Circumference . . .

The most curious of all in the texts of Scève and Pelletier, is not that they take up, sometimes word for word, the texts of the Pythagorean and Neo-Platonic thought. This is a matter of course and only continues a tradition uninterrupted throughout the Middle Ages. But, in addition, the poems of Scève and of Pelletier tend to constitute a new poetry, whose originality consists in the perfect adequation between an abstract language and an abstract thought, in brief, purely mathematical poetry. Moreover, and what is perhaps even more important, this mathematical poetry is also a genetic poetry, that is to say a poetry in which the mental realities come forth—the ones from the others—in the same way that physical realities have emerged from each other under the creative action of the power of God. Therefore, the movement of poetical thought is strictly analogous to the movement of nature, for both one and the other are obedient to the same process. The universe and the poem that sings of it develop from the same point, following the same lines. The cosmic genesis and the poetic genesis have the same principle and the same development.

Such is the dominant theme in the majority of the vast scientific poems which appear toward the end of the sixteenth century, and whose authors mostly are Huguenots. Mr. Albert-Marie Schmidt has made an excellent study of them.

Du Bartas, describing God prior to His creation, does not present Him other than does Maurice Scève. God,

perfect circle
Of which the center is everywhere and over all its round outline.[8]

He describes him in the following manner, in the *Seconde Semaine:*

I am He Who is in Myself, for Myself, by Myself . . .
The principle, the end and the middle of All,
But without beginning, without in-between, without end;
Though all is comprised in Me, and even indeed in Whom all things
Are and shall be enclosed as in their own matrix . . .[9]

Principle and matrix of things, the God of Du Bartas is the center
from which creation develops, as it is also the circumference in which
it is contained. This central and punctual character of God is even
more apparent in another cosmic poem of the period, inspired, furthermore, by Du Bartas, the *Uranologie* of Edouard du Monin.
Addressing himself to the Macrocosm, Du Monin salutes it in these
terms:

I salute thee, O Globe, once, twice and three times,
Globe well recognized by the eternal Voice,
Since creating this Whole formed upon all things thy model,
It chose thy round pattern, whose beautiful shape
Encloses a point in itself (mark of the powerful God)
For [in the same way] as this Point, neither deep nor wide nor high,
Notwithstanding commences and completes all lines
Of equal significance drawn from the center
Toward the encirclement: So is the Lord
The head and tail of this great roundness
Even as eternity supported on a point
By depth, width or height, though high, is not measured:
This All springs from this Point, this Point limits the All,
As of the All God is the point and endless end without end.[10]

And a few lines further on the poet exclaims with astonishment:

To see a solid body in a point have its ground
In a point, which has no point, if one thinks it over!

But of all the poets who, at the end of the sixteenth century, have
been haunted by the emblem of the God-point and the God-circle,
there is none more profuse in developments of this kind than the
Catholic Guy Le Febvre de la Boderie. He was suffused with Plato-
nism and Neo-Platonism. With his brother Nicolas he is the author
of translations by Marsile Ficin, Pic de la Mirandole and Franciscus
Zorzi. He lived for a long time in the milieu of Plantin, at Anvers,
that publisher who had for a motto a circle traced by a compass.
Almost without exception, all the poems by La Boderie are poems
of the center and the circle. One may notice this even in the titles
of his works. For example, in *Encyclie des secrets de l'éternité* the

word encyclie signifies a series of interlocked circles; in the *Galliade,
ou révolution des arts et des sciences,* the word galliade is presented
by him as having been taken from the Hebrew *Galal,* signifying *to
return.* All the cantos that make up these two poems are labeled
circles. La Boderie sees circles everywhere. Suffering from a periodic
fever, he consoles himself by considering the cyclical aspect of his
illness. In a sonnet in his *Divers mélanges poétiques,* he formulates
thus the main object of his poetry:

> God be the principle and be the end and the center
> Of my songs: His wise Providence
> Be the argument of my apprenticeship
> And of my Rounds be the Center and the axle.[11]

From the debut of his *Encyclie,* that is to say the long poem in
which he sings the cycles of creation, La Boderie fixes our attention
on this unique "center and axle" of all his Rounds.

Here is a bit of dialogue between the poet and the Muse Uranus

> "— Is not the world eternal in every point?
> — In no Point.
> — One greater hence did make it; is it God, then,
>   this point?
> — Yes this point."[12]

With Bruno in Italy and Traherne, a little later, in England, La
Boderie is of all writers the one who has multiplied the greatest
number of variations on the theme of the circle or of the sphere of
which the center is everywhere and the circumference is nowhere.
Here are two examples. The first is taken from a poem on the Trinity, which forms part of the *Hymnes ecclésiastiques,* published in
1578. A significant detail, the poem is dedicated to another friend
of Maurice Scève, Pontus de Thyard. God is, says La Boderie:

> The infinite Sun, whose prime roundness
> Perennially produces rays of light:
> Thus from the roundness as well as from the precious ray
> Comes forth eternally the eternal warmth.
> It is the unlimited Round, of which the central point
> Is found in every place, whose spherical contour
> Is found nowhere, and from whose center and circuit
> The rims or rays ensue all around.[13]

But the most surprising passage is, perhaps, this one, which, taken
from the seventh Circle of the *Encyclie,* at a place where, in the

margin, La Boderie expressly sends the reader back to the *Parmenides* of Plato:

> O happy spectacle! io, io, that I enter into
> The profound infinite which turns within its center
> Its center moves in it, and yet it does not move itself
> That which one calls the Universe, of its Center is the Point:
> How is it then that in oneself is folded
> The non-encircled Circle encircling the Encyclical?[14]

Paradoxically, God is at once the center from which the universe comes forth and the infinite sphere which contains it as a point. Following the tradition of Cusa, God is at one and the same time the minimum which is the point, and the maximum which is the sphere. This maximum and this minimum coincide. The final God is identical with the initial God. The circumference is equal to the center, and every point of the sphere is the center.

It thereby follows that in the very epoch in which, because of the Copernican revolution, man seemed to lose the central position he had occupied up until that time as an inhabitant of the absolute center of the world, at the very same time, on the other hand, he could regain it and even acquire a more advantageous position, since from no matter what point of the world and of time, where he might find himself, he could transform this point into a center of universal investigation. In the infinite every point is a center, or to speak as did Bruno, "the universe is all center."[15] This is what an eminent French disciple of Nicolas of Cusa, Charles de Bouelles, teaches from the beginning of the sixteenth century, in particular in a Latin poem, *Hecatodia de nihilo,* of which the following lines may be quoted:

> Omne nihil pellit, vacuumque exterminat omne:
> Mola sua complens, quod locus omnis habet.
> Totque potest mundos, quotquot numerabis in illo
> Centrorum notulas, signa vel exigua.[16]

One may translate it in approximately the following manner:

> Its All fills nothingness, abolishes emptiness,
> Pervading with its mass all the places of ether,
> Hence comes that every infinitesimal part of space
> Of its own universe is the center and mark.

In every infinitesimal point of space the human soul can thus constitute itself as the center of that space, and make use of it as a springboard by which to attain and apprehend the whole. This is what Pic de la Mirandole was affirming in his *De Dignitate,* a discourse which was to be commented upon by the whole of the sixteenth century, up to and including Bérulle, who, in 1599, in his *Traité des énergumènes,* was to say: "Man is like a point and a center, to which all parts of the world are related." Center of the world, like divinity, the human mind, again like divinity, can propagate its influence excentrically; and be likened therefore to the enlarging circles produced by a stone falling into a pond. This is the very image used by Le Febvre de la Boderie in the sixth Circle of his *Encyclie:*

> Thus though of the heart and Center of the world
> The very soul seethes and surges, and breathes all around
> Among the intestines and limbs of the great Body
> Interlocked one with another, and all amongst them
> > twisted:
> And even though more than one Spirit draws patterns upon
> > its lid
> As sleeping water little by little and ring by ring,
> By the throw of a pebble begins to undulate,
> And from there ever further pleat on pleat deploys:
> Or as the throat's articulated voice
> In the spacious air to the compass vibrates:
> Yet without the aid of a hidden Motor,
> Spiritual circle to no body attached
> Of which the center is everywhere, and the circumference
> Is in no existing place (this is the difference
> Of the Soul with it)—the Soul could not run through
> The open pores of the invigorating World.[17]

The world is therefore an open field, which man invades with his thought. More and more, he is conscious of the singular power which he possesses, to be able to send a force out, into a space which he scours with successive waves. "Glory is like a circle in the water— which never ceaseth to enlarge itself . . ."[18] writes Shakespeare. Another Elizabethan, Chapman, compares the quivering of a kiss to a perpetual self-propagating movement.[19] Besides, the inebriating emotions of love are not the only ones to benefit from this power of diffusion. It is equally the same for fear, desire, or anguish. A contemporary of Malherbe, Jean-Pierre Camus, imagines a sort of Emma Bovary of the time who dreams of a handsome gallant whose image haunts her life of a recluse:

"The imagination of our confined one," he writes, "was like stagnant water, multiplying to infinity the circles on its surface, from the smallest pebble which may fall into it."[20] —The friend of Camus, François de Sales, writes in the same vein: "And all this seems to resemble the circles that water makes when one has thrown a stone into it, for it makes a small circle, and this one makes a larger one, and this other, still another."[21]

Doubtless, in most of these texts, the space in question is not exterior space. It is often in a sort of imaginary expanse that the Renaissance man diffuses his humors and his thoughts. But for our concern this is hardly important. Whether it be outward or inward that the circle of which he is the center enlarges itself, man is conscious of an enlargement and that is all that counts. Around him, the limits of the circle become more and more remote.

The same image of the stone in the pond is employed by Du Bartas to describe humanity's progress:

> For as the polished pebble that falls into the water
> Of a dozing fishpond, forms a little ring
> Around the place of its fall, and thus also compasses,
> By the gentle movement gliding on the surface
> Of this undulating marble and tremulous crystal,
> A series of rounds which go ever spreading . . .
> So Man day after day nursing his wisdom,
> Causes to flow all arts by the circumference
> As he grows, and as in divers flocks
> Scatters his seed throughout this great universe.[22]

Thence circular spreading of the macrocosm from the creative and divine center, therefore becomes, by analogy, the no less circular blossoming of the human microcosm. Every soul is a growing and irradiating center, creator of its own spherical activity. In itself, it virtually holds all, is all. But this virtual totality must be developed and realized. Already Nicolas of Cusa had written: "Human activity consists in unfolding everything beyond itself into its own circular field, in making everything come forth from the virtuality of the center."[23] Paracelsus will say laconically: "Man is a pip, the universe, an apple."[24] What does this mean, unless it be that man can become the universe, that he is already one in potentiality? "The minimum is virtually the maximum,"[25] says Bruno.

There is more than one way for the minimum to become the maximum. The most direct is that of the conquerors. Man becomes the universe quite simply by taking it over. A whole book should be written[26] on the myth of the conquering hero at the time of the

Renaissance. The conqueror's force is even more expansive than acquisitive. It is a point which diffuses itself in the circle. Or, more precisely, it is a point which is so swollen with power that it is no longer content to be a point, but must explode and expand without limits. Thus is, for example, the conqueror dreamed of by Marlowe, Tamburlaine.

Still, there are other ways, less coarse and quite as effective, of conquering the world. Incidentally, it is no longer a case of the terrestrial world only. Man is now in an infinite universe, in which, because it is infinite, every point is the center. Even more, this infinite universe is the dwelling place of God Himself: "When thou imaginest beyond the world this imaginary space," writes the Jesuit Kircher, "it is not necessarily the nothingness that thou hast conceived, but the plenitude of the divine Substance."[27] To be at the center of the world, is therefore to be at the center of the infinite, to be at the center of God. Every moment of our lives, every place that we occupy, can thus become the point of view and the point of departure from which a prodigious diffusion of the spirit is realizable. If the soul extends itself, it is in the divine immensity. An immensity in which universes are contained like other things. God's space is not empty. It is, on the contrary, full of beings. In every one of them, an aspect of God is revealed. Space is the infinite coexistence of forms in which God makes manifest the inexhaustible variety of His nature. In no matter what place in the world that one may be, in no matter what moment in the duration of one's life in which one may be living, one is in the center of the indescribable spheric totality where God reveals Himself. It is therefore man's duty in some manner to seize upon an ecstatic consciousness of this whole which discloses itself in every one of its points of existence. Quite at the end of the Renaissance, in Italy with Bruno, in England, a little later, with the "metaphysical" poets, one finds the admirable expression of this relativism at once theological and cosmological. Nowhere else is its expression so elevated, so enthusiastic, and so continuously making use of the symbol of the circle, as in the verses of Thomas Traherne.

"A free man," he writes, "moves in a sphere of marvels."[28] For Dante also the divine sphere was marvelous; but it was composed of permanent marvels, marvels which furthermore did not reveal themselves to the voyager until, precisely, the moment when he had finished his journeying, to immobilize himself in the contemplation of the eternal beauties. With Traherne, it is the very reverse which happens. He moves in the miraculous sphere; he therefore constantly changes its center, and, at the same time, in his view, causes it constantly to change its aspect. Hence no one better feels the whole variety of points of view which it presents; as no one, either, except perhaps Boehme, has to such a degree the faculty to hold in every moment of ecstasy the maximum of space and duration. In the Latin sense of a term which he loved above all others, he is truly the poet of capacity:

> Infinite Love cannot be Expressed in finite Room: but must have infinite Places wherein to utter and show itself. It must therefore fill all Eternity and the omnipresence of God with Joys and treasures for my Fruition. And yet it must be Expressed in a finite Room; by making me able in a Center to Enjoy them. It must be infinitely expressed in the smallest Moment by Making me able in every Moment to see them all. It is both ways infinite, for my Soul is an Infinite Sphere in a Center . . .[29]

> O Joy! O Wonder! and Delight!
> O sacred Mystery!
> My soul a Spirit infinit!
> An image of the Deity!
> . . . .
> A strange extended Orb of Joy,
> Proceeding from within
> Which did on every side convey
> Its self; and being nigh of Kin
>   To God, did evry way
> Dilate its self even in an instant, and
> Like an indivisible center stand,
> At once surrounding all Eternity.[30]

But if the soul is a center, God is the center of centers. And all other centers turn avidly around Him and tend toward Him. The poetry of the Renaissance is not only a poetry of the center, it is also a poetry of the revolutions which operate around the center: "As the skies turn and are in perpetual movement on an immobile point," writes the first Margaret of Navarre to Champvallon, "my thoughts, my desires, my affections, conducted by that great demon (Love), turn and continually move around our idea, principle and end of all our desires."[31]

One would think one was reading a paraphrase of Scève's *Délie*. But this is a current thought of the time. Half-a-century later, Jean

le Sponde speaks in the same terms of the gyrating movement
of love:

> It turns around the point of constancy
> As the heavens turn around their point.[32]

The divine is therefore not only the emanating center of the
universe or of human thought; it is also the pivot and cause of its
gyration. In *Astrée,* Tircis explains to Hylas that Love is a God, and
that he can therefore desire nothing outside of himself: "He is his
own center."[33] Center in so far as it is the desired object, Love is
circumference in so far as it is the eternal movement of desire
around the object of desire. This is what Urfé writes in verse as
in prose:

> The air is my will, that, free in its power
> Around my faith continually moves.[34]

This fashion of representing the activity of love in the form of a
mobile circle around a fixed center was so common from the time
of the Renaissance, that Du Bellay parodied it:

> Some other one also, having subtly
> Found the accord of every element
> Fashions a circle tending from all sides
> Toward the center of his soul!
> His firmament is painted on a beautiful brow.
> All his desires swing round and round
> His arctic and antarctic poles, these are
> His lady's fine eyes.[35]

Nevertheless, in despite of railleries, the fashion of the circle
erotic, cosmic, and theological, persists until the mid-seventeenth
century. Lazare de Selve begins a sonnet by remarking that

> As this great world has a circular form,
> Every part, too, is an active circle . . .

From there, gradually, he lifts himself to the contemplation of
God, infinite circle:

> This great Course, of which the Center is everywhere so perfect,
> And of which the circle is such that no one can encompass it.

And he concludes:

> Man, contemplate in thyself two precious circles,
> The soul, which comes from Heaven, must return to the Firmament;
> The body, of ashes made, must to ashes return.[36]

The body in returning to matter, the soul in returning to God, thus accomplish, one and the other, a circle and a cycle. But the return of the soul to God is not only representable in the form of a peripheral movement. God, infinite circle which the soul invades and traverses, is also God, infinite center into which it sinks. The return of the soul is a return to the center. Point of departure, the center is also the point of abutting.

This is what is expressed by Jean de la Ceppède, in one of his sonnets from his *Théorèmes,* from which the first two lines are given here:

> Intelligible sphere, it is indubitable
> That thy center is everywhere, that in it
> all finds an end.

Commenting himself on this sonnet, La Ceppède adds: "Now, the center of this sphere is everywhere (let us say with Trismégiste,) that is to say that in it all finds an end. And neither more nor less than all the lines are drawn from the center to the circumference, by the same token all created things come from and proceed from God, as from their center, and give themselves to Him . . . and as the things created cannot rest perfectly, nor enjoy themselves, unless they are conjoined to their center; so the spirit of man can never be tranquil nor take delight in any perfect ease, unless it is brought to and joined to God, as to its center."[37]

Another poet of the counter-Reformation, the Jesuit Lemoyne, says the same thing. His favorite image is that of the sea, but if one can so express it, a central sea, toward which all rivers converge and in which they lose themselves:

> Sea without shores, he said, inexhaustible center
> From which all comes, where all goes, from which
> all comes forth, and to which all [things]
> return . . .[38]

And in another poem, speaking again of the sea:

> Always it gets fuller, but without ever overflowing:
> And by this token it is alike to the great Center
> From which all things flow out, to which all things return.[39]

This re-entry and re-absorption in the divine center became one of the preferred themes of the French mystic of the seventeenth century. As with Ruysbroeck, Saint John of the Cross, or Juan de los Angeles, the essential movement of the soul for the French Quietists is the passage from the periphery to the center, the progressive disappearance of all surface characteristics, the simplification of the soul, its sinking into a central bareness where there is only God.

Saint John of the Cross sings:

> O sharp flame of love
> How you wound me with tenderness
> In the most profound center of the soul!

In the admirable commentary which he gives on these lines, John of the Cross develops his doctrine of the center: "In ordinary language," he says, "we call the most profound center of the soul the extreme point to which a being's virtue can reach, the force of his working and of his movement and beyond which it cannot go. So it is with the fire and the stone. They possess a virtue, a natural movement and power in order to arrive at the center of their sphere beyond which they cannot go, but which they do not fail to reach and there remain unless they are prevented by some obstacle . . . Now, the center of the soul, is God."[40]

In a very beautiful line, François Malaval was to write:

> The soul seeks its center and the body its tomb.[41]

This quest for the center is a favorite theme of Madame Guyon, who recognized very clearly the symbol of the infinite sphere:

> Being of an unalterable essence;
> Circle without principle and without end,
> Having no circumference,
> Since its center is to be found everywhere.[42]

Pure love, for Madame Guyon, is a return to the center:

> . . . Love draws us
> From the circumference to the unity . . . .
> First it draws, unites and concentrates
> The rejoined forces in a point:
> When God entirely possesses the center
> The senses receive, dissipating nothing.[43]

But perhaps the most admirable of the Quietistic poets is Jean de Labadie, that strange personage who passed through all religious forms, Catholic and Protestant, without being satisfied by any, perhaps precisely because he dreamed of a religion without forms, a circle without limits and abyss-centered. He too knew and loved the symbol of the infinite sphere. Speaking of God he writes:

> In a most perfect circle, without beginning and without end,
> Which, without circumference, has its center everywhere:
> He has all, is in all places, is a supreme All,
> Which being nothing, is Everything, and is but the
>   very Being.[44]

One of the finest of Labadie's poems is that in which he describes the progressive union of the soul with this Nothingness-All, which is the God-point. It is the Third Exercise of the First Decade of his *Quatrains de piété chrétienne.* Herewith are two quatrains:

> Source of multitude! Adorable unity!
> From whom as from a point all numbers unroll,
> Toward which as toward their center they once more roll,
> With them receive me in thy Immensity . . .
> O God! Who alone art All, one and All without doubling,
> Source without effusion, without moving center!
> When in Thy unity dost Thou wish my line to enter,
> And my tide to rest in Thee and flow no more?[45]

But the epoch of Labadie and of Quietism is already close to the eighteenth century. One does not only fulminate, with Bossuet, against the Quietists; one chaffs them, and to chaff them one mocks their centers and their circles. This is what Fléchier does in a parody in which he accuses a partisan of pure love to speak in this way:

> As for me, I go straight to the divine essence;
> I stop only at God, not at His power,
> At His mercies, at His eternity;
> I know how to gather my all in His unity;
> In the sublime orison where pure love enters,
> The lines are nothing, one must go to the center.[46]

II

THE BAROQUE PERIOD

To Marcel and Claire Raymond

THE MOVEMENT of expansion which, from the time of the Renaissance, inflates thought, does not manifest itself alone under the form of an enlargement of the spiritual scope. This new space must be occupied and furnished. Perhaps among the diverse categories of the Baroque art, there is none more important than the multiplicity of forms by which the architect, the painter, the sculptor, the poet feels compelled to fill the space that he deploys before him, around him, or within him. This space extends itself inordinately beyond all forms, but to make it evident, to give it, if only in imagination, some reality, it is necessary to fill it as full as possible with material objects, whose mission is less that of existing in themselves than of conferring on the space which contains them the vastest possible power of envelopment and of encompassment. A crowd of figures encumbers the expanse; an infinity of details there disposes itself in tiers; a universal thrust traverses it. Yet this space is never totally filled. It is a container larger than its content. Hence, the more Baroque art and poetry multiply the detail of the intensity of this content, the more the transcendance of the containment becomes manifest. A growing gap stands out between what is represented and what is suggested. And it is not forcing terms to maintain that in the furious deployment of forms which constitutes the most evident trait of Baroque art one must observe less a sign of the conquest of space by the mind, than of the impossibility for the mind finally to accomplish this conquest. Space is not a boon that one can appropriate by force any more than by any other manner. It is only just possible to invade it. And all the attempts by which one may try to take possession of it by pouring into it the greatest number, or the largest possible volume, of forms, only end in making more obvious the

15

contrast between the real immensity of space and the false immensity of volume or of number. In the presence of space everything which occupies space shrinks or decays. Multiplication becomes division, mass a plurality of parts. Space filled is immeasurably surpassed by space unfilled.

This plurality of detail scattered in the enormity of the whole appears, for example, with great clarity in the play of fountains and rainbows which one so frequently finds described by the Baroque poets. Jean Rousset has admirably shown that this poetry loves nothing so much as the spectacles of running, iridescent water. In it he sees the manifestation of the Baroque taste for everything which expresses the metamorphosis of the forms and the variations of duration. At every instant the preceding form gives way to the following form. A new instant is born in the fading of the anterior instant. Thus each moment, like each drop of water which reflects the prism, avers its own particular existence beyond the death of all other instants. Other instants, in their turn, precipitate themselves toward life and toward death. And this perpetual birth and death have the effect of forming a temporal universe wherein all instants live their instantaneous life, but are never able to constitute a continuous web of duration. Now it is the same with space. Every form comes to life in it, and in its springing into life affirms an individuality which distinguishes it from all others; but all have an equal originality, so that a discrete multiplicity finds itself spread throughout space, without ever being able to identify with it, nor form in itself a homogeneous mass. Such is the effect made, for example, by iridescences of light in a fountain described by the chevalier Marino:

> But the marvel, then, while it exalts itself,
> Imprints on the sky an arc as beautiful as Iris.
> The fluid and aqueous humor metamorphosizes
> Into ray, comet, star, a wonder.
> Here dart *globes,* or bubbles shoot out;
> There without a break turn *minute spheres*;
> All germinates, oozes, the jets multiply themselves,
> All undulates and streams, spurts and flows.[1]

The phenomenon one witnesses appears, at first sight, a phenomenon of sheer multiplication. Instead of the divine sphere, unique and infinite, there is a growing plurality of "minute spheres." The movement which traverses the poem is an optimistic movement. It would seem that the germination and the gushing forth of spheres will never stop and that they will end by filling with their number the infinite sphere of which they remind us through their forms, though not by their dimensions. However, if everything gushes, everything also flows away. Number can never equal true grandeur. Moreover, or even worse, the over-abundance of smallness only exaggerates the vice of littleness. As all becomes more numerous, everything becomes more miniscule and more fragile. The prodigious proliferation of things is only a proliferation of *bubbles*.

Nevertheless the writers of the Baroque period cannot help but be fascinated by this resemblance between the infinitely large and the infinitely small. As the macrocosm is represented by the microcosm, and the rainbow by each one of the drops of water which compose it, so the immense sphere of the universe can be rediscovered, reduced but curiously like, in objects *which man's science engineers, in order to reproduce, on a small scale,* cosmic space or solar time. Astrolabes, terrestrial globes, planispheres, and clocks are abridged universes, orbs in which the cosmos is drawn back to the minuscule. If there is an immoderate movement by which the mind stretches to the limit of things, there is the inverse movement by which these limits are shortened and coincide with the natural limits of the human mind. A planisphere, a terrestrial globe, a clock are an immensity which has contracted, without ceasing to manifest its total circularity.

This is probably what delights the Jesuit Father François Binet in a passage of his *Essays des merveilles de nature et des plus nobles artifices:*

> The mind of man gives itself the air of a little God and prides itself on making worlds of crystal, and counterfeits the miracles of the Universe. . . . And whatever great cannot be said of this divine science which knows how to mimic the azure vaults of the skies, and to light them with a thousand thousand Stars. This it is which makes liars of those who dared to maintain that there could not be two Suns in the world; for making use of the hands and mind of Archimedes, it has set in a crystal firmament a second Sun, companion or younger brother of the other, coursing over the glass and gilding with its golden rays in the same cadence as the other, making a little crystal year by its turns and revolutions, as the other measures the great year by its courses which run over the sapphire vaults in its normal course. This it is which by the force of its daring mind, bordering on omnipotence, has built a scarf of glass, peopled it with twelve terrestrial images, and like a Zodiac has girdled with them its *little*

earthly Sky. . . . What a strange thing that this science by secret
links should have so well harmonized this *Sphere* with the ca-
dence and swingings of the Heavens, that a little mannikin
makes by himself on earth all that the angelic intelligences make
in Heaven, where they make the orbs spin through the great
vaults of the Universe. By this means Art has begot a tiny bit
of a machine pregnant with a great world, a *Portable Heaven
and Paradise, a great Universe in a nothingness of glass,* a fine
mirror where nature preens itself, astonished to see that by this
stroke Art has surmounted and practically engendered nature.[2]

In fact, that on which Father Binet is congratulating himself, is
that art (or science) counterfeits nature, and, to counterfeit it, reduces
it to the minimum. Not that Father Binet seriously considers this
reduced version as superior to the larger. He simply makes himself
happy with the idea that a reduced universe is more manageable—
let us use his own word—more portable. Like the volcano of Super-
vielle's hero, one can put it in one's suitcase; or hold it in the hand
like an apple, such as one sometimes sees done with certain divinities. Not only that, in submitting to this reducing operation, the
universe has lost nothing of its perfection. It functions just as well.
It is even, in a sense, preferable, because when reduced to its new
size one may the more easily watch it function. The eye with ease
takes in the whole. Not that it stops at superficies. The portable
universe also has the merit of being transparent. From the outside,
one can see all the cogwheels inside. When one contemplates it, not
only does the glance go from top to bottom (instead of going from
the bottom to the top, as it does when one contemplates the macrocosm), but this glance penetrates without resistance to the interior
of the object. One possesses it therefore at one and the same time,
both from within and from without. Lastly, if this world is transparent, it is because it is made entirely of crystal. The crystal is the
sign of the transformation the universe has undergone in passing
from the maximum to the minimum and from the natural to the
artificial. As Gaston Bachelard has shown, crystal, glass, mother-of-
pearl, the ice of frozen water (even to a certain extent the metal of
the wheels of the machine) are the indication of a process by which
for the organic is substituted a matter at once mineral and luminous,
in brief, a spiritualized matter. When Father Binet rejoices to see
the universe reduced to minuscule proportions, he rejoices as much
to see it reduced to an abstraction. The globe has become globule,
the form (spherical) has become a formule. A magical formule, since

the globule contains the globe, and the Nothingness the All. It is in a similar spirit that Marino was to say in speaking of a world map:

> The great wheel of the All is in a little Round.[3]

So a simple clock can inspire the same feelings. Another Marinist poet writes:

> As the highest sphere turns in the sky,
> Which in its circle encompasses lesser circles
> And whose action revolves the spheres
> Which in their courses follow its trace;
> So the major wheel causes to turn with itself
> The minor wheels, and sets them in motion;
> And just as in heaven, there turn within,
> Opposite movements and wheels within wheels.[4]

The clock is an Ezekiel's chariot. In it one finds wheels within wheels, and if the lesser circles turn within the greater, they reproduce on their scale the form and movement of the larger ones.

The small world is then a faithful image of the great world. And it is even thanks to this reducing operation that it is possible to understand how the larger functions.

Nothing is more frequent among the Baroque poets than this process of reduction, exactly the inverse of that by which they try so often to inflate their thought and to give it universal dimensions.

So in a sonnet by Ciro de Pers, another Marinist, one finds a woman winding her thread from a large spool to a smaller one. The heart of the poet tosses in these wheels, in which passes the thread of his existence:

> And if of old my life spread in large circles,
> At present she gathers it and wants it united
> With a single beautiful face to live and to breathe.[5]

The shrinking of the circle of existence can therefore be a happy process, the recalling of forces dispersed in a too-vast space, the concentration on a nearby object that can be possessed. But, most often with these Baroque poets, the concentration has an entirely different emotional meaning and represents the spiritual catastrophe by which the being which had over-extended itself finds itself brought back to the quasi-nullity of its true dimensions. This is what one sees, for example, in the most dramatic of all the Baroque poets, the English Catholic poet, Richard Crashaw. In an *Ode on the Death of Mr. Staninough* he exclaims:

Come then youth, Beauty, and Blood, all ye soft powers,
Whose silken flatteryes swell a few fond hours
Into a false eternity, come man,
(Hyperbolized nothing!) know thy span.
Take thy owne measure here, downe, downe, downe, and bow
Before thy selfe in thy Idea, thou
Hugh emptinesse contract thy bulke, and shrinke
All thy wild Circle to a point![6]

Dramatically, the immense extension taken by the forces of the being appears as an illusion, like an untrue distention. The balloon deflates, the sphere finds itself reduced to a point. Man is a hyperbolized nothingness! The infinite graph that he traced in space, and by which he thought to become equal to space, is a decoy, a myth. Refuting in advance Mallarmé's pretention to give oneself a hyperbolic existence (but without foreseeing in which ironic sense one must consider it), Crashaw pierces the windbag and lets the air escape. Man is at one and the same time an immense hollow and a simple point, i.e., to say, twice nothing.

In a flash Crashaw makes man pass from absolute expansion to the absolute absence of expansion. The transformation and the disillusion show an extreme suddenness, as if the reduction of space also implied an equivalent reduction of duration, a reduction not only to a point not only without dimensions but without time. And this is certainly the effect that Crashaw wishes to create, since he starts with the false eternity obtained by the inflation of a few cherished hours. Divine eternity, as has been seen, is a sphere of which the center is an eternal moment and of which the circumference contains the totality of times. But in the false human eternity, a few hours only are enclosed, and it is their illusory inflation which permits one to suppose that they constitute a perfect temporal totality. The sphere deflates, the inflated hours are instantly brought back to a single instant. And this human instant is a point, a center, but with nothing around it, without any rapport with a circle of hours. A bald, naked instant, absolutely isolated in the emptiness of times, and the contrary to the eternal instant by which God is always in rapport with all times.

In another poem Crashaw interpolates the same dramatic movement of reduction, without giving it, however, the same suddenness of execution. It is a Latin poem entitled *Bulla,* in which one sees the appearance of a theme of great importance to us, the theme of the

soap bubble. I cite some fragments from the translation of Jean
Rousset:

> Sphere, not of glass,
> More brilliant still than glass,
> More fragile still than glass,
> More glassy still than glass.
>
> I am the brief phantasm of the wind,
> I am a flower, but a flower of the air,
> A star, but from sea water,
> A golden game played by nature,
> Strange fable and brief song . . .
>
> I ramble, I bounce around
> I am a motley
> Of snow and roses,
> Of water, air and fires.
> Painted, gemmed and gilded,
> I am, oh! I am but a nothing.[7]

The similarity between the two poems is striking. In one as in the
other an inflated spherical illusion gets dissipated, and all returns
to nothingness. In the last of the two poems, however, Crashaw introduces a quantity of nuances left out in the first. The *Ode on the
Death of Mr. Staninough* is a poem of suddenness, of instantaneousness. In *The Soap Bubble,* on the contrary, what matters is to show
the illusion while it lasts. It is on the whole of man's existence that
Crashaw directs our gaze. If life is an illusion, it is an illusion which
prolongs itself. Its duration is rendered tangible by the number of
events that succeed one another. Rambling, bounding, the bubble
moves about in space as well as in time. Composite, formed of different elements which ceaselessly combine and separate in the terrestrial
world as in its little world, it receives successive tints from the light.
It lives a life constantly renewed, but always discontinued, it is like
the iridescent drops of Marino's fountain. Its duration is most different from that of the celestial or divine sphere, because the life of the
bubble is always alterable, always altered, a life composed of an infinity of little deaths and terminated at last by total dissolution.

Thus the soap bubble, akin to the planisphere of Father Binet by
its crystalline character and smallness, differs from it radically, since
this crystal is pure appearance. "More fragile than glass," "Brief
dream," the bubble has a little circle of duration and a little spheri-

cal surface, which reflect something of Eternity, of Immensity. But it is hollow, it is also as brief and fragile as could be conceived. A shock, the least breath, and it is no more; for it is only surface, only a play of appearances.

There is no theme more frequently used by the Baroque poets—and even the Rococo—than the theme of the bubble.

For example, this madrigal by a compatriot and contemporary of Crashaw, William Drummond:

> This life which seems so fair
> Is like a bubble blown up in the air
> By sporting children's breath,
> Who chase it everywhere,
> And strive who can most it bequeath.
> And though it seem sometime of its own might,
> Like to an eye of gold, to be fixed there,
> And firm to hover in that empty height,
> That only is because it is too slight.
> But in that pomp it doth not long appear,
> For even when most admired, it is a thought
> As swelled from nothing, doth dissolve in nought.[8]

The intention of these poets is evident. They not only wish to describe the minute character, ephemeral and illusory, of the human sphere. They wish to contrast this brevity and this untruth with the immensity, the eternity, and the truth of the divine sphere. It is the perfections of this latter which they constantly hold in mind and which they silently oppose to the false perfections of the bubble. These poems are not only moral. They are truly religious.

It is therefore not surprising to even find this theme in Madame Guyon. There is, in her *Poésies et cantiques spirituels* a curious poem entitled *Le Saint Enfant en jouant souffle des bulles de savon*. It is evidently a question here of an emblem. Madame Guyon tries to give a meaning to the figure of the divine Child surrounded by bubbles:

> It seems to me, divine Child,
> That You amuse Yourself with frivolous things.

Then she overcomes her first movement of surprise and almost of reprobation. She has found the sense of the emblem:

> These bubbles are the image of an inconstant world;
> Far rather do I love to hear Thy words.
> Is there in the world anything more fragile and
>   more vain

Than these soap bubbles are?
Man who is only made of clay
Should find in this, a fine lesson.
Let us never depend upon ourselves,
Let us depend only on Jesus;
He alone, has the supreme strength:
Any support outside of Him would be wrong.[9]

In cheap verses Madame Guyon draws from the theme of the soap
bubble one of her favorite conclusions. Since we are bubbles, which
is to say inconstant and inconsistent beings who hold in themselves
no fixed principle of existence, and who are buffeted by all winds,
let us abandon ourselves to these winds; for they all come from the
Lord, and we should go where they send us. This is the doctrine of
the Quietist surrendering, which elsewhere Madame Guyon often
expresses by means of other symbolic figures, no less "circular" than
the bubble: the symbol of the weathercock and that of the balloon.
A balloon rolling in every direction, but under the divine impulse,
a weathercock turning to the four corners of the sky, yet whose pivot
is fixed in God, the Quietist soul is a mobile roundness, of which
the circularity signifies no true perfection, but simply the capacity
to go in any direction that God pushes it with the least possible
resistance and the greatest docility. It is round because it has a
center. The mobility of its gyrating movement is in constant relationship with a fixed point, which is God. God is at once the center
of every soul and the sphere which envelops the spheres of all souls:
infinite center, infinite sphere.

Thus, in one way or another, the religious thought of the seventeenth century tries to establish a rapport between the infinity of the
divine sphere and the infinity of human spheres. In a poem cited by
Henri Bremond, Father Martial de Brives deliberately confounds
these different little spheroid entities such as tears, pearls, and drops
of dew:

Crystalline grains, pure dews
Of which are composed,
During their morning festival,
The crowns of the marjoram and the thyme,
Liquid pearls of the Orient,
Heaven's tears, which cause
The watered silk and enamel of our fields
To smile, bless God Who by tears
Gives back to our withered souls
The lost glow of their primal colors.[10]

Drops of dew are even smaller and more fragile than soap bubbles; but their fragility and tininess are redeemed, because they are akin to the tears of Christ Who redeems us. Our puniness is a marvelous puniness. By divine grace we are transformed into pearls; into those pearls which, Saint Francis de Sales tells us, draw their luster, not from the sea, but from celestial light. Between the minute sphere of human existence and the heavenly sphere there is therefore a relationship which is more than an influence. For in the shape of a tear it is truly the divine immensity which comes to bestow its brightness, its purity, even its configuration, to human smallness. The Heaven reflects Itself, even more, if It incarnates Itself in the minute. The drop of dew is divinity in miniature.

There is an admirable poem by the Puritan Andrew Marvell, who, by the same symbol expresses ideas very close to those of Martial de Brives. One must quote the poem in its entirety:

> See how the Orient dew
> Shed from the bosom of the morn
> Into the blowing roses,
> (Yet careless of its mansion new,
> For the clear region where 'twas born,)
> Round in itself incloses;
> And, in its little globe's extent,
> Frames, as it can, its native element.
> How it the purple flower doth slight,
> Scarce touching where it lies;
> But gazing back upon the skies,
> Shines with a mournful light,
> Like its own tear,
> Because so long divided from the sphere.
> Restless it rolls, and unsecure,
> Trembling, lest it grow impure;
> Till the warm sun pity its pain,
> And to the skies exhale it back again.

Then comes the application:

> So the soul, that drop, that ray
> Of the clear fountain of eternal day,
> (Could it within the human flower be seen,)
> Remembering still its former height,
> Shuns the sweet leaves, and blossoms green,
> And, recollecting its own light,
> *Does, in its pure and circling thoughts, express*
> *The greater heaven in an heaven less.*

In how coy a figure wound,
Every way it turns away;
So the world-excluding round,
Yet receiving in the day;
Dark beneath, but bright above,
Here disdaining, there in love.
How loose and easy hence to go;
How girt and ready to ascend;
Moving but on a point below,
It all about does upwards bend.
Such did the manna's sacred dew distil;
White and entire, thou congealed and chill;
Congealed on earth; but does, dissolving, run
Into the glories of the almighty sun.[11]

No one has known better than Marvell how to marry and merge into one another the significances of spherical minuteness. The drop of dew is enclosed in itself, refuses all contact with the external world, wishes to have no communication except with another sphere, this one immense, and immensely removed. The first impression, therefore, is that of absolute separation and, in the absence of all intermediary meeting grounds, with the maximum of distance between greatness and smallness, between the sphere of God and that of the soul. But in its smallness the sphere of the soul mirrors, and in an exclusive way, the sphere of God. Even more, despite its smallness, it is of the same nature as that of the immensity from which it has issued. When it encloses itself in its roundness, it encompasses the roundness of the immense; so that when the sun comes to dissolve it, it does not vanish, it only loses its smallness. And the last line of the poem is that by which all at once there is restored to the sphere of the soul its true dimension, which is that of the infinite.

Fallen into smallness, restored to grandeur, the dew drop therefore possesses two existences. Condensation and expansion, the two contrary movements cross one another and find a meeting place which is the aim of all Baroque poetry. But to the dynamism of the action is also allied the static of the figure. As long as divine grace does not transform the terrestrial status of the drop of dew, it stays where it is put *on the point of arising,* but without the power to do so. Here, we are in a place and in a moment which are the narrowest possible; the point at which the drop touches the flower, the moment at which it touches eternity. The action which will take place is still suspended and as if fixed in the state which precedes its start. The moment when the flight will take place is still frozen in this place. The drop is a delayed fluidity, and it is this provisional, but indefinitely prolonged, delay that preserves it from any impure admixture. It is eternally pinned to the point of departure from which it will come to expand.

Another poet of the Baroque period, Father Lemoyne, uses nearly the same image as Marvell:

> Pearls, those curdled tears
> Which fall from the Sun's eyes . . .
> They are hearts fallen from the skies,
> Souls of pure light,
> Spirits white and precious.[12]

By the metamorphosis of tears into pearls, as inversely of, drops into vapor, the divine action pursues a double end, successively protective and redemptive. Around the souls it builds an envelope which protects them from their own fluidity and from contamination by the world into which they have fallen; they are thus permitted to retain, under a minute form, a principle of grandeur. Moreover, at a set moment, they will be withdrawn from the world and from their smallness; they will be given a circumference equal to that of the sun.

But it is not only by a supernatural action that the Baroque poets try to safeguard a principle of grandeur within smallness. The same Andrew Marvell who describes the saving and preservative action of God in the human soul is also he who describes the simple human action by which the soul saves itself, or at least protects what is most precious in itself, from the destructive forces of the exterior world. In a celebrated poem, addressed to his "timid mistress," and where he develops the old theme of time devouring all, Marvell incites his mistress to profit by the present moment, not because it will pass, not because one must enjoy it as it passes (as Horace and Ronsard would have it), but because it is possible, by the concentration of the whole being on this brief moment of pleasure to fasten it in its form, and to confer on it an absolute character:

> Now therefore while the youthful hue
> Sits on thy skin like morning dew,
> And while thy willing soul transpires
> At every pore with instant fires,
> Now let us sport us while we may,
> And now, like amorous birds of prey,
> Rather at once our time devour,
> Than languish in his slow-chapt power.

> Let us roll all our strength and all
> Our sweetness up into one ball,
> And tear our pleasures with rough strife,
> Through the iron gates of life.[13]

The act by which the spirit, instead of resigning itself to wait to be devoured by time, goes ahead of it and seizes upon it, is an act of fixation and determination. Instead of being carried away and devoured, the moment is possessed in itself and taken out of the game. Brief, and fluid though it be, it is grasped and rolled into a ball. Instead of falling from the sky like manna, the drop of duration hardens under the action of the human will. Solidified by this act, the human instant carried away by time does not disintegrate.

But this deliberate crystallization of moments of duration by the act of man is not due only to amorous desire. It can be an effect of art. Another English poet of the seventeenth century, Abraham Cowley, addresses this invocation to his Muse:

> If Past, and Future Times do thee obey,
> Thou stopst this Current, and dost make
> This running river settle like a Lake,
> Thy certain hand holds fast this slippery snake.
> The Fruit which does so quickly waste,
> Men scarce can see it, much less taste,
> Thou Comfitest in Sweets to make it last.
> This shining piece of Ice
> Which melts so soon away,
> With the Sun's ray,
> Thy verse does solidate and crystallize,
> Till it a lasting mirror be.
> Nay, thy Immortal Rhyme,
> Makes this short Point of Time,
> To fill up half the Orb of Round Eternity.[14]

River issuing into a lake, ice changed into glass, fruit transformed into comfits, the transitory substance of the instant is, through the operation of language, metamorphosed into an eternal substance. The movement stops and becomes a state. But even more significant still than this fixation is the inverse operation which completes it. Hardly has language detached the instant from flux, isolated it, immobilized it, rendered it similar to a permanent drop of time, than the same mutative force gives to this "brief Point of Time" immobilized, an incomparable force of expansion: "Thy verse does not solidate and crystallize, / Till it a lasting mirror be. / Nay, thy

Immortal Rhyme, / Makes this short Point of Time, / To fill up the Orb of Round Eternity." Without ceasing to be set in itself, detached from all other times, the globule of duration formed by art dilates itself, invades the future, fills, hemispherically, all time to come. Its minute spherical reality becomes the roundness of eternity.

But this proud pretention of the mind is far from being that of all the Baroque poets. The majority content themselves with the symbol of the bursting bubble, and the vanishing dew, of the spinning weathervane or the deflating windbag: narrow space and brief moment. Here is how the Marinist poet sings of the minute circles described by a firefly in the air:

> Charming firefly,
> While you play round and round,
> Make of your luminous rings
> A collar for the shadow.[15]

A light not divine, pure terrestrial movement that in its gyration only envelops a little shadow, circles traced with the grace and economy of a Japanese poem.

Or this other poem, as graceful and of the same kind:

> Of a white humor, this frozen mass,
> Take it, press it, make of it *a brief globe*;
> Then garnish thy hand with it, adding to the white snow
> A warm and animated snow.[16]

The snowball is, like the drop of dew and the soap bubble, a minuscule and ephemeral sphere. As with Marvell, the Marinist poet tries by a human action to coil the instant in his hand, to communicate to its purity, warmth and life. But differently from Marvell, the Marinist knows well that the conjunction of life and purity in a perfect sphere can only end in the destruction of one or the other. No matter! It suffices to live the brief moment of perfection, even though to live it, be to die. The instant can only be lived in the "brief globe" of the instant.

A globe so brief that it reduces itself at times to being no more than an imperceptible point. One of the most beautiful Marinist sonnets (of which the author is Tommaso Gaudiosi) describes a circle of players grouped around a table. The cards fall, one by one. In the spinning points and numbers, says the author, lies "the will to win and the art of contesting." Finally all the cards have fallen, destiny has been decided. The wheel which has spun from player to player suddenly settles on one to the exclusion of all others. Circling time becomes immobile. For nothing has really happened in the movement of duration. Everything has been decided, everything has been fixed in a single moment. "The fugitive moment, the indivisible point."[17]

The circle or the sphere which human thought embraces tends more and more to contract, to condense itself. And at the same time, too, this circle or this sphere seems more precarious, more fragile, more imperfectly preserved in its thin envelope from the world which surrounds it. Snowball, dance of fireflies, dewdrop, tear, the tiny sphere seems likely to melt, to evaporate, to scatter, to be lost, whether in the exterior void, or whether in its inner futility. No doubt, throughout the whole course of the seventeenth century, religious thought maintains the rapport between the "brief globe" of human existence, and the sphere of eternity. But with the end of the century the symbol of the infinite sphere loses all signification and all energy, it disappears from theological and philosophical language, so that the little sphere in which human thought is formed is condemned now to float without mooring and without a model, and to reveal even more gravely, its insignificance. If we pass from the Baroque age to that of the Rococo, we again encounter, for example, the theme of the soap bubble, dear to Crashaw and to Drummond. But it goes without saying, one discovers it now emptied of religious significance. The fragility of the man-sphere is no longer compensated by the immutability of the God-sphere. Smallness is lost in an immensity which is no longer the divine immensity, but the cosmic immensity. Ephemerality has no further rapport with eternity. The soap bubble therefore becomes purely a spectacle of "passing nuances," which unroll themselves in the void. This is how it is in a poem by Bernis, *l'Épitre sur les moeurs,* which begins in the following manner:

> An inconstant divinity
> Animates and conducts us all;
> This it is which in the same age
> Renews our tastes a hundred times.

Quite evidently we are no longer in the presence of Divinity, eternal and immutable sphere, as was conceived by Crashaw. Bernis continues:

> So, to paint the origin
> Of our reviving caprices,
> Watch a troupe of children,

Who, by different pipes,
In the swill where soap has dominion
Form transparent globes;
A breath on these light bubbles
Brings the brilliant blaze of flowers,
From their passing nuances
A breath nourishes the colors:
The air, which fills and colors them,
Fluttering under our wainscotted walls,
Gives them the freshness of Flora,
Or the amber tint of Aurora,
Or the inconstant green of Iris;
But this useless chef-d'oeuvre of Aeolus,
Which a light breath has produced,
In the instant it shines and flies,
Because of a breath, faints away.[18]

At this point we are as far as possible from Platonic and Christian
symbolism. Nevertheless this has furnished the theme which the poet
has borrowed, without knowing its antecedents. The little sphere of
perceptive life finds itself bereft of all causal or analogical rapport
with the great sphere of the divine life. It is both of a breath, of an
anonymous caprice; and not having any true substance of its own,
it is content to be by turn whatever the colors of the exterior world
around it may make of it. It is a minuscule and sensitive event which
replaces, without apparent reason, other tender, impressionable
events. Therefore it is too much to say that the bubbles of Bernis
have a life. At the very outside, the most that they possess is a
particle of existence. Each one follows the disappearance of preceding ones, in such a way that they never constitute a chain of instants,
nor an association of places. There is therefore neither space, nor
even time, possible, no continuity and no permanence. And if the
bubbles are spherical, this is not to suggest that they have any particular perfection, but simply that each one being enclosed in its
own little locality and particular moment, it is absolutely impossible
for them to find themselves related to each other externally. In the
place of the medieval universe where the lesser spheres were hierarchically encased within wider spheres, in the place of the Baroque
universe where by expanding and contracting, spheres could rejoin
and mingle one with another, now here is a universe where spheres
do not join, do not mingle, do not even link, but are quite simply
content to float alongside others. Less a universe than a dust of a

universe, a world of unlinked atoms, condemned to flutter without attachment and without ever forming a real world.

This reciprocal independence of spheres is so radical that it even becomes impossible, at the final count, to decide if they are really small. One loses the notion of their attenuation, as one has relinquished assigning them any grandeur. Size and smallness are relative ideas. Micromegas is alternatively a dwarf and giant:

And now a bubble burst, and now a world,

writes Pope in his *Essay on Man*.[19] If one wishes, the bubble is a world; the world is, if you wish, a bubble. Fontenelle amuses himself at transforming the universe into a collection of bubbles or balloons, which now dilate and now contract, but which never cease to remain bubbles or balloons:

One may therefore imagine that the Universe, as much as is known to us, is an amassment of great balloons, great stretched elastic bodies bound one to the other, which inflate and deflate. . . .[20]

This is the same Fontenelle, incidentally, who mocks the divine symbol of the infinite Sphere: "An infinite Sphere," he says, "would imply contradiction, since every figure is what is terminated exteriorly." And Fontenelle adds that it would be better to replace the idea of the infinite sphere by that of an "infinity of finite spheres."[21] This infinity of finite spheres, these are soap bubbles.

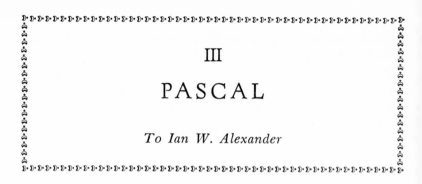

III

PASCAL

To Ian W. Alexander

I

ONE KNOWS that the celebrated fragment *Disproportion de l'homme* was to form a part of a chapter *Transition de la connaissance de l'homme à Dieu*. By transition one must understand the movement of the mind by which it passes from one object of knowledge to another. Now, the initial expression of this movement has been lengthily described by Pascal under the title of *De la misère de l'homme*. All understanding of self is, for man, an understanding of his own misery, and this understanding "without that of God creates despair."[1] To escape from this despair, there is, therefore, but one issue: one must pass from the understanding of oneself to that of God. But how to do it? What way must one take to pass from so much known misery to such unknown grandeur? This common ground, this only intermediary, Pascal indicates, is the God made man and rendered knowable: "The knowledge of Jesus Christ creates the milieu because therein we find both God and our own misery."[2] But for those who do not know Jesus Christ, is there a milieu and a transition possible? The whole passage of the *Disproportion de l'homme* has as its goal the answer to this question.

The starting, therefore, is the understanding of our own misery. One knows the terms in which Pascal has depicted it in a passage in the *Copie des pensées* which immediately precedes that of the *Disproportion*:

> When I see the blindness and the misery of man, when I look at the mute universe, and man without light, abandoned to himself, and as though having strayed to this corner of the universe, without knowing who put him there, for what reason he came there, what will become of him when he will die, incapable of any understanding, I become afraid, like a man who has been

brought while asleep to a fearsome desert island, *and who awakes without knowing where he is,* and without any means of getting away.[3]

The first understanding is therefore more of a nonunderstanding. Cut from his origins, ignorant of his future destiny, incapable of locating the place or the moment where he is amidst the durations and the spaces enveloping him, the being who finds himself here without light and abandoned to himself, is not without a tragic resemblance to the Heideggerian or Sartrian being. Like them, he is subjected to dereliction and contingency. But more exactly, with his absence of future or of past, by the darkness of the mind which isolates him, he is like the personage who, in the beginning of *A la recherche du temps perdu,* wakes in complete darkness: "And when I woke in the middle of the night, *as I had no idea of where I was,* I did not even know in *that first instant* who I was."[4] In Pascal as in Proust, there is therefore a first moment of consciousness in which the sleeper who awakens, apprehends himself in ignorance, incapable of knowing who he is, because he is incapable of situating himself in creation. On the one hand, there is the mute and distant universe; on the other, there is a moment and a place where one is, but without knowing where he is; so that between the place, the moment, and on the other hand all the other parts of space and duration, there is no common measure. If one does not know who one is, it is because one knows neither in what place nor what moment one may be. To know it would be to know what the entire universe is, in its spatial and temporal expanses. Such is therefore the first aspect under which is manifested the Pascalian anguish. Under an infinitely more piercing form, it is of the same nature as the "Where am I?" of Proust and the "I don't know where I am" of Marivaux. Here there is the place, the moment, there an indistinct immensity. How to link them, how to place them in rapport one with another? How to establish a *proportion?* Proportion which in any case, as these immensities themselves, could be only cosmic. For here it is a question not so much of a truly religious anguish, as much as a *straying* in the precise sense of the term, that is to say the anguish of the being who finds himself lost, powerless to give himself any points of reference, without hold on any world larger than the narrow circle of his island or of his cell:

Why is my understanding limited, my height, my duration to a hundred years rather than a thousand? What was nature's reason in making me so, and in choosing this milieu rather than another in the infinite in which there is no more reason to choose one place than another, nothing more tempting than another?[5]

And elsewhere, in an almost identical development:

When I consider the short duration of my life, absorbed in the eternity which precedes and follows it, the little space that I fill and even that I see, engulfed in the infinite immensity of spaces of which I am unaware, and which are unaware of me, I am frightened and astonished to find myself here rather than there; why now, rather than then?[6]

Thus, not only do the infinities of space and time oppose themselves irremediably by their dimensions to the point and the moment that I occupy, but they filch their reason for being, they deprive them of having any landmark in the whole, they uproot them, toss them into the unknown. Where am I? This is the essential question, the one to which I cannot give a reasonable response, unless I discover the means of linking this kind of floating point where I am, to the totality of things, and even to the intelligence of Him Who in creating it has chosen to place me precisely in this moment and this place. To know who I am, I must know where I am, and to know where I am, there is no other means possible, I must by thought embrace all which is and the very Being which is the reason of what is. Such is the reason of the vertiginous unfolding of thought which constitutes the substance of the passage on the *Disproportion de l'homme*. Vertiginous deployment, for it is not a matter of simply enlarging by ever so little the sphere of human understanding. A larger island would not be any the less an *island*, and a *desert*, it would no less be incommensurably separated from the world and from God by the same absence of rapport. It is on this point that Pascal differs absolutely from Proust, for his sleeper waking on a desert island cannot be satisfied by linking it through memory to the archipelago of the past. Here, memory proves itself miserably ineffectual. It could only, by the vain miracle of affective reviviscence, transport us from island to island, from moment to moment, and from place to place. Never, for any moment nor for any place, could it tell us who put us there, nor what we are doing there. Only a world understanding, a universal presence, can suffice for our needs and our exigencies. To know where I am, it is necessary for me to leave the place where I am, stretch out myself indefinitely by thought in space, so that having possessed myself of this space, I may at last, coming back to myself, strong in my universal understanding, determine with assurance, through the proportion which I have established with the universe, where and what I am.

Such is the significance of the Pascalian unfolding motion. Its excentricity, its outward sweep, has little to do with the expansion of impersonal science. What matters here is not knowing for the sake of knowing, but knowing for the sake of knowing oneself. The world and God Himself are, here, only objects of inquiry only because this secondary knowledge is the indispensable condition to the first, which is self-knowledge.

Nothing differs more from Cartesian thought. For Descartes the *Cogito* is an act which not only precedes the knowledge of the universe, but is such that in order to accomplish it it cannot be preceded by any knowledge of the latter. It is while voluntarily abolishing all relationship with the world, that the thinking subject discovers itself, in itself, to be immediately possessor of its essence, in a moment and a mental place of perfect plenitude, not a desert island but one filled with substance, and such that it is not necessary to imagine other expanses around it, since it is without expanse or other moments, since it is independent of moments of time. Inversely, the Pascalian *Cogito* discovers in the being only the insufficience of its moment and its place, leaves it without reason for being, and consequently obliges it, in order to acquire reason and sufficience, to have a double movement by which, moving transitively from itself to the extremity of the universe where God is, it comes back again from this extremity to itself. Here the knowledge of the universe is not the second part of a metaphysical treatise, entitled "Knowledge of Nature," a supplement to the knowledge of oneself; it is the *sine qua non* condition of this, the only possibility which man has, in constituting himself knowledgeable of a universal science, of situating himself where he is, so perfecting the miserable rough sketch of the science of self that is his first *Cogito*.

But from the beginning, before even attempting the venture, Pascal knows that this possibility is not really a possibility. In fact, he has no other design than to demonstrate the impossibility of this possibility. Thus, one could say that Pascal's intention, here, is precisely to reveal the vanity of Cartesian thought. If, as Descartes believes, the first question is to know oneself, the very act of the knowledge of self, contrary to what Descartes held, leads us at once, either to despair through the comprehension of our misery, or else to catastrophe by making obligatory the impossible, that is to say, universal knowledge. A catastrophe of which it is well to become a victim, so that we shall be aware of the immensity of our ignorance and the totality of our aberration. From the beginning of this attempt, its catastrophic character appears. For if, on the one hand, leaving its mental island, thought sees growing above and around it the dimensions of an infinitely opening world, on the other hand, the thinking being, far from leaving the place where he is, sees himself shrinking on the spot as fast as the sphere of his contemplation enlarges:

> Let man then contemplate the whole of nature in its full, high majesty, let him withdraw his view from the base objects which surround him. Let him look at this brilliant luminary, placed like an eternal lamp to give light to the universe, let the earth appear to him as a *point* in comparison with the vast circuit described by this star and let him learn with wonder that this vast circuit itself is but a very minute *point* in regard to that embraced by these heavenly bodies, rolling in the firmament.[7]

On one hand, then, passing from the circle of the baser objects to those described by the sun, and from that of the sun to that described by the stars, the gaze of the contemplator sees the circular limits of the universe unroll; but on the other hand, too, as fast as these limits unroll, all that they overtake and contain tends to contract and to mingle with the point of view of the spectator. Two opposing movements are accomplished at the same moment: one, centrifugal, by which the periphery of the universe sinks further and further away from the being who looks and who thinks, and the other, centripetal, by which all of circumscribed space tends to close upon the spectator, to identify itself with the place he occupies, to reduce itself, with him, to the dimensions of a simple point. And to this double movement, by which on the one hand, all flies outward, and on the other, all falls inward, no limits can be fixed by our imagination:

> But if our gaze stops there, let the imagination pass beyond: it will sooner be wearier with conceiving, than nature with supplying. All of this visible world is but an imperceptible mark upon the ample bosom of nature. No idea can approach it. In vain we inflate our conceptions beyond all imaginable spaces, we beget but atoms in comparison with the reality of things.[8]

From the outset, therefore, the catastrophe happens. Double catastrophe, since the two halves of a split universe are thrown in opposite directions, at whose extremities in the final count, the eye and the mind can no longer distinguish anything. The more the thinking being inflates his conceptions and tries to pass beyond them, the further he sees receding above him, a universe whose final limit is nowhere; while conversely to this infinite flight, there occurs an infinite reimplication, by which everything which is seen, thought, even imagined, in the interior of this total universe, surges back, is reabsorbed, closes itself on the place where one is, on the point which one occupies. Infinitely, over and above all perception and all thought, there is a natural order whose circumference is nowhere. And at an infinite distance this side of the circumference, there is a mark, a point, a central atom, which is nothing in itself, and merges with the spectator. Space is only a maximum of distance between a point and a circular line. And what is true of space is true also of duration: "The eternity of things in themselves or in God should also astound our short duration."[9] Space and time become the transcendent field of an objective, anonymous immensity and eternity, while at the center there is nothing more than a subject reduced to the instant and the point: "I see only infinities on all sides, enclosing me like an atom and like a shadow lasting only an instant without a return."[10]

The attempt then to acquire self-knowledge through knowledge of the universe, ends in total failure, in the consciousness of a maximum disparity. At one extremity there is nothing more than a *nowhere* of circumference, at the other, an *anywhere* of center, and between them a space now stripped of all content, an incommensurable distance. To be the center here, is not to be the generating place of a circle, the privileged point from which all is measured and from which everything is brought back. Anywhere and forever, it is to be at an infinite distance from the infinite circumference. Like the Peripatetics and unlike all Neo-Platonic thought, Pascal, here conceives the center as situated at the lowest possible point, in the most remote place, in the worst position of all, since in no matter what place one may be, it is always the furthest from the limits of reality.

Hence, when, following so many thinkers, Pascal again takes up the famous phrase: "It is an infinite sphere of which the center is everywhere, the circumference nowhere," he undoubtedly uses it in a very different sense from that which had been conferred on it by these thinkers. Far from expressing an objective conception of God, it expresses here the most rigorously subjective conception of a universe which one cannot imagine without seeing the periphery of it vanish in the distance from the central point where one looks at it: so that there is no way of finding proportions between it and oneself. Here, therefore, center and circumference do not express a rapport as they do in mathematical figures; on the contrary they represent the impossibility of establishing this. In the first draft of this passage Pascal had written: "We beget only atoms in comparison with the reality of this *infinite vastness*. It is an *admirable* sphere . . . ." The sphere here, therefore, is not God, not even nature, but the vastness of what is. Vastness whose infinity expresses itself precisely by the impossibility of conceiving the limits of it from no matter what point where one may find oneself. So that the great Plotinian and medieval *topos* on being taken up again by Pascal, sees its significance reversed. Instead of representing, as with Saint Bonaventure, Eckhart or Ficino, the supernatural reality of a God Who, being at one and the same time everywhere and above all, is simultaneously center and circumference, it represents on the contrary, at the precise place in the text where Pascal has put it, the limitation of human knowledge since in whichever place this knowledge sets itself as center, it always finds itself at the same infinite distance from the circumference of the knowable. Such a distance is the inexorable affirmation of the disproportion existing between human thought and what it is incapable of encompassing.

It is true, nevertheless, that if the sphere here is no longer the symbol of God, it is at least still the symbol of this symbol. For no sooner has Pascal identified the sphere with the infinite vastness, than he adds: "Finally, it is the greatest witness to the omnipotence of God that our imagination loses itself in this thought."

Thus, for Pascal, according to a thought which he develops farther on in the same essay and that should be considered in its place, the admirable sphere, by the same token that it is the symbol of the divisible infinity of space, is not without representing, too, something of the indivisible immensity of God, since space is an imperfect but perceptible representation of Him. Over and above the divisible and infinite sphere of nature, there is therefore something like a reminiscence of what the Neo-Platonic scholastic had conceived as the infinite indivisible sphere of God. Farther on and elsewhere in the *Pensées,* this reminiscence is to become stronger and take on all its force. But no sooner does Pascal indicate it here, than he takes away from it any cognitive value for human thought ("Our imagination is lost in this *incomprehensible* thought") and hurls man back to the opposite extremity, which is the infinite smallness of his own being in this remote province of nature.

"What is man in the infinite?"

II

Man is a point, an atom. From this point, equally, infinitely, in concentric circles which vanish in depth, a spatial and temporal abyss unrolls, from beyond which is spherically extended the even more "abysmal" reality of God. All is emptiness, all is silence, all is infinite distance: "The infinite distance of bodies from minds illustrates the more infinite distance of minds from that love which is supernatural."[11] Among these expanses the human atom is lost and engulfed: "Engulfed in the infinite immensity of spaces of which I know nothing, and which know me not . . .".[12]—"I see these terrifying spaces of the universe which enclose me."[13]—"What an appalling distance!"[14]—"The finite annihilates itself in the presence of the infinite."[15] Everywhere in the *Pensées* these phrases recur which convey the essential terror. It seems that as soon as he attempts to leave his desert island, the Pascalian being only discovers outside, infinitely, the same desert. Everything empties before the gaze. Everything comes back to being nothing more than this empty space, of which, speaking of his experiments in physics, Pascal said that he contented himself with pointing it out.[16] Now, as soon as he has pointed it, there is nothing left but it. There is nothing more striking, in Pascal, than the movement of the mind by which, as soon as it contemplates the world, everything perceptible which he finds in it perishes by engulfment in the incommensurable dilation of a thing without substance, which, said Father Noël,[17] is "at once everywhere and nowhere," which is the void. "Through space the universe encompasses me and engulfs me *like a point*."[18]—And yet, by my thought, this space, this void, this infinitude of distances, precisely because I am a point, can I not say that I understand it? There is still a recourse, that which I find in the dignity and the grandeur of my human thought. Lost, engulfed in space, may I not affirm myself as the center of this space? Am I not a thinking reed?

Here again, it is possible to compare and oppose Pascal and Descartes. For the universal reduction of the exterior reality to the void of expanse is not without analogy, not with the positive world of whirlwinds, but with the negative world, the kind of mental vacuum in which Descartes sets his *Cogito*. It is truly at the center of a vast nothingness caused by the hyperbolic doubt, that Descartes places like a luminous point from which all will reappear, a thought which, comprehending itself, will then comprehend the infinity of space and the universe. The "thinking reed" is the violent transformation of a Cartesian expression. It would not be impossible to imagine at this stage Pascal's thought just as ready to anticipate that of Leibnitz, as to prolong that of Descartes and of Giordano Bruno. For if in the middle of the universe thought discovers itself as a center and a point, if all thought is thus the indivisible place from which the rest is disposed, there is nothing which impedes one from understanding the rest. The Pascalian God could talk to man in the terms which Pic de la Mirandole puts in his mouth: "I have placed thee at the center of the world, so that thou canst the more comfortably look around thyself at everything that is in the world."[19] For human thought, no matter where, would always then be the authentic center of the infinite universe. "The immense divine sphere," said Charles de Bouelles, "has an infinite number of centers."[20] If man is a point, this point is the center, and from there, in a sense, space, the universe, God Himself, become comprehensible again. A human measure of the total reality is possible; it follows, therefore, that both my thought and myself are saved.

But nothing is saved of itself, and it is precisely to put aside this last final possibility of natural salvation, that Pascal goes from the first to the second part of his exposé. When I conceived the vastness of things as an admirable sphere, I had to conceive myself as the central point of it. But as soon as I bring my gaze inward on myself, I am no longer a point nor a center, I am that from which, interiorly, deeply, I must go and sink in order to find the center.

> But to show him an even more astonishing prodigy, let him seek among things he knows the most minute. Let a mite offer him in the littleness of its body parts incomparably smaller, limbs with joints, veins in these limbs, blood in these veins, humors in this blood, globules in these humors, vapors in these globules . . .

Let us not allow the image of the mite to hide from us here the essential idea. It is not from the mite that thought proceeds, it is from itself, that is to say, from man, a thinking subject. Just as earlier he came forth from himself, excentrically, to try to measure the spaces of the infinite, it is once more from himself—for he has "come back to himself"—that he sets out on another quest, which is to be that of the infinitely small. And the first object which he encounters in this quest does not differ physically from himself, except through its smallness, for in the mite as in man are found limbs with joints, veins with blood, and in the blood, globules and vapors. In looking at the mite, man is not ceasing to look at himself. He distinguishes, reduced to minuscule proportions, the internal world which constitutes his body; and this same world itself envelops others, which envelop still others; so that from envelope to envelope and from body to body, it is always himself, and with himself the exterior immensity surrounding him, that man sees to be disposed in ever-receding circles, enclosed one within another, in the interior spaces of the infinitely small!

> I will show him therein a new abyss. I will picture to him not only the visible universe, but the conceivable immensity of nature, in the *compass* of this abbreviation of an atom. Let him view therein an infinity of universes, each one of which has its own firmament, its planets, its earth. . . .

The scene has changed and yet it remains the same. It is still an abyss which reveals itself. But it is an interior abyss. It is no longer a case of *"embracing the circumference of things,"* but of *"arriving at the center."*[21] In its movement toward the abyss, thought, here, no longer leaves an initial and central point. It is in the search for this point that it now moves inward. Instead of placing man at the center of the excentric unfoldment of his thought toward the circumference of things, Pascal describes it here as directing itself concentrically toward the center of these things. And instead of showing in the progressive dilation of nature the corresponding constriction of all that it contains, Pascal shows here in the progressive shrinking of his center, the gradual dilation of successive points of view from which this is contemplated. So that from point of view to point of view and from object to object, as thought sinks down toward the receding point of the infinitely small, the very subject of this thought sees surging back toward it, every object as monstrously amplified. Their inflation is his inflation. The onlooker becomes mountain, earth, firmament, universe. Or rather, while thought endeavors to attain at the end of its vertical movement the central point of things, these things, rising from their depth, come one by one to stretch and inflate the surface, transforming it into a circumference which threatens, also, to be infinite. Thus the subject of this thought now discovers itself, before and behind, not anymore as the center, but as the very periphery of that which it wishes to contemplate. It is from this periphery that man tries to pierce, circle after circle, the concentric layers which veil from him the central verity. His gaze no longer diverges in space. He must make it converge from all the points of its surface toward a center; and this center is similar to the point of an immense inverted cone of which the lines would sink indefinitely into the depths. Depths which englobe worlds, but which are themselves englobed. A reversed universe disposes itself like the other under the form of concentric spheres, where paradoxically globules enclose globes, and mites, the stars. The more the mind loses itself in smallness, the more man marvels at seeing himself so enormous:

> For who will not marvel that our body, which for a while was not perceptible in the universe, itself imperceptible in the bosom of all, is now a colossus, a world, or rather, an all, in respect to the nothingness at which it is impossible to arrive?

Man now is a colossus, a world, an all. He is the very sphere which embraces the totality of things. And since the center of this sphere is at an infinite distance from the circumference, the circumference is also infinite. No matter where man places himself, he is always at the surface of the imperceptible; the circumference is in all places, the center in no place.

In citing, at the end of his development on the infinitely large, the phrase: "It is an infinite sphere of which the center is everywhere, the circumference nowhere," Pascal could not help but think of the radical inversion to which he would have to submit if he wished to apply it to the inverse development on the infinitely small. For in the infinite sphere of the infinitely small, it is the center which is nowhere and it is the circumference which is everywhere.

Now, the circumference is man. Man seems to himself to be like a colossus, like a world. This world encompasses the infinite, but it encompasses it without understanding it. Just as there could be no possibility of comprehending the world for him who fixes himself at the center without attaining the circumference, by the same token there is no possibility of understanding the world for him who places himself at the circumference without ever arriving at the center. The ignorance of the minimum is equal to that of the maximum. On the one hand as on the other there is an absence of rapport. Totality without unity equals unity without totality. The absolute *dispro-portion* is always the same.

When one puts oneself at the center, the circumference disappears; when one places oneself at the circumference, there is no center. The two ways of thinking end in the same volatilization, in the same engulfment. The only possibility of freeing oneself of the paradox would be to be able to place oneself *at one and the same time* at the center and at the circumference; but man is incapable of it. So that in no matter what place he may locate himself and in whatever manner he may think, the world escapes him in either height or in depth. One after the other the circumference and the center of things appear as being nowhere. Finally, man finds himself in a world emptied of all possible rapports, somewhere, in the center of a sphere of which the circumference and the center "fleeing with an eternal flight," are never in any time nor in any place. On all sides there is the same ignorance. The catastrophe therefore seems total. The transitive movement by which thought had hoped to reach the truth both excentrically and concentrically, results only in throwing the thinker back "into the middle of extremes," at an infinite distance from the center and from the circumference, on the same indefinite shore from which he took his starting point. "This is where knowledge of nature leads us."[22]

III

"That is to say, in a word, that whatever movement, whatever number, whatever space, whatever time, there may be, there is always a great and a lesser than these so that they all stand between nothingness and the infinite, being always infinitely removed from these extremes."[23]

Such, therefore, it would seem, in the final point of the dialectic of disproportion. Between the largest and the least, between nothingness and the infinite, there are the spaces, times, durations, movements, and numbers; and there is man endeavoring to find with them proportions. They are upheld, and man also, but as though suspended in the middle of the void formed by their own remoteness from the extremes. It is as though all truth and all absolute existence had been withdrawn from one and from the other, in the infinity of a circumstantial limit, or in that of a nothingness of grandeur. Above, below, everywhere around and everywhere within, there is the "infinite chasm which can never be filled."[24] Now, this was precisely the work which, according to Pascal, human thought had given itself: to fill up the chasm, invade the void, "to search out from among those things absent what one cannot obtain from things present,"[25] to attain, without allowing anything to escape from the intermediary milieux, the ultimate height and the primal point of reality. To know, could only be to fill, and to fill, to handle.[26] In fact, it is striking that in the Pascalian epistemology there can be no place for knowledge at a distance, for a knowledge which would attain its object without stretching toward it. To know, is to enlarge the point, to elongate the lines, extend the surface, dilate the masses; or else it is to gather everything up in the seizure of a principle. And by the same token, to measure, is not to gauge distances, it is simultaneously to touch the place where one is and that toward which one aims, while occupying the interspace. Like that of a child or the blind, the Pascalian knowledge remains essentially tactile. The eye and the thought are not to be conceived here as otherwise than as an antenna on the forehead, a lengthening for the fingers. Hence, the tragedy of the void is not, with Pascal, as with Baudelaire or Hugo, the fear of wells into which one falls, but the horror of the desert island, which is to say a cell without walls within which there is nothing to clutch. This is why he must try tirelessly to find ways of touching the untouchable. If he sends out without respite, excentric and concentric waves into the void, it is because it is their express function to fill it up. But despite his efforts, this universe always rings hollow. Nevertheless, if nothing finite exists which is not lost in the infinite and incapable of filling it, the infinite is no less, in all its parts, in all its ampleness, traversed: "The least movement is of importance to all of nature; the whole sea changes for a stone."[27] Thus the stone, in a sense, is successful in doing what intelligence cannot; it propagates its waves to infinity; it fills the void; it joins through a hundred effects the infinitely small with the infinitely large.

Why, therefore, by intelligence, or else by moral force, can one not, as the stone does, fill the world, touch the extremes, be both circumference and center? Pascal dreams, while reading Montaigne, of the existence of Epaminondas, in whom the excess of a virtue implied excess of its opposite:

One does not show one's grandeur by being at one extremity, but by *touching both extremes at one, and filling all the interspace.* Yet it may be that it is only a sudden movement of the soul from one to the other of these extremes, and that the soul is never, in fact, but in one point, like a whirled firebrand.[28]

Here again reappears the image of the circle; but this time, it is a false circle, since it never exists entirely at one time. This is what Duns Scotus pointed out to Saint Thomas: "If in its circular movement the point does not allow to the circumference any other existence than its own, so that the moment it ceases to be in a certain place, the circumference also ceases to be, there will never be a circumference whose different points make themselves feel present at the center, but only a moving point."[29] The false circle therefore never closes itself and never unites the extremes; it contains nothing. Far from having a real circumference, it is only a point which through motion tries to fill all and to be all, but which, finally, wherever it is, is always only a point. So it is for all virtue as for all knowledge. An inexhaustible series of nuances fragment them into an infinity of exclusive points of view which one can neither embrace nor weld:

> When one wishes to pursue the virtues to extremes on the one hand or the other, vices present themselves which insinuate themselves by degrees, imperceptibly, on the side of the little infinite: and there present themselves a host of vices on the side of the great infinite, in such a way that one loses oneself in vices, and one no longer sees the virtues. Thus one turns against perfection itself.[30]

One turns against perfection as one turns against truth. Moral as well as physical knowledge implies the necessity to fill all the interspace while touching the extremes, to be at once center and circumference. Now, for that, one would need a supreme agility! To have a mind which "would see by a single look and not by the progress of reasoning,"[31] which would "see at a glance."[32] Such is the "esprit de finesse." Yet it is only a "sudden movement from one to the other of these extremes." As in the example of the whirling firebrand, here there is no circumference of which all the points are simultaneously present at the center, but only a moving point. The whirling point of thought can only create an illusory circle. For man, the extremes remain infinitely remote.

But they are remote only for man. He alone is fixed where he is, he alone cannot pass beyond. All things are "caused and causing, aided and aiding, mediate and immediate," all "keep in touch with one another by a natural and imperceptible bond which *links the extremes.*"[33] The Pascalian universe no longer looks hollow but full of things. Everything is in everything. Everything is linked to everything. If the whole sea changes for a stone, there is therefore a rapport and a linking of the stone to the sea and of the sea to the seashore. The center and the circumference in reality touch one another; their interspace is filled. In the plenitude of this stoic universe man alone introduces a kind of void; he alone is unable to perceive the relation and linking of all the parts. But this relation exists, the extremes are in close contact. What intellect, therefore, will seize them in their interrelations? An intellect capable of "touching both at once and filling the interspace"; divine intelligence.

In the autographed manuscript of the *Penśees,* immediately after the passage in which he describes human thought as a movement of the soul from one to the other of the extremes, Pascal throws in this phrase without a verb which by its shortness suggests something of the lightning suddenness with which a truly divine thought, far from going from one to the other of these extremes, immediately joins them:

> The infinite movement, *the point filling all,* the moment of rest; infinite without quantity, indivisible and infinite.[34]

It is suitable to connect this phrase with the following text, which perhaps is its source. It is taken from the *Morales Chrétiennes* of Father Yves of Paris:

> The faster movement is, the closer it gets to rest, and if one made an infinite movement, it would be also perfect rest, since it would outdistance this succession of parts which follow each other in ordinary movements.[35]

This passage is manifestly inspired by Nicolas of Cusa, to whose *Excitations*[36] Father Yves expressly refers. One can also cite this other passage of Cusa:

> Since the maximum is like an infinitely large sphere, we clearly see how it is the absolutely simple and adequate measure of all that the universe contains. . . . God is thus the absolutely simple, unique definition, of the entire universe . . . He is absolute repose, in which all movement is repose, and this absolute repose is the measure of all movement, as absolute straightness is the measure of all circumference, and as the greatest present, which is to say, eternity, is the measure of all time.[37]

Also with Giordano Bruno:

If, therefore, God is really all that He can be and possesses all which He is apt to possess, He will be at one and the same time both everywhere and in everything, and so perfectly mobile and rapid, that He will also be perfectly stable and immobile.[38]

Repose that is the measure of all movement; being which is indivisibly everywhere center of itself and of things; thought which, no less indivisibly, from its initial and final fixity, fills without transition the circular totality; eternal point to which, as with Saint Thomas and Dante, all times are present; an act so prompt that its starting point and all the circle of its action coincide; final coincidence of contraries, which, for Pascal, as for Nicolas of Cusa, is the human definition of God:

Do you believe that it is impossible that God could be infinite without parts?—Yes.—I should like to make you see something infinite and indivisible. This is a *point moving everywhere with an infinite speed;* for it is in all places and is wholly present in each of them.[39]

To express this image of the point moving everywhere, like the wave from a stone thrown into a liquid, Pascal had at first written *a point stirring in all directions.* A center instantaneously stirring even to the extremity of its infinite periphery, God is therefore exactly He of Whom Pascal said that "His tangible character" appeared symbolized in the reality of things. Now, for a mind which situated itself in the center of creation, this vastness appeared as an infinite sphere of which the center is everywhere, the circumference nowhere. For a mind, on the contrary, wanting to establish itself in its circumference, creation revealed itself as a sphere no less infinite, of which the circumference is everywhere, the center nowhere. But such as yet were only the opposed aspects of the world of the divisible infinite, in respect to a mind which, in order to think an extreme, must establish itself in the extreme opposite. So that for such a mind, one of the extremes could never be but the negation of the other. But in the indivisible infinite, which is God, the extremes merge. "If one considers," says Charles de Bouelles,[40] "sometimes the center, sometimes the circumference of the immense divine sphere, it is easy to state about God contrary verities . . . . And yet in so doing one does not divide His nature. For the divine sphere is indivisible without parts; thus it is altogether everywhere, and altogether nowhere."

God is therefore at one and the same time principle and infinite limit, center, and circumference. He is "the indivisible being without parts,"[41] the point which fills everything, which mingles everywhere; He is the sphere of which one can say that the center and the circumference are both together and nowhere. For the sources and the infinite are only one. Taking again an idea of Nicolas of Cusa which was introduced in sixteenth century France with Charles de Bouelles and brought into their own epochs by Bérulle[42] and Yves de Paris, Pascal organizes around the symbol of the infinite circle a theology which rests on the principle of the identity, in God, of contraries. He expresses it in a phrase in which the whole argument of the essay of the *Disproportion de l'homme* culminates, and in which one finds affirmed the absolute *proportion* of the infinity-circle and of the source-point:

> These extremities touch one another and join because of their remoteness from each other, and are found in God, and in God only.[43]

The extremes do not touch one another and do not simultaneously find one another except in an indivisible reality, of which the universe is but the symbol: neither in nature nor in man, but in the supernature and in God:

> . . . Nature having engraved its image and that of its author in all things, they almost all take after its double infinity.[44]

The transitive movement, passing, by way of nature, from man to God, does not end, in the final analysis, in a total catastrophe, since it ends in God. Without a doubt, as Father Yves de Paris has said, "the creatures are incapable of God's infinite unity, which at the same time is the point and the quantity, the center and the circumference."[45] But their incapacity is not so radical that it is not able to conceive the existence of a truly divine capacity. "By which," as Pascal says, "one may learn to evaluate oneself at one's true worth, and form reflections worth more than the rest of geometry itself."[46] The God of Christians "does not consist of a God Who is simply the author of geometrical verities";[47] He surpasses them by a species of divine geometry, in which the extremes coincide, and coinciding, fill the interspace. "The infinite chasm cannot be *filled* except by a finite and immutable object."[48] The gulf that is God, can be filled only by God. If we are incapable of seeing this in nature, we can at least see it in ourselves, when grace, in fulfilling us, adjusts us to the center and the circumference of the divine sphere. "It is a God Who *fills* the soul and the heart of those He possesses."[49] Filling the soul, creating the milieu between God and our misery, there is the grace of Jesus Christ. "Every effort of Pascal, from then on," says Albert Béguin, "was to tend to prove that man can, even in a world with no common denominator with himself, together find his *own measure* and a haven of peace."[50]

IV
THE EIGHTEENTH CENTURY

I

A Marinist poet, Giuseppe Battista, describes a cavalier who makes his lady a present of a ball:

> This globe, which often I throw into the air,
> Where of my sighs I hide the breath,
> Here it is, Nice, accept such a light weight
> And may this gift fulfill thy wish.
> While playing with the young Hyacinth
> A thousand times the blond god made it turn.
> It is the world's idea, if not the world,
> And the mobile prisoner of the wind.[1]

This ball offered by the player to his lady represents a principle of unity. It is the symbol of a unique thought, of an exclusive love. But it is also "the mobile prisoner of the wind." Here, there, this little world puffed up with love has been tossed about in the vast world, where it described a variety of curvetings. In a like manner, in Bernis' poem cited earlier, different breezes blew soap bubbles about in the sky. Nevertheless, in the Marinist poem, the mobility of events is counterbalanced by the fixity of the thought. The roundness of the balloon, still holds something of the homogeneity of the Eleatic sphere. On all sides, the same emotive substance swells this toy which rolls in every direction. But in Bernis' poem, the bubbles, following different itineraries and reflecting different countrysides, have also for sources divers puffs of wind. From the Baroque poetry of the seventeenth century to the light, sensationalist, poetry of the eighteenth century, a movement is accomplished which, accelerating the variations of experience, at the same time diminishes the importance of the principle of unity which linked them. The little spheres of de Bernis do not draw from the fact of being spheres the slightest character of cohesion or of permanence, only a greater facility in changing aspect and direction. The curve which bends their surfaces, and those they ceaselessly draw toward new points of the horizon, tend to mingle in a single line which is not any more circular, but simply sinuous. Scarcely has the eye been able to note on the surface of the bubble a continuing curvature which seems to end in a sphere, than it distinguishes, as if prolonging it, the differing curvature by which, in changing direction, the bubble bends its trajectory. The eye easily glides from one to the other of these curves. It takes pleasure in seeing always belied, and always reestablished on new bases, the circular regularity which had struck it in the first place. Instead of a fixed form, there is an incessant genesis of forms; instead of a circle, a continuous generation of contours. The bouncing ball, the bubble veering at the wind's whim, are no longer spheres, at the most, attempts at spheres; forms unceasingly effaced and rebegun, a principle of variety substituting itself for the principle of unity. Such had already been the principle of beauty for Leonardo da Vinci. Such is, for the people of the eighteenth century, the grace "more beautiful even than beauty." Grace, or rather, the graces, the mobility of gesture, nuance, inflection, by which a sinuous plurality comes to take the place of the circular continuity and of the constant rapport of this with the center: "I am I know not what," states an allegorical personage of Marivaux, "the I know not what which pleases in architecture, in furnishings, in gardens, in all which can make taste its object. Do not look for me under any form, for I have a thousand, and not one is fixed: this is how one may perceive me without knowing me, without being able either to seize me, nor to define me. I am just sensed, never unravelled."[2]

The I know not what has no fixed form. It is the contrary of the circle, and yet it starts from the circle, returns to the circle, plays at being, not a circle, but an infinity of circles. It can be conceived at one and the same time like a going out and a coming back, like a capricious faithfulness to an always loved and always forgotten pattern. It is variety in unity and unity in variety: "Man," says La Motte Houdar, "is the friend of symmetry; but even more so of variety. One must therefore, in order to satisfy him, present him with exact proportions, but always offer different ones."[3]

The man of the eighteenth century therefore applies himself to presenting everywhere proportions that are always different. In architecture, in painting, in sculpture, in novels or poems, the artist sets himself to draw curves which are engendered one from another, but of which not one closes upon itself to imprison unity. In 1745, on the frontispiece of a book of engravings, Hogarth designed on the palette of a painter a serpentine line with this device: *the line of beauty*. A few years later, he explained this symbol: "The serpentine line," he wrote, "by its waving and winding at the same time different ways, leads the eye in a pleasing manner along the continuity of its variety, if I may be allowed the expression."[4]

Burke was to develop this idea in a famous essay on the Sublime and the Beautiful. It became universally applied, in particular, in the landscaping of gardens. The fashion of English gardens of the eighteenth century faithfully reflects the taste for the serpentine line. One finds a reflection of this taste in the poetry of Delille. The bard of gardens loves

> Sinuous paths and indecisive ways;[5]

counter to this he detests uniformity and rigidity:

> Rich variety, delights of the eye,
> Hasten; come to break at last the insipid level,
> Break the sad T square and tiresome tracing-line.

Sinuosity is therefore the enemy of the straight line, of the great rigid avenues in the park of Versailles; but it is no less an enemy of that other tiresome and monotonous line which is the circular line:

> By a happy mixture of bays and protrusions
> The borders of the wood wish to be embellished.[6]

At once bay and border, concavity and convexity, beauty and fantasy, the variegated line is the only one which is charming and alive. It is the very line of nature and of life.

"Artists," says Wickelman, "have found in beautiful bodies the source of beauty in unity, diversity and harmony. For the aspects of a beautiful body are determined by *lines whose center incessantly changes,* in such a manner that even if one would prolong them, they *would never make a circle;* they are therefore more simple, but also more diverse than the circle, which, large or small though it may be, still holds the same center and encloses other circles or is enclosed by them."[7]

Nothing differs more, therefore, from the human body such as it was viewed by Vitruve or Leonardo, than the human body for the artist of the eighteenth century. The body is no longer an ensemble of proportions which attach themselves to the circle described around the separate members, it is a multiplicity of curves which are those of the very countryside. The human body is an English garden. And it is the same, too, with human thought, for, since Locke, philosophy and literature describe this thought as a series of movements of which the curve ceaselessly changes. The greatest novel of the eighteenth century is perhaps Sterne's *Tristram Shandy*. It is, in any case, the one which best embodies the sinuous variety of thought which is the most evident trait of the psychology of the epoch. And it even doubly represents it, in the first place, by telling the history of a person whose thought is pure sinuosity; and in the second place, by writing a history which is in itself sinuous in form, which incessantly diverges from its line and proceeds from digression to digression.

The novel of Tristram Shandy is emblematically represented by the complicated flourish which the cane of Corporal Trim describes, a flourish which Sterne has graphically reproduced in one of his chapters. Balzac's imagination was so struck by this diagram, that he used it in his *Peau de Chagrin*.

It is significant that Trim accomplishes this flourish at the moment when he is discoursing with Uncle Toby on the idea of liberty. The flourish is a representation of free thought: free to think what it wishes, free not to think what it no longer wishes to think. The sinuous line is the line invented "on the spot" by somebody freed from the obligation of following a determined direction, who turns from the straight road, and takes crossroads when it pleases him. The line of beauty is thus also the line of liberty; in any case, of that liberty which consists in following one's own caprice, in adopting the changing itineraries which fancy proposes to the mind. But this liberty of spontaneity is secretly contradicted by a principle of necessity which dominates it. If I am free to follow the curve of my caprice, the caprice itself is determined in advance by a whole mechanism of external and internal laws. The sinuosity of my thought depends on the exterior conditions in which I find myself, on perceptible experiences which modify me, and finally on the law of the association of ideas which does not force me to fix my thought, nor to cause it to turn in a circle, nor to make it follow a straight line, but that insidiously constrains it, by the contiguity of points in common, to move from one idea to another, as one passes from a concave to a convex curve at the point of coincidence. It follows, then, that the liberty of the sinuous caprice in the eighteenth century is no more than an illusory liberty. It does not consist, as with Stendhal later on, in a principle of action, a center of human dynamism. It is a passive variety, an inexhaustible capacity to become what hazard orders it to be. The hero of the eighteenth century novel, (up to Laclos) is not endowed with the faculty of arranging his life, or organizing his *self*. Both disappear in a jumble of lines so complicated that reason renounces deciphering anything, unless it be the extraordinary facility with which the mind can elude the very rules it has set itself.

The construction of existence in the form of a sinuous line, therefore, ends in failure, not from the non-obtaining of the objective, but by the absence of all objective. The sinuous line goes nowhere. It is a hieroglyph without signification, a scribble, a complicated but futile gesture. Unfaithful to the circle, erratic, supremely excentric, it becomes encumbered in its network, exhausts itself by the multiplicity of turns and returns, ends like a wearied river by dividing itself and becoming sluggish in some delta. A frequent happening in the eighteenth century is that of the exhaustion of caprice, the interruption of an activity which, from twisting and untwisting, tires of its spinning and stops no matter where.

II

But the eighteenth century is not only the epoch in which the shifty line of ideas and passions is developed. More orderly structures can also be distinguished therein. On the themes of the soap bubbles, ball, and serpentine lines, is superimposed a theme, analogous and yet quite different, the theme of the *spiderweb*.

To understand in what sense it is used in the eighteenth century it is useful to see how it was treated in the preceding epoch.

Here is the debut of a Marinist poet:

> From branch to branch, a minute animal,
> From its entrails, spins and composes
> An ingenious embroidery.
> Made of innumerable threads,
> It disposes such a spherical work
> That, ornamented with rays, it resembles the sun.
> But while at its graceful and delicate design
> Consuming itself, it gives itself to its task,
> Now a fortuitous breeze,

Shaking the mobile structure,
Breaking the frail threads,
In an instant, destroys the beautiful work.[8]

The spider web is not without rapport with the drop of dew and the soap bubble. Like them, a frail structure, it exists but a moment and is destroyed by the elements. It is a little world which, in spite of its roundness and its perimetric perfection, does not possess the indestructibility of the great world. Nevertheless, it is comparable to the sun. There is, in a poem by Hugo, a spider in its web, which God transforms precisely into a sun. For the spider, like the sun, has a round body "ornamented with rays."

Now, there are two advantages to a body furnished with rays. They traverse space in all directions, thus giving it a kind of structure; and they immediately make apparent the existence of a center. There are no rays without a center from which to be deployed. The cobweb, like the sun, is fitted with rays. Consequently, it not only (as the drop or the bubble) has a circumference, it has a center, and more than that, a living center. Thanks to this remarkable property, the symbol of the spider in its web (of stoic origin according to Chalcidius) greatly pleases the thinkers of the eighteenth century, or, at least, those among them who do not wish to shut themselves up in a moment without duration or to give themselves to the sinuous multiplicity of existence. No doubt, there is not a single writer of the time who does not accept Locke's principle, according to which the feeling of existence manifests itself in a *point* of consciousness, and there is not one, either, who is not persuaded that the incessant repetition of this point in every moment of time will form a sensible plurality of which the detail can never be enumerated by the mind. But for certain thinkers the problem consists, precisely, not in joining these different and particular points by capricious and vagabond lines, but in establishing between each one of these points and all the others, an ensemble of intelligible and structural relationships. Speaking symbolically, the cobweb offers a marvelously clear representation of this ensemble of relationships. Just like the sun, (that, in mythology, is not only an astral body but a living spirit), the spider web has the advantage of having, as a center, not only a base of operations and of convergence, but a cognitive and receptive force by whose operation what comes from outside is seized and experienced within. The cobweb is formed by a peripheric network which intercepts and annexes a certain number of objects. But it is also made of an animal and intelligent centrality, in which these objects find themselves metamorphosed in sensations and in ideas. The striking image which it offers therefore is of an external peripheric world, incessantly felt and rethought by a central consciousness. The spider not only devours, in a literal sense, the insects that it captures; it absorbs them also figuratively. It does this by an action difficult to comprehend and yet of which, to a larger or smaller degree, all sensible beings are capable, in transferring to the inside, to the mind, what is outside, in the web.

The spider is the consciousness of the universe of its web. It is the web itself, not under the aspect of the objective and exterior reality which the latter embraces, but under the form of a conscious centrality, of a subjective reality without space and without external objects, but where, by an act of consciousness, these objects are collected, transformed and redistributed in a space which this time is entirely mental.

Psychologists of the eighteenth century were naturally prone to represent to themselves the spider, first as torpid, being empty of sensations and of consciousness, in the center of its web. Yet let the shock of an insect's wing make it tremble, and behold! the creature awakens and gets called to feel its existence. If the sensualist Cogito can correctly be expressed by the formula: *I feel, therefore I am,* the result is that the creative sensation of the consciousness flows from the exterior, but surges up at the center of the interiority. Thus, each moment in which this creative action manifests itself becomes, as it were, a perceptible point situated at the extremity of a line or a thread coming from the exterior. And if to the first sensation others are added, if they multiply and combine, the whole web is set in a commotion. From all sides, peripheric vibrations converge toward the center.

"The soul is in our bodies," says Montesquieu, "as a spider in its web. It cannot move without disturbing one of the threads stretched out in space, and, too, one cannot shake one of these threads without moving it."[9]

Pope was to say the same thing:

> The spider's touch, how exquisitely fine!
> Feels at each thread, and lives along the line.[10]

Because it is the center, the soul therefore exists in the whole web. The center is the moment and the place where the threads meet. But the center is *aware* along all the rays and consequently at all the points of the circumference. I am the center, the spider in its web, and I am also the web, since all the web makes itself felt in me at the point where I am: "The present moment," says Turgot, "is a center to which a host of ideas, linked up one to the other, converge."[11] Buffon defines animal life in the same way. It is, he says, "a center to which everything is brought, in which the whole Universe is mirrored, an abridged world."[12]

Rivarol was to say the same thing: "The self in animals and in man is a fullness of feeling; it is produced by the convergence of the faculties toward a unique point."[13]

Here, therefore, is re-established, thanks to the symbol of the spider in its web, a satisfying image of the cohesion of the spiritual experience, be it only at the lowest level, the level of sensation. If the symbol of the spider is of stoic origin, the conception of a special sense which would centralize the experience of all others, comes in a direct line from Aristotle. Be that as it may, for the philosophers of the eighteenth century the perceptive being feels unitively, indivisibly all the divers sensations which are brought to him by his exterior senses, and this unification of experience takes place at the center, which is organized for it. The perceptive being is not a bubble or a balloon, a hollow thing. He is not, either, a drop, something flowing or melting. Finally, he is not a pearl, a substance enclosed within itself and ignorant of the outside. The human being is a center toward which the outer reality converges and gets synthesized. Thanks to this organization, the outer is linked to the inner and the circumference to the center. The mind is capable of extending itself as far as the universe and the universe of converging upon the mind.

"An extended mind," says Vauvenargues, "will consider beings in their mutual rapports; it seizes at a glance all the ramifications of things; it unites them at their source and in a common center; it fixes them under the same point of view; finally it diffuses light upon great objects and vast surfaces."[14]

III

This common center, this point of view from which one seizes the ramifications of things, does not only appear in the sphere of the psychological life. One sees it radiating everywhere, in the contemplation of objects of art and the beauties of nature, as well as in the philosophical meditations on the Newtonian cosmos. Thus, in the same manner in which in the eighteenth century there is an aesthetic of *I do not know what*, of fleeing contours and the serpentine line, there is an inverse aesthetic, that of the clarity and the vigor of the rapports uniting the circle to the center. Already in the middle of the seventeenth century the German poet Catharina Regina von Greiffenberg had conceived art as a seeming disorder, dissimulating a true order; when one acceded to the center, she said, one saw the chaos coming to order around this point:

> The disorder of art
> Is full of the most beautiful order. From the center of the sphere
> Springs a point of view; when one draws the rays
> As far as this point, the united form
> Appears with a perfect clarity.[15]

Such was to be the opinion of Dryden. Commenting on the Aristotelian rules governing tragedy, he writes: "As in the laws of perspective, so in Tragedy, there must be a point of sight in which all the lines terminate."[16] And a few years later he returns to the same subject: "The hero is the center of the principal action; all the lines drawn from the circumference converge upon him alone."[17]

This converging motion of the work of art is again affirmed by him whom one may call the father of modern criticism, the Zuricher Jakob Bodmer: "The poet," he says, "creates a whole in which all the parts are held. Every work of art should thus have a center."[18]

The importance of this remark goes beyond the limits of aesthetic theory. If the work of art has a center, around which the other parts distribute themselves to form a whole, it becomes possible to analyze the rapports which the center maintains with the different parts of the whole and to remake the synthesis. The work of art is an organic togetherness, which must be understood as such. A new sort of critical appreciation is therefore possible. All German criticism, beginning with that of Goethe and Humboldt, comes from this.

But perhaps the most ingenious reflections on the perspective center and the work of art are those of the Englishman Addison, which appeared long before in an issue of the *Spectator:*

> Among all the Figures in Architecture, there are none that have a greater Air than the Concave and the Convex, and we find in all the Ancient and Modern Architecture, as well in the remote Parts of China, as in Countries nearer home, that round Pillars and Vaulted Roofs make a great part of those Buildings which are designed for Pomp and Magnificence. The Reason I

take to be, because in these Figures we generally see more of the Body, than in those of other Kinds. . . . Look upon the Outside of a Dome, your eye half surrounds it; the entire Concavity falls into your Eye at once, the Sight being as the center that collects and gathers into it the Lines of the whole Circumference.[19]

Thus, the ancient Platonic aesthetic reappears in the middle of the eighteenth century. The beauty of the circle is greater than that of all other figures, because one can immediately perceive in it the relation between the multiplicity of the peripheral points and the simplicity of the central point. Addison speaks no differently than Plotinus, Saint Augustine, Saint Bonaventure, or Marsile Ficin. Yet for these last named, the final reason for this beauty was the analogy between the center of the circle and the divine unity whose infinite richness radiated in creation. Therein lay an eminently theological reason. For the writer of the eighteenth century there could be no question of reasoning in this way. The circle is beautiful because, from the center where he situates it, man's eye can easily embrace the whole shape of it. Such is the explication given by Addison. It comes from a thought which cannot place itself except in the domain of psychological relativism and of perspectivism.

But if all is perspective and point of view, nothing, therefore, is more important than to place oneself properly in a point of view, and to look carefully around oneself. In so moving the eye circularly over the world, man discovers that there are no fewer spheres and circles in nature than in art. Of all the writers of the eighteenth century, the one who has been most sensitive to the beauties of *natural circles* is Bernardin de Saint-Pierre.

Flights of birds, petals of flowers, trunks and foliage of trees, all seem circular to him: "The most beautiful of forms," he says, "is the spherical form; and the most agreeable contrast which it can make, is when it is in opposition to a radiating form. You will frequently find this form and its contrast in the aggregation of flowers called radiated, like the marguerite, which has a little circle of white divergent petals, environing its yellow disk."[20] And elsewhere: "Of all the movements, the most agreeable is the harmonic or circular movement. Nature has diffused it in the majority of its works, and has even rendered susceptible of it the vegetation of the earth. Our fields offer us frequent images of this spectacle, when the winds create on the meadows, long undulations similar to the waves of the sea; when they gently rock, on mountain summits, the high crests of the trees, causing them to describe bits of circles. Most birds form great circles as they play in the plains of the air, delighting in tracing there a multitude of curves and spirals."[21]

One sees that Bernardin knows how to happily marry the aesthetic of the sinuous line and that of the circle. One is but a variation of the other. Further, he has, to a very high degree, the sense of the *harmonic* relationship between the circle and the center. All of nature is for him, as for Kepler, a music of moving forms, which by turns become circumferences and centers, which combine together to create the same effect: "The harmonies of every force cross one another, and every one of them is circumference and center by turn. The disc of a daisy offers us one image: every one of the florets of its circumference is the center of a semi-circle of florets, which pass through the center of its disc. All together they represent the harmonies and forces of nature spherically conjoined; and their central floret, surrounded at a distance by white petals, is a naïve image of the sun, projecting its rays around its own system."[22]

Naïve image of the sun, naïve image, too, of man. For man, far more exactly than the sun, is the center of creation. All its harmonies dispose themselves around man, they are combined only for him. Man is the center, because he is the *end* of creation. From this point of view, which is that of finality and not that of efficient causality, the order of things finds itself reversed; the sun becomes peripheral and man, central: "Such are the two extremities of the chain of forces, that forms, by its revolution, the sphere of harmonies. The sun is the circumference, and man is the center: *it is in man that all rays end.*"[23]

For Bernardin as for Addison the harmony of things cannot therefore be grasped unless one understands that they have been formed to be disposed around a center and the eye of an onlooker. It is in this central eye that they join and become intelligible. And what is true for objects of art and for things of nature is so even more for nature itself, taken in its totality. "In our Speculations on infinite Space," Addison writes, "we consider that particular Place in which we exist, as a kind of Center to the whole Expansion."[24] No doubt, from this point, which is repeated everywhere, we are scarcely able to embrace an expanse whose circumference may nowhere be distinguished. But God Who is everywhere, and everywhere at the center, does not have our difficulties. Addison knows the old adage on the infinite sphere, of which the center is everywhere and the circumference nowhere. He cites it in another number of the *Spectator*,[25] where he identifies it with the divine *sensorium,* which is to say, infinite space, according to Newton. God is space, because He is, everywhere, the center of space, and from this center He feels and sees all that is in space. The great matter for Addison is to conceive how God perceives the world. God is a sort of universal regard, which embraces everything all at once. God is a center which is present in all parts of the sphere. God is a general glance on the whole of the spectacle.

Speaking this time, not of the ubiquity, but of divine eternity, Condillac also finds the same point of view: "We can imagine intelligences which perceive at once ideas which we read only successively, and we can arrive in some fashion at a mind which embraces in an instant all knowledge . . . . *It will be as a center of all the worlds . . .* in an indivisible and permanent instant to which the instant of creatures coexist."[26] One sees by what a curious road Condillac here rejoins the ancient scholastic conceptions of the *totum simul.* The eighteenth century does not necessarily overlook theology, but it needs to reconsider it in the frame of a relativist philosophy.

But if God, simply by looking at the world, can constitute Himself the center of it, it is much more difficult to do so for us than for Him. It is true that we can content ourselves in looking at the solar system. Since Newton, its circular organization appears more vigorously, more mathematically, more clearly than ever. The law of gravitation imparts to the center of this system a greater prestige and an infinitely more dynamic character than it had heretofore, even with Kepler. The force which attracts the planets is the principle which regulates all their motions. Now, this principle is immediately comprehensible, at least in its applications. The astronomer sees the sky, literally, so to speak, obeying his calculations. Hence one can say that man, possessor of the secret of the solar universe, participates in thought in its government.

When Voltaire writes:

> In the dazzling center of these immense orbs
> Which have been unable to hide from us their
> road and their distances,
> Shines that astral body of light which God
> Himself has lit,[27]

Voltaire sets in the same center God, creator of the sun, the sun, governor of the world, and even man, coadjutor of the sun, since he knows how the world is governed. In the mind of the eighteenth-century writer there is a sort of good conscience which springs from the fact that astronomy is known, and that, thanks to this knowledge, one can place oneself at the center of things and embrace it advantageously from this point of view.

But when other poets, such as André Chénier, begin to speak, not of *the* sun, but of the *suns,* plural, the situation changes strikingly. For, in this case, it is very possible for the poet to transport himself in imagination to one or the other of these suns (or comets), to "journey with them in their immense circle," but from the moment when they are made to move and be uttered in the plural, the suns are no longer suns nor centers, they are, at the utmost, huge planets:

> An invincible weight
> Curves them under the yoke of irresistible laws,
> Whose power, sacred, necessary, inflexible,
> Causes them all to pursue an irresistible center.[28]

There is, therefore, still, in immense space, an "irresistible center," to the attraction of which suns, dethroned from their central position, are submitted. Lebrun-Pindare (André Chénier's master) celebrates this center in terms which once again recall the *topos* of the infinite sphere whose circumference is nowhere:

> O nature, o my mother! O eternal Goddess . . . .
> It is thee, Daughter of the Gods, thee whose fecund hands
> Form the immense chain of the Times and the worlds.
> Thy supreme Will is thy supreme law;
> Thy illimitable reign has no boundary but thee.
> Far beyond the Skies where thy flames circle,
> It is thy hand that sowed under thy radiant steps
> Their starry powder on the vast Fields of the Skies.
> Light of mortals the prideful ignorance,
> O *Center! which never had a circumference* . . .[29]

If Lebrun's verses seem to us cold and pedantic, it is not because of the misuse of rhetoric which we find there; though such an abuse may be something in our own way of thinking. No, the true reason of our reaction may be in the fact that through the false enthusiasm, we can perceive there the uneasiness of a man who would like to find a *point of perspective,* and who cannot. For either there is an objective center of the universe, or there is not. And if there is one, where is it, how does one conceive of it, how can one in imagination place oneself in it? Newton, who defined and centralized the solar system so well, declares elsewhere that space is illimitable, thus, without a center. In the presence of infinite space, the imagination loses itself and reason can find no fixed point of view. The universe is unimaginable and unthinkable. No circumference and no center:

> In vain We measure this amazing Sphere,
> And find and fix its Centre here or there;
> Whilst its Circumference, scorning to be brought
> Ev'n into fancied Space, eludes our vanquish'd
>   Thought.[30]

What the English poet Prior says here in verse, Shaftesbury says in prose:

> O glorious nature! . . . Thy being is boundless, unsearchable, impenetrable. . . . Wearied imagination spends itself in vain, finding no coast or limit of this ocean, nor, in the widest tract through which it soars, one point yet nearer the circumference than the first center whence it parted.[31]

This is a Pascalian theme. The manifest circumference of the universe flees before the glance, although the apparent center, the first point of view where one had placed oneself, seems less a starting point than a fast ground, from where, no more than the swan of Mallarmé, one may fly. One can find analogous texts in Haller, Young, and *tutti quanti*. It is a common setting of the epoch. It is striking that the eighteenth century should have at one and the same time both a good and a bad cosmic consciousness. Good, when it considers the circle and the center of the solar universe, which it thinks to possess by thought; bad, when it searches for the center and the circle of the total universe, and finds them nowhere.

Kant is the only person who, in an essay which appeared in 1765 entitled *General History of Nature,* presents a hypothetical solution to the problem. It stems from the idea that in infinite space the masses began by being unequally distributed, in such a way that by the exercise of the law of gravitation a hearth of attraction constituted itself somewhere, there where the density of the masses was greatest:

> It is true that in an infinite space *no point, properly speaking, has the right to call itself center;* but following the essential differences of density which had to exist in primitive matter, and according to which, when they were created, they had to be accumulated more densely in a certain place, and in a more disseminated way when it receded from this, *such a point merits to be called center,* and ends, really, by so becoming in conse-

quence of the formation of the central mass under the action of the attraction exercised on it. It is at this point that all the rest of elemental matter is linked; consequently, as far as in the *infinite sphere of creation* the development of nature can extend, it makes of this great whole, one system.[32]

Kant is nearly the only thinker of the eighteenth century who was able to imagine the world from a center. His cosmology, however, was to have no real influence on his time. It will be necessary to wait for the German romantics, Poe, and Claudel, for as coherent a version of the total universe, or at least something equivalent to be established in literature.

IV

The eighteenth century therefore remains a relativist century. Truth consists in a series of points of view, and the supreme point of view, the only one which could embrace the cosmos, is the point of view of God. This does not prevent all the points of view being true, and all places and moments being centers of a circle which envelops some part of the truth. Thus relativism is a doctrine of great elasticity. This becomes manifest in particular in the conception by the epoch of the great chain of being. From animal to man, from man to the angel, and from the angel to God there is a long series of perspective fields that vary according to the length of the intellectual beam and the relative eminence of each being, but which, by definition, always goes from a center to a circumference. Still, the man of the eighteenth century is never satisfied to recognize the variability of the length of the beam. If the beam is variable, why not make it vary? If our field of perspective is less than that of superior minds why not try to extend it and to draw closer to those who are above us? As Arthur Lovejoy has shown,[33] the old Platonic conception of the chain of being, for the philosophers of the eighteenth century, is not any more a series of degrees where every species has its place allotted and can neither go up nor come down. A sort of vast progressive and ascendant movement seems to sweep all creation along from the bottom to the top. The chain of being is an escalator which simultaneously brings everybody up without mixing the ranks. Now, if it is so in ontological reality, why should it not be the same in the sphere, or rather in the spheres of knowledge? This progressive and expansive movement of the mind can already be seen in the child, from the moment of its birth. To have consciousness of self and the world, is first to discover the point at which one is and a little bit round about; then to apprehend more, and still more. If man is a spider, he is a spider tormented by the necessity constantly to enlarge its web: "As we like to see a great number of objects," writes Montesquieu, "we should like to extend our view, be in several places, wander through more of space; in a word our soul flies all boundaries, and would, so to speak, *extend the sphere of its presence.*"[34]

The human mind is a sphere which tends to dilate itself. This dilation is very different from that which one observes in the Neo-Platonic or Baroque literature, since here it no longer is an ideal movement or an illusion of the mind. It is a real phenomenon, a clearly defined occupation of space and the world by sense and intelligence, like an army taking possession of a larger and larger territory by the process of pushing its advance posts more and more ahead of it. It is clear that the progress of science consists, above all, in the enlargement of its field of observation. No doubt, not everyone accomplishes this progress. Some do not leave the narrow sphere which nature or their own laziness has prescribed for them. But others make the effort to open their mind, to give it the vastest possible range, and so to meet the immensity of the field of consciousness: "A great soul," said Vauvenargues, "loses sight of nothing; the past, the present and the future are immobile before his eyes. It sends its sight very far; it embraces this enormous distance . . . . It possesses everything; everything touches it; nothing is foreign to it."[35]

For Vauvenargues, therefore, if knowledge can increase and enlarge, it is because there is no hiatus in the knowable. Things are attached one to another, as the threads of the spider's web at the points of intersection. Everything is linked with everything else, and it is this liaison which permits passage from one thing to another by a constant ramification of investigative movement. But Vauvenargues does not yet conceive any other movement than this. In the passage which has just been cited, only the "great soul" moves, or, more precisely, its gaze which is incessantly carried further away. As to the field of knowledge and to the objects found in it, they await the gaze, they themselves do not move. Yet others, and Diderot in the first rank, realize that everything moves, the spectator, his gaze, the objects, and space itself into which everything is inserted. In addition, the universe of Diderot is a molecular universe. Not only is everything held in it, but everything is filled, and the movement diffuses itself everywhere by waves, as in a gaseous or liquid medium. Everything propagates itself; everything influences it. Knowledge, feeling, sympathy, are, like the rest, undulations which start from one point to influence all other points.

> I exist like a point. . . . Here is the last term of the concentration of (my) existence; but its ideal *dilation* can be without limits.[36]
>
> There is a circumscribed happiness which remains in me and which does not extend beyond. There is an *expansive* happiness which *propagates* itself. . . .[37]
>
> Do not let us narrow our existence, let us not circumscribe the *sphere* of our pleasures.[38]
>
> Let us not forget for a moment the point which we occupy in space and in duration, and let us extend our view on the coming centuries, the furthest regions and the peoples yet to be born.[39]

Diderot's movement of thought is therefore precisely *excentric*. No moment or point of existence, for him, could ever be changed into a closed place, in the interior of which heart and mind would find their sufficiency. Every moment must put itself in relation to all other moments, as each place with every other place. Nothing is stranger to Diderot's metaphysical system than the image of the bubble. For the bubble is a little closed universe, and the worst of it is, a universe which is not susceptible to enlargement without exploding. Diderot's thought, on the contrary, wishes to remain as elastic as possible. Elasticity of the idea or of the feeling which dilates, elasticity too, of all the other sensory points with which the idea or the feeling comes in contact: "I am a little cluster of sensory points, which everything impresses on me, and which I impress on everything."[40]

In a famous passage, Diderot takes up the comparison of the mind with the spider in its web. The "large or small spider" of which he speaks in the *Rêve de d'Alembert,* a spider "of infinite netting," whose threads extend to everything, is it the consciousness of Diderot or that of Mademoiselle de Lespinasse, that of God, that of the world, or is it all consciousness? For all is consciousness, or all can constitute itself in consciousness, that is to say in a nervous sensory center, from which one can "carry oneself to the extremities of the netting."[41] The universe is not only a conglomeration of contiguous molecules, but an interlacing of all the strands, which from one extremity to the other of this world, a multitude of webs entangles. Whether or not there exist a center of centers and a matrix of a web, each particular center remains in constantly renewed communication with the ever mobile ensemble. From the "fluent point"[42] where it oscillates and which involves it in an indefinite succession of points of view and points of contact, every consciousness is capable of grasping, in the immense space environing it, everything going on, given that "everything is linked, contiguous."[43]

Yet this discovery of the absolute contiguity of things also reveals that the comparison with the spider's web is not absolutely exact. Even in imagining a mobile or indefinitely extensible web, or an infinity of webs, one is only able to conceive in this way a universe which at the most is furrowed with the strands of spirit; not the plenary movement by which reality converges into consciousness, by which consciousness extends itself into reality. Light, it is true, diffuses itself equally and universally, but this metaphor which is so natural to the Neo-Platonic thinkers, is less suited to sensationalist thought. No doubt, since Huyghens, the conception of light has changed. To the hypotheses of emission, formulated by Newton, Huyghens opposes an "undulatory" theory. Light propagates itself by waves: "I call them waves," says Huyghens, "because of their resemblance to those which one sees forming in water when one throws a stone into it."[44] Luminous waves, sonorous waves, magnetic waves (with Gilbert), modern science is full of waves. Why should the universe not be filled with them?

To convey the phenomenon of universal intercommunication, the perfect image, the favorite image of the philosophers, is not that of the spider in its web, but that of the stone thrown into water, and the circular waves it there creates. "All beings flow one within the others" writes Diderot.[45]

Of all the philosophers of the century the only one who holds reservations on the idea of an infinite propagation of all movements is Voltaire. Not that he denies the existence of propagation. He only denies its infinity.

> One must realize that all is not filled in nature, as it has been shown by Newton, and that all movement does not communicate itself from near to near, until it has circled the world. Throw into water a body of similar density, you may easily calculate that at the end of a certain time the movement of this body and that which it communicates to the water, are annihilated.[46]

A stone thrown in the Baltic sea produces no effect whatsoever in the Indian sea. There are a thousand effects which annihilate themselves like the movement in fluids.[47]

It suits Voltaire to arrange some discontinuity in his universe. A world in which everything would never stop propagating itself would no longer furnish the mind with the occasion for pauses and resumptions, for the annihilation of empires and the volatilization of ideas; or at every instant for starting in a new direction. Voltaire rather belongs to the group of those who prefer the sinuous line to the circular wave. Even, with him, sinuosity often cedes to angularity. His world and his thought go by leaps and bounds. It is a world of ricochets and stones in a frog's bog.

Still, in spite of Voltaire, the idea of infinite propagation had the greatest success in the eighteenth century. "Everything in the world is linked," writes Madame du Chatelet; "every being is related to all those other beings which coexist with it, and to all those who have preceded it and who must follow . . . . The impressions which objects make on us, continue at whatever distance they may be placed, because *in the plenum of things all movement must produce waves going to infinity, like the stone which one throws into the Ocean* . . . . and these waves propagated and dilated to infinity must necessarily reach us . . . . We receive the impressions of all movements which occur in the universe."[48]

These are Leibnizian ideas: "The Universe," Leibniz had written, "being a fluid matter, all of a piece, and like an ocean without shores, all movements are conserved and are propogated to infinity, even though imperceptibly, as the circles . . . *made by a stone thrown into the water.*"[49]

But if this image suits the Leibnizian idealism, where every monad embodies an adequate representation of all that takes place in the universe, it suits even better sensationalist and materialist thought for which every perceiving mind is the emitting and receiving center of concentric waves. The example of Pope will suffice to illustrate it. The image of the stone thrown into the water and producing circles recurs three times in his work: first, in an imitation of Chaucer, to represent the propagation of rumor in the world; then in his *Essay on Man,* to describe the sympathizing movement by which the human soul progressively embraces all creatures, from parents, neighbors, closest friends, to the whole human race; finally in the *Dunciad,* to express the opposed affective movement, that by which ennui spreads throughout the whole world.[50] For Pope, as for Locke, the passions, by which is meant the first motive of action, are the condition of all thought. They create around themselves by circle, eddies of activity. Let them be extinguished and around the center which has disappeared ennui and corruption will propagate themselves.

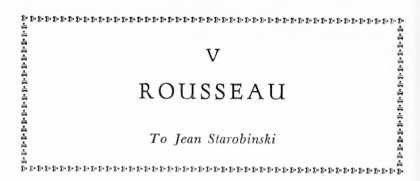

V

ROUSSEAU

To Jean Starobinski

I

Every man, for Rousseau, has "his particular circle or horizon of which he is the center."[1]—"There is not a creature in the universe," he says, "which one could not, to some degree, regard as the common center of all the others."[2]

Man is therefore a center, center of expansive life. Now, as to this center, it is first fitting to consider it in itself, independently of the regions in which it is called upon to shine. Because, before keeping up with the surrounding world of multiplicity of relations which will be the effect of the activities of the expansive soul, this center already exists, at least in a virtual fashion. It is the place from which, as soon as it has the power, the soul begins its enlargement. Nevertheless, at first, it has not as yet this ability. It is without power: "We are born feeble," says Rousseau, "we need strength."[3] Far from being able to extend ourselves in the exterior world, it is from the encroachment of this latter that we must be protected: "Soon, create an enclosure around the soul of thy child," Rousseau counsels a young mother.[4] An exiguous space, around which rises a defensive barrier, this is the initial expansion of the infant soul. And still it is too much to attribute to it the least possible space, for, concentrated in itself, incapable of imagining anything beyond what immediately touches or surrounds it, the soul of the child (or of the savage) is more similar to a point without dimension, to a center without periphery: "Let us suppose that a child at its birth had the power and the stature of a grown man, . . . he would not perceive any object beyond himself. . . . All his sensations *would unite in a single point*."[5]

It is from this unique point that everything begins, and from which everything needs must commence. The exigence of extension which, according to Rousseau, is the characteristic of every human soul, is only so large and so total, because, initially, it is without any extension whatever. Withdrawn in itself, it has no true territory. Everywhere is the outside. Everywhere there extends what it does not possess, what it is not. Everywhere space extends, which it can invade and possess.

It would be an error, however, to imagine that the human being begins by coveting some external good, of which inwardly it feels the absence. It does rather the opposite. As with the Pythagoreans and the Neo-Platonists, the soul, with Rousseau, first affirms itself as an incomparable center of energy. If it radiates, if it overflows, if it springs beyond, it is not to acquire being, but rather to extend it; for it possesses being within itself, it witnesses its outpouring, it lets go its flood. Thus, as soon as it has passed beyond its initial frailty, the child, for Rousseau, enters "that state of strength which carries us out of ourselves, and which makes us carry elsewhere the superfluous activity of our well-being."[6] It becomes "an active principle," of which the life is "overabundant, and expands in the outside world."[7]

Nevertheless, the child still ignores the nature and dimensions of this outside world. He does not know if it is empty or filled up, nor how far it spreads. But from the outset he sees in it a field which opens to receive him. The outside is the place where his being will unfold. And this unfolding seems to him, if not illimitable, at least as being susceptible of being indefinitely pursued, without fatigue or obstacle.

> At first, [says Rousseau speaking of early childhood] we are only concerned with that which touches us, *and that which immediately surrounds us;* all at once here we are traversing the globe and leaping to the extremities of the universe! This leap is the effect of the progress of our powers and the inclination of our spirits. In the state of feebleness and insufficiency, the care of conserving ourselves *concentrates us within ourselves;* in the state of force and power, *the desire to extend our being carries us outside of ourselves,* making us soar as far as we possibly can.[8]

Nothing, therefore, is more striking than the contrast between the concentration of the being at his beginnings, and the vast dilation of which he becomes the subject, as soon as he begins to develop himself. It is like a flight, an excentric leap. And in such an abrupt movement, one could see something prefiguring the great effusions of

the adult, if it did not become clear that this movement is less that
of a soul gliding imaginatively in space, than of an intelligence
tightly linked to the body and dependent on it to proceed to its
expansion. For this, in the first place, is an expansion of the senses.
In describing the progressive invasion of the world, which is every
juvenile's experience, Rousseau wrote: "Our thought goes no further
than our eyes, and our extending *only extends with the space it
measures.*"[9] It is to link, as the whole of the eighteenth century did
link, the progress of the mind to that of the senses. For Rousseau, as
for Locke and Condillac, the sphere of intellectual knowledge never
ceases to coincide with that of perceptible experience. As far as the
senses put out their antennae, the being extends its presence, and no
further.

Let us take care, however, in imagining that the sensations it
experiences, have for their exclusive end, to furnish to the sentient
being indications on the surrounding world. They bring to him too,
which is infinitely more precious, continual information about himself. To feel, is to feel oneself. To feel everywhere, is to feel oneself
everywhere. At the extremity of the antennae that the man of feeling
stretches out, everywhere, there are not only things, there is the self
that perceives the things. Thus, sensation is the universal means
through which a human being extends himself in space, and, in so
diffusing himself, everywhere gains consciousness of himself.

This excentric movement "of a naturally expanding soul"[10] manifests itself in more than one admirable passage at the beginning of
the *Confessions.* Thus the young Rousseau crossing the Alps for the
first time, not only discovers the beauty of the world, but diffuses
into it his own being:

> No accident troubled my journey; I was in the happiest con-
> dition of body and mind in which I have ever been. Young,
> vigorous, full of health, of security, of confidence in myself and
> in others, I was in that short and precious moment of life in
> which its *expanding plenitude extends our being, so to speak,
> by all its* sensations, and embellishes the whole of nature to our
> eyes by the charm of our existence.[11]

In the plenitude of the exterior world, therefore, is rediscovered
the inmost aspect of being. One is of the same kind as the other.
The only difference is that the inner being, considered in itself,
appears as though folded back into its center, while on the outside it
unfolds, it takes the measure of its development. From the center of

the self, to the ultimate points of the countryside embraced by the onlooker, a same environment extends, which is swept over by the sentient. Nowhere does it encounter any difference of nature. The outside is the inside. Here, for Rousseau, is the true joy: to be at the circumference what one is at the center; from the central home of the self to let be diffused the impression of existence on the surrounding universe: "He feels, so to speak, enough life in himself to animate everything surrounding it."[12]

The animation of the surrounding world by the center of sensibility, this is what matters above all in the text cited above. If nature appears there as radiant, one does not see it illuminate the soul of the adolescent and confer on it by its beauty a supplement of being. On the contrary, it is the soul of the young Rousseau which is veritably creating and recreating the external world which it discovers; it distributes life; it embellishes beauty. Things become vivid from the moment the eye touches them, as if this had the magic power of light. Moreover, in this lighting up of the world, the irradiating consciousness is neither shackled nor slowed by any obstacle. It is by a continuous movement that the animating force accomplishes the trajectory transporting it to the extremity of its rays. Finally, beyond the limits reached by these rays, there is nothing of which the mind seems to surmise the existence. The universe extends itself no further than the eye. It is entirely penetrated by the senses. Between them and the world no distinction is possible. It is not without reason that there is uttered here the word plenitude. Indeed, it would be hard to conceive an external space which, by the very act of thought, could be more effectively transformed into an internal space, in the subjective place where the soul reigns alone, for it has in it its own seat and its exclusive habitation:

> When everything was in order about me, when I was satisfied with all that surrounded me and with the sphere in which I had to live, I filled it with my affections.[13]

The expansive movement shows itself here at its point of perfection. The exterior sphere of the universe has become the interior sphere of the soul. The world is a void filled up, a pellicule which the breath of the mind has puffed up like a gas.

But no sooner has Rousseau written these lines than he adds:

> *My expansive soul extended itself on to other objects,* and, ceaselessly drawn outside by a thousand kinds of tastes, by pleasant attachments which ceaselessly occupied my heart, I

forgot, so to speak, my existence, devoted myself wholeheartedly to what was unfamiliar to me, and in the continual agitation of my heart experienced all the vicissitudes of human things.[14]

Is there not here the exact opposite of the phenomenon described immediately before? For if the sensation can be represented by the act by which consciousness absorbs all that it feels, transforming it into its own being, on the other hand it is also possible to conceive it as the process by which the same consciousness allows itself to be permeated and absorbed by everything which makes it feel. In one sense, I am a force filling all, diffusing in the all; in another, it is the objects of sense experience which, drawing this force into themselves, make use of it to imprint upon my spirit their own characteristics. So that sometimes the world seems to me to be an integral part of myself, and sometimes I seem to be an integral part of the world and to identify myself by turn with the thousand objects which it contains and which make themselves apparent to me.

The better to understand this curious alternative of diffused thought, one must return still once more to the symbol of the circle or the sphere. Nothing in the young Rousseau's experience, as we have seen, gives a more adequate image of happiness than the phenomenon of the "expansive fullness" of the mind. Thanks to it there takes place in the universe the delightful unfoldment of the self. From this point of view, which is that of the spectator accompanying the "active principle" in its diffusion, the circle or the sphere of the world appears as if it were opening on all sides from the center the field where, so to speak, the mind will make its career. The circumference is only the limit reached by the expanding source of power.—But let us reverse the point of view. Let us no longer regard things in the unity of the center of consciousness, but in the infinite multiplicity of aspects which they offer to the fatally divergent gaze. Is it not obvious then that diffused thought appears in the simultaneous or successive dissemination of the objects of perception? Thus the experience of the expansive fullness of the mind metamorphoses itself into its opposite, in an experience of dispersion in which the disappearing self tends to become absorbed and lost in the impalpable dust made up of the multitude of minute perceptible events. Instead of being a joy, the diffusion of the soul therefore becomes a suffering and a danger.

Whosoever surrenders himself to self-expansion through the senses, is obliged, to employ Rousseau's expression, to experience the vicissitude which does not cease to agitate the sphere of the external life. But as this coincides with the sphere of the interior life, the result is that the continual agitation which is created in the one, is also created in the other. To the external vicissitude is added the thousand eddies it provokes in the heart of him who is its plaything. Sensations perpetually engender emotions. And, as in the expansive existence, the man of feeling experiences sensations in all the points of his universe, in every one of these points, with a species of ecstatic or dolorous ubiquity, he begins to undergo delights or sufferings. To feel becomes a sort of scattering of affections in a multitude of objects, all susceptible to arousing pleasures or sorrow. So it goes for example, with Saint-Preux, when, introduced into Julie's antichamber, he finds there a hundred occasions to pour out his passion on the objects round about:

> Here am I in thy chamber, here am I in the sanctuary of all that my heart adores . . . How charming is this mysterious sojourn! Everything in it humors and nourishes the ardor that devours me. O Julie! it is filled with thee, and the flame of my desires *pours out on thy every vestige.*[15]

In pouring itself out on vestiges recalling to the mind the burning image of Julie, the flame of desire in Saint-Preux becomes charged now with an ardor more dangerous for himself than for the objects which awaken or kindle his passion. The invasion of the abode of the beloved and the perception of everything in which she has left a little of herself, have as a direct outcome, for the lover, a multiplication of emotions. As one who is jealous discovers in every uncovered secret not only a new reason to be jealous but an ever new way of so being, thus Saint-Preux invents new ways to love passionately, and soon enough, sorrowfully. Among these new ways, there are none more fatal for the peace of mind than those furnished by the lover's own imagination. Imagination, with Rousseau, proceeds in the same manner as sensory activity. This too, is a focus of energy, from which the being radiates into a milieu which it animates with its own life. The only difference is that the milieu here is created by the very one who spreads himself in it. It is as though a center were inventing its own periphery: "Love," writes Rousseau, "creates its own universe, so to speak; *it surrounds itself with objects that do not exist,* or to which it alone has given life."[16] In passion, therefore, nothing distinguishes the real from the imaginary objects. On one and the other the lover's fire courses with the same ardor. It is worthy of note, however, that, in the latter case, the soul's move-

ment springing toward what it desires, does not only imply an occupation of space, but also, as Pierre Burgelin has so well shown, an
invasion of time.[17] One remembers with what promptness Rousseau's
thought—especially in his youth—sprang toward the future. An
always disquieting future, always coveted or distrusted, in which,
sometimes in spite of itself, the anticipating thought rejoices, and
which, for an aged Rousseau, disabused by his over-frequent forays
into the future, will finally represent the true dwelling of misfortune:

> Foresight! foresight *which carries us ceaselessly beyond our-*
> *selves,* and often places us where we shall never arrive, that is
> the true source of our misery. What mania has a being as transi-
> tory as man, to always look ahead into a future which comes so
> rarely, and to neglect the present of which he is certain?[18]

> Reflection only serves to render man unhappy, without
> making him either better or wiser: it makes him lament past
> good fortune, and prevents him from enjoying the present: it
> presents to him the happy future, to seduce him through the
> imagination, and torment him with desires,—and the unhappy
> future, to make him feel it in advance.[19]

In short, in no matter what manner imagination may disclose to
him the abode of the future, this discovery can never do otherwise
than throw man into the heart of misfortune. His foray into duration
is a discovery of the true domain of suffering. The more man enlarges the area in which he feels he exists, the more he enlarges the
perimeter of his disquietudes, of his griefs, of his disappointment.
Worse still! at the very interior of this mental space where thought
spreads out, the movement of the imagination produces a rupture
of equilibrium and finally a grave distension. For the invasion of the
future implies a corresponding relinquishing of the present. Between
the present where one is and the future of which one dreams, there
is a hiatus:

> As soon as these potential faculties are in action, imagination,
> the most active of them all, awakes and precedes them. It is
> imagination *which extends, for us, the measure of possibilities,*
> whether for good or for evil, and which consequently, excites
> and nourishes desires by the hope of satisfying them. But the
> object which at first seems to be at hand, escapes more quickly
> than one can pursue it; when we think we have attained it, it
> transforms itself and appears again far ahead of us. Not noticing
> the country already covered, we discount it; the part of it still
> to be got over enlarges and extends ceaselessly. Thus one ex-

hausts oneself without ever arriving at the goal of our exertions; and the more we gain upon delights, the more happiness withdraws from us.[20]

The movement of propagation here becomes a pure movement of scission. No doubt, there is a part of the self which moves freely on the crest of the wave, which extends itself in the space of the future in constantly growing circles. But there is another part of the being which measures the disparity separating it from this self so vast and more and more fabulous. Between the circumferential self and the central self a growing interval widens; and, in the final analysis, seeing disappear at the horizon the myth of a happier and illusory self, the real central self, finds itself back at the same place, forced to recognize that it has never moved. The experience of the propagation of self by the imagination can only end in the consciousness of the radical distance which separates the soul from its desire and spreads out an immense hostile and insurmountable space between the imaginative center and its imaginary projections. The dilation of thought becomes similar to spirals of smoke which arise out of some burning but immobile core. Between the center and the periphery there is no longer either contact, nor measure, nothing but the feeling of a void which grows larger and larger.

II

Far from leading to happiness, expansion through the sensations and through the anticipatory imagination has unhappiness as its inevitable end. Such is the lesson which Rousseau draws from his own experience. Whoever says expansion, says multiplication of all the misfortunes, imaginary or real, from which man suffers:

> *Everyone spreads himself out, so to speak, over the whole earth, and becomes sentient over the whole of this great surface.* Is it surprising that our misfortunes multiply themselves at all the points by which we may be hurt?[21]

In the following passage Rousseau with particular ingenuity formulates his condemnation of the fatal movement by which man becomes sentient over the whole great surface. He expresses it, by means of an image familiar to us, that of the spider and the web:

> When I see each one of us, endlessly occupied with public opinion, *expanding his existence all around him, in a manner*

of speaking, scarcely preserving anything of it for his own heart, I seem to see a little insect forming from its own substance a great web by the means of which alone it seems to be aware, while one would think it dead in its hole. Man's vanity is the spider's web *which he spreads all about his environment;* one is as resistant as the other; the least thread one touches starts the insect moving.[22]

What is singular in this passage, is that, while absolutely conforming to the symbolism of the time, it says nevertheless the opposite. For the men of the eighteenth century, as we saw, the soul is like a spider at the center of its web. From there it maintains an infinity of relationships with the world round about. A Montesquieu, a Pope, a Diderot represent by this what for them is the essential function of man: to construct as extensive a network as possible, a web which puts the center in communication with the whole universe. But for Rousseau there is no more dangerous folly than this excentric development: "Do not imagine that in extending your faculties you are extending your forces; you are diminishing them, on the contrary, if your pride extends beyond them. *Let us measure the ray of our sphere, and stay at the center like the insect in the midst of its web;* we shall always be sufficient unto ourselves."[23]

When for Montesquieu or Diderot the spider is a center because, from this point it enters more easily into communication with the periphery, Rousseau, himself, wants his spider to stay in the center, as one would stay at the bottom of one's burrow, as one chooses the most solitary place, the furtherest removed from all points of the periphery. The spider's web loses here all receptive virtues, all diffusive force. Far from wishing to extend its web, the disenchanted insect does not even hope to catch its prey in it. It counts on drawing its subsistence from itself. It renounces all extension or importation. It is a spider which pulls in its threads, a center which gathers in its rays:

> Let us begin by being ourselves, by *concentrating ourselves in ourselves, by circumscribing our soul* within the same limits as those which nature has given to our being; let us begin, in a word, by *reassembling ourselves where we are,* so that in searching to understand ourselves, everything composing us comes *at one time* before us.[24]

Of this ingathering of the being an unexpected aspect is the contraction, around it, of the places which it inhabits or frequents. In fact, often, with Rousseau, the countryside gathers itself, sometimes even clusters around a center. Thus, in the *Lettre à d'Alembert,* Rousseau mentions, "in the environs of Neuchâtel a rather pleasant spectacle, perhaps unique in the world, a mountain entirely covered with habitations *of which every one is the center of the grounds which depend on it.*"[25] Nothing pleases Rousseau more than this disposition of human geography, in which the soil is seen to be divided into a quantity of small holdings. It is that every one of these farms or cottages, in Rousseau's eyes, is a hermitage. Here the social intercourses, without being suppressed, leave much time for "contemplation and retreat." And the winter season, in isolating these farms by creating barriers of snow, "takes away from them easy communication," so that "every one is shut in very snugly, with its numerous family, in his clean and pretty wooden house."[26]

In this family separated from the world and grouped in the center of its little domain, one can see, on the social plan, the equivalent of the psychological contraction which we have just noted. This equivalent one can find again, under another form, in the preference which Rousseau accords to English gardens above French gardens. If he prefers the first, it is less because he shows a positive taste for sinuosity which is the principle of their construction, than because of his mistrust toward the straight line, present in all gardens of the type of Versailles. The straight line has the fault of drawing the gaze toward the distances: "The man of taste," Rousseau writes in the *Nouvelle Héloïse,* "will not care about piercing afar fine perspectives; the taste for points of view and distances comes from the propensity most men have for being pleased only with the places where they are not: they long always for what is far away from them . . ."[27] In brief, if men like French gardens it is from the same perilous inclinations which make them abandon themselves to the deliriousness of expansion. With their long, divergent avenues these gardens incite the walker to seek anywhere in the distance what is close to him. They are invitations to dispersion. Inversely, intimate, compact, folding upon itself, the English garden is pleasing to the man with a domestic leaning. "Contented by what surrounds him," all he wishes is to have a walk at the door of his house. To make a garden for himself, *"he will gather together,"* says Rousseau, "water, greenness, shade, and coolness, for nature too gathers these things."[28]

One may experience some surprise to find in a work which invented the taste for the vast landscapes of lakes and mountains, a panegyric consecrated to little walks and limited horizons. But after the lyrical effusions of the first part, what Rousseau pursues in the *Nouvelle Héloïse* is precisely a dream of limited happiness: happiness which would be obtained by a contraction and a reassemblement of the being on itself, in a place which for him would be restricted and regrouped.

Nothing, therefore, is more important nor more typical than this movement of folding in and contraction, which is the very reverse of the antecedent expansion. What causes it is bitter disappointment. Nevertheless, it is far from being devoid of all feeling of hope. It is not in vain that the soul has "made itself sentient over the whole great surface." Dispersion has taught it the value of concentration. The fatigues and difficulties of over-long and too often multiplied excursions, have revealed to it how restful, charming, and restoring is the way home. Finally, if the imagination, which projects the being into the four corners of the future, is a dangerous and baleful activity of the mind, how is it possible not to praise the contrary movement, by which man is recalled to the center of his activity, and made to gently retrograde to the sources of his being? There is no doubt but that, from this point of view, in Rousseau's life memory plays a role exactly opposed to that of the anticipatory dreams. Imagination disperses, memory reassembles. It brings man back to his primitive concentration, there revealing to him his essential being.

In his failure Rousseau finds fresh resources. Forced to turn in upon himself, he takes up contact with this self. To the desperation of realizing that no further expansion is possible, hope soon follows, and even better, the sweet certitude of discovering in himself, at the *center,* and nowhere but the center, a marvelous sufficiency. From his reverse Rousseau draws a new philisophy of happiness:

> The real world has its limits, the imaginary world is infinite: *not being able to enlarge the one, let us contract the other;* for it is from their difference only that all the sorrows spring rendering us unhappy.[29]

> O man! *narrow thy existence within thee,* and no longer wilt thou be miserable.[30]

> It seems to me that I have truly lived *more when my feelings, so to speak, pulled in around my heart* by my destiny, did not *evaporate outside* on all the objects of men's esteem . . .[31]

I am daily more convinced that one cannot be happy on this earth but in proportion as one withdraws from things and draws nearer to oneself.[32]

III

The taste for solitude and contemplation burgeoned in my heart with the *expansive and tender feelings* intended to nourish it. Tumult and noise constrict and suffocate them, calm and peace reanimate and exalt them once more. I need collectedness in order to love.[33]

It comes to this: reanimated, exalted by collectedness, the need to love that I experience will make me come forth from my recollection.

In sum, Rousseau therefore explains to us here that if expansion ends in restriction, the restriction, in its turn, ends in expansion. He who, disappointed in the world, withdraws into himself, finds in himself a strength of feeling which inspires in him the desire to once more make contact with the world and to open his heart to it once more.

Nevertheless, in this second expansion, there are new factors which one must not neglect. The being who, after having been concentrated within himself, begins again to open his heart, is now marked by an experience which he previously lacked. No longer is he the impassioned adolescent of the beginning. He knows that the possession of the world is not obtained by a unilateral movement, without limit and without restraint. Added to this, the return to solitude, the deepening of the dream, even the feeling of detachment with which the solitary becomes used to consider beings and things, all this insensibly transforms the aspect under which these are now viewed by him. These beings and these things no longer are simply objects to be acquired or milestones to mark the progress of a conquest, they have become imbued with mystery and attraction in proportion to the very measure they have been withdrawn from the ascendancy of desire. With them it becomes possible to establish relations which are no longer based upon covetousness. Consequently, a new kind of effusiveness of the self in the world is revealed, which no longer is the expansion of the senses. It is sympathy.

Certainly, in Rousseau's life, as in the progress of his tales and the chronology of his other works, it is difficult and sometimes arbitrary to distinguish between these two forms of expansion. Rousseau himself has a tendency to confuse them. All one can say, is that, more complex, more thoughtful, less naïvely spontaneous than the other, the theme of expansion by sympathy has a tendency to appear not quite as soon. For example, in *Émile* or the *Nouvelle Héloïse*, it is appreciably later than the theme of expansion that one sees appear in the analysis or the story.

When looking at it at first, the theme of sympathy does not seem very original with Rousseau. As one knows, it is one of the most popular themes in the literature of the century. Yet one may perhaps venture to say that Rousseau is more inclined than any other to believe that souls all around are just as disposed to be penetrated as his soul is to penetrate them. But the conception of the world in the form of an open plenitude that emotion traverses and impregnates is a current idea of the epoch. On this point Rousseau does not differ in any way from, for example, Diderot or Pope.

The latter, in his *Essay On Man*, describes the propagation of sympathy in the following manner:

> Self-love but serves the virtuous mind to wake,
> As the small pebble stirs the peaceful lake;
> The centre moved, a circle straight succedes,
> Another still, and still another spreads;
> Friend, parent, neighbor, first it will embrace;
> His country next; and next all human race.[34]

It would be difficult to conceive a text closer to Rousseau's ideas. Rousseau, like Pope, believes that sympathy's point of departure is self-love:

> *When the force of my expansive soul identifies me with my fellow-creature,* and I feel myself, so to speak, in him, it is in order not to suffer that I wish him not to suffer; I interest myself in him for love of myself . . .[35]

Love of self, (that, naturally, is not to be confused with "amour-propre") therefore holds the central place. It is the starting point from which the circles of sensibility propagate themselves. In *Émile,* Rousseau gives a fully elaborated method to help the development of sympathy in the adolescent:

> To nourish and excite this nascent sensitivity, to guide it or follow it in its natural bent, what have we to do unless it be to offer the young man objects on which the *expansive force* of his heart can act, *which will dilate it, which will extend it toward*

*other beings, which will let him find himself everywhere outside
of himself* . . . which is to say, to excite in him, goodness, humanity, commiseration, benevolence, all the engaging and gentle
passions which attract men naturally.[36]

Gentle and engaging passions which dilate the heart and which
let it find itself everywhere in the outside world, such is the principle
of Emile's education. This is also the principle of Julie's existence:

> . . . It was Julie herself who *shed* her invincible charm on
> everything surrounding her.[37]

> . . . *The gentle influence of this expansive soul affected people
> around her* and even triumphed over insensibility.[38]

Those who surround Julie are, to the highest degree, aware of the
beaming influence which she exerts upon them: "Thy heart *vivifies
all those that surround it,*" Claire wrote her one day, "and bestows
on them, in a manner of speaking, a new being for which they are
forced to give it credit, since they would never have received it
without it."[39] And, in more general terms, but still apropos of
Julie, in a previous letter: "This is what should happen to all souls
of a certain temper; they transform, so to speak, others into themselves; they *have a sphere of activity in which nothing resists them:*
one cannot know them without wanting to imitate them, and from
their sublime elevation they attract to themselves all who surround
them."[40]

Julie's character therefore merits more than another (and certainly
more than Saint-Preux) the title of the central character of the novel.
It is around her that the other characters group themselves. The
sympathy which emanates from her person attracts the others, penetrates them, changes them, yet holds them at a distance, in their
place, which is that of planets in the solar system. Everything is
bathed in the light of her feelings. All participate in the marvelous
principle of radiating unity, which she incarnates. In her, once again,
Rousseau finds an adequate image of happiness: happiness is a central principle of benevolence which irradiates upon beings around
it, which interiorizes them, so that in their ambience the mind finds
itself as if in an interior space emanating from it.

Of this fine role which Rousseau entrusts to her, and which consists in being a central generating power of happiness, Julie herself
has full knowledge. One day, not long before her death, feeling in a
highly significant way the need to recollect in her mind those beings

on whom she exerts her influence, she writes the following lines to Saint-Preux, who has become the most docile of her satellites:

> I shall never forget one of this winter's days, when, after having read together the account of your voyages and those of the adventures of your friends, we had supper in the Apollo room, and there, thinking of the felicity which God sends me in this world, *I saw around me* my father, my husband, my children, my cousin, Milord Edward, yourself, not to mention Fanchon, who did nothing to spoil the picture, and *all these assembled together for the happy Julie.* I said to myself: this little room contains all that is dear to my heart, and perhaps all that is best in the world; *I am surrounded by everything that interests me; the whole universe is here for me;* at one and the same time I delight in the attachment that I hold for my friends, in that which they return to me, and in that which they hold for one another; their mutual feelings either come from me or are connected with me; *I see nothing which does not extend my being,* and nothing that divides it; *it is everything that surrounds me,* there is no portion remaining without me; my imagination has nothing left to do, I have nothing more to desire; to feel and to delight are for me the same things; *I live at once in everything I love,* I sate myself on happiness and the joy of living.[41]

In this passage of the highest import, one sees that Rousseau and his heroine are calling the roll of their little world, assembling souls together in exactly the same way that Marcel Proust was to make the synthesis of his romanesque universe at the end of *Time Regained.* For, in one case as in the other, what is realized (there by the intervention of memory, here by the action of sympathy), is the complete unification of the mind and of the place where it diffuses its feelings, a complete unification of the center and of the circle. In the same manner that, from the top of the steeple of Combray, Marcel's gaze can embrace *at once* both the direction of Guermantes and that of Méséglise, so Julie's gaze embraces and reconciles those on whom her soul is spread. Simultaneity and homogeneity: with Rousseau these are the two attributes of the sentient being.

To render this similitude between the fullness of human affection and divine eternity more striking still, Rousseau has chosen to make Julie die at the precise instant when she reaches the highest consciousness of the state of sympathy which unites her with her milieu. Suddenly, without taking the smallest lapse of time to do so, by the power of her feeling, Julie's soul fills all others: a ubiquity obtained in an instant so absolute that it does not need to be continued. Even Julie herself, on her death-bed, is conscious of this: "I have found the way to *extend my life without prolonging it.*"[42]

Existence therefore appears here to be at one and the same time an extension of the being in space and its retreat beyond time. It is a purely nontemporal diffusion. In this consists the miracle of sympathy: it transforms ambient space into a place where the spirit finds itself instantaneously diffused.

A concrete example will illustrate it. It is that of the village or town dweller's festival: "Is there sweeter joy," Rousseau writes in his *Rêveries,* "than to see a whole people give themselves up to joy on a festival day, and all hearts opening out to the supreme rays of happiness which pass rapidly but profoundly across the clouds of life?".[43] This passage illustrates well the extra-temporal character of the fête: if public pleasure passes rapidly, at least while it lasts it constitutes a privileged and brilliant moment, detached from ordinary time, and around it as a center there spreads not any stretch of a long duration but the vastitude of human happiness.—The word *opening* which explains this phenomenon, returns in another passage of the *Rêveries* devoted to the theme of the fête: "Well-being, fraternity, concord dispose hearts to open up and often, in the transports of an innocent joy, strangers accost one another, embrace, and invite one another to enjoy the concert of pleasures of the day."[44] —In the precious editions of the *Oeuvres* by La Pléiade, a note joined to the text sends us to a third passage, which, in the *Lettre à d'Alembert,* describes a military fête at the square of Saint Gervais:

> Soon the windows were filled with spectators who gave an added zest to the actors; they could not bear to stay long at their windows, they came down; the ladies of the house came to see their husbands, the servants brought wine, even the children, awakened by the noise, ran half-dressed between their fathers and mothers. Dancing was suspended: there was nothing but embracing, laughter, toasts, caresses. The result of all this was a general emotion which I do not know how to depict, but which, in the universal cheerfulness, is experienced quite naturally *in the midst of all that we hold dear.*[45]

The fête, as Jean Starobinski says, is "the optical milieu in which all become transparent: minds simply present for each other, with nothing interposing between them." An open space where there is an instantaneous communication of all the world; even more, a simultaneous diffusion of the feelings of each toward all and of all toward each. Hence everybody can consider himself the center from which his particular feelings of sympathy spring out and cast themselves into the universal happiness, and toward which, from all sides, happiness converges to inspire him to a new sympathy.

In the fête everyone "is in everything that surrounds him," everyone plays the role of Julie.

IV

Nevertheless, the fête is an exceptional event. On the other hand, Julie, in whom the force of sympathy "triumphs even over insensibility," is a purely fictitious character. Yet, in ordinary life, how may one triumph over the insensibility of others? This is a grave question, and such that the absence of answer would amount to the failure of the movement of expansion by sympathy. When what truly mattered was the invasion of the exterior world by feelings such as sensation, passion, the anticipatory imagination, disastrous though this enterprise was, at least it required only one actor. But there is no sympathetic movement which does not require reciprocity. And there is no universal sympathy which does not require a universal reciprocity. The success of the movement of expansion by sympathy is therefore not possible except in a universe where all the souls are of a sentient nature, not only those of an expansive turn, but also those which are ready to open to expansion. For all must vibrate in unison, feel the same thing, receive the communication of any peripheral movement.—But what if they should refuse the communication? If, to the circles of emotion which propagate and come to them, they oppose the wall of their insensibility and their hardness? Then what happens? The movement is interrupted, the circle broken, the wave repulsed. The world is no longer a quiet, liquid surface along which the circles sent out from the center can indefinitely enlarge themselves. It forms a limit, a barrier, against which feeling jostles and collides. To spread outside is no longer to shed one's joy everywhere; it is to discover the surrounding wickedness of men, and to learn that in leaving one's home joy transforms itself everywhere into sorrow.

If there is, says Rousseau, an active sensibility which "seeks to *extend and to reinforce the feeling of our being*," there is another, "negative or repelling that *compresses or shrinks* the one felt for others . . . . From the first are born all gentle and loving passions, from the second all heinous and cruel ones."[46] Such are, he says elsewhere, "envy, covetousness, hate . . . which torment those who experience them."[47]

Thus the agitation of a misunderstood heart, disillusion, repression, a thousand wounds of all kinds cause Rousseau to discover the existence of a world which is exactly the contrary to that in which he wished to expand through sympathy. This new world appears to Rousseau more and more somber and closed. There are, he says twice in the *Dialogues,* "triple walls of shadow which are erected around me."[48] Surrounded by a network of snares and conspiracies, shut up in a circle of opacity and silence, Rousseau now discovers a new kind of center. The center is the hated entity, which the whole circle represses and from which it draws away. The center is alone. It is this solitude of the center which is described in a whole series of passages in the *Dialogues:*

> There had been found an art to make for him of Paris, a more frightful solitude than caves and woods, where, *in the midst of men,* he finds neither communication, consolation, nor counsel, nor light, nor anything which might help him to conduct his life, an immense labyrinth in which he is not permitted to see through the gloom anything but false paths which draw him even farther from the true way. . . . If he enters a public place he is treated as one who is pestilent; *everyone surrounds him and stares at him, but draws away from him* and without speaking to him, only to act as a barrier.[49]

> I have seen him in a unique and almost unbelievable situation, *more alone in the midst of Paris than Robinson Crusoe on his island,* sequestered from the commerce of men by the crowd *even eager to surround him in order to prevent him from acquainting himself with anyone.*[50]

The mythical transformation of the environing world now becomes so grave that all movement of re-establishment proceeding from it is at once interpreted as a sign of obstruction or aggression. From the point of view of this delirium of interpretation, the most extraordinary passage in the *Dialogues* is perhaps the following, which depicts Rousseau crowded by the throng at the theater:

> See him going in to the theater *surrounded in an instant by a narrow enclosure* made of taut arms and canes in which you may imagine how little he is at his ease! Of what use is this barrier? If he wishes to force it, will it resist? Probably not. So what is its purpose? Uniquely to give the people the amusement of seeing him shut up in this cage, and to make him feel that

all those surrounding him are taking pleasure in being warders and bowmen.[51]

The center is a prison, the circle is a cage or a wall. Wall or abyss, these are the two terms by which Rousseau now designates the environing space, *isolating* space:

> They have dug out between themselves and me an immense abyss which nothing any longer can fill up or cross, and I am as separated from them for the rest of my life as are the dead from the living.[52]

From the center to the circumference no further communication is possible, no further feeling can make itself felt. Center and circumference are absolutely separated one from the other. And the distance which separates them no longer is traversed or annulled by the wave of emotion. It is a desert, a frightful silent solitude. Such is the universe which, "with a secret horror," Saint-Preux penetrates, when he thinks he must separate himself forever from Julie. For it is the very universe of separation: "My soul in the press, *searches to pour out, only to find itself everywhere restricted.*"[53]

Of all the writers of the epoch Rousseau is perhaps the first to experiment and to depict the tragic antipathy between the self-center and the peripheral world, which, from Balzac to Poe and to Baudelaire, was to hold such an important place in romantic literature. And he is also the first to undergo and to express the painful constriction of the self which is like a hideous transformation of the happy concentration in self, of whose benefits he himself boasted. On the other hand, it would be a mistake to confuse this narrowing of the being with the reduction of man to his true dimensions, of which one has seen numerous examples in Baroque literature. The narrowing with Rousseau never holds the aspects of a deflating nor of a collapse. It is not the disappearance of the illusory substance of a being brought back to its essential and real nullity. With Rousseau, it is the folding back, the forced return to the center, the investment of this center with a peripheral reality become wicked and hostile. The contracted being is a surrounded being.

V

> The confederacy is universal, without exception, without return, and I am certain to end my days in this frightful proscription without ever being able to penetrate its mystery.

It is in this deplorable state that after long anguish, instead of the despair which seemed to be my portion, I have once more found serenity, tranquillity, peace, happiness itself. . . . Reduced to myself, I have finally taken up my basic position. Pressed upon on all sides, I remain in equilibrium. . . .[54]

At the time of misfortune, Rousseau therefore rediscovers peace and equilibrium. For he has refound the center. It is also that to the hate of others he has refused to respond by hatred. The center, and, consequently, in the center, the force of expansion which is held by it, have remained intact: "I love myself too much to be able to hate anyone, no matter who it may be. That would be to *restrict* my *existence,* and I should prefer to *extend it over all the universe.*"[55]

The old dream of expansion begins over again. It begins again each time, because each time, in falling back on himself, Rousseau becomes once more enamoured of a dream which asks for nothing better than to fill out its sails. Rousseau is reduced to living in a point. But this point can once again inflate and enrich itself with all the fantastic life which the imagination deploys in it. Imagination which must not be confounded with the avid anticipation and disquiet of which it has been spoken in the beginning. For now what matters is a "creative imagination"[56] susceptible of throwing the mind "into the country of chimeras," and of making it "glide in the empyrean in the midst of charming objects" with which it surrounds itself. "There is no more seductive point of attraction," says Rousseau, "than those fictions of a loving and tender heart which, in the universe which it has created to suit itself, *dilates itself, and spreads out freely,* released from the hard shackles which *compress* it in our own world."[57]

This new effusion is a compensatory dream. To the restricted and inward-turned being it brings a space that, even though fictitious, is no less deliciously encroachable and available to explore, a free space. And when the tone of the reverie rises, this space becomes deeper, purifies itself, extricates itself from the fantasies which encumbered it, and so reveals itself even more vast than the cosmic expanse. One remembers the terms of the letter to Malesherbes: "In imagination, I liked to lose myself in space, my heart narrowed in the limits of the being found itself too tightly held, I suffocated in the universe, I should have liked to have thrown myself into the infinite."[58]

Thus, for a long time, at the depths of the self, in the profundity of the center, one takes pleasure in unfolding an imaginary universe, and the sweeter to conceive as, "with it one gets identified." On the one hand, one lives as a recluse, in the narrow sphere of a life, which is more and more solitary and turned in upon itself, and on the other, in the immense sphere with which the dream makes us coincide.

And so one goes on until old age. Old age, that grave epoch of life, particularly when one lives in the alternative of the expansive dream and the contraction into oneself. For, with old age, the dream changes its nature. The imagination runs dry, "the soul no longer has the vigor to throw itself forward, as before, beyond its old envelopment."[59] In other terms, Rousseau must say farewell to his great peripheral dreams. Let life remain narrowed into the center. One must get back to it just at the time when one is forced to acknowledge that the self is not an inexhaustible source, and that in this center where one is constrained to live, barely does a little heat exist which cannot radiate anymore.

Rousseau's last powers attempt to reassemble around this focus of heat. In the distance the wickedness of men continues to erect a wall which it would be useless to try to penetrate. Nearer, however, much nearer, a few very simple objects still form a little friendly circle. When Rousseau's heart, as he says, "constricted *by distress, brought together and concentrated all its movements around itself* to conserve this remaining warmth ready to evaporate and to be quenched,"[60] the plants, rocks, the humble things, all close, at a hand's reach, still attracted his attention. "My imagination which refuses to open itself to painful objects allows my senses to give themselves to the light but gentle impressions of *surrounding objects*."[61]

No longer the surrounding world, but surrounding "objects." The diameter of the circle has definitively been shortened. And it is at this moment, which is the final moment, that Rousseau for the last time, finds a kind of happiness. No longer in the delirium of expansion of a young heart, no longer in the propagation of a feeling of benevolence, no longer in the dilation of a cosmic dream, but in the simplest sort of contact with the things of the earth:

> My thoughts are almost nothing now but sensations, and the sphere of my understanding does not go beyond the objects with which I am immediately surrounded.[62]

VI

ROMANTICISM

To Albert Béguin

I

AT THE very end of the eighteenth century, describing the pain suffered by a perceptive soul, Tieck wrote:

What most depressed me in my sorrow, was that nature and all surrounding objects seemed so cold and unfeeling. *In myself there was found the center of all sensations,* and the more I removed myself from myself, the more these sensations diverged from one another, which, in my heart, remained tightly clustered against each other.[1]

At first sight, the situation which one finds described here does not seem to differ greatly from a number of others described by the writers of the eighteenth century. As with Montesquieu or Pope, as with Diderot or Rousseau, the center of which Tieck speaks is purely a nucleus of sensations. Once more, the human soul is conceived of as the focus of impressions which radiate outside. The only universe that the man of feeling can conceive is a universe also composed of men of feeling. All feeling seeks to pour itself outward and to communicate with the external world. How would it be possible to feel, without experiencing the need to share with all peripheral sensibilities the emotions at the center?

But at once differences appear. First, what is described in this text is not the success of the sympathetic movement but its failure. One would say that the wires which tie the sending station to the exterior world, are cut off, even cut off not very far from where it sends its threads outward. The world is there, all around, but nothing reaches it, nothing spreads itself in it. On one hand, there is the self, and on the other, distinct, closed, cruelly removed from the self by its lack of communication with it, there is a peripheral universe. Far from being linked, center and circle are separate and opposed. No doubt, in the history of feelings, such a situation is not new. Have we not just seen Rousseau denouncing the contrast between the generous, expansive life of the center, and the hostility of the environing world, characterized by antipathy and opacity? Nevertheless, the situation which is spoken of here is not exactly the same. It is at one and the same time more serious and less serious. Less serious, since to the sorrow of Tieck's hero it is not the hostility of the world which responds, it is uniquely its indifference. More serious, since the simple indifference of the exterior world is sufficient to paralyze the movement of expansion. From the inside to the outside, communication is not therefore the invariable rule. The circle is not spontaneously and infallibly associated with the center. A natural affinity does not render them inseparable. For the first time there clearly appears the consciousness of the non-identity which distinguishes the self-center from the circumferential non-self.

But from the moment when the fact of this non-identity imposes itself on the consciousness, a double mystery there appears. The circumference is no longer similar to the center; what is it, then? The coldness of nature, its refusal to participate in our real emotions, confer on it a character of a depth difficult to penetrate. The effusion of the heart no longer appears as the easiest possible movement, that by which one passes from the self to a milieu no different from the self. On the contrary, the center must now, not without difficulty, put itself in quest of the circle. Before the eye, a limit which recedes, a barrier which rises up, an obscurity which thickens and gets unfathomable, the non-self screens itself against the invasions of the self. It protects its true nature, it refuses to allow itself to be intermingled with the diffusive mind. To be at the center of things no longer matters except to measure how different the center is from things. Thus the romantic hero (whose thoughts here greatly resemble those of the idealistic philosopher), going one step beyond sensual monism, experiences the fundamental duality of the mind-center and of the peripheral-reality. Willy nilly, he must say goodbye to the seductive conception of a world resembling a sensitive web, where vibrations propagate themselves without obstacle. Such is not the reality. Reality is something else. Else than the self, else than the center. Its otherness makes it diminished and withdrawn. The center, constrained to remain center, becomes aware of its isolation.

But to become aware of its isolation is to find itself in the presence of a fresh mystery. If external nature becomes enigmatic in our eyes in the same degree as it becomes foreign to our minds, it is on the contrary in the very degree with which we take a more intense consciousness of ourselves that this self fills for us with mystery. How to know it, since we are unable to refer it to anything known? The more we contemplate it, the less we understand it. We never seize it except in its essential difference. It does not conform to anything. It does not resemble anything. As there is a mystery of light, there is a mystery of the center. If one scrutinizes it too much it disappears. It flees before our gaze. But it does so without moving. It is no longer out of the self, far from the self, that the quest must be pursued. Against the remote depth of the peripheral world there stands in contrast another depth, the intimate depth of the center. Introspection is not like expansion. Rather, it is more like a contemplation. Contemplation by a mind which no longer is in haste to spread itself out in space, but which remains, here where it starts to think, in a meditative immobility. Perhaps there is no better definition, if not of romanticism, at least of one of the most important sides of it, than in saying that it is a taking possession by consciousness of the fundamentally subjective character of the mind. The romantic is a being who discovers himself to be a centering point. What matters more is not that the world of objects is out of reach, it is that at bottom there is in the romantic something which, as he knows, is inassimilable to an object and which is the subjective and most authentic part of his self, that which he most readily recognizes as his own. Deprived of the periphery, the romantic will slowly familiarize himself with the self, with the center. It is true that, long before the romantic era, the consciousness of self had already attained two or three times, in the history of the mind, an exceptional intensity or quality. But for Descartes, as for the majority of his disciples, the act of knowing held less value in itself than as a general principle of comprehension. To know oneself was nothing more than a preliminary step; to know the world was the essential goal. Barely was the self assured of itself (and of God) in the *Cogito,* than it hurried to leave these introspective regions to extend in the world the exercise of a power, subjective, certainly, in itself, but important only in its application to a world of objects. In the same way, the eighteenth-century sensationalists gave themselves as their goal, not to isolating the feeling of the self in itself, but, on the contrary, the mingling of it with the sensations provided by the external world. Different though the Cartesian and sensualist positions may be, they are both characterized by the same wish never to consider the subject in itself, the subject without object, the center without its periphery. Even Rousseau, in the most ecstatic or withdrawn moments of his existence, had never dreamed of cutting the bond which joins the consciousness to the outside world. In the ecstasy of Saint-Pierre island, as in the moments of contemplation of the last years, no matter how disengaged from his environment he might wish himself to be, and however purified the feeling of existence became for him, Rousseau invariably joins it, in spite of everything, to one sensory event or another, the splashing of water, the sight of a flower, the springing up of a remembrance. The subject is never purely a subject, it never frees itself from a certain liaison with the objective world. And even, in a sense, one can maintain that what Rousseau had done very precisely is not to describe consciousness freed from any datum, but, on the contrary, to show it embarrassed by a multitude of equivocal relationships.

Now it is exactly this sort of relationship which a little later Maine de Biran wished to reject. And he wished to reject it through finding in the mind a point which should be unquestionably beyond the reach of all the influences, suggestions, metamorphoses, and other compromises engendered by the world of objects. A point where the mind, freed from emotional and organic fluctuations, should be pure subject, central and fixed: "I am happy in solitude," he writes, "because *I feel myself depending on this central point of my being* which rules and makes itself present to all."[2] Whatever the all is which is mentioned here, we may be sure that it is held at a distance by the dominating subjectivity. A deliberately sought after solitude, infinitely deeper than habitual isolation, spreads its double series of ditches between the self and the world. First of all, there is the withdrawal of the soul, detaching it from everything which directly linked it to the world; then there is a second sort of withdrawal, detaching it from that part of itself in which it felt the influx of objects. The soul reduces itself to what is most central in itself; it no longer exists except in the awareness of its own inner activity. One cannot even say that it sets itself as an object. Nothing is perceived anymore in it except the activity of pure subjectivity, which is its true being.

Still, if the subjective consciousness reaches in Biran an exceptional degree of purification and condensation, perhaps it is, at least at first, at the cost of the inner depth of feeling. For a long time, Biran had the tendency to restrain the consciousness of the self to the intense, if limited, perception of the act of will by which it constitutes and maintains itself in existence. It is only much later that at the very root of the self, in the voluntary act, Biran was to distinguish the intermittent intervention of a more powerful and a more profound will than that of the personality. Through this he entered upon a road, neglected for a century, but long frequented by mystics, which, sinking into the depth of the center, leads to a God who secretly operates and dwells in it; not an exterior objective God, watching on the good working of His external Providence, but the God more interior to ourselves than ourselves and more central than we could ever become.

Besides, almost simultaneously, at that time, in France, in Germany, in England, the romantics were discovering or finding again the essentially religious character of human centrality: "I am the central point, the blessed source"[3] Astralis cries out in the novel by Novalis. Man is the source, and a sacred source. In the depth of his centrality is mingled in an indescribable manner the mystery of his true being and that of the Divinity who wishes to associate himself with it. To withdraw to the center is not to renounce the plenary life, to condemn oneself to a diminished life, it is, as Maurice Scève and the Platonic poets of the Renaissance had done, to return to the original forces, to go to the fountainhead. And by a phenomenon for which the reason is too evident to need amplifying, the retreat of the mind into itself, far from exterior nature, becomes the very principle of a fresh return toward nature, and consequently, to a new blossoming of the mind beyond the center where it is reinvigorated.

Nothing is more important in Romantic literature and thought than this intuition of the source, principle of a new expansion of life. One finds it, in particular, in a form of thought which recommences, at this epoch, to have a great influence—occultism. Saint-Martin for example, writes this: "I was amazed as to how this universal source animates all beings, and confers upon each of them the inexhaustible fire, from which everything has drawn movement. Every individual formed a center, in which all points of its individual sphere were reflected."[4]

So, therefore, between the divine source and the individual sources there is identity of origin and identity of growth. The human being, like the divine being, develops in the manner of a generating principle, "throwing at once outward the innumerable and inexhaustible multitude of its rays."[5] Every hour of existence, every place, no matter how tenuous it may be, occupied by the most fragile entity, becomes a center of irradiating energy, which, as Saint-Martin says, "grows simultaneously on all sides; occupies and fills all parts of its circumference."[6] From this "explosion of the center"[7] one finds many examples in the poetry of William Blake:

> *Thou perceivest the Flowers put forth their*
> *precious Odours,*
> *And none can tell how from so small a center*
> *comes such sweets,*
> *Forgetting that within that Center Eternity*
> *expands*
> *Its ever during doors . . .*[8]

> *To see a World in a Grain of Sand*
> *And Heaven in a Wild Flower,*
> *Hold Infinity in the palm of your hand*
> *And Eternity in an hour.*[9]

As with the poets of the Renaissance, most of all with Boehme, each point of creation, each particular moment of duration reveals here a capacity for expansion that is truly infinite. But what is striking is that the imagination of the poet is endowed with an equivalent force. A grain of sand which becomes a world, a rose which fills space with its perfume, the mind of man possesses the same power of dilation as that which God puts into the objects of creation. There is an unfoldment of the mind, as there is a blossoming outward of things. Everyone can draw from himself an eternity and an immensity truly internal. Love is a perfect example of this extraordinary spatial and temporal extension conferred by feeling to a psychological reality previously without either dimension or duration. One sees it in a famous passage of Benjamin Constant's *Adolph:*

> Love compensates for the lack of memory by a kind of magic. All the other affections need the past. Love creates, as though by enchantment, a past which surrounds us. It gives us, so to speak, the consciousness of having lived for years with a being who, before, seemed almost a stranger to us. Love is only a *luminous point,* and yet it seems to master time.[10]

The being who loves, therefore, sees growing around him space and duration. Or rather, it is at the interior of himself that he feels a double growth of existence. Love is an enlarging of the field of thought, a way of feeling one's being overflowing from all sides the point of time and extension in which he has been placed. Let us refrain, however, from mistaking it for the movement of expansion to which the eighteenth-century sensible soul used to give itself. This would be to confound Romanticism with a sensationalism now left behind. The expansion of the self engendered by Romantic love has in fact little to do with the phenomenon of undulating vibration through which, in the eyes of the sensationalists, the center of emotive life communicates its agitation outside. A purely psychological phenomenon, profoundly different from the extension of the internal being described by Benjamin Constant. With the latter, what is of importance is not the propagation of feeling outside but its growth within. The enlargement which is spoken of here is purely interior. Even more, one feels that in this case love is a very different thing from mere passionate feeling, and that what is discovered through its intercession is the action of energy coexisting with the human being and perhaps identical to it. For the Romantic, man first of all is a self generative force. He is a living point destined to become a circle. His expansion is therefore not simply psychological. It is really ontological. To expand, is to realize one's being. It is to bring out from the central point that which, potentially, it contained. Such is the new point of view, from which man is now contemplated. "In the whole of every man," says Jean-Paul, "scintillates and springs forth, a source, an essential point, a *punctum saliens,* around which the secondary parts will gradually take shape."[11]

There in incomparable fashion appears the depth of German intuition. It, and it alone (with the exception of certain ideas of Coleridge, Nerval, and Guérin) is capable of bringing itself back to the central and initial point of man, of conceiving him in the manner of a seed of which there is foreseen and estimated the gradual growth. For German thought, all reflection on the being takes almost inevitably a genetic turn. From Boehme to Schelling, the occult and philosophical tradition tries to conceive, and in some way, to follow intellectually, not only the genesis of creation, but that of the Creator, of God himself. Hence the entire scheme of life appears as the development of an enveloped God, so that the cosmos and the very expanse it presents become illustrations of a divine dilation to which a new contraction succeeds, and so on to infinity. "The whole cosmos extended in space," Schelling writes, "is but an expansion of the heart of God, of which the uninterrupted pulsations, due to invisible forces, alternately produce dilations and contractions."[12] And Lamennais was to say the same: "Perpetual effusion of God, the Creation comes forth from Him, pours out at Him like an immense ocean and within it, beings link themselves to beings in their successive production endlessly and without respite and without end, as waves are born from waves in a continuous movement which engenders them all and pushes them forward, enlarging ceaselessly their mobile circle toward eternally fleeing shores."[13]

Man therefore does nothing more than to repeat the process of divine and cosmic generation. In himself, from the contracted version of himself which is his original state, he contains in embryo God and the world. To rediscover man at this first point, is to rediscover, under a condensed form, the divine immensity and cosmic totality. As Paracelsus said, everything comes from man and all ends in him. He is, according to Herder, "the central point of the circle, where all the rays seem to converge."[14]

Now, just as the peripheral totality makes its rays converge on man, man makes his rays diverge toward totality. Of this effulgence one must follow the generative progress step by step. Man's final span can only be estimated if one retraces the progressive metamorphoses which cause him to pass from the state of the point to that of the circle or the sphere. Man is only intelligible if one grasps him in the gradual unrolling of his history. An unrolling that is an enlargement. Who develops himself in duration also develops in space. To become is to have place and to occupy more and more places. It is to exteriorize in the expanse that which, at its beginning, was without expanse. The historian who relives by thought the genetic movement of man, sees deployed a world of human realizations which take up more and more room. The history of humanity is not linear. It is the history of a point which becomes a sphere.

But it is also the history of a sphere which, one must never forget, has come forth entirely from a point. This point has therefore determined all the rest. But who has determined it? For Herder, the center of animal life and that of the spiritual life, coincide in the original point. Primitive man is a *punctum saliens,* animated by a *scintilla mentis.* It would therefore be tempting to imagine this point as entirely submissive to the double predetermination of the two principles of causality which encounter one another therein: divine will and biological determinism. The deployment of the circle may already be contained in the center. It is the greatness of a contemporary of Herder, the philosopher Fichte, to have seen, to the contrary, a true symbol of human liberty in the point. A point has no direction. It contains in itself all possible directions. It is an infinite possibility for action. But it would be wrong to take it inversely for a purely virtual entity, for the sheer potentiality which is one of the aspects of freedom. The point is concentration. In the midst of the indefinite diffluence of space, it represents willful and well-regulated autonomy. The point wills and wills itself: "All interior energy," writes Fichte, "appears in immediate consciousness as a concentration, comprehension and contraction of the mind, previously disseminated elsewhere, in a point, and as a persistence of itself in the unity of this point, which opposes itself to the constant and natural tendency to reject this contraction and to diffuse itself once more outside. . . . Briefly, the fundamental image of the autonomy of the mind in consciousness is that of a geometric point which eternally forms and vitally maintains itself."[15] And in another passage: "Freedom can only be conceived formally as a concentration of the flowing plurality of virtual light on a central point, and as the diffusion of light, from this central point, in a multiplicity that is sustained and lit only in this way."[16]

Thus, free man is an autonomous source of light and power, a will which projects itself from beyond its original contraction. First the "I" takes shape in its initial punctuality, then it radiates in the circle of the "not I." In this manner there appears a first solution of the problem stated at the beginning of this chapter. If, in fact, the world and the "I" distinguish and oppose one another, if to take consciousness of oneself as center, is to take consciousness at the same time of the nonidentity of this center-subject with the universe-object, what must one do? Fichte replies: one must freely will the conformation of the non-self to the self. To will, is to act, and to act, is to diffuse the self in the non-self.

To the identifying expansion of the self in the universe Fichte invites the free man. In 1794, more than three hundred years after Pic de la Mirandole, Fichte gives a discourse on the dignity of man, imitating the great Florentine. One recalls the theme of Pico's discourse. Man is the center of the world, because, from that point of view, he can the better see the world, distinguish its perfections, and model himself on them. Such was the thought of the man of the Renaissance. To rediscover or remake in the self, which is to say in the center, what one perceives outside oneself, this is to say the circumference. Let us now listen to Fichte:

> Philosophy teaches us to search for all in the self. It is thanks to the self that order and harmony have been instituted in the inert and unformed mass. It is uniquely thanks to man that order extends around him to the very limits of his control. . . . It

is thanks to him that the celestial bodies assemble and form an organized Whole, thanks to him that the astral bodies accomplish their harmonious revolutions. Thanks to the self there is constituted the immense hierarchy which runs the scale from the sprig of moss to the seraphim; in him there is situated the entire world of spirits, and man expects rightly that the law he gives himself and the world, will rule over the latter; he relies rightly on the universal observance which from this moment, shall be kept of this law. In this self there resides the pledged promise of *extending outward* with an infinite order and harmony, in places where neither the one nor the other as yet exists; in such a way that with man's growing culture, the culture of the universe will grow correspondingly. . . . At every moment of his existence, *man attracts to himself some new element in his circle* until all is integrated; until all of matter bears the imprint of his action and all minds, with his, form a single identical mind.[17]

One can see the differences between Fichte and Pico. Despite the similarity of the subjects, they could not be greater. No doubt, for one as for the other, man is a free being. But Pico's free man uses his liberty to model himself on the image of the macrocosm according to his own image. With Pico, human dignity consists of assimilating the world, with Fichte, in imposing itself on the world. One transfers the resources of the periphery to the center, the other fashions the periphery to suit himself.

In place of the opposition of the self and the non-self, here, therefore, is the *imposition* of the self upon the non-self. Such is Fichte's solution. It is entirely in favor of man and at the cost of nature. The relations of the circle to the center are determined solely by the will of the center. Peripheral nature morally and legally must submit itself to the empire of the human center.

But other solutions are possible. Thus for Schelling, perhaps opposition of the center and of the circle is not insurmountable. Are they not, after all, substantially identical? Does not human consciousness already hold, potentially, the entirety of the objective world? Is not everything which is, virtually so in the world of thought? In short, "the center is the entire circle, conceived only in its ideality or in its affirmation; as the periphery is the entire circle, but only conceived in its reality."[18] Nature in itself is an object without a subject, a circumference without center; detached from nature, the self is a center without circumference. Now it is enough to recognize the identity of the center and of the circumference to accomplish the synthesis of the circle. This is what we are shown by mathematics, in the figure of a circle so small that the periphery coincides with the center.

Schelling's philosophy of identity is therefore a philosophy of the identification of contraries. German Romantic thought takes up the celebrated theses of Nicolas of Cusa. It nevertheless mixes with it a human dynamism that is entirely new. Situating the non-self, or nature, at the periphery, and the self in the center, it confers a value to the circle not only more human, but more explicitly subjective; for, at bottom, if the center is the self, this self, that is human consciousness, reigns over the circle. It is no longer a question of the cosmic circle, where the earth with its creatures would be situated in the middle, the empyrean at the circumference; it is even less a question of the theological circle, in which God would be at the center, and what is farthest away from God, matter, at the circumference. It is a question of a truly epistemological and homocentric circle, where nature is placed at the periphery, because it is the object of a thought which, being essentially a center of activity and of investigation, has as mission the need to recognize itself little by little in the properties shown by every one of the attributes of the circle. All philosophy therefore becomes a study of the similarities existing between center and circle, and even more, of their dependence one upon the other: "Just as," writes Frederic Schlegel, "the center is center in relation to the periphery, and the periphery is periphery by reference to the center, thus the Self and the Non-Self exist only by their reciprocity."[19]

Mirror of the circumference, the center reveals to the circumference its true perfection, in the same way that the circumference, in reflecting the center, flashes back to it an infinitely amplified image of itself. While mirroring itself in the circle, the center discovers its true depth, and, consequently, the possibility of being able to transform it in extent. It is in this sense, no doubt, that one should understand the words of Novalis: "We carry within us a singular tendency *to open outward in every direction from a center infinitely deep.*"[20]

Sometimes, as with Hegel, this new conception of the circle is limited to a theory of knowledge. The center is the consciousness surrounding itself with the circle of its ideas. But as for Hegel, consciousness coincides with the idea, and the idea itself, in developing itself, transforms itself into an even vaster idea; the Hegelian thought can be conceived, and moreover is often described by its author under the form of circles fitting one within the other: "Those of which infinity is the self," Hegel writes, "are themselves infinite, reflections of themselves on themselves, not simple circles, but circles which contain their principle in other circles, and which are the circles of these circles."[21]

In such a conception of the circle, the circumference remains a pure object of knowledge. It is therefore not itself, as such, that matters, it is rather the movement by which thought is carried toward it and projects upon it a light having emanated from its own source. There is therefore a sort of centrality radiating from thought. All of Romanticism, not Germanic alone—but European, takes account of it. "Man's genius," writes Chateaubriand, "does not move in a circle from which he cannot escape. On the contrary . . . he traces concentric circles which spread out and whose circumference will ceaselessly grow in an infinite space."[22] In the same way, Lamartine's poetry is essentially like a limitless expansion of thought and word in space. "Man," he says, "is but a point," but this point

> of the Infinite, by thought is master
> And, limitlessly rolling back the confines of his being
> Spreads himself through all of space and lives in all
> time.[23]

Man is therefore simultaneously center and circle: center by the active principle of his thought, circle by the infinite content of it. This is precisely what Shelley says more than once in his theoretical writings: "Each is at once the center and the circumference, the point to which all things are referred, and the line in which all things are contained."[24] And elsewhere, in a more condensed and more brilliant formula: "Poetry is at once the center and circumference of knowledge."[25] Keats writes in a similar way: "It is an old maxim of mine that every point of thought is the center of an intellectual world."[26] No one, finally, had more lively awareness than Wordsworth of the advantage there is in fixing one's thought forever in a central position from which the world discloses itself, in depth as surfacely, as a sphere enclosing truth:

> . . . Hither come and find a lodge
> To which thou may'st resort for holier peace,—
> From whose calm center thou, through height or depth,
> May'st penetrate, wherever truth shall lead.[27]

II

Of all the English poets, he on whom the theme of the circle has exercised the greatest fascination since Traherne, incontestably, is Coleridge. A deep knowledge of German idealism, the practice of Neo-Platonic philosophers from Plotinus to the Cambridge school, even, in a paradoxical way, the first influence of the Hartleyian associationism, all this combines to give in his instance to the theme of the circle an exceptional complexity and inflection. It is therefore useful to make a more extended study of him.

Let us take the famous poem, *Kubla Khan*. In effect, it is linked, in an indirect but indubitable manner, to the theme of the circle. Let us think of the glass dome, the coilings of the subterranean river, the triple circle described by the demon; but above all let us consider the fact that according to Coleridge, the poem had begun by having, in his mind, an explicit unity: "On awaking, the author appeared to himself to have a distinct recollection of the whole," Coleridge says.[28]

Nevertheless, as it stands *Kubla Khan* is not an ensemble, it is only the fragment of an ensemble. The circumstances of this fragmentation are well known. In the preliminary note which he attaches to his poem, Coleridge tells us that having, in a dream, composed the two or three hundred lines of the entire poem, he had put down on paper about fifty when when he was interrupted and was never again able to remember the rest. It does not matter much if these are real or fictitious circumstances. What is important, is to remember that the poem is expressly presented to us as having had a unity, which he later lost. In this way the preliminary note attached by Coleridge to his fragment is, in reality, a postscript whose purpose is to explain to us why we have only a fragment in place of a whole.

It is on this point that it would be wise to reflect. Coleridge's poem is an interrupted and broken unity. It is a whole of which nothing finally remains but a fragment. The crystal dome which contained the gardens, the chasms, the sacred river, and which drew around them a continuous limit, this dome existed, but exists no longer. It was shattered. And the better to make us understand this disappearance, the poet uses the following comparison: "All the rest had passed away like the images on the surface of a stream into which a stone had been cast."[29] Thus *Kubla Khan,* such as it existed in the mind of Coleridge, consisted of a vision whose unity was undone in a sort of spiritual fragmentation similar to that which one sees in water disturbed by the fall of something into it.

But not content with giving us this image, Coleridge sends us back to another of his texts where the same phenomenon is described. In the preface of *Kubla Khan*, he cites a corresponding passage of another poem entitled *The Picture*. The two poems having been linked by Coleridge himself, must be compared. Now, what is the subject of *The Picture*? One finds in it a lover who, to free his mind from the obsession which is oppressing him, takes a long walk in the country. He comes to the edge of a stream, in "A silent shade, as safe and sacred from the step of man as an invisible world."[30]

But in this secluded shelter, which is that of day-dreaming, a woman's form is suddenly outlined on the surface of the water. It is the nymph of the locality. She has the haunting face of the beloved one. For an instant this figure remains in the stream, inspiring in him who is contemplating her, delicious desires. Then the very ardor of his passion produces in the delicate reflection a movement similar to that which a breeze on the surface of the water would set in motion in letting flowers fall upon it. At once the adored image vanishes in a confusion of ripples:

> And suddenly, as one that toys with time,
> Scatters them on the pool! Then all the charm
> Is broken—all that phantom-world so fair
> Vanishes, and a thousand circles spread,
> And each mis-shapes the other.[31]

These lines are cited in the preliminary note to *Kubla Khan*. In both cases, they depict the destructive movement by which fragmentation substitutes itself for union, and multiplicity for unity. Contrary to what we have found everywhere else, the circle here is a symbol not of a coherent whole, but of a diffused plurality.

Now, if there is, with Coleridge, one trait which manifests itself more precociously and frequently than any other, it is that of diffusion. For him alone a thought which freely communicates with the universe, is capable of attaining the divine spirit immanent in this universe. It is therefore necessary that thought liberate itself from its narrow fixation, that it enter into relationship with the surrounding cosmos. A not impossible task, Coleridge thinks, for whom

> . . . by sacred sympathy . . . makes
> The whole one's self! self, that no alien knows!

Self, far-diffused as fancy's wing can travel!
Self, spreading still![32]

Thus Coleridge's thought tries to diffuse itself emotionally in every direction, in movement which, making it participate in the life of the universe, makes it also possess, at the same time, the spirit of God that animates it. The passage just cited is taken from *Religious Musings*, but many years later, in the rough drafts of his *Logic*, Coleridge was to repeat it in an approximate way: "Personality is a circumference continually expanding through sympathy and understanding, rather than an exclusive center of self-feeling."[33]

This movement of human thought is therefore similar to that nature which, says Coleridge, "is more truly represented by the ladder, than by the suspended chain, (since) she expands as by concentric circles."[34]

Coleridge is not unaware of the grave dangers which are implied by illimitable expansion of thought. A thought without boundaries is, in effect, a thought without coherence. It is also a verb condemned forever to engender and pursue its monologue. All his contemporaries describe to us the unfailing flood of words which issued from the lips of the lecturer-poet. But we possess the word of Coleridge himself, in which precisely the image of the circle reappears. Speaking of his celebrated soliloquies, Coleridge says: "I go on from circle to circle till I break against the shore of my hearer's patience, or have my concentricals dashed to nothing by a snore. That is my ordinary mishap."[35]

But the dangers of length and monotony are not the only ones which give rise to a thought which abandons itself to a limitless diffusion. Going from circle to circle, from digression to digression, abandoning itself to each of the suggestions which fortuitous sympathies may propose, it becomes the toy of all the accidental combinations of external causation and of all involuntary associations of memory. For having been its consenting victim for years, no one has understood better than Coleridge the harmfulness of Hartley's associationist system: "One whole life would be surrendered either to the despotism of outward impression, or to that of senseless and passive memory."[36] Each moment of existence becomes the meeting place of an infinity of images which erupt in the mind, and which, by their number and their confusion, neutralize it: "What a swarm of thoughts and feelings, endlessly minute fragments, and, as it were, representations of all preceding and embryos of all future thoughts, lie compact in any one moment!"[37] And if all the moments are filled in the same way, how otherwise to conceive existence than as a tight succession of similarly inflated moments, in whose march there is never a pause, so that there is also no possibility of either rest or reflection? Human duration is therefore nothing more than "a scudding cloudage of shapes."[38]

But there is still more. He who lets himself be carried away by diffused thought, not only abandons himself to the continuity of its flow but also to the discontinuity of the elements which compose it. It is a succession, but as J. H. Green, the most intelligent of Coleridge's disciples, says, it is "a succession of fragmentary and unconnected phrases."[39] The flood of confused thoughts which traverse the mind, is at one and the same time composed and broken by an inexhaustible multitude of unconnected forms which at times have not the slightest relation to one another. To the external incoherence there corresponds an internal incoherence. This is what Coleridge indicates by the term *fancy,* that is to say "the arbitrary bringing together of things that lie remote."[40] The movement of the mind is ceaselessly broken by upspringings, ripples, leaping out of unpredictable images. Such is "The shifting current in the shoreless chaos of the fancy in which the streaming continuum of passive association is broken into zig-zag by sensations from within and without."[41]

This last image is already very close to the one in the poem, *The Picture,* already mentioned, in which the continuity of the moving surface of the stream is interrupted by the proliferation of circles. Here is another example, taken from *Anima Poetae*:

> Now the breeze through the stiff and brittle-becoming foliage of the trees counterfeits the sound of a rushing stream or water-flood suddenly sweeping by. The sigh, the modulated continuousness of the murmur is exchanged for the confusion of overtaking sounds—the self-evolution of the One, for the clash or stroke of ever-commencing contact of the multitudinous, without interspace, by confusion.[42]

Confused continuity, broken by the discontinuity of details which thought isolates, such is the constant character of Coleridge's reverie. It ends in a disruption and a fragmentation, which, in an unexpected way, causes it to resemble, at least in the opinion of Coleridge himself, scientific knowledge. This, disseminated in encyclopedias, is, says the poet, "divided into innumerable fragments scattered over many volumes, like a broken mirror on the ground, presenting, instead of one, a thousand images, but none entire."[43] "Man is inevitably tempted," he writes elsewhere, "to break and scatter the one divine and indivisible life of nature into countless idols of the senses."[44]

The diffuse movement of thought therefore becomes more and more anarchic. Instead of an enlarging circle, there are now a multitude of broken circles. It is a scattered totality, existing only in pieces.

Nothing is more tragic in Coleridge's eyes than this fragmentation of reality: "The universe itself! What an immense heap of little things! I can contemplate nothing but *parts*, and parts are all alike. My mind feels as if it ached to behold and know something great, something one and indivisible."[45]

All of Coleridge's effort of thought was therefore to be directed toward a reconstruction of divided unity.

No doubt, as it takes place in the poem, *The Picture*, sometimes the reverie of itself, after having decomposed, reforms anew:

> Stay awhile
> Poor youth, who scarcely dar'st lift up thine eyes!
> The stream will soon renew its smoothness, soon
> The visions will return![46]

It therefore sometimes happens that a sort of spontaneous synthesis is accomplished, which restores the dream and saves it from fragmentation. For example, there forms in us, "a confluence of memories," thanks to which, Coleridge tells us, "we establish a center, a center, as it were, a sort of nucleus in the reservoir of the soul."[47] But this fortuitous and still involuntary reconstruction is the index of more fundamental and more stable power which resides in our souls. What spontaneously forms or reforms in us, would form even more firmly still under the action of our explicit will. Now, this will, when it is exercised on the images in order to link them together, and, from its center, imposes on them all a unique form, we know is the very inverse of *fancy,* and that which with Coleridge carries the name revered above all of *imagination.*

An "esemplastic" power, which gives "unity to multiplicity," Coleridge's imagination, too, must be represented under the form of the circle; not, certainly, under the form of the assemblage of the entangled circles which fancy engenders; but under that of a unique circle, deployed from and around a fixed point, and of which the circumference never ceases to be in rapport with the latter.

The imagination is a circle; but chiefly, it is the center of the circle; a center from which radiate outward lines which place the central unity in rapport with the peripheral variety; in such a manner that one can say of the space which they embrace, that it is at once united and divided, multiple and organized.

Coleridge's imagination is therefore essentially irradiating. Contrary to fancy, its diffusion is the projection of a unifying force. Into the disorderly and evanescent mass it introduces the aggregation principle indispensable to the transformation of plurality into beauty. It is a circle of which the center is fixed, the circumference uninterrupted, and the rays distinctly drawn. Thus understood, the circle is, for Coleridge, the symbol of beauty:

> An old coach-wheel lies in the coachmaker's yard. . . . There is beauty in that wheel. . . . See how the rays proceed from the center to the circumference, and how many different images are distinctly comprehended at one glance, as forming one whole, and each part in some harmonious relation to each and all.[48]

A work of art is like a wheel: it is a circle of which the rays are well delineated. But it is the same with all other forms of life. "Organization," writes Coleridge, "is nothing but the consequence of life . . .; it is, in truth, its effects, formed by the infinity of radii which proceed from that as a center, and which taken collectively, form the circumference."[49]

Nature and art resemble one another, in the sense that one and the other have as their foundations organized phenomena. At nature's origin, as at the origin of art, the central reality of the mind is perceived. "There is a central Phenomenon in Nature," Coleridge writes, "and this requires and supposes a central thought in the mind."[50] The mind is center. It is the center of the circle which its perceptions and conceptions form around it. "Man's mind is the very focus of all the rays of intellect which are scattered throughout the images of nature."[51] The mind therefore preserves, with the variety of images it arouses or perceives at the horizon of its thought, a link which prevents them from scattering. "The principle of unity must always be present, so that in the midst of the multeity the centripetal force be never suspended, nor the sense be fatigued by the predominance of the centrifugal force."[52]

Profoundly in accord with the Romantic thought of his own epoch, Coleridge conceives a spiritual universe, at the circumference of which all the combinations of fancy can play. They do not scatter into a thousand fragments, provided that at the center of the circle, imagination, the principle of unity, maintains the action of its formative power.

III

Everything takes place as if human thought, when it finds itself given over to a centrifugality without control, begins to break up in small fragments, or to turn in circles and become crazed. At the end of this movement thought slips away, or it vanishes in its own fragmentation, or else it becomes the prey of a kind of demented vertigo. With how many Romantics does one not encounter the delirium of the whirlwind or the disappearance of the self through vaporization? Vigny, Lamartine, Nerval, Poe, Baudelaire, Mallarmé, Rilke, are the victims of one or the other of these two catastrophes, as we shall see later on. But there is also the inverse example, that of the mind which, fleeing centrifugality, falls into the opposite excess. This is the case of Guérin, of whom we have spoken elsewhere, and it is also most particularly that of Amiel, who is to carry by turns excentricity and concentricity, to unimaginable extremes. But first of all it is the case of Schopenhauer, of whom it is necessary now to say a few words.

"All efforts of the mind which do not obey the intentions of the will," Schopenhauer writes, "are akin to madness, and such a tendency merits the name of excentricity."[53] Now all the activities of the mind, as one might say by definition, escape the control of the will, from which, nevertheless, they have emanated. To think, is to distinguish; to distinguish, is to separate. Once again, there can be perceived the image of the rays which, in going away from the center, separate themselves one from another, thus distorting by an endless parcellization of reality, the original unity. The more our thought diversifies and exteriorizes itself, the more it individualizes itself and becomes vulnerable. To think is to suffer. The more one thinks, the more one multiplies on the surface of the sphere the points of sensitivity and the chances of suffering. Only one recourse is possible. This is the movement by which the being retracts the rays it had projected outside and abandons the great spherical surface, on which the game of suffering and appearances is played.

"But from the instant in which we entirely withdraw ourselves from this surface, consciousness escapes us—in sleep, in death, and in a certain measure also, in the state of somnambulism or magic; all of this *makes us go back to the center.*"[54] The center of Schopenhauer's world is therefore localized beyond conscious thought. It is the obscure point around which an activity of the mind, ill-starred, desperate, and mad, spins the illusory wheel of fire created by a whirling brand. But entirely opaque and unconscious as this center is, what is its nature? It is the power which hides itself behind appearances, the occult kernel of the universe, the dark eternity surrounding the cycle of life and death called time: "The will, insofar as it is a thing-in-itself, is entirely undivided in every human being, as the center is an integral part of every ray; but whereas the peripheral extremity of this ray at the surface is, simultaneously with it, drawn into the most rapidly gyrating movement, which represents time and its content, the other extremity, on the contrary, remains still, at the center, in the place where eternity resides."[55]

One must then return to the center, and to do that, renounce the surface, light, and consciousness. Such is the solution Schopenhauer proposes to remedy the peril of dispersion. This remedy is absolute concentricity, the circumscription of the being in a point more tightly closed than a tomb.

Yet one can imagine the inverse: instead of absolute concentricity, absolute excentricity. This would be to transport the being, forever, far from the obscure center into the great sun of the surface. It would also be to deliver it to the cycle of life and death. Let us accept the moments of life, says Nietzsche, let us will them. Consciousness in the sense of an existence which ceaselessly makes and remakes itself, which in the uninterrupted succession of its eclipses and rebirths, participates in a prodigious circular dance. The eternal return is nothing but a circle; but it is a circle of which the only points which matter are the ones placed at the circumference. Not the totality of cyclical time but, simply the fact that thanks to the movement of the cycle, every moment of which it is composed returns an infinite number of times into the field of consciousness. Thus, by a paradox better realized by Nietzsche than by any other (but of which Nerval already had a very clear intuition), every moment of time is at once peripheral and central. Peripheral, since it is but a point situated at the circumference; central, since this point, returning an infinite number of times to the same place, makes of this place a fixed and eternal point: "At every moment existence begins, around every Here turns the sphere of There; the center is everywhere."[56]

In extreme excentricity Nietzsche therefore discovers a kind of concentricity; in the same manner in which in the very depth of the center, Schopenhauer found an annihilation of the mind no different from peripheral vaporization. But these two solutions are both a choice of extremes, and a solution of despair. Between the central subjectivity and the peripheral objectivity is there no way of establishing a relationship no longer theoretical but instead, practical? Is there no way of finding the example of a life which presents itself as an orderly and harmonious development between the two extremes?

This example is that of Goethe: "Every instant of his existence," says Gundolf, "possessed the faculty of serving as a center and a pivot to the totality of his existence."[57] There is no more accurate remark nor one more universally applicable to Goethe's existence. Even before one could speak of Goethe's existence, from the prime of his youth, which his life had not yet been long enough to give to him who was living it an appreciable expanse, his every moment already characterized itself by the immediate ability possessed by the young poet to transform it into a center of time and of space. The point where invariably the young Goethe placed himself, Gundolf again remarks, "is always the central point of the universe . . . ."[58]

Thus the centrality of the moment of existence, has, with Goethe, at least in his youth, an incomparable capacity of extension. It is as though at the median point of things a power surged up each time, of such vehemence that in its aggressive violence it came to threaten the world and the gods. To affirm oneself the center of the world, is to affirm one's centrality against the world, and it is to affirm one's right over the world. Thus, when Prometheus asks the gods the following question: Can you make me grow to the size of a universe?[59]—knowing beforehand their negative reply—he raises himself above those whom he interrogates, for he knows that there is in himself a force which renders him capable of accomplishing that which the gods are powerless to do. It is not upon the gods but from himself alone that the Promethean mind depends in order to

> put the vast space
> of sky and earth
> like a ball in one's hand.[60]

Nothing, therefore, would be more tempting than to see in Goethe's expansibility the sheer expression of a titanic appetite.

This would, however, be an error. Goethe is neither among those who wish to absorb the world, nor of those either, who wish to diffuse into it their own temperamental moods. Even in the most imperious moments of his youthful existence, Goethe never dreamed of impregnating the world with his own mind, to metamorphose it into his own nature. One could rather say that with him, as later with the young Claudel of the *Tête d'Or,* the invasion of the world by the mind is simply the most direct means for it to put itself in contact with the exterior regions, not so much to make of them a field of conquest, as to find in them a terrain of action. From this point of view Goethe is closer to Fichte than to Schelling. His intention is not to establish (by the absorption of the one into the other) an identity between the center and the circle, but rather to utilize the circle in the manner of a space naturally designed for the central activity which is deployed within it. It is nevertheless true that, with Goethe, the characteristic of the central activity is not, as with Fichte, the pure expansion and affirmation of the self in the world of the non-self. For Goethe, the exterior space has no uniquely negative value. It is not an anonymous expanse, a virgin territory, the place of impersonal resistance opposed to the self by the non-self. It is, on the contrary, a circle of concrete realities with which it is the duty of the mind to establish rapport and with which it draws the inestimable advantage of being able to define itself. Even if Goethe's thought abandoned itself to the titanic need of subduing the universe it could not covet a limitless universe. Goethe's cosmos is naturally limited because it is an ensemble of limited objects, which, by their very limitation, delimit, also, the desire to possess them.

Accordingly, the excentric movement of thought with Goethe never runs the risk of dispersing itself in the infinite, of vaporizing in space. Space is a furnished expanse filled with objects which hold the gaze and invite the mind to establish stable relationships with them. Why go beyond? It would be no less uncongenial for Goethe to by-pass these objects and come out into free space, than for the eye of the traveller to pierce through the screen of foliage in a wood, in which he is entangled. No matter how vast Goethe's horizon may be, it is a limited horizon. But the presence of these limits in no way suggests an interdiction imposed from outside. They reveal, on the contrary, the will to circumscribe from within the area explored and occupied by thought. There is nothing tragic, then, in the experience of the limits observed by Goethe. One has rather the impression of the satisfaction experienced by an owner determining the boundaries of his domain: "The mind projects its rays from the center to the periphery," Goethe writes. "If it runs against the latter, it stops, and recommences to draw from the center new lines of force; so that if it is not allowed to pass beyond the limits of its circle, it is at least able to know it and fill it as best it can."[61]

The concern of the center is to project its rays within the limits of the circle, not outside. Goethe is, in every sense of the word, someone who contents himself with living in the interior of his circle. This may be clearly seen in his correspondence: "I concern myself almost not at all, at present, with what is outside my circle"[62] —"Such as I am, I am happy. Business, the sciences, one or two friends, such is the entire circle in which I am wisely withdrawn."[63]

To be in a circle, is to be happy. The circle of the sphere is the very image of happiness:

One is accustomed to calling happiness round like a sphere, by reason of its great mobility, and this expression is doubly exact, for happiness may be compared to the sphere for quite a different reason. When it is still, the sphere presents itself to the eyes of the spectator in the aspect of a self-sufficient substance, perfect, enclosed in itself.[64]

The perfect, happy existence is therefore that which presents itself in the form of a circle or a sphere, even more, it is that which takes consciousness of itself, of the space it occupies, the beings and objects with which it associates, of the continuity of duration of which it feels itself a part, under the form of a similar spherical totality. If one senses so just an adequation between the self of Goethe and the world of which he is the center, it is that this self and this world are a part of a system whose unity one immediately recognizes. "Self-sufficient substance, perfect, enclosed in itself," indeed, these are the right epithets. An admirable coherence of all the elements which compose life, the universe, Goethe's work, immediately appears to the gaze.

But so that there shall be this coherence, it is necessary that the opposition between the subject and the object, the center and the circumference, be entirely surmounted. We have seen elsewhere that this can be done by the triumph of the subjective principle. In this case the objective world becomes centralized, subjectivized. Such is emphatically not Goethe's solution. Has he then adopted the contrary solution, that which implies the victory of objectivity? For an instant one would be inclined to think so if it were not that one realizes instantly with what intensity Goethe's consciousness persists in being. The central principle with Goethe not only survives the pressure of objectivity but finds in the consciousness of this pressure its essential characteristic. In other terms, consciousness never exists here in itself or for itself, it does not conceive of itself otherwise than as a consciousness of objects.

The center thinks the circle. There is no shorter or more exact way to describe Goethe's attitude. The circle is the object of the center. Neither the circle nor the center can independently be conceived. Hence one could define this attitude as a happy reconciliation of the two component antagonists. There remains, however, an important problem to settle. With Goethe is it possible for the center to seize itself as such? Absorbed as it is in its peripheral object, is Goethe's consciousness condemned to remain exclusively the consciousness of its object and never to be the consciousness of the subject?

One might be tempted to reply in the affirmative. Yes, Goethe is bound never to arrive at the pure consciousness of self. Hardly ever, does one sees him place himself in the interiority of the center. Barely, in the enormous mass of his work, is it possible to find a brief couple of lines in which there is an act of introspection:

> *The moment that thou turnest thyself inward,*
> *Thou shalt find thyself inside the center . . .*

However, one has only to go on in one's reading to perceive that it is by no means a question here of psychological or metaphysical consciousness, but simply that of moral sentiment:

> There no law is lacking,
> For *autonomous conscience*
> Is the sum of the *moral* day.[65]

Goethe here, therefore, only paraphrases Kant (or Fichte). He does not try to take possession of himself in his most intimate depths, but to perceive in himself an ethical principle, whose value lies less, indeed, in its subjective essence, than in the empirical part it plays in the outer world.

Is this to say that Goethe never has an awareness of Goethe? Nothing could be more erroneous. As a matter of fact, it would be right to say that Goethe never loses sight of himself. But the expres-

sion which we use here should attract our attention to the specifically optical aspect of this understanding of oneself. Goethe never
lets himself out of sight. He is the one object, among all he contemplates, which his eyes follow with the most constant assiduity. Now
this is to say that the knowledge he holds of himself is not a consciousness of self but a contemplation of the self. In its way of functioning, as in its nature, it does not differ in the least from the act by
which Goethe looks at the world. In short, if the first step of thought
with him consists in the movement by which it becomes objective
knowledge of the circle, one could say that the second movement consists in a return of the thought toward the center, *without thus reversing its direction it ceases to present the character of objective
comprehension of the real, which is his when it applied itself to
exterior objects.* In other words, Goethe sets himself before himself
and studies himself like a central object of which he would be the
peripheral observer. So that, between the movement by which he
goes from the center to the periphery and that by which he comes
back to himself, which is to say the center, it is impossible to perceive any difference.

Goethe is, therefore, in his own eyes, a pure objective center. But
nonetheless, in his eyes, he is *a* center and *the true* center. Quite
rightly, in the center of the tableau, he takes the place of honor.
This is also the commanding post, the structural center, the point
on which the rest leans in order to find order and power. No one is
more convinced than himself of the importance of this nucleus
which we form and the necessity to build a circle around it:

> It does not matter at all in which circle we begin our culture,
> it is perfectly indifferent from which place we orient the de-
> velopment of our ulterior life, provided that there is a circle and
> provided that there is a starting point.[66]

From the Goethe-center, there is a homogenous development of
the Goethe-periphery. Between the fixity of the central principle
and the mobility of the peripheral principle, there is no conflict, but,
on the contrary, rather the feeling of the solid bond tying one to the
other. One would think of someone who, without moving, would
spread out and go over ceaselessly, the circle of his actions and
investigations. These form a vast gyrating movement. No matter
how rapid or how simple these may be, the bond which ties them
to the pivot never lessens or breaks. In a word, with Goethe, center

and circle continually adhere one to the other and together form an order at once stable and moving, of which the spectacle never stops interesting him who is both the audience and the subject.

As early as 1780, in one of the rare pages of importance in his journal, Goethe noted this:

> I must more closely observe the circle of good and bad days which turn in me to produce passions, attachments and divers penchants. Invention, execution, disposition, all change and form a regular cycle. Serenity, trouble, vigor, elasticity, weakness, poise, appetite, do the same. As I am following a diet, the course of my life does not vary, and I must still decipher in what kind of succession and order *I move around myself*.[67]

In the same way in which there is an observable order tying the being which one is to the active and affective life which one leads, there is a relationship no less intelligible between man, taken in isolation, and the life of the cosmos which surrounds him:

> How can man measure out himself to infinity, how, unless it be in uniting in the depth of himself all the spiritual forces which lead in so many directions, and in telling himself: Canst thou dare only to conceive thyself at the heart of this eternal order of life, without also revealing within thyself a wonderful gyrating motion around a pure center?[68]

When facing the infinite, Goethe's reaction is not to throw himself into it, but to establish with it definite relationships. The infinite is not a gulf, it is an order, and a sort of superior limit: somewhat like the cupola of an edifice in whose center Goethe places himself. Center and circle support one another. Mobility and fixity together form a structure.

A structure which incidentally is the same which life imposes everywhere. Let one observe the plants, the bones of animals, the social institutions, the cosmic order. A double principle manifests itself there, one of change, the other of permanence. Centrifugal force and centripetal force, centrality and excentricity. Speaking of the faculty of metamorphosis as what is found everywhere distributed in nature, Goethe shows it counterbalanced by a contrary force: "It leads to amorphousness, it destroys knowledge and disintegrates it. It is akin to centrifugal force, and would lose itself in the infinite if it did not have a counterpoise: I make allusion to the need for specification, this obstinate capacity of persisting as such which is inherent in all those who come into existence, centripetal force whose depths cannot be troubled by any exterior things.[69]

Two powers, therefore, compensate and limit one another. In his old age, Goethe liked to follow in the development of plants and animals the combinations of the spiral and the vertical tendencies. The plant is a center vertically constructed, but also a coiling and a winding around this center. Exactly in the same way in which he contemplates the gyrations of his own activities and of his own humors around the obstinate immutable part of himself, Goethe observes, around the stiffness of the vegetable stem, the supple rotation of leaves and branches:

> Yet swift, still without leaves, the delicate
>   stalk lifts up,
> And a marvelous form ravishes the spectator.
> All around, in a circle, are then disposed,
>   numbered and numberless,
> The slender leaves, all neighbors, and all alike.[70]

Movement of the ascending spiral, multiplication of lifting circles. This image is found almost everywhere in the *Second Faust,* and in particular, in the classical *Walpurgis Night,* in the lines at the end.

Here, for example, is the arrival of the Nereids:

> In a gentle movement, in a measured haste, around the chariot, in concentric circles or intertwined, line by line, undulating by rows, you approach, hardy Nereids.[71]

The Nereids are plants, and consequently they obey the double principle which makes them turn around themselves and raise themselves from their center. A movement which penetrates and lifts nature, but which also goes beyond nature, since it is that which finally carries Faust toward the superterrestrial regions:

> Come! Lift thyself toward higher spheres . . .[72]

The spiralling movement of the spirit therefore moves from circle to circle and from sphere to sphere, turning around its own axis: "The highest gift we have received from God and nature," writes Goethe, "is life, the rotary movement of the monad around itself." And he adds: "The need to enclose and to cultivate life is ineradicably implanted in every being."[73]

Now, this essentially organic need for growth shows itself nowhere as clearly as in literature. A work of Goethe's is, too, a developing plant, a winding around a center. Such is the aesthetic principle which Goethe had retained from the teaching of his friend Moritz. A work is a focal point, multiplying its relations with a circumference. A principle of which Goethe found the application in the work of Shakespeare: "All his plays," he said, "turn around a mysterious point."[74] But it is a principle whose application Goethe's followers were to find particularly in the works of Goethe himself. Speaking of one of them and of them all, Friederich von Schlegel said: "One can grasp at a glance, in its multiplicity, the whole circumference, as being joined, so to speak, to the center."[75]

VII

LAMARTINE

To Alan Steele

I

Not a mental tension, not an expectation, not a concentration of vigilant thought, but simply the initial inertia of a soul absorbing nothing, in which nothing lives, from which, it would seem, all withdraws in order to leave it to its vacuity, as a sail that, in turning, discloses the expanse:

> My heart rests, my soul lies in silence;
> The world's distant noise dies as it comes,
> As a far sound is enfeebled by distance,
> Brought by the wind to an uncertain ear.[1]

Without a doubt, in this constantly recurring moment in Lamartian poetry, the soul's vacuity is not total. Something resounds with it, a murmur is heard which a breeze has carried to the threshold of consciousness. But one would be wrong to imagine that here there is a true motion overtaking the mind, similar to a wave running toward the shore to pour onto it its rich weight of water. There is nothing here of the immediate profusion that one finds in the great singers of sensibility, a Shakespeare, a Keats, a Rimbaud. On the contrary, if any distant sound reaches the ear, it is less to recall the existence of the exterior reality, than to announce its retreat. The outside murmur arrives attenuated, half emptied of its substance; and as soon as it comes it expires; it only manifests itself to betray the immateriality of its non-presence:

Here the last sounds of the world come to die. . .[2]

As in Josephine Soulary's sonnet, one may distinguish in Lamartine's poetry two intersecting processions. Living and dying touch each other, going in their opposite directions. On one side, there is that which is arriving, but what almost no longer exists; it fades at the instant it touches our senses; on the other, there is life that continues to resound, but farther and farther into the distance: flight of external reality, carrying its presence—less and less perceptible—elsewhere, while what flows back to the abandoned soul is like an insubstantial shadow left by the vanishing thought in the mind.

> And the evening breeze, dying along the beach,
> Brought back to me thy songs prolonged on the
> waves.[3]

Does what is felt here, only if the song is prolonged, have an essentially excentric movement? The vibration of sound propagates itself, but in withdrawing from the auditor. Nevertheless, the breeze brings back the echo of the fading song. It is as if there were two voices, of which one was sustained in the distance, and the other came to die with the wind in the center of the perceptive field. Such is the curious scission that one notices in Lamartine's poetry. One might say that in it, the human being is condemned to separate himself in two distinct ways from ambient reality; in one way, in allowing himself to flee to the horizon; and on the other hand in seeing die at his feet the forms he has abandoned in his flight. Extinction of sound, retreat of sonorous life, a farewell mingling with the silence, and, at the same time, a corresponding diminution of light, a fading of light:

> The sun of our days fades from its first dawn;
> On our languid foreheads it barely still sends out
> A few trembling rays to combat the night. . . .[4]

Very often the paling and the deafening combine:

> To the soft clarity of the serene arch
> We will sing together seated under the jasmine,
> Until the time when the moon, gliding toward Misena,
> Loses itself, paling in the morning fires.

> She sings, and her voice dies at intervals,
> And, the chords of the lute more lightly struck,
> The subsiding echoes give to the zephyr
> Only dying sighs, broken by the silence.[5]

> Half of the sky paled, and the breeze
> Weakened in the sails, immobile and without voice,

The shadows ran, and under their grey shade
All on the sea and sky was at once effaced;
And in my soul, paling and measured,
All sounds here below fell with the day . . .[6]

What pales, what falls silent, what fails with the day, is every minute of existence. No one experiences as does Lamartine, in the often-repeated manner, the sense of duration as a running flood: "Time escapes me, and flies!"—But, in escaping me, where does it fly to? It flies far from the present, far from me, into the past, into space. Universal phenomenon! A great poetical meeting ground! Who has not sung of this effacement accomplished in the soul and in space, at one and the same time? But no one, unless it be Lamartine, had *begun* by being a poet of effacement. Ordinarily, one begins by singing of that which lies around one and beyond, which, in appearing, causes a similar life to appear in the soul. The theme of disappearance comes later. But, with Lamartine, it seems to have been there from the beginning; it is the great original theme. For Lamartine, to think and to sing, is to think and sing a reality which, *already* given, *begins at once* to be withdrawn. In other words, it is only when that which one enjoys is protected in one's grasp that Lamartine shakes off the kind of happy stupor in which he would willingly spend the rest of his days, to take consciousness of a world which exists for him only from that moment when it is in danger of no longer existing.

Lamartine is, par excellence, the poet of a dissolving reality. This dissolution of the real manifests itself in the first place by what one could call cloudiness.

This cloudiness is the metamorphosis of the world into clouds. As soon as things appear with Lamartine, they mist over:

Already I see life, through a cloud
Fade for me into the shadow of the past . . .[7]

As the cause precedes the consequence, cloudiness precedes fading. Seen through a cloud, life itself becomes a cloud. It loses its solidity. It changes itself into a species of cotton. Nothing in Lamartine is more striking than this lack of consistence, revealed by the objects of the exterior world. At the instant when the poet discovers them, it would seem that they had already undergone a first process of disintegration which causes them to pass into a liquid state. Now they are ready to change into vapor. This incessant renewed vaporization of the Lamartian universe, and of all he comprehends, could make one think of the no less famous Baudelairean vaporization. But the two phenomena possess only superficial similarities. With Baudelaire, the vaporization is caused by the transformation of perceptible forms into an infinity of droplets of which each one is a mirror and a prism; in such a way that the melting of things accomplishes itself in the magical intensification of the light, the multiplication of colors and the powdering of a thousand iridescent particles. But it is quite different with Lamartine. The vaporization with him is rather a gaseousness than a pulverization. Or rather, if there is a pulverization, it is less crystalline and mirroring than flaky. It is not a state, even though transitory. It is a movement by which things hasten to their dissolution; comparable to a wave whose crumbling dust

> In flakes of light
> Rolls and disperses in the distance all these fragments
>   of the day.[8]

Fragmentation, therefore, with Lamartine, does not have the effect of the substitution of a multitude of distinct fragments for the shattered entity. The primary substance does not disintegrate in sharp and sudden bursts. Quite on the contrary, one has the impression of an almost imperceptible disintegration similar to the ravelling of clouds. Every form, less and less precise, seems to have been given over to an element which wears or gnaws at it, which tears it shred by shred, obliterating the details of its contours and leaving it without recognizable characteristics. Speaking of the Ossian world, to which his own has such a strong resemblance, Lamartine writes: "I involuntarily assimilated into myself the indeterminate, the revery, the oblivion in contemplation, the look fixed on confused apparitions in the distance. For me it was sea after shipwreck on which floated by moonlight patches of debris; in which one saw a few faces of young girls lifting their white arms, loosing their damp hair onto the spume of the waves; on which one could distinguish plaintive voices broken by the roar of the surf against the reef." And he adds, speaking now more particularly of his own thought: "This is the unwritten book of reverie whose pages are covered with enigmatic characters, in which the floating imagination makes and unmakes its own poems, as the dreaming eye in the clouds makes and unmakes its countrysides."[9]

Like the mythical book of reverie, the Lamartian poem is made up of clouds and debris, vague faces given over to the fluctuations of an aquatic and misty world. A world rapidly unravelling itself, even though it is covered over by a liquid element, or a mist, even though in withdrawing, the fogs or the waters take with them the forms that seemed to float therein. Thus, with Lamartine, everything softens and weakens, brings itself to an end, or enters into the element enveloping it. Everything unravels under the thickness of the veils or in the absence of forms. Above all, everything is confounded. Far from ending at the multiplication of the real, the dissolution of things has for effect the reduction of them to unity. A unity, naturally, as different as possible from the Neo-Platonic unity, and which has, as principle, not as with Amiel the concentration of all the virtualities in the monad, but on the contrary, the absorption of these in the universal mass, absolutely undifferentiated. Also, no matter how distinct the visual or auditory phenomena by which Lamartine begins making a minute description, almost at once we see them lose their true identity to participate in a sonorous and luminous movement infinitely vaster and more imprecise than themselves, in which they are soon diluted as a drop of wine in the sea. —Here are two examples:

The first, concerning light, describes a sunrise:

> In proportion to the lifting day, the distinct brilliance of the azure or flame color of the luminous bars *diminish and melt* in the *general gleaming* of the atmosphere; and the moon which had been suspended over our heads, rosy and the color of fire, *dims,* takes on a mother of pearl tint and *sinks into the depths of the sky,* as a silver disc whose color *pales* in proportion to its penetration into deep water.[10]

The second is relative to sound and reproduces the murmur of a town:

> All these sounds, already *weakened* by the advanced hour, . . . *melt instant by instant into one voiceless and indecisive humming,* forming a harmonious music in which human sounds, the stifled respiration of a great dozing city, *mingle, so that one can no longer distinguish them* from the sounds of nature, the distant reverberations of the waves and gusts of wind that bend the sharp crests of the cypresses.[11]

General atmospheric gleam, the humming of a whole town—almost always one sees appear with Lamartine some vast confused entity, that, surging above the multiple manifestations of perceptive phenomena, opens its broad breast to make them welcome, to make room for them, and to unify them while transforming them into the same substance as itself. Everything mingles and is confounded into a single mass, everything rapidly permits itself to be identified with a whole, at once both homogenous and indistinct. A moment before they disappear, one can still see the condemned forms detaching themselves from the depths in which they will be lost. Some final characteristic permits of their recognition, such as the debris which Lamartine saw floating on the water. For it is in effect a species of supreme floating, so to speak, at which we are assisting:

> And before my eyes floating at random
> With pieces of sky, and shreds of nature![12]

Detached, in shreds, already inconsistent and changing face, the floating forms have the appearance of being supported in space as petals glide on the surface of the water. But a breath draws them, their aerial navigation takes them farther and farther from the gaze, until their contours end by blurring in some grisaille, to mingle with the ambient immensity of the very horizon's line.

Suppressed at the horizon, the forms let nothing subsist except the horizon. Never, with Lamartine, does the gaze fix itself before they have attained this absorbing mist in which they are consumed and which constitutes the border of the unique countryside the poet describes. If, in the first place, quite near one, it would be possible to make out a host of precise details which would swell the description, it would suffice on the contrary, as it invariably does with Lamartine, that the eye be carried farther and farther away, so that it should perceive less and less of things and see the last of those subsisting, melt at the horizon line. Of this centrifugal and purely negative movement, where it is a question of ridding oneself of all forms along the way, one can find dozens of such examples in Lamartine.

> In the evening, the moon floated with its flecks of light on the tepid tides of the river. The dreaming astral body opened, at the extremity of the Seine's bed, luminous avenues and fantastic perspectives *in which the eye lost itself in vaporous and shadowy views.*[13]

> At my left, the valley, in dropping toward the shores of the sea, widens and presents to the gaze its hilly flanks, more and more wooded and cultivated; its serpentine river between the

breasts of the hills crowned with monasteries and with villages. *Farther away*, the palm trees of the plain lift up, behind the low hills of olive trees, their plumage of a yellow green, intersecting the long golden line of sand bordering the sea. *The gaze loses itself at last in an indefinite distance*, between the sky and the waves.[14]

But the most beautiful sentence perhaps, is this, on the temples of Baalbek:

> The great temples were before us like statues on their pedestals; the sun struck them with a last ray that withdrew slowly from one column to another, like the shadows of a lamp which the priest carries to the depth of the sanctuary.[15]

Admirable image, one of the purest that one can find from Lamartine's pen, and which very exactly expresses what is essential in him, the movement by which every image drifts toward absence, as the day glides toward nightfall. Such is really the thought or, if that word is too strong, the fundamental experience of the poet, retreat, the gradual engulfment of all that which is and has forms in the immense negative entity of formlessness. An invariable scheme presides at these descriptions. First, in a light essay, the glance of the poet goes from form to form. But nowhere is it gratified nor does it linger. The impetus by which it carries itself forward to meet the exterior world is less the radiantly regular and progressive movement of a conquest, than an effusion similar to a movement of flight. There is nothing here resembling the action of a center taking possession of the expanse. In proportion as it excentrically displaces itself toward the periphery of the horizon, the attention of the poet completely turns away from the place from which it has emanated, so that contemplation with him is not so much an aggrandizement of the zone embraced by the glance, as an evacuation of the territories which he has successively seized and abandoned. So that the field of vision is comparable to a circle of which the circumference ceaselessly augments, but in such a way that a kind of vaster and more visible *no man's land* separates it from the center. In this indefinite retreat of vague thought there is no more striking example than the following text, taken from the *Voyage en Orient*. One distinguishes in it with particular clarity the different stages followed by the Lamartian glance, before ending in the final vaporization of all forms in the absolute centrifugality of a horizon, beyond which it seems that the universe is in flight:

At my feet, the valley of Jehoshaphat stretched out like a vast
sepulcher; the dry Cedron furrowed a whitish cleft . . . ; somewhat to the right, the Mount of Olives hid itself, letting, between the sparse links of the volcanic cones and the naked
mountains of Jericho and Saint-Saba, the horizon *extend and
prolong itself* like a luminous avenue between the tops of the
unequal cypresses; the gaze sent itself out, drawn by the azure
brilliance and the leadenness of the Dead Sea, which shone at the
feet of rising mountains, and, behind, the blue chain of mountains of Arabia Petraea bounded the horizon. Yet *bounded* is
not the word, for the mountains seemed transparent as crystal,
and one saw or thought one saw *extend far off a vague and indefinite horizon swimming in ambient vapors* of an air colored
purple and ceruse.[16]

How can one speak here, still, of the *line* of a horizon? In the same
way that at the interior of this line all things have the tendency to
lose their contours and to merge one with the other, now even the
trace of the line of the horizon shivers and one no longer knows if
what one glimpses beyond still belongs to the world of the earth, or
to that of space.

II

Nevertheless the falling evening holds serene languors
Which the end gives to all, to joys as to sorrows . . .
For our senses, this hour offers gentle impressions
Like muffled steps on mosses:
The bitter-sweet kiss of farewells.
The crystalline and transparent air is limpid,
Mountains of vaporized azure drift, liquid,
Melting into the azure of the skies.[17]

From the muffling of sounds to the unification of colors, everything participates here in the same phenomena of identification
with vaporization. It would be an error, however, to imagine that
the mountains mingle with the sky for the simple reason that they
become the same color. First of all, something which seems to be
vaguely suggested by the text is that the distant mountains, situated
at the very back of the perspective, are like a last vestige of the
world, progressively engulfed in shadow, so that it is the earth
itself, or rather what remains of it, that goes into the distance to
unify itself with the azure air. But this is not enough to say, and the

identity of colors should be taken here as an indication of a more general identity, which is an identity of substance. If the earth is indistinguishable finally, from the sky, if, like the sky, it takes on a truly celestial and aerial tint, that is because, at the very farthest reach, it has become something aerial and celestial. Thus there clearly appears the decisive reason for the phenomena of vaporization in Lamartine. His express goal is to spiritualize the ambient world. The vaporized world is a world dematerialized. When the operation has succeeded, when the alchemy of the poet has sufficiently etherealized the forms and blended the colors, nothing is left to oppose the identification of visible reality with the infinite extent in whose chasm it lies. From one end to the other, from the point of departure from which radiates the gaze of the spectator, to the indecisive zone it reaches, where the earth becomes sky and the sky vapor, all is now of the same nature. Earth and sky, and all they support and contain, with the prodigious variety of the objects of creation, seem to be mingled into a homogenous continuity, like the surface of a lake or an atmosphere cleared of all exhalations. In the same way as there is in Lamartine an initial, but still terrestrial, point of repose which is the languor of a soul letting the trouble caused by pleasures of sense be lulled, there is also in him, but more tardily, a second point of rest, more exalted, more serene, which is the quietude of a soul liberated from the senses, liberated from forms, attaining, by a stripping down, realized with a strange facility, to the consciousness of a world so purged of all matter that it differs in no respect from the purity of space. With Lamartine, the vaporization has no other goal: it reduces the world to space. Space which appears finally as the unique reality, omnipresent, omniform, and omnisubstantial, in which end, as rivers in the sea, the thousand cogitations of poetry. Poetry discovers space; even more, it transforms everything into space. Everything it feels, everything it thinks, everything it imagines, all that it sings, becomes space.

The Lamartian volatilization does not only operate on the concrete forms of creation. It is, at base, so efficacious, so universal, and so contagious that it even infects the words which are the equivalent of it. When Maurice Blanchot, for example, asserts that all language replaces presence by absence in substituting the abstraction for the reality, he does not consider the extreme case of Lamartine. In fact, with Lamartine the transformation of the real into the unreal does not stop there. The abatement of sounds, the fading of light, the retreat of things, the growing indistinctness of contours, all these phenomena by which, as we have seen, the concrete realities metamorphose themselves in Lamartine into their ideal reflections, into their verbal images, all this pursues to the very heart of the images, and the verbal flux which expresses them, its insensible work of deteriorization. In such a way that one can say that, with Lamartine, not only the world of real things is abolished by the negative magic of writing, but also the world of the word, this too, is gravely affected. The deafening, the paling, become a deafening and a paling of the language itself. What is now blurred is not simply the universe imagined by Lamartine, it is the universe of Lamartine's word. Speech, which little by little is divested of everything it could conserve that still might be distinct, becomes in the final accounting the vaguest language there could be: a sort of long modulation, of which the harmony is not made up of independent elements linked to one another by a measure, but the unrolling of one sonorous web which, like the general background of certain pictures, spreads and stretches out on all sides to give the most smooth and indefinite surface possible to the continuity of the verbal space.

Lamartine, poet of pure space; or, even more exactly, poet whose words, verses, stanzas, poems, seem less to succeed one another than to continue indefinitely, one into the other, as those undifferentiated parts, without substance and always similar, which altogether form pure space.

But is this to say that Lamartine is the poet of *empty* space?

It would certainly seem so. In fact, has not all this poetry for its final goal to efface the universe, to make space appear? Consequently, is this not a poetry of a deprived universal space, deprived of things, of a space haunted, like that of Mallarmé's poems, by the disappearance of the vivacious and the *bel aujourd'hui*? A space without life, similar to those of the ice fields or sidereal expanses?—Is it really this, however? In contrast to the Mallarméan extents, one feels certain that, in spite of their denuding, the expanses sung by Lamartine are not frozen or uninhabitable. On the contrary, a warm breath moves over them. A temperate climate favors them, and, even more than climate, an atmosphere, tenuous, it is true, but dense enough so that the winged creatures can breathe and fly in it. Far from being a vacuum, the Lamartian space seems to be occupied by a quintessential matter, uniformly distributed, which could well be the residue of the volatilization of the real. By an imaginative process whose chemistry is far from clear, it appears that the world, in

vanishing, has become truly divine. As solids become liquid in order
to next become gases, this dematerializing matter becomes soul, to
push on its substantial refinement to a state similar and perhaps
identical with that of divinity. This, naturally enough, does not
present itself as a definition of the system of beliefs formulated by
Lamartine, always supposing there is one. The famous pantheism of
the poet, denounced by his critics, is only a rather clumsy idea, pro-
posed *a posteriori* by the author of *La chute d'un ange,* to explain
a phenomenon, for him, indubitable, and perhaps more exalted
than any other, which is the *universal diffusion of the spirit in
space.* Lamartian space is only initially and imperfectly the place of
material and concrete things. After that, it is definitively, substantially, naturally, thanks to a dematerialization process of matter,
the place where the divine life of the spirit is spread and animated.

It is not otherwise, in what is *reasoned* but in what is *imagined*
in one of the most faithful of the Lamartian dreams, the Socrates of
the *Meditations:*

> Perhaps really, in the immense expanse,
> In everything mingling, *a soul is poured out;*
> And these brilliant heavenly bodies sown above our heads,
> Are living suns and living fires;
> And the Ocean, striking its frightened shores,
> With its growling waves rolls an angered soul;
> *So our fragrant air flying in a pure air*
> *Is a spirit floating on azure wings;*
> So the day is an eye distributing light,
> The night, a beauty veiling her eyelid;
> And at last in the sky, on the earth, in every place,
> Everything is intelligent, all lives, all is a god.[18]

Animism, panpsychism, it is easy to give a name to the system of
ideas which these lines express—moreover, with an uneven merit—
representative of the Lamartian genius. Yet if one compares them
to other verses which translate the same animism, for example to
such poets of the Renaissance as Du Bellay, Belleau, du Bartas, and
above all, Ronsard, one can see the difference. The animism of
Ronsard is before all else a vivifying principle, a quasi-animal energy
working in the interior of stones, of trees, of men, to make them
exist and realize themselves. The world is the result of its efficacy,
the living witness of its virtue. Neither Ronsard nor his friends
would have dared, even in thought, to detach such an animal force
from the terrestrial or cosmic flesh it animated.—But take Lamar-

tine. From the brilliant heavenly bodies, already so little material in their aerial and distant perfection, thought glides to the ocean, to fragrant air, to the light. It seems that the soul pours itself out more with more ease when its habitation is more spiritual; until the moment when it finds its perfect situation, far from bodies, even though celestial, in space.

If the Lamartian space is animated, it is, therefore, by a life reserved by preference to spirits or the spirit. Space is the ideal place for the existence of discarnate entities. It is not without reason that Lamartine's imagination has turned toward angelology. Apart from the souls of the dead, of which he makes frequent use, and apart from, naturally, God Himself, soul of souls, king of angels, immanent in space, he has only the birds and the angels with which to enliven space; and even the Lamartian birds are submitted, like all the rest, to the process of dematerialization, resembling angels, rather than birds in flesh and in bone. Lamartian space is also filled with angels; and one could even say that, the better to people it, all the world is angelicized. The famous title, *La chute d'un ange,* is the reversing of the process familiar in the Lamartian universe: the movement by which the fallen being rediscovers its wings, becomes once more an angel, and thus repairing the effect of its fall, ascends again into its ancient spatial territory.

But since space now appears as the natural place for liberated minds, there is no further reason for the poet to remain on earth and to look *from afar* into space. If Lamartine's poetry is in the first instance poetry of the progress of things, of the flight of forms, of an ascension of all the objects of contemplation, it becomes in the second place a poetry of the very mounting of the poet himself, rejoining, so to speak, everything he has caused to precede him. Perhaps there is nothing more moving in this poetry than the moment when he places himself between the lifting of the image and the more tardy ascension of the being who at first had been content to see them rise. A moment of pause and silence, a moment when the being, at last understanding that he has exchanged the world of things for a world deserted by things, begins to love this beautiful aerial desert that things, in withdrawing themselves, have disclosed to him:—*"Come, the enamoured silence occupies distant space . . . ."* —The invitation of space has, for Lamartine, the accent and the voice of sirens. In his universe, the angels are like sirens of the sky: sirens whispering in the ear not voluptuous sub-marine promises, but the pleasures of souls without bodies, the pleasures of space:

Lift yourself up, voice of my soul,
With the dawn, with the night!
Spring forth like the flame,
Spread yourself out like sound![19]

In the main, the pleasures of space for Lamartine are no different than those tasted today by the amateurs of skiing. Altitude, the virginity of the situations and the matter, the exquisite abolition of the body consumed by the facility with which it can move, as if it floated in a pure expanse: in a certain sense, certainly, skiers are souls or are angels. Not being able to glide on snowfields, Lamartine has done what, imaginatively, comes closest to this exercise; he is transported into the beyond. There is no dream more often taken up again, more intensely lived by Lamartine, than his dream in which he finds himself dead and liberated from his body:

I love to let myself be rocked in this silence,
To feel myself no longer living or thinking,
To believe that the mind, which in vain the body recalls,
Has quit beyond return its mortal husk
And forever swims in the rays of the sky . . .[20]

Thus when our soul, to its source flown,
Leaves its terrestrial valley forever,
Every beat of its wings lifting it to the skies,
It enlarges the horizon which spreads beneath its eyes . . .[21]

On the rays of the evening, on the wings of the wind,
It rises to God like a living fragrance . . .[22]

Here, therefore, at last, is the soul of the poet emplaning in space. —But what is it to emplane in space? For Baudelaire, for example, it is to continue to vibrate. To fly, swim, roll, all these terms serve him to express a sort of *Cogito* of the dilation of the senses. Like a tightened cord which prolongs waves of sound while amplifying them, Baudelaire is conscious of the sensation which swells, which propagates itself, which fills environing space; and, at the same time, he feels the sensation which lifts and transports him, so that on the crest of his wave he follows the same course and participates in the same swelling forth. This invasion of space is therefore entirely determined by the intensity of sensation. The more acute the sensation, the more inhabited space is enlarged.—Now it is not the same with Lamartine. His poetry has as principle, as one knows, obliteration, fading, which is to say not a *crescendo*, but a *diminuendo*, and even finally, the extinguishing of sensation. Also, with Lamartine the expansion of the spirit does not depend on something positive, but, quite the contrary, on a negation and an abnegation. It is, in fact, as we have seen, in ridding itself of its forms, in lightening itself of the weight of matter, that this poetry succeeds in elevating and dilating itself. Its expansion follows an *unballasting*. He who takes clear orders wins the field of play. Space is an opening plain for the gambolling of the spirit. "I soar in freedom in the fields of the possible,"[23] cries Lamartine. If the fields of the possible are much more spacious than those of the real, it is precisely for the reason that they are cleared of all reality. They are pure vacancy. Nothing in them is in opposition to the infinite progression of the spirit:

> He mounts up, and the horizon grows with every instant,
> He mounts, and before him the immensity is spread
> As if under the gaze of a new dawn;
> At every step a world seems to germinate under his eyes,
> Up to the supreme summit where his enchanted eye
> *Takes hold of space and soars in liberty.*[24]

Elsewhere Lamartine says:

> Spreads into all of space and lives in all of time.[25]

When all is said and done, as in Newton's hypothesis on the irradiation of light, the movement of growth which is the question here, does not proceed by translation into fullness, but by diffusion in an ethereal milieu. The soul overflows itself. To grow is for it a thing as natural as for water to pour. Give it immensity, and it becomes immensity:

> It seems to me, my God, that my oppressed soul,
> Before immensity, grew great in me . . .[26]

> Already, already, I swim in waves of light;
> Space grows before me . . .[27]

Growing space, and I grow in space. External space? interior space? Who could tell! Does it have to do with the *sensorium* of God, of the habitation of elected souls, or again of this sort of expanse which is the profundity and the duration and in which simultaneously are all remembrances refound? Perhaps of these three kinds of space at once. In that case, they form an uninterrupted medium in which thought freely extends itself in the manner of circles:

As for us, we are not astonished at this power of repercussion of the human soul sounding across all souls and all ages; there are in the heart of the hero, the poet or the saint, impulses of force that break the sepulcher, the firmament, time and *that travel, like the eccentric circles of the pebble thrown into the sea,* slowly to die on the farthest shores of the ocean bed. The heart of man, when it is moved by the idea of God, *carries its emotions as far as the ocean* carries the undulations of its margins.[28]

The lake, the beautiful ideal lake of Lamartine and Elvire, has therefore become an ocean, along whose immense surface, in circles, human emotion develops. It develops itself in tending toward a distant periphery, which is called God.

III

Thus Lamartine refinds or conserves something of the great theological symbol of the infinite circle. For him, too, God is

The limitless circle in which all is written.[29]

One could even say that this boundlessness particularly suits the poet's conception of divinity. There is in fact nothing more natural to Lamartine's effusive thought than a peripheric God; nothing is more natural to him, too, than to conceive this periphery under the least determined form possible. In a word, Lamartine interprets the definition of God, namely, God is an infinite circle, in the following manner: God has indefinite contours, God is a Being infinitely vague. Even more: for Lamartine, God is that which is at the extremity of a thought which in dilating itself dilutes itself in such a way that God is perhaps this final dilution of thought or of its disappearance when it has expended its expansive force. Now in this extreme place, where the first impetus "comes to die on the last beaches," in this most peripheral of all places, what is left? There remains a thought which vanishes in the very feeling of its weakness, and an object which is still withdrawing, which is retiring beyond the circle, which proves itself unseizable. In the final reckoning, as with how many other poets, there is the experience with Lamartine of an overtaking and abandonment. That is to say, no matter how great the force of the expanding spirit, it is always surpassed by the power of evasion of the object he covets. Lamartine is one who goes on to the pursuit of that of which he dreams, knowing already from the moment of departure that no matter how long the course, he is beaten from the beginning, and, as we say, *laissé au poteau* [left at the post]:

> How could I not, carried by Aurora's chariot,
> Vague objects of my desires, leap as far as thee![30]

Is it a matter here only of Elvire, or a higher object, with whom, by fleeing and being lifted in flight, she ends by confounding herself? Be that as it may, there is in Lamartine not simply a flight of things, a flight of beings, but a very flight of God. It could not be otherwise. Since on the one hand all this poetry stems from a movement engendered by the retreat of the being, and not by its presence, and as on the other hand it is not possible to assign any limit to this retreat, the result is that Lamartine's poetry can only be that of an infinite flight, not alone a flight *to* God, but a flight *of* God. It has been held to be a poetry of divine immanence. This is perfectly true, but it is of a flowing immanence, fleeing, as water disappears through the fingers. Certainly, it is not amiss to say that God is everywhere present in the Lamartian universe; but He is present as mountains that rise up, yet that, at the same time, merge and are lost. God is immanent, but His immanence never ceases to fade away in its transcendence.

It is true that, tired of imagining this eternally peripheric God, Lamartine tried to conceive a God-center. Let us push aside, he says, the thought of a God entirely diluted in the infinity of His creation:

> Not that second chaos which a pantheist adores,
> *Where in the immensity even God evaporates.*
> Made of brutally confused elements, pell-mell,
> In which good is no longer good, and evil is no longer evil;
> But this whole, *God-center of the universal soul,*
> Subsisting in Its work, and subsisting without it.[31]

A very rare apparition with this poet is the word *center*. For the whole movement of his poetry is accomplished in the form of a continual flight toward an ever-fleeing circumference. One barely has the right to consider it as a movement emanating from a center. Rather one should understand it under the aspect of a radically excentric movement, a movement that does not in the least try to establish a coherent coming-and-going between the center and the periphery, but which *forgets* the center, that without respite diffuses itself toward a singularly decentered God. In several other passages, as well, Lamartine rejects the anarchic cosmos which is his, as he also rejects the orientation toward a peripheral God, which was that of his poetry. Now, like Dante, he reverses the perspective, transforming the excentricity of his essential approach into an unexpected concentricity.

Already, in the *Meditations,* he asks if the "divine ray" of the soul should revivify itself in a series of reincarnations on earth,

> Or whether, seven times changing destiny and sphere,
> And mounting from star to star toward its *divine center,*
> An *ever fleeing goal which it endlessly approaches.*[32]

Historically this is the question that divided Pierre Leroux and Jean Reynaud. But what matters to us is that, of these two hypotheses, it is manifestly the second that Lamartine prefers and that he is to develop elsewhere throughout his great unfinished epic poem. In the Foreword to *La chute d'un ange* he writes: "I believe that the sole work of humanity, as a collective being and as an individual being, is to gravitate toward God, *approaching Him always.*"

One doubtful point is that Lamartine's poetry pretends in these instances to become the contrary to what it is. It is a poetry of amortization, in brief, of *withdrawing.* Now here it wishes to become a poetry of *approaching.* But in the lines just cited, one expression reveals to us that Lamartine is incapable of frankly exchanging vaporization for centralization. If the soul approaches the center, he says, it is by an endless movement in the direction of "an ever-fleeing goal." The divine center, therefore, is behaving like the divine periphery. One must consider not Dante, but Pascal here. Periphery and center flee in an eternal flight. And in flying, they do what all objects of thought do in the Lamartine universe: they pass from presence to absence.

An absence that now seems a goal of all poetic movement. Absence of things, absence of the world, absence of words, absence of God. And completing this series of absences, there is the absence of the very one who had gone in pursuit of those absent; for, at the limit, losing turn by turn every one of the objects of grace to which he still held with some firmness, it is the poet himself who dissolves in his own absence:

> . . . .
> The remains of my soul *evaporate*
> In accents *lost* upon the airs . . .[33]

> The more I sound the abyss, alas! the
> more I *am lost therein!*[34]

Such, to put it rigorously, is Lamartine's final experience. After the loss of all objects comes the loss of the self-subject. The vanishing of the soul is, in fact, the consequence of the vanishing of things. It becomes as impossible to hold any possible distinction between self and non-self, as between the world and the world beyond. Nothing is no longer separated from nothing. Everything being merged with everything, all is at one and the same time full and void. There is a general flight of the being, and in a vague movement of flux and reflux, a no less total absence of forms.

Here, in a sense, is an extraordinary success. Poetry has never been so completely removed from the Cartesian spirit that makes of the clear and the distinct not only a principle of truth but a principle of beauty: "Poetry," Lamartine says magnificently, "has stripped itself more and more of its artificial form; *it has no other form than itself.*"[35]

Therefore, with Lamartine, one comes to this new, disconcerting, perhaps contradictory, thing, a poetry almost without external forms, *a poetry,* in consequence, *of the inform.*

But a poetry that sinks into the inform rapidly becomes inexpressible.

By dint of diluting his song, Lamartine can no longer sing anything, can no longer sing:

> *My soul searches in vain for the words with which*
> *to pour itself out . . . .*[36]

> *All words expire in impotent efforts.*[37]

Lamartine's impotence is not so different as it seems at first sight from the sterility of Mallarmé. Their torment is the same. The poetry of the inform becomes a sort of glib discharge, no less futile and substanceless than the mute contemplation of a blank page. And Lamartine prolongs even longer than Mallarmé, his poetical aphasia, broken at long intervals by this temporary resuscitation of forms which one calls memory.

VIII

BALZAC

To Hillis Miller

> Was I in a fit state to search for
> the laws by which we send more or less force
> from the center to the extremities?
> —Balzac, *Théorie de la démarche*

"THE WORK OF ART," says Balzac, "is, in a little space, a frightening accumulation of an entire world of thoughts."[1] Elsewhere, for Balzac, thoughts or passions (in his vocabulary these words are interchangeable), are "the most profound cause of the disorganization of man and consequently of society."[2] From these two texts it follows that to Balzac's eyes the work of art and the society that it reflects, are, within their respective limits, a frightening accumulation of disorganizing forces. At the beginning of the *Fille aux yeux d'or*, that carries as epigraph the following phrase: "All exorbitant movement is a sublime prodigality of existence,"[3] Balzac describes the ravages of social life in the following manner:

> Is not Paris a field ceaselessly shaken by a tempest of interests under which whirls a harvest of men that death mows down more often than elsewhere . . . all extenuated, all imprinted with the ineffaceable signs of a breathless avidity?[4]

Since Taine, the critics have often drawn our attention to this exorbitant movement of the Human Comedy. They have set in relief the factors of disorder which it comprises. Without a doubt throughout its ninety volumes, the Balzacian work never ceases to represent a tempest of interests and a whirlwind of wills. But the words "tempest," "whirlwind," suggest in common a world deprived of constant relationships, of limits and of center, a formless and anarchic world. Is this really the Balzacian universe? Is it by definition a universe of excesses, of public unrest, a movement of illimitable and disorganized forces? Or is there in the Human Comedy, a principle that rules these forces and that renders this spectacle not only intelligible but even admirable?

A first remark is that the Balzacian world is not a world that reduces itself to the pure diffusion of its movements. One could conceive of a universe that would simply be constituted by the free expansion of limitless energies. But the Balzacian world is not only a world of expansion, it is also a world of the reaction to this expansion. To rephrase it, it is world in which there are upsurges, and also resistances to these upsurges. In consequence, in Balzac's apparent energetic monism, one sees a principle of duality introduced. How many of Balzac's novels are realized, either in their entirety, or in the most significant of their episodes, as "a duel between two wills,"[5] of which one attacks while the other resists? Paris and province, nature and society, private life and political life offer the same fundamental combination, "the battle of two forces that produce life."[6] "In going thoroughly into all human matters," Balzac says, "you will find in them the frightful antagonism of two forces that produce life."[7] "Is not life the battle of two forces?"[8] he says elsewhere. And in another place: "Life results from the play of two opposed principles."[9] Finally, in *Louis Lambert,* which of all Balzac's works is that in which he tried to formulate in the most systematic way his conception of the world, Balzac writes: "Movement, by reason of resistance, produces a combination that is life."[10]

A disordered life without a doubt, a life condemned to exist only in and by the shock of contrary tendencies; but a vital principle that is at the same time a principle of universal intelligibility. All Balzacian novels are immediately comprehensible under the form of an engagement in which two forces come to grips, one which attacks while the other braces against it. A precarious equilibrium, it is true, but calculable, the result of the exercise of movement and of resistance. The moral life is not a chaos of entangled forces if the law governing the movement of bodies applies as well to the world of wills. There is in the Human Comedy a prime factor of coherence and intelligibility, and that is, properly speaking, a dynamism of the spirit.

To this first factor another is added. A world that is made up of pressures and resistances is only possible because there exists between the elements composing them a *milieu* that permits these pressures and resistances to operate. One could imagine an entirely different universe, a Proustian universe, for example, in which ideas and beings would never be in contact, but would glide one over the other without exercising pressure or without violently repulsing one another. But this would be only the artifice of a vacillating magic lantern in the void of the spirit. Now the Balzacian world is not empty, and it cannot even tolerate a void: "The void," says Balzac, "does not exist."[11]—"Our globe is full, all is contained in it."[12]—"Nature is one and compact."[13]—"All is linked up and in command of itself."[14]—"Man is linked to everything."[15] Instead of a Newtonian universe which supposes the existence of a cosmic void across which the particles of light precipitate themselves without resistance, Balzac prefers the universe as Herschel conceived it, a universe filled by "an etheric substance, without weight, spread out into every part of space, whose repeated undulations carry to our eyes at great speed the sensation of light, as the vibrations of the air produce sound for our ears."[16]

The Balzacian universe is therefore a world without a continuous solution of continuity, a homogeneous world in which everything seizes hold and is repulsed, and in which, in consequence, nothing is unaffected by the slightest movements that are therein produced; finally, a world in which undulations propagate themselves, gaining ground nearer and nearer, over all points of space, in such a way that every particular perturbation influences the whole, but the whole in turn also exercises its action on every determined point. The Human Comedy is a sphere of which every part is put into relation with all the others and with the whole by a movement extending to the circumference, as the whole places itself in relation with every part by a pressure even greater since that part is close to the place where all the pressures converge, which is to say the center.

This sphere even has an atmosphere, that is to say a thick covering of opinions, of tendencies, and of customs that weigh upon the social world and form around it a second spherical belt:

> The earth is not determined by its exact geometry, it cannot be separated from the atmosphere surrounding it, and it has shown that not one of its productions, either man, or animal, or plants would exist in their conditions without this gaseous belt from which they draw their nourishment and which gives them their forms, their varieties . . .
>
> Here is the most complete image of social law. The social law taken in its most extended acceptance is certainly that of the right to live morally and physically in a certain *milieu,* in a certain expanse, under a residuum of customs . . .

The analogy is not only exact, it is perfect . . .
Everyone draws from the atmosphere according to his strength, lives there according to the laws of his own organization and *submits to the conditions of the situation in which he places himself.*[17]

The human being, for Balzac, therefore, depends on his situation. He is conditioned by the physical and moral atmosphere that he breathes:

There is an *atmosphere of ideas.* In a Court of Justice the ideas of the masses weigh with the judges, on the juries, and reciprocally.[18]

Countrymen . . . submit, without being aware of it, *to the action of atmospheric circumstances and of exterior factors.* Identified with nature in a way, in whose midst they live, they are insensibly penetrated by the ideas and feelings it awakens, reproducing them in their physiognomy, according to their organization and individual character. *Thus molded and slowly fashioned by the objects that continually surround them,* they are the most interesting and true book for whoever feels himself drawn toward this little known but fecund part of physiology, which explains the relationship of the moral being and the exterior agents of nature.[19]

The following is the most revealing of the passages in which is explained the determining relationship between the social sphere and the individual it encloses. It is taken from the *Envers de l'histoire contemporaine:*

The *sphere* in which he lived had a positive action on Godefroid. The law governing physical nature relative to *the influence of atmospheric milieux* on the conditions of the beings developing therein, equally governs moral nature. . . . He was taken with a desire to imitate these unknown heroes.[20]

In the preceding example, the atmospheric milieu is constituted by a beneficent association. The influence that is exercised on the will of the central personage is therefore a good influence, with which he agrees to associate himself. It is not the same in the other history of association, that is the *Histoire des treize.* Thirteen young men secretly unite their forces to exercise a powerful influence over society. From the periphery where they hide themselves, to the center of their activity, which is the common object of their desire they send out waves of converging energies. Balzac has always been haunted by the idea of a gigantic secret society that would possess the world by surrounding it with a network of their wills. Following this thought he even wrote a *Histoire des Jésuites.* If the world is in fact a collection of forces, and if the property of power is to lead to ends, amongst all the possible combinations there is none more efficacious than that in which the different forces find their effort directed toward the same end. The directional cumulation of energies ends in the most decisive result: "There where you see bodies," says Balzac, "I see forces that lead from one to the other by a generative movement . . . . The life of worlds *is drawn toward the centers* by a hungry aspiration, as you are pushed by hunger to nourish yourselves."[21] And elsewhere: "Everything here below has its virtue, that is to say its force . . . . These forces, corresponding between one another, *go toward the centers.*"[22] In the plurality of movements that compose the Balzacian universe a natural grouping is arrived at. The forces associate together because their objective is the same. All around one knot of attraction, forces turn and amalgamate, forming a continual peripheral mass that envelops the center, that presses on it. — But then the moral problem presents itself. What happens, if, in fact, instead of being, as in the *Envers de l'histoire contemporaine,* a good society, a beneficent society, or, as in the *Histoire des treize,* a society in itself neither evil nor good, the association of converging wills is one of maleficence, destructive of those over which it exercises its power? Then the movement appears as a coalition of the strong against the weak, as an organization of acquisitive wills directed against fatally crushed and flayed individuals. Such is the combination that Balzac has described in a few of his most famous novels. For example, this is the story of Cousin Pons:

> Hazard decreed that nothing in this world should be lacking against this poor musician. The avalanche that was to roll over him was to hold everything: the Chamber of Peers, the Chamber of Deputies, family, strangers, the strong, the weak, the innocent.[23]

This too is the story of General de Montcornet, against whom, in *Paysans,* the whole surrounding countryside is in league:

> Imagine that this league of a whole canton and of a little town against an old general, . . . set itself up in more than one

department against the men who wished to do well. This coalition incessantly menaces the man of genius, the great politician, a great agronomer, in short, all the innovators![24]

"Have we not to foil this permanent conspiracy of evil?" Balzac wrote elsewhere.[25] Conspiracy, coalition, the assemblage of covetousnesses that willingly forms in an association of forces leading to the same end. In almost every one of Balzac's novels, around a figure which is at once a victim and an object of envy, a circle of avid wills constitute themselves, as, for example, in the novel of the *Vieille fille,* toward whose human center "so many interests," Balzac says, *"were converging."*[26] Balzac is the admirable painter of what he calls "collective feelings,"[27] those which exercise their action simultaneously from all sides, from a circumference toward a center. And Balzac is a no less admirable painter of the investment of the center condemned by the dynamic social encirclement that wants a coalition to be more important than an isolated individual.

To the inherent weakness of the situation of every being hemmed in by society is added the inherent weakness of his true nature. For assailed by society, and yet constrained to find in it his distractions and his food, man, says Balzac, "is obliged continually to go *from the center to all points of the circumference;* he has a thousand passions, a thousand ideas, and there is so little proportion between his base and the extent of his operations that at every instant he is taken in a misdemeanor of weakness."[28] But to suppose on the other hand that the individual, instead of a thousand passions, has only one; this dangerous concentration of all his interests can also give to the enemy an occasion to attack him at a vulnerable point:

> Concentrate on a given point a few violent ideas, and a man is killed by them as if he had received a dagger's thrust.[29]

> Similar in its caprices to modern chemistry which recapitulates creation by reference to a gas, does not the soul compose terrible poisons by the rapid *concentration* of its delights, of its forces, or its ideas? Do not many men perish under the blast of some moral acid suddenly poured out in their inner being?[30]

Thought is therefore a weapon and a poison. It is, Balzac says, a fluid that, *"by its affluence on a single point,* acts like a bottle of lye, and can cause death."[31]

The point at which force accrues to the mortal blow is certainly the vital center of the being: "What we call our soul," says Balzac, *"the geometric point at which all roads converge which traverse our* sensation."[32] These routes are also borrowed and used by the enemy. Man in society is therefore doubly vulnerable; because in the heart of a hostile country he is as though in a besieged place; and because his own passions cause him to open his defenses and sometimes to reveal their weak point where the attacker will concentrate his effort.

Nevertheless, Balzac does not always represent the conflict between the society surrounding him and the central individual under the form of an immediate crushing of the latter. If, for him, life is essentially a struggle between two tendencies it will not do that one should be too rapidly vanquished by the other, and that all the social tragedy or comedy should reduce itself to the subjugation of man by the milieu in which he is situated. For, in this case, in the last analysis, there would soon no longer be a struggle, nor in consequence, life. On the contrary, the writer must bestow on the enemy energies an almost equal power for defense as for attack. The individual is not always crushed by society. It even happens that he crushes society. In fact, he disposes great resources which in periods of peace he can accumulate, and which in moments of peril he can plumb. If the Balzacian being often weakens in allowing passions to carry him to all the points of the circumference, he also often reinforces himself by abstinence, the economy of thoughts and desires, which Balzac terms "the *concentration* of interior forces."[33] The most resistant natures for Balzac, are the "virginal natures:" "The Virginity, like all monstrosities, has special riches, those of absorbing grandeurs. The life whose powers are economized has given to the virgin individual an incalculable quality of resistance and of endurance."[34] Fixity, moral or physical, the contemplative life, the simplicity of needs, the absence of passion form for Balzac a sort of prime state of being. The latter, hoarding not spending its powers, bringing them back to the center, living no more than a virtual and punctual existence, is like a spring wound tight and ready to discharge itself violently when necessary:

A logical and simple deduction from his principles had made him know that Will could, by a contracting movement of the inner being, pull itself together; then, by another movement, project itself outside.[35]

Certain souls . . . do they not try to *concentrate* their forces in a long silence, in order to reappear ready to govern the world, by Word or by Action?[36]

But this silent concentration is still only a prime and virtual state, potential force, not acting force. Inversely, there are, with Balzac, a thousand places where we can seize upon the passage, often overwhelming, of the force of action, the concentration now acting from all the energies of the being onto an object, which is the object desired:

> With what violence my desires mount to her! If during the preceding days the universe had grown for me, in a single night it had a *center*. To her were attached my wishes and my ambitions.[37]

> In these moments, my entire life, my thoughts, my powers, mingled, uniting in what I call a desire . . .[38]

Sometimes a concentration operates in a genius:

> Let us examine thy state: thou art young, thy faculties are great and beautiful, their force is incalculable, thou hast always directed them toward the same end, *toward a point*, amassed . . .[39]

Sometimes it takes place in a frustrated being; but the result is the same:

> The phenomenon explained above, that of the *moral forces* in all the coarse people who do not use their intelligent faculties, as well as the society people, which by a daily expenditure, finds them strong and forceful at the moment when in their mind the redoubtable weapon called the *fixed idea* comes into play, manifested itself in the Cibot to a superior degree. Just as the fixed idea produced miracles of evasions and miracles of feeling, this door-keeper shored up by cupidity became as strong as a Nucingen at bay, as witty under his stupidity as the seductive La Palférine.[40]

So, without transition, in a moment of duration, but which, more often than not, later orders the whole of existence, the fixation of desire produces in the Balzacian character the concentration of a type differing completely from those who preceded. For it is no longer a case of a slow accumulation of forces that are still unemployed, but of the brusque and total orientation toward a new point around which the whole of life will organize itself:

> . . . The savage and the child *make all the rays of the sphere in which they live converge to one desire;* their life is monophile and their power comes from the prodigious unity of their actions.[41]

The power of the individual is therefore the direct reason of his united action; and this unity is represented by Balzac in the form of the sphere of which the rays, which are the different faculties of the soul or the varieties of the situations in which the being finds itself, are brought back to the same center, that is the object of desire. The sphere of the soul is a solid of which all the peripheral points pierce, at the median point, all converging equidistant lines. Such is the real structure of the famous Balzacian monomaniacs. Balthasar Claës, Hulot, Grandet and so many other characters of *The Human Comedy* are constructed like the spokes of a wheel fixed in their hub. From whatever point of perspective one may look at them, in whatever phase of their existence one surprises them, they always appear to be orientated toward the same object, finding their unity in the same point of convergence.

But it is not only the unity of their structure that is manifested here; it is also the intensity of their force. Reducing themselves to a single mobile existence, putting all their activities at the service of a unique desire, the Balzacian monomaniacs arrive by concentration at an almost infinite multiplication of vital energy:

> It seems to me to have been proved that under the dominion of a passion, which is will *gathered to a point,* and brought to incalculable power of animal force, as are all electric forces, man can carry his whole vitality, whether for attack, or for resistance . . .[42]

> The *concentration of moral forces,* by no matter what system, doubles the effort tenfold.[43]

Sometimes—rarely—with Balzac, this active concentration is artificially realized, in the sense that it is produced by the action of an excitant. It is thus, says Balzac, that "the opium absorbs all the animal forces, *reassembles them at one point,* takes them, squares or cubes them, carries them to I know not what power, gives to the entire being a creation in the void."[44]

But Balzac does not interest himself in the least in creations in the void. What do interest him are creations or projections in the filled. Opium only permits a futile dilation in imaginary spaces. Much more worth while is a world of obstacles and of pressures, actions and reactions. When, in the Balzacian universe, a being discovers himself to be in mortal peril, he immediately reassembles his forces, takes possession of physical and mental resources that up to

that time were unsuspected, and opposes to the surrounding menace
an almost immeasurable force of resistance or of counterattack:

> Extreme danger has . . . an effect on the soul as terrible as
> those of powerful reactives on the body. It is a charge of moral
> voltage. Perhaps the day is not far off when one can grasp the
> method by which feeling *condenses* itself chemically in a fluid,
> perhaps similar to electricity. . . . This dying, despondent
> woman, who had not slept, this duchess so difficult to dress,
> recovered the force of a lion at bay, and the presence of mind
> of a general in the midst of battle.[45]

The environing pressure here therefore plays a reactive role. To
the concentric movement that pulls in to the invested center, is
opposed an inverse movement, excentric, by which the menaced
being moves to the attack and repulses the invader. This is what
occurs in the *Cousin Pons,* where one suddenly sees the old dying
musician stripped, beaten down by the weight of lusts, get up from
his sickbed, and, with an energy of body and spirit totally at odds
with his earlier state, direct an offensive against his enemies that for
a time is victorious.

In the Human Comedy, such are the reversals of direction caused
by the dynamism of the will. "The soul loses in *centripetal force*
what it gains in *centrifugal force*,"[46] and inversely. The soul does not
possess centrifugal force except in measure as it condenses itself pre-
liminarily by its centripetal force. Its power of deployment depends
on its power of withdrawal. It is only when a being can concentrate
himself in a point of force that he can thereafter project himself
outside, pass, by action, from the center to the periphery, transform
himself into a sphere of activity that progressively enlarges itself
around him.

All those who are willful, that is to say all strong beings, are, with
Balzac, capable of this double movement of withdrawal and diffusion. Louis Lambert is such a type:

> Lambert possessed the gift of calling to himself, at certain
> moments, extraordinary powers, and of being able to assemble
> his powers *in a given point* in order to project them.[47]

> . . . Nothing resists this certain power when a man habituates
> himself in *concentrating* it, and in managing its sum total, in
> order constantly to direct toward other souls the mass projection
> of this fluid.[48]

One may then distinguish in the Balzacian novel a form of composition which is exactly the inverse of the novel of conspiracy. Such a one describes a process of compression, the other, a process of diffusion and of expression. Nothing is more recognizable in *La Comédie Humaine* than the projection of the individual force multiplied tenfold by concentration. In Balzac, all those of great passions and ambitions have invariably been represented as emitting around themselves a mesmeric fluid, a perturbing and dominating essence which incessantly augments on the field of action. At first, it is usually the mental and physical life of the characters that is found to be affected; next, their immediate surroundings and entourage, wife, children, mistress, or friends; next, acquaintances, the social ensemble of which they form the center; until at last their will cracks the framework and the whole of society becomes the field of their activity and possession:

> I have decided that man could project beyond himself, by all the acts stemming from his movement, a quantity of force that would produce any effect whatsoever in his *sphere of activity* . . .
> If, in fact, as the most wonderful genius has said, the geometrician who has listened most acutely at the doors of the sanctuary, a pistol shot at the edge of the Mediterranean causes a movement which can be felt as far as the coast of China, is it not probable that if we project beyond ourselves an abundance of power, we shall either change the atmosphere and conditions around us, or necessarily influence, by the effects of this live force that seeks its place, the beings and the things with which we are *surrounded*?[49]

> Thus the entire force of a man should have the property of reacting on others, and penetrating them with an essence that is not their own, if they do not defend themselves against such aggression."[50]

The roles, then, are reversed. The environing world is now on the defensive, and it is the isolated individual who is the aggressor. In the Balzacian novel every human being can suddenly constitute himself in active and offensive power, determining around himself an infinite series of effects. Sometimes these are monstrously evident by reason of their violence and of the quasi-comic range to which they unroll; sometimes, on the contrary, it is the insidious and almost invisible manner in which they succeed one another, not without finally tending toward the same universality; for, as one knows, in a world which is crowded and thronged, a movement engendered at the edge of the Mediterranean propagates itself as far as the coasts of China, which is to say throughout the entire universe. Every one of our desires, no matter how feebly we may express it, unchains undulations that go on out of sight. Even without wishing it, we influence the world. We pour our soul into it. Thus we determine it and imprint our own image upon it:

> Do we not imprint our customs, our thought, on all that surrounds us . . .?[51]

We imprint them by our acts, our words, our gestures, by a simple motion of the hand:

> A hand is not only attached to a body, it expresses and continues a thought . . .[52]

> The hand transudes life, and everywhere it touches, it leaves traces of a magical power. . . . It exhales, more than any other part of the body, the nervous fluids or the unknown substance that one must call *will,* in default of another term.[53]

Expansion therefore implies, too, expression and impression. Man really projects his imprint, far from himself, in the exterior world. He writes in the ambient air the history of his desires:

> In the same way that bodies really project themselves in the atmosphere leaving to subsist in it the spectre seized by the daguerreotype which stops it in its passage; in the same way ideas, real and agitating creations, *imprint upon what one must call the atmosphere of the spiritual world,* producing effects there that live spectrally. . . .[54]

Effects that can compare themselves, yet another time, to the successive wrinkles imprinted on the surface of the water by the stone thrown into the pond. For example, the springing up of a love is a communicable shock which transmits its vibrations in the double expanse of time and space, which imprints its trace in a circular field endlessly enlarged:

> Both, during this rapid instant, felt one of those lively commotions of which the effects on the soul may be compared to those produced by a stone thrown to the bottom of a lake. The gentlest of reflections are born and succeed one another, indefinable, multiplied, without end, agitating the heart, *as the*

circular wrinkles that for a long time fold the wave from the
point where the stone has fallen.[55]

In this passage the dilation once again is interior. It is in spiritual
space, known only by lovers whose emotion is propagated from the
center to the circumference. But more often Balzac does not content
himself with describing a diffusion entirely held within. It seems
that with him the sensitive movement must almost always go beyond
the frontier of the invisible and the visible, the interior and the exterior. In enlarging the circle of its effects, emotion goes beyond the
limits of the body and manifests itself around, outside, in the form
of a halo:

> . . . A rendez-vous had never irritated his senses more, had
> never before revealed more daring voluptuousnesses, had never
> so well caused love to spring from his center to *pour itself out*
> *like an atmosphere around a man.*[56]

Here, the atmosphere is no longer, as before, an ambient milieu
that, from the exterior, molds and fashions the beings who are
plunged into it. It is exactly the inverse that is accomplished here.
Man, cause and center of his own emotions, creates around himself
his own atmosphere. Of this, Balzac is very much aware:

> . . . Let us recognize that if the *atmospheric milieux* have
> authority over man, man must all the more strongly exert
> authority, in his turn, over the imagination of his fellows by the
> vigor and force with which he projects his will *which produces a*
> *veritable atmosphere around him.*[57]

But if man projects a particular atmosphere around himself, this
atmosphere must be perceptible to others. It must form in the air a
sort of luminous globe that envelops him from whom it emanates,
and that is visible to the spectator. Multiple passages of Balzac attest
this visibility of a spheric aura liberated by the passionate individual:

> From whence comes this *flame that radiates* around a woman
> in love?[58]

> She threw (into the music she was playing) the feelings moving
> her. In a manner at once both suave and dreaming, her soul
> spoke to the soul of the young man, enveloping it like a *cloud*
> by almost visible ideas.[59]

These ideas that so often float like *vapors* in the neighborhood of souls . . .[60]

An indefinable grace, an inexpressible charm, light as air, penetrating as fire, gentle as a blessing, spread over this scene of love; a sort of celestial *cloud* surrounded them. . . . One would have said around the (slightest objects) this *aureole* reigned, with which one surrounds the inhabitants of the heavens when they descend here below.[61]

. . . Thy work, thy scissors, thy basket, seem to me *environed by a supernatural light* that escapes from every part of thy being, forming a light *cloud*.[62]

Every gesture of the young girl gave another charm to my sight; she appeared to move in a *luminous atmosphere,* and her slightest movement brought a new undulation to the light.[63]

The Balzacian being is therefore capable of diffusing around himself a flame, a cloud, a luminous atmosphere. He is, says Balzac,

a poor firefly who, unknown to him, allows light to escape from his every pore. He moves in a *brilliant sphere* in which every effort brings another shock of light and defines his movements by long traces of fire.[64]

Among the innumerable examples of this singular luminous diffusion, with which, like Swedenborg's angels, the Balzacian characters possess the faculty of being able to surround themselves, there is none more striking than that of Père Goriot disclosing to Rastignac the fullness of his paternal passion. At this moment he is lit by fires which are not only perceptible to his interlocutor, but which affect him, propagating in him the emotion that makes them shine, by this power of contagion of feeling that Balzac knows and whose immense amplifying action he likes to describe:

Père Goriot was sublime. Eugène had never been able to see him *illumined by the fires* of his paternal passion. One thing worthy of remark is the force of the infusion that feelings possess. No matter how coarse a person may be, the moment they express a true and strong emotion, they exhale a particular fluid that modifies their physiognomy, animates their gestures, colors their voice. Often the most stupid being is capable, under the effort of passion, of the greatest eloquence of ideas, (thought), if not of language, and seems to move in a *luminous sphere*. At this moment, there was, in the voice and the gestures of this man, the communicative power that signalizes a great actor. But are not our fine feelings the poetry of the will?[65]

In its spherical deployment, the will, luminous fluid, therefore penetrates and influences weaker wills. The passionate person does not only pour himself out into space. He communicates his passion. The whole work of Balzac is filled with these extensions of the affective force.

But the extension with which we have to do is not only the extension of an emotion. It is also, almost always, the extension of the will itself: "I felt in myself," said the country doctor, "I know not what need of expansion . . . . I had tasted the cruel delights of maternity, I resolved to give myself up to it entirely, to gratify this feeling in a more *extended sphere* than that of mothers, in becoming a sister of charity for a whole country . . . . I love, in extending my hand, to sow happiness and joy."[66]

Here is an example of will lavished upon good deeds. More often Balzac describes the movement by which a maleficent will extends its empire. Such is the passage of the *Femme de trente ans,* in which a criminal, by only casting a glance over a family, seizes their minds and hearts: "All at once . . . the indefinable empire to which the stranger belonged, in spite of himself perhaps, the principle and the effect, poured itself out around him with the rapidity of an inundation."[67]

But, criminal or well-wisher, in extending around him the empire of his action, the Balzacian character never ceases to remain in the center. He directs the play from a distance:

> Skillfully to employ the passions of men or women like springs that one causes to move to the profit of the State, to put in movement the wheels of this great machine that we call a government, and to please oneself by enclosing the most indomitable feelings like the triggers that one amuses oneself by watching, is it not to create, and like God, to *place oneself in the center of the universe?*[68]

Like Corentin or Vautrin, the Balzacian being therefore likes to be enthroned in the center of a world from which his will radiates. He is at once by concentration in a point without extension, and, by projection, everywhere that his radiations extend. Thus Goriot is where he is, in the Pension Vauquer, and at the same time every-where that his love for his daughters carries him:

> —Shall I tell you a curious thing? Well, when I was made a father, I understood God. He is wholly *everywhere,* since crea-tion has come from Him. Sir, I am thus with my daughters.[69]

As Goriot is wholly everywhere that his daughters may be, so Balzac is entirely everywhere with the creatures of his mind. He it is who accompanies his own word, who pours himself out with it in the spaces which it animates, who participates in the more and more numerous and distant existences that his word causes to gravitate to his universe. And he is also he who swells his own word, who inflates his text like a balloon. Similar to the angelic spirit that he describes in *Séraphita,* Balzac "disposes of motion and associates himself with everything by *ubiquity.*"[70] Like the satellites and planets of a solitary world disposed in circles and epicycles, the multiple figures of the Human Comedy are illuminated by a central projector which trans-mits immediately to them its own light and energy, no matter what the distance and the differences of nature that separate these creatures from the creative power. Every one of these planets con-stitutes a particular sphere, having its own center and its own law. But all these spheres are grouped and maintained in motion by the will of a unique pivot:

> Every world had *a center to which all the points of its sphere tended.* . . . The different parts of the Infinite (formed) a living melody; and every time the chord made itself felt like an im-mense respiration, the worlds swept along by this unanimous motion, inclined themselves toward that immense Being, Who, *from Its impenetrable center, caused all to go forth and brought all back to Itself.*[71]

This impenetrable Cosmic center, which causes all to come forth from It and which brings all back to Itself, is, in the last analysis, the genius of Balzac himself. Balzac is not content to deploy around him-self the Human Comedy, he has reflected it in himself, he has con-centrated it. There is not only in Balzac's work a concentration of forces, there is, as well, a concentration of ideas. The mind con-stitutes itself an intellectual center in which everything it embraces comes to be unified.

It is what Balzac calls (after the Latin word *speculum:* mirror) the *specialty,* and what, more exactly perhaps, one should call the *centrality:*

We are one of the greatest of God's works. Has He not given us the faculty of being able to reflect nature, of *concentrating* it within ourselves by thought?[72]

The poet, to be complete, must be the *intelligent center* of everything, he must epitomize in himself the luminous syntheses of all human knowledge.[73]

These are the princes of art, they carry in themselves a mirror to which nature comes to reflect itself with its slightest occurrences.[74]

The specialty consists in seeing the things of the material world as well as those of the spiritual world in their original and consequential ramifications.[75]

And above all, this passage, where the Balzacian symbol of the center and the circle finds its most complete expression:

One must . . . possess the glance that causes *phenomena* to *converge toward a center,* that logic which *disposes in rays,* that measure serving never to discover *one of the points of the circle* without observing the others, and that promptitude which takes everything in at a bound from head to foot.[76]

To employ Leibnitz's expression, which he repeats endlessly, Balzac constitutes himself, or constitutes his work, as a *"concentric mirror."* The universe comes to be reflected and absorbed in it. The circle is in the point, the point is in the circle. Far from being only a "tempest of interests" and a whirlwind of disordered movements, the Balzacian work is at once the expansion of a center toward a periphery, and the concentration of this periphery in the center. It is this incessant movement, both "expansible and contractible."[77] What we see in it, is, in Balzac's terms, "the despotism with which a mind constrains us to submit to the effects of a mysterious optical illusion which grows, shrinks, exalts creation."[78] For "the soul has the unknown power to extend as well as to contract space."[79] Balzac also always affirms, directly or indirectly, the principle of centrality which dominates his work. In the Introduction to the *Études de moeurs,* written under his inspiration by Davin, the reader finds himself warned that he will finally discover between these Études "a link that will cause them all to *converge toward a luminous center.*"[80] Criticizing the *Brutus* by Lethière, Balzac rejoices to find in it a multiple activity that *"tends toward a center* which is called unity, and without which there is no work of art."[81] Finally, in *César Birotteau,* in which Balzac pleased himself by constructing it to follow the pattern of the *Symphony in C* by Beethoven, all the action is arranged by the novelist around a central episode which exactly corresponds to the last movement of the Beethoven symphony. It is the episode of the Birotteau ball:

> When, after the slow preparations of the sublime magician so well understood by Habeneck, the gesture of an enthusiastic orchestra conductor lifts the rich curtain of this decoration in summoning from his bow the dazzling motif *toward which all the musical forces have converged,* the poets whose hearts then beat understood that the Birotteau ball produced in his life the effect that was produced in their souls by this fecund motif, to which the *Symphony in C* perhaps owes its supremacy over its brilliant sisters.[82]

The Balzacian novel is therefore a movement, but an ordered movement. It leaves from a point and returns to a point. It unfolds a life, or an ensemble of lives, that, issued from a center and propagating themselves around a center, return to the center. It seeks to establish that perfect accord of which an amateur of music speaks in *Massimilia Doni.* This accord "leads us forward further into the *center of life,* on the flood of elements that reanimate the voluptuousnesses and that *carry man to the center of the luminous sphere from whence his thought can convoke the whole universe.*"[83]

In causing all the elements of its universe to converge toward the center, the Balzacian work comes, in the final analysis, to an extraordinary unity and even to a pure abstraction. By a paradoxical return to its deployment in the vast sphere of the concrete, Balzac's novel often tends elsewhere to rarefy itself, to impoverish itself, to shrink itself, to be less at the center of the luminous sphere of the reality it has created than to be the central abstract principle of which the peripheric images are but the reflection and effect. Everything is reabsorbed in the principle, everything is only the previsible resultant of a unique idea, which, finally, alone matters:

> A first principle exists! Let us surprise it at the *point* where it reacts on itself, where it is one, where it is principle before being creature, cause before being effect; we shall see it absolute, without form, susceptible of clothing all the forms we see assuming it.[84]

In seizing the movement at its first point, one finally risks being unable to seize the movement, only the point. Again, cause without effect, principle still without form, the One absolute is the Plotinian God with which Balzac's thought tends to identify itself. But the God of Plotinus is not really a creative God. If the world emanates from Him, this emanation has in its last term so little importance, and even reality, that it has the insubstantiality of a dream. Finally, there remains only a principle without a form, a God without a universe, a central point without periphery, without radiation, without space. It is true that "the abstraction contains all one nature in germ."[85] But this nature is only in germ; it is virtual; it does not exist. When Balzac arrives, as he does sometimes, at the extreme point of his development, which consists in reducing everything to the central and causal principle, to the point from which all the lines flow, but where all the lines also *disappear,* he replaces the marvelous circular development of concrete figures that fill the Human Comedy, by the inverse, which is to say by their absorption in a point where there is no longer anything and which is nothing.

VIGNY

To Austin Gill

The march of the mind is not direct. If its flight were in a straight line, without detours, it would lose itself in the infinite beyond of the atmosphere. . . . From the moment of his awakening every day, man's mind is errant and glides like the swallow, turning, mounting, descending, fluttering, beating, suddenly rising to highest heaven.[1]

No MATTER HOW high it lifts itself, Vigny's thought never runs the risk of losing itself, for it never goes up in a perpendicular flight. By comparison with the thought of Lamartine, it never disappears beyond the horizon. Ascending, descending, covering with an oblique flight a sky that the eye embraces and measures, it never ceases, in the meanderings of its flight, to be a visible object. It never reaches fusion or dissolution. The flight of images is, by consequence, not a disappearance in the distances of thought, but their distinct spinning at a measurable distance. To this turning movement that never stops, as the aerial objects that accomplish it never cease being visible, there corresponds the need to find the fixed place where, from all directions, the images may attach themselves, as a mobile wheel to an axle-tree. "He sought in the immensity a point of support on which he could fix his always errant thoughts."[2] Vigny's originality is to have identified this point of support, this central resting place of the spiritual life, not only with himself, with the reflexive force of his own thought, but with the constant object of that thought, namely, the Idea. From the moment when the mind represents itself as the habitat for a unique idea, in which it succeeds in in-dwelling itself with an invariable thought, it matters little that all the rest of mental life, images, remembrances, premonitions, are dispersed to the four corners of the sky. The wandering activity of the mind becomes an orientated activity. Everything turns, but around the idea. Thus the topography of the Vignian imagination constitutes itself under the symbolic form of the compass or the clock: around one part firmly set in the center, the other runs from moment to moment and from place to place.

Now, between these two so different parts of the being, is there a link, and if so, what is it? How, for example, can the round exterior of images bring anything at all to the central idea? Without a doubt, the images of the sensible world, as well as those engendered by dream, could easily be conceived as a mobile frame which, enclosing the idea, would confirm it by outside limitation, and consequently, definition. All around it, these images dispose their variations and variegations, not to dispute with the idea the privileged place it occupies in the mind, but, quite simply, it would seem, to indict by their fluctuations, spatial wandering and ephemerality in time, the essential contrast between the swirling periphery and the central fixity. Such would be the unique contribution of images to the life of the mind: its horizon bordered by a multicolored moving fringe. But first, if it was uniquely so, there would be something strange in seeing an element composed of a mad and capricious mobility serve as the limiting and formative principle to a thought already in itself very imprecise. What is striking, in fact, in Vigny's mental life, is that, to the contrary of other lives, his hard, determined, stable, and resistant element is found to be situated in the center, and what is soft, transitory and vague, to be superficial. In brief, provided with a solid kernel, the thought of Vigny in no way has a need to be limited from the outside. His central reality holds itself compact in itself, and without it there would be a peripheral life which would be menaced by the loss of all consistency and fade into formlessness. — On the other hand, what kind of exterior enrichment can this whirling bring to the central fixity? Do we not find ourselves in the presence of two contradictory modes of life, that take place simultaneously, but at distinctly different levels of existence? Perhaps it would be useless to want to try to find a relationship between all forces? And yet Vigny is the very one who, with a remarkable persistence, has tried to put into communication these two modes of life, the mobility of the surface and the permanence of the depths. From this paradoxical communication between the ways of mutually exclusive existence, one can see the first example of the role which the circumference plays in relation to the center. Certainly, the life which the being leads on the surface is of a velocity as absurd as it is exhausting; but this life is really alive. Vigny has, to the highest degree, the feeling of all the affecting variations through which thought passes, the perception of the fugitive tints that color a nuance, ceaselessly retouching the changing humors of the spirit. But such is life, or such at least is the only tangible witness that we have of it. It is like a blush that now is effaced and now revived on a cheek, giving away, by the fantastic character of its apparitions, the successive movements of the heart. An almost uniquely affective animation unfolds itself, a pure shivering of the surface, a gliding of furtive forms, through which, as through a veil of mist inundated with light, is divined the entirely different form of the idea that inhabits the depths of the spirit.

Now it is in this that there consists with Vigny the contribution of the circumference to the center. The clamor of the surface descends to the silence of the depths. A sort of warmth comes to animate a region whose solitary purity would soon be icy otherwise. Even more, one might say that the sensible qualities which are those of living, the forms, the gestures, above all, the colors, interpose themselves in a way between the gaze and the object brooded over. And as the figures are the most transitory in the world, and they replace themselves with a singular promptness, nothing is more varied than the spectacle which they present in simply defiling against the immutable background toward which the eye is directed. So the orientation of the gaze of Vigny reveals itself as being almost always interior and concentric; and if in his field of vision, the external world and the superficial regions of the being find themselves in an embrace, with him the point of view is usually so highly situated, it is so far and so peripheral, that on the road the eye travels in sinking toward the center, it must necessarily encounter a series of zones disposed in layers around about.

Also, with Vigny, the glance is at one and the same time of an extraordinary scope and a no less remarkable profundity. Like Moses, from the top of Mount Sinai, Vigny contemplates a world whose first blueprints are made up of the sky and clouds, by the spread of the desert and of a thousand shades; but progressively tightened perspectives converge toward a promised land. An *interior* promised land, an underground treasure of thought, that draws the gaze like a lover, yet meanwhile between this one and his object unfolds the fantastic movement of life in full daylight.

But to this contrast, to this double vision the contribution of the circumference to the center is not reduced. It is not content to *inter-*

pose itself between the gaze and the center, it truly *deposits* around the center and on the center the best of the images that it had caused to pass through. There bursts forth what is perhaps most admirable in Vigny's vision: not only does this force designate the eternal beyond the transitory, it covers it, without hiding it, with the covering with which the momentary envelopes it. So that the eternal, far from manifesting itself in an utter nakedness, reveals itself dressed and decorated with ornaments, transitory in themselves, but through association with it, acquiring the eternal character of the very object which they adorn. The most surprising thing of all, there is with Vigny, thanks to the support of the peripheric and ephemeral, a knowledge of the center, a perceptible development of the eternal.

This development is marvelously expressed by the symbol of the pearl:

> Poetry, O treasure, pearl of thought!
> The tumults of the heart like those of the sea
> Could not hinder thy shaded robe
> From *amassing* the colors which must fashion it.[3]

Every wave of the sea adds a whitened veil to the beauties of a pearl, every tide works slowly to make it more perfect, every fleck of spume that balances on it leaves it a more mysterious shade half-gilded, semi-transparent, where one can only divine an interior ray that comes from its heart.[4]

If one bears in mind only the first of these two passages, one would suppose that the circumferential tumults simply abstain from troubling the formation of the pearl. But this formation consists in the acquisition of colors that have no other origin than the tumults of the external life. The second text tells us so formally. Every wave of the surface adds a layer of nacre to the roundness of the pearl, which grows and is enriched by reason of its direct support from the external life. The circumference therefore embellishes the center, it surrounds it with a complex stratification, delicate and animated, it makes of the central point an even more minuscule sphere, which slowly grows. Certainly, what is affirmed in these two passages is the beneficent influence of the peripheral life over the central life. The movement is from top to bottom and centripetal. But it is also centrifugal, since what shows itself with great clarity is the swelling of the idea, its patient growth from the point without dimension that it occupies in the human mind. Here, we are no longer in the presence of a whirlwind of images around an immobile point. It is a point which mingles with all the parts, without renouncing its fixity and its centrality. The growth of the pearl is comparable to that of a plant; it has regularity, and a sort of organic growth; with this difference, that it is without root and without stem, and that instead of growing in a spiral according to the process described by Goethe, it grows equally in all directions. Finally, although its growth does not bring it to the surface of the exterior world, it presents the spectacle of an enclosed sphere growing in the interior of another. Between one and the other a proportion is established. The curvatures of the great surface find themselves repeated in the convexity of the small one. As with the Baroque and Metaphysical poets of the seventeenth century, for Vigny, the pearl is a microcosm reflecting the macrocosm on its polished walls as in a mirror.

In this network of reciprocal support, lie the relations established in Vigny between the central idea and the external life. A rich and happy relationship, more especially since the related boundaries remain distinct one from the other and are destined not to mingle. Different from Schelling's universe, there is here no danger whatsoever that the growth and gradual enrichment of the idea will cause it to coincide with the surface world; as the external world comes to deposit its own reflection on the idea, it is always at the surface, never at the center. As two nations that would lose everything by joining together, still have the advantage of establishing between one another a system of alliance and commerce, center and circumference proceed, with Vigny, to their multiple exchanges.

But what occurs if there is no exchange? What happens when, by reason of circumstances more often than not fatal, the poet finds himself incapable of establishing between the fixed center to his thought and his daily life, the numerous but delicate and precarious rapports which we have seen?

Then, in their respective isolation, both circumference and center follow their particular sort of existence. The peripheral rotation of thought becomes a whirlwind without an object, a foolish gyration which no fixity moderates: "Under the bony box of the skull," says Dr. Noir, "ceaselessly circulates, like an invisible storm, the poor soul who cannot get out except with a great deal of trouble and cannot stay without a great deal of boredom. It whirls, it turns, it makes sounds, it moans . . ."[5] Elsewhere, in the Journal, one finds:

"Obstinate work, perpetual, born with me, and of which the great wheel turns in my brain night and day . . ."[6]

But it is not only in the brain that the wheel is turning. The exterior world is in itself a whirlwind. How often does one not see surging up in Vigny's poetry a vast exterior force, hostile and tempestuous, that envelops the poet and his idea, threatening to carry them into a fatal circle? Then the central part of the being feels itself to be endangered. It seems to it that the circle is tightening. The soul sees itself to be besieged, oppressed on all sides, in mortal peril:

> And there you are *encircled* in the growing ring.
> It is the Law that *advances and presses in upon you.*[7]

At all costs, one must protect the center; one must oppose to the circumferential assaults the resistance of an enclosed precinct. Crystal protector, the transparent dress and armor of the idea, a defensive circle forms to face the offensive circle of the enemy. So the bottle, thrown into the sea resists the multiple shocks of the waves, in a curved wall of glass conserving its hollow at the center, "like a phoenix under a crystal."[8]

It is a crystal whose transparence permits the perception of the idea in its primitive purity, which, nevertheless is tinted—like the pearl—with all the varieties of colors projected upon it by a world that has been unable to destroy what it was protecting: "This crystal is transparent, and, through the rosy lustres, gilded, irised, brought to it by the torches of the astral bodies that give it the aspect of a marvelous lake or of an unknown sky, discovered in shadow, one continues to perceive the immobile face of the mummy."[9]

Thus, once more, circle and circumference are rejoined. One shows through the crystal. The other places its own images on the crystal. But the re-encounter of these two elements is not a true re-encounter. It is a conjunction in separation. For between the multicolored world whose reflection is projected upon the crystal, and the immobile object the image of which the crystal allows to show through, no direct contact is possible. Things and the spirit do not touch one another. It is only that the *images* of the one join the *idea* conceived by the other.

Between the circumference and the center, therefore, what Vigny sets up is a rampart and a mirror. Let us say more exactly a pro-

tective and transforming milieu. Like the Mallarméan pane, the
Vignian crystal defends the entrance to a sacred place, to which
nothing can penetrate but objects and the beings that have submitted to a truly poetical idealization. One recalls Vigny's definition
of poetry: "A voluptuousness covering thought and rendering it
luminous by the brilliance of its conserving crystal."[10] When the
magic of poetry has completed its work, when the idea has begun to
scintillate and the forms of affective life no longer present themselves except by an idealized reflection, then a curious phenomenon
of mental juxtaposition is produced: the idea we have conceived is
revealed to us in the midst of the colorings the images confer upon
it; and inversely the disordered sound of images is controlled in us
by the inflexible attention with which the mind follows the evolution. Our poetical life is therefore composed of a double reflection.
Sometimes it seems to us that poetry itself has its birth in us out of
some deep center, like the flame of a pulsing hearth whose prismatic
forms come to full flowering at the surface; sometimes, and now and
again at the same time, it seems to us that our mind puts forms and
colors aside to plunge toward a center in which there is only light;
and then again, our thought appears to ourselves as the synthesis
of a progression toward the center and a flowering at the surface.

Now it is to this synthesis that Vigny attaches the greatest value
and gives the fullest attention. Of all Vigny's texts that have to do
with the theme of the center and the circle, there is none more
charged with significance than that in which he compares two sorts
of beings, those, like Marie Dorval, incapable of synthesizing center
and circumference, and the others, who, like Vigny, attain it thanks
to an intense application of mind:

> There are two kinds of souls among us. The first kind rejoice
> in the present moment and forget at the very instant when they
> are possessed of this intoxicating emotion, both what has pre-
> ceded it and what will follow it.
> The point at which they can arrive is a complete withering
> of the heart. A perpetual giddiness renders for them one impres-
> sion as good and as lively as another; they give themselves up to
> it without reservation. A soul of this sort, as soon as it sees the
> moment approaching when it will feel in its heart the remorse
> and fright of the emptiness of its life, makes haste to stupefy
> itself and to throw itself into whatever exaggerated action pre-
> sents itself, or else search for an occupation that will absorb
> it. . . . A perpetual chameleon, this soul ends by being neither

happy nor unhappy, but only a flame lighting itself from the movement of others, and by having no life of its own remains incapable of *being,* and merits no more being counted upon than a *soap bubble* that is always carried away by the wind and colored by the objects it encounters.

The contemplative Soul, on the contrary, is attentive to the three points of existence, the past, the present, and the future. . . . It knows, it sees, and it feels *profoundly.* It carries to the heart the emotions giving it its triple view and at this *center of love and of goodness* is *ceaselessly perfected* the grandeur and force of its being. The *higher and wider* this intelligence, the more its goodness grows and is purified, the more it *spreads around* itself a limitless and measureless intelligence. But also the more there is accumulated in equal *depth* a disdain of the human nature which it pardons, and the sadness of being condemned to the humiliating spectacle of degraded individuals and peoples. It feels, *at the center of the world, solitude extending around it.* Its thought produces this like the flame hurled by the American savage who throws it at his feet onto the prairie grass to make it *form around himself a boundless circle.*[11]

Of the two souls of whom Vigny here gives symbolic portrait, the first is extraordinarily restricted in its mental space. It has, so to speak, no dimensions. It is a minuscule sphere, ephemeral and mobile, incapable of dilating itself, only capable of mirroring itself, and of floating in the wind, a soap bubble.

The soap bubble is just the opposite to the pearl. If, like the pearl, it is a little colored globe, nothing in the soap bubble adds to itself; everything is replaced. Hollow, toy of winds, living only in the reflections that the exterior colors on its surface subject to an indefinite number of metamorphoses, it is only what it is in the place where it happens to be at that moment. It is "incapable of being," because it is incapable of lasting, of ripening, of growing, of extending in time and space. Without a fixed place, without a central principle of permanence, it is carried away in a whirlwind itself homeless. It is only a *nunc fluens,* a mobile point.

Wholly other is the soul gifted with the "triple view." It is a "large and high intelligence," that "sees and feels profoundly." Possessing width, height, and depth, it is susceptible of having volume, of occupying the three dimensions. It develops itself in every sense by a process of circular dilation. "A forebearance without limits and measure spreads itself around it," from a "center of love and goodness." Nothing in Vigny is more moving than this invasion of space by the movement of love and union that takes its flight from the most intimate point of the being and goes off freely to find its expression beyond the horizon. From this point of view, space seems the unifying milieu, thanks to which the central being attains the periphery of the objects of its feeling. But at the extremity and from this extremity back to its initial center, by a reflux and a characteristic returning of the Vignian thought, the movement of love changes itself into one of disappointment and disdain. In very proportion as "the goodness grows," also grows "in equal proportion the scorn of human nature." The place of union becomes a place of exclusion and separation. In proportion to the growing indulgence with which the thought turns toward other beings, there is also augmented the lucidity with which it considers them, and the mental detachment that permits, and constrains it to judge them. The more it tends toward them, the greater seems the distance that separates the conceived ideal and the feeling of the original love. Then "the soul feels, *at* the center of the world, solitude *extending* around it." Instead of being a movement which rejoins its peripheral objects, thought becomes an action that establishes and completes their absolute withdrawal. No longer is it love diffusing itself, it is solitude spreading all around. Here we are very close to Mallarmé's early attitude. Space is a glass which opposes a transparent obstacle to the object dreamed. But with Mallarmé this object is purely ideal, and the incapacity of attaining it has for a consequence, the condemnation, not of the ideal, but of that which finds itself impotent to lift itself up to it. The jet of water sinks, a kind of heaviness overwhelms the center, which has been culpable of not being able to identify itself with the peripheral ideal. While with Vigny, it is, on the contrary, toward the periphery that is borne the condemnation of thought, it is the circumferential zone only, which, finally, is struck by *scorn*. In such a way that the movement of expansion which the center pursues, ends, with Vigny, by becoming the movement by which the center pushes the circumference further and further away. Nevertheless, no matter how clear the difference may be between Vigny's experience and that of Mallarmé, one may establish in the one as in the other the same severance between subject and object, center and periphery, and understand for what reason, in both cases, this severance has the inevitable effect of the solitude of the central subject. Solitude that grows without measure, a species of negative space, beyond which is outlined the presence of repressed forms, and in the midst of which stands an ivory tower. Instead of being a "perpetual chameleon," an ever mobile and peripheral point, here thought remains immobile and at the median point of an activity to and from which, simultaneously, it both links and separates itself. And, by its double action of relation and separation, it ploughs up everything between, and traverses the whole length of its furrow. It is striking that in order to oppose to the "soap bubble" soul the soul of an inverse tendency, Vigny should use also an image of sphere or circle: it is that of "the flame which an American savage throws at his feet on the prairie grass and which forms around him a *boundless circle.*" Here the circumference of the circle is no longer orientated toward the exterior; it is no longer a simple reflective and mobile surface. Infinite, it disposes itself around a determined hearth. Instead of receiving its life and its color from the environing world, like the bubble, the flame itself engenders and radiates its own clarity in the desert. Not a pearl, but a flare, a star, or a diamond.[12]

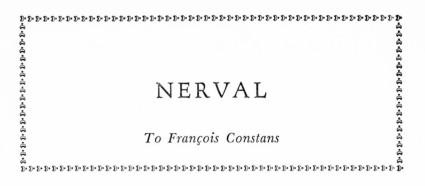

NERVAL

To François Constans

I

"The thirteenth return . . . . It is still the first." When he writes this in the margin of the verse: *La treizième heure, pivotale,*[1] Nerval dreams, as has been said,[2] of the dial of the Touraine clock that he owned, or of a bas-relief of Diana, eternally leaning on her elbows, presiding over the circle of hours which, achieving the number twelve, recommence with figure one or figure thirteen, equivalent numbers. On the dial where, "the enamelled numbers of the hours were displayed on a smutty background,"[3] two by two and twelve by twelve, all the hours coincide, in such a way that the identity of the moments of time does not only appear on the circumference of the dial in the identity of the one or the thirteen, but also as a pivot, either one or thirteen, and all the hours mingle in one figure and one moment; as in the Euclidean Commentary by Proclus, in which all the points of the circumference find themselves again at the center of the circle; that is their principle and their end. Thus the thirteen reduces itself to the one, as it recommences, and the peripheral diversity of the duration contains a moment in which all times are united, and which is nevertheless itself eternal and beyond time.

Time of day, time that conjoins the variations of the light and the night:

> . . . beautiful as the day by the fires of the footlights that lit her from below, pale as the night, when the lowered footlights left her lighted from above under the rays of the chandelier, showing her as more natural, more brilliant in the shadow of her beauty, *alone,* like the *divine Hours* that cut out stars to wear on their foreheads, on the brown backgrounds of the frescoes of Herculaneum.[4]

Reduced to herself, brilliant in the shadow of her beauty alone, queen of a moment only, the pivotal hour is described on the indeterminate background of all the others. She recapitulates them all. She is at once one or the other of all the particular hours that scintillate in the night as in the day, and the central hour, unique, in the presence of which the others are dimmed and withdraw to the periphery.

Before this image, which is that of the procession of the Hours in the frescoes of Herculaneum, how is it possible not to think simultaneously of the alternative title that Nerval gave to the sonnet *Artémis: le ballet des heures,* and to that other Ballet of the Hours which constitutes one of the happiest episodes of the long drama that Nerval wrote in collaboration with Méry, under the title of *l'Imagier de Harlem?*

However, it is not certain that Nerval is the unique author of the Ballet of the Hours of *l'Imagier de Harlem,* nor of the poem that, on an air by Adolphe Degroot, was sung in it.[5] But who does not know that all that Nerval touched, became part of himself? And nothing could more naturally become a part of himself than the image of twelve graceful figures representing, by their evolutions and by the song that accompanied them, the symbol of an action that recommences epoch by epoch and "of which all the personages," says Gautier, "seem to have existed from all time and to extend themselves in ever-enlarging undulations toward the ocean of the ages."[6] Renewed orbs enclosing an instant that is always the same, the hours form by their concentric movements and endlessly varied ensemble, endlessly similar, "collective animated figures,"[7] ballet or successive bouquet of flowers, which, like the personages of the Herculaneum frescoes, go from night to day and from day to night:

> The hours are the flowers that blossom one after
> > another,
> In the eternal hymen of night and day.[8]

Hours that pass and turn, cycles of successive hours, but from which the present hour detaches itself to take on a unique importance:

> In its rapid flight, embrace the best,
> Always that which is about to strike.
> Foster it well according to your will
> As the *only instant that your soul will dream,*
> As if the happiness of the longest life
> Was in the hour that goes.

However, the poem degenerates very quickly, taking on an epicurean and somewhat banal significance. One must profit by the instant before it has flown. But it is perhaps not without worth, to find in the preceding verses a sketch of the first quatrain of *Artémis*. *The only instant that your soul will dream,* is already near: *And it is always the one—or it is the only moment,* as: *O thou, the first or the last* is prefigured by the following strophe of the *Ballet:*

> You will always find *from the first hour*
> *Until the hour of night* that speaks twelve times,
> The *vines* on the mountains, inundated with light,
> The *myrtles* in the shadow of the woods.

Alternative plants of the Nervalian universe, the fronds, branches of the vines and the myrtles, inundated with light or with their somber verdure, compose a duration which, twelve times repeated and extending from the first hour to the sainted hour of the abyss of the night, are wholly refound in the moment in which one dreams, and that, each time that it is renewed, is the only moment.

The ballet of the hours, the circular dance of time, has therefore the mission to create at the center an eternal hour, a unique hour,— unique and yet "composed of all."[9]

What is this unique hour, nevertheless eternal and total? Many of Nerval's texts give us an indication. Here are the oldest, that are found in letters to Jenny Colon:

> What a fine novel I should make for you, if my thought was calmer! but too many things *together* offer themselves to me, at the *moment* that I write to you. . . . There is a storm of thoughts in my head, by which I am dazzled and unceasingly tired, *there are years of dreams, projects, anguishes that would compress themselves in a phrase, in a word.*[10]

> . . . The excess of emotion for an *instant mingles* all the resiliences of life. . .[11]

In a variation on this last phrase Nerval had written: excess of emotion *contracts* all the resiliences of life. — The significance is the same. The dreamed or lived instant is not complete unless it opens to the richness that compresses it, unless, in the central point that constitutes it, they come to mingle together, like a storm that abases at the center of its gyration, the years of dreams, projects, anguishes, *mingled* or *contracted* in a single moment.

Years of dreams, projects, anguishes. What finally gives validity to a moment of existence, are the years of existence. What contracts itself into the present, is a vast environing space of the past and of time. The Nervalian moment has the strange characteristic of being at one and the same time unique, eternal, replacing all the others, and yet depending for what is its intensity and even its existence, on an identical past that it must conjure around itself to give itself signification and life:

> I cannot interest myself in places that I see without trying to raise the spectre of what they were in another time.[12]

> ... I imprint my feet in the traces of my old footsteps.[13]

> There is nothing more attractive than to still find on the way a figure already encountered, a personage already imprinted in remembrance; at its sight, one recommences in imagination the course suspended or achieved. . . .[14]

The Nervalian past is therefore not only the object of a distant remembrance. There is not even, as with Proust, a lost time, refound by the mysterious act of an affective memory. Far from being a difficult or fortunate reviviscence, it is that which, from all sides, freely, lifts itself up and approaches, to bring to the present the grace of a similar life, of a life not lost but always present, faithful, transmissible and ready to be relived. The being that discovers itself in the present moment, sees itself repeating a gesture, a dream, a series of spiritual events, that on their side are also repeated by a chain of remembrances. It finds itself environed by itself. Its past revolves around it.

Also, the revolutions that so often encompass the Nervalian being are not only composed of actual figures. Young girls of different ages take hands. And if these figures transmit themselves, as has been so well shown by Jean-Pierre Richard, a universal sympathy, the magnetic current that they communicate to one another, does not only pass through the fingers of the living beings. From grandmothers to mothers and from mothers to daughters the same gestures, the same inflections of voice glide in a movement like that of the dance that endlessly reforms on the lawn: "It forms a serpent that changes first into a *spiral* and then into a *circle,* and that tightens around the auditor;" auditor "moved to tears in recognizing in the little voices, intonations, trills, delicacies of accent, heard at other times—and that, mothers to daughters, are identically conserved."[15]

Around its pivotal hour, what the Nervalian being therefore sees unfolding, is the round composed of all the elements of the past: a turning spectacle, ballet of hours and ages, in which the epochs give one another their hand. And the faster the round turns, the more different ages seem susceptible of being confounded and able to reveal their essential identity. Then thought becomes a mad clock. All the hours, all times seem to wish to be everywhere present at the same time. A phenomenon which is ceaselessly reproduced in the work of Nerval and that is almost invariably expressed by the symbol of the movement of a clock whose chain is broken:

> There are times when life multiplies its pulsations despite the laws of time, like a mad clock whose chain is broken.[16]

> . . . The eternal clock . . . will put itself out of order, like a movement of which the chain is broken, that will perhaps next indicate a century for every hour.[17]

> The chain was broken and marked hours for minutes.[18]

But this breakage of the chain is not—or not yet—its rupture into a thousand fragments. What is broken is chronology, as also the ordinary progress of the time of pendulums. Nevertheless the hours and the centuries, indistinctly linked by the rapid movement with which they succeed one another, tend to form—as in the experience of the spark from the fire—a luminous curve around the center of gyration. Time loses its destructive force. It is only a moving and circular line, at whose interior the Nervalian being rediscovers its eternal youth. This is what is revealed in the unknotting of the pieces of the Funambules where the protective genius of love "ends by uniting the lovers in a temple with rose columns, at the back of which *ingeniously turns a sun of golden paper*,"[19] — "turning sun" that reappears at the end of an episode of *Sylvie* where the fairy lets fall her wrinkled mask to reveal eternal youth.[20]

Everything rejuvenates itself, is repeated, turns and recommences to live, in the Nervalian world. A self-same event is reproduced, a self-same star scintillates, a self-same sentiment recomposes itself, constellating the same horizon. All is always the same, always recognizable. The fountains begin again to run, time brings back order to the old days. What has happened happens and will happen. The same events that have occurred, occur, and in the same detail. Eternal return of the gods, incessantly recommencing the world, hymen forever renascent of the earth and the sky: "It is the world that repeats itself, it is man who *turns in the abstract circle* indicated by Vico."[21] — "It seems to me," says Gérard, "that in the past few months, I have gone back over the *circle of my days*."[22] If he has gone back, it is the very heart of the instant itself that causes the temporal circumference to turn around him; so fast that there is no more time, no "night of time," nothing except the enveloping presence of a duration whose events repeat themselves. Thought that thus seizes at a glance the evolutions of the ballet of the hours, "traverses at an easy wing-beat atmospheres of inexpressible happiness, and this in the *space of a minute that seems eternal,* such is the rapidity with which its sensations succeed one another."[23] A rapidity in which everything hurries, joins, grouping around the "eternal minute" the ensemble of existence.

"This state often permits one to see press forward in a few moments the most telling pictures of a long period of life."[24]

II

"Gérard," Arsène Houssaye used to say, "turned toward the past to *seize his life again* and to think himself still alive, . . . and like a traveller who sees night falling, he would *turn to send still one more look on the travelled ways.*"[25] This phrase is perhaps only a reminiscence of Nerval himself, when he speaks of the isolation of the voyager detached from his habits, who *"looks at his life from a point unique and sublime,* as one moves over with one's eyes, from the height of the clock tower of Strasbourg, the road one has painfully come along during the whole of a long day."[26]

One thinks also on Baudelaire's lines:

> As a traveller who turns his head aside
> Toward the blue horizons of the morning left behind . . .

But to the difference of the Baudelairean landscapes, the horizons that Nerval's glance embraces do not have precise contours. Instead of forming a limit, they constitute a sort of indeterminate circumferential region, whose veils open, inviting one's gaze to penetrate farther. In the Nervalian landscapes the perspectives willingly take flight. The eye finds itself drawn into stranger and stranger districts that yet remain the natal country. Behind the first circle of the horizon others are discovered, and so on, as in the northern countries where, behind "the horizon of woods bathed in grey vapors," may be perceived other woods bathed in other vapors. Now, in Nerval, the circle of time conforms to the same laws as the circle of space. Its area grows endlessly, and beyond its near remembrance emerge others, as if, without stopping, the being sinking into his memories, who goes back degree by degree to the first years of his life, finally, almost without realizing it, goes beyond these frontiers. Thus, continuing to remember, he remembers a time when he did not exist. Between the real and the imaginary remembrance there are no precise limits, but rather a troublous zone which the mind recognizes with difficulty. Yet it is in these regions that Nerval's thought most willingly adventures, as though it were behind these last veils of remembrance that the truth of existence hides itself and that one could discover it all at once, white and naked; as in those verses of the *Alchimiste,* signed by Dumas but so beautiful and so purely Nervalian that it is inconceivable that Nerval had not touched them:

> My old existence offered itself to my eyes
> Like a beloved phantom, pale but still beautiful,
> Which God permitted to leave the tomb.[27]

The lived past has therefore drawn back beyond death into a prenatal region. But even more often too, it is a past never lived, a dreamed-of past, that appears in the profundities of "another world:"

> Among the young girls present at this little fête I had recognized the accented eyes, the regular traits, and, so to speak, classic, intonations particular to the country, that made me dream of my cousins, of friends of that time, as if, *in another world,* I had refound my first loves.[28]

> . . . This divine face was known to me. Where had I already seen it? *In what world* had we met one another? What *anterior existence* had put us in rapport? . . . Now and again I thought I had grasped across the ages and the shadows *semblances* of our secret affiliation. Scenes that had occurred before the apparition of men on earth, returned to my memory . . .[29]

All of Nerval's work is therefore bathed in a paramnesiac atmosphere: "Is it remembrance remaking itself here? Or the same events that have occurred, are they reproducing themselves a second time with the same details?"[30] To tell the truth, it is both one and the other. On one side, in the present, is the very center of the Nervalian being, when it discovers its secret affiliation with "the series of all its anterior existences,"[31] and feels the accomplishing in itself of an extraordinary intensification of its actual existence. And, on the other hand, it is all around this revived center that, precisely to cause it to revive, dispose themselves, in their tiered series, all these existences. Thus the ballet of the hours grows. Like Cazotte's room in which the dead were added to the living in such numbers that one could no longer distinguish one or the other, the ballet of the hours ceaselessly accumulates new figures representing the immemorial hours, and the circle of time turning around Nerval enlarges itself measurelessly, finally embracing all time:

> . . . And as though the walls of the hall had opened onto infinite perspectives, I seemed to see *an uninterrupted chain* of men and of women in whom I existed and who were myself; costumes of all peoples, images of all countries distinctly appeared *at the same time,* as if my faculties of attention had been multiplied without confounding one another, by a spatial phenomenon similar to that of time which *concentrates* a century of action in *a moment* of dream.[32]

Around the center of the "moment of dream," all interlinked time therefore *co-existed,* deployed in a sort of immense psychic space. On the one hand, these times repeat themselves, one upon the other, in such a way that history and prehistory are no more than a series of levels of revolutions perfecting their "cyclicreturns" further and further; but also these levels of circles seem like creation itself "to always move fading in this illimitable space," and *"in a series of concentric regions* extend around the material world."[33] All the past, all the shadows of the past swell and people the extent. They "are wandering somewhere in the immense spectre that their century has left in space."[34] Every one has its "circle of existence," and every one of these circles ceaselessly enlarges its ring.

But in Nerval's mind this incessant swelling and peopling of the void of the vast extent are not yet sufficient. For the void would signify a space-abyss, where communications would be impossible, and also one duration-night, in which epochs would be forever separated one from another in the shades of oblivion. Also, space and time constitute, for Nerval, not only the place where the visible images of the past and nature dispose themselves, but that which is still crowded by the presences, no less numerous, but occult, of phantoms and spirits. "All is filled, all is living." Everything is filled with the inhabitants of an invisible world which presses from all sides on the visible world and on the being who, at the center, submits and thus looses universal events: "The soul of every creature corresponds to a chain of spirits . . ."[35] — "The invisible world presses upon us from all sides . . . . Every one of our ideas, both good or bad, puts in movement a corresponding spirit, as every one of the movements of our body shocks the column of air that we support."[36] — "Here is the first link of the chain, all the others should be similar to it except for position."[37] Taking up again and mingling Cazotte's and de Towianski's ideas, and those of Quintus Aucler, Nerval conceives a sort of mental universe similar to a liquid sphere, where from the periphery to the central point and from the central point to the periphery, concentrically and excentrically everything propagates itself, everything is in a moving and mysterious rapport of identity: "The water that one has placed in a round vase, Dante said, carries itself from the center to the circumference or from the circumference to the center, according to whether one agitates it from within or without."

To the "constant series of impressions that link themselves to one another"[38] add, while lengthening it, "the uninterrupted chain that links intelligences around the world."[39] To the levels of remembrance are linked the "stages of minds:"[40] one and the other are disposed in "successive layers" of which the piercing bases touch the "edifices of different ages."[41] The *"turning circle"* therefore becomes *"a growing spiral:"*[42] "My soul grew in the past and in the present."[43] If Nerval peoples with a crowd of visible and invisible forms his spatio-temporal universe, it is so that this universe ceaselessly enlarged should be, across all the fields of time and space, simply the fulguration of his own thought, creating an image of itself multiplied and dilated to the cosmic scale, without this mental creation ever stopping from faithfully sending back to its creator the image of what it is. Every being, every consciousness, for Nerval, is the author of a universe which, like that of Leibnitz, is the mirror of his own existence. From the center of his present thought to the infinite horizon where his stars turn, the Nervalian spirit touches all the points of his cosmos:

> The magnetic rays emanated from myself or from others traverse without obstacle the infinite chain of created things; it is a transparent network covering the world, of which the unfettered threads communicate by degrees to the planets and to

the stars. Captive in this moment on the earth, I keep in touch with the choir of the stars, that take part in my joys and my sorrows.[44]

Magnetic rays, network of veins and arteries, serpentining vessels, circulating and vibrating, fading of a central fire in an *"interior orb,"*[45] Nerval's thought incessantly spins a web of which it is at once the thread, the fly, and the spider. Always further away, but always interiorly, it develops the variations of its central identity. Center and God of the universe of his dreams, it only diffuses itself in itself. Mingled form of the lover and the loved, hermaphrodite being that in multiplying its stolons reproduces itself in all points of the great extent, it is comparable to "an immense vine that extends its runners around the earth."[46] History and nature are but the same theater, where, always higher, always lower, always farther, at all stages, a myth recommences which can have but one protagonist. From the central point of its infinite circumference, by continuous undulations, the ballet of the hours continues its round:

> *Immense circles traced themselves in the infinite like the orbs that troubled water will form after the fall of a body;* every region, peopled by radiant figures, was colored, moved, and mingled one by one, and a divinity, always the same, smilingly refused the furtive masks of its diverse incarnations, finally to take refuge, unseizable, in the mystic splendors of the Asian sky.[47]

Let us not deceive ourselves, the divinity that thus extends itself in the infinite like a series of successive orbs, is not here alone the image of a woman or a goddess; it is the very symbol of Nerval's thought, which, from its center, diffuses itself, always like itself in the diversity of its imaginings: "Nerval's every word," excellently says André Rousseaux, "is the center of a constellation or of a circle of waves that propel themselves across the dream, as if on calm water."[48]

III

My day has begun like a song by Homer . . . . Imagine—but what shall I tell you?—dream of all the pomp in the world bursting in a corner of the sky; then of this burning, fiery line *enlarging itself on the circle of the waters,* from which blossoming rose rays come in sheaves to revive the azure of the air

that, higher, is still somber. Would one not say that the brow of
a goddess and her extended arms lift, little by little, the veil of
the sparkling night?[49]

Between Nerval's preceding passage and this one the resemblances
are striking. In one as in the other, a light or a central energy
propels itself circularly. In one as in the other, and by a paradox
which is the very basis of Nerval's work, the more the irradiation is
diversified, the more numerous are the falling masks, the lifting
veils; the more central thought is unknotted. "Unity, diversity";
"follow the same traits in different women;"[50] cause a new image
or a new love to delineate itself on the variegated texture of the
others; see that the "variations succeed one another to infinity;"[51]
such is certainly the central motif of the Nervalian thought. To
achieve it, it was necessary for him, like Proteus, to take form after
form, constantly further to disseminate the series of his avatars, and
syncretize in an immense Nerval the variety of the universe: "I then
had the idea that I had become *very large.*"[52] All of *Aurelia* is filled
with these enlargements. Now under its masculine form, now under
its feminine, now again under that of giants or of monsters, the
Nervalian being absorbs time and space, makes of one and the other
its own measure. But this growing absorption, in which nature and
history find themselves, in the final analysis, drowned in the cavern
of the being, has its counterpart which is the announcement of the
disaster to which Nervalian thought already runs. For the enlargement is a fading. As soon as each new image is captured by the ever
vaster net of thought it needs must identify itself with all the others.
It loses its own identity. From variety it passes to unity. Such is
perhaps the signification of certain notes of the *Carnet de voyage en
Orient:* "Enlarge my choice. Grow." And, further on: "Elle. I had
fled from her, I had *lost* her. I had *made her large.*"[53] There is
nothing more striking than the rapport between *largeness* and *loss.*
It is from growth that the being dissipates itself and that thought
loses its distinction. This double theme is constantly found in
Nerval's work:

> . . . The chimera *grows in effacing itself,* reaches the summit
> of the temple and fades in the depth of the walls, like the
> shadow carried by a man lighted by a vanishing torch.[54]

> At the moment when he extended his arms to seize her, she
> faded in a cloud of perfumes.[55]

Then she sprang forward rejuvenated, from the tawdry finery that covered her, and her flight lost itself in a sky empurpled from foundation to columns. My floating mind in vain wished to follow her: she had disappeared for eternity.[56]

Already their ravishing forms mingled in confused vapors; these beautiful faces paled, and these accentuated traits, these sparkling eyes were lost in a shadow in which still shone the final flash of a smile.[57]

At the extreme limit of thought there is no longer even an image, nothing of the palpable or imaginable to which to attach the mind. The mind loses everything, indulging itself in its interior immensity. This phenomenon is described in detail by Nerval in one of the most beautiful passages of the first part of *Aurelia:*

The lady I followed, involuting her slender waist in a mirroring of changeable taffetas, gracefully curved her bare arm around the long stem of a hollyhock, and *then she began to grow larger* in a clear ray of light, in such a way that little by little the garden took her form, the flower beds and the trees became the rosettes and festoons of her clothes; while her face and her arms imprinted their contours to the sky's empurpled clouds. I *lost sight of her,* as she became transfigured, for she *seemed to vanish into her own grandeur.* "Oh! don't disappear!" I cried . . . "for nature dies with you!"[58]

A passage whose sad beauty perhaps consists in the fact that there simultaneously appear the two facets of Nervalian thought: the glorious face, a movement truly divine by which the creative thought continually and triumphantly develops itself further and further in nature, which it absorbs; and the tragic movement at the same time, since by absorbing all, this thought is no longer thinkable. It fades in its own grandeur, leaving the anterior universe in death and in night.

Recapture and deepening of a word of Apuleius, which incidentally Nerval had cited: "The invincible goddess disappears and withdraws into her own immensity."[59] In identifying his thought with the immensity of nature and beings, Nerval loses at one and the same time both the variety of beings and his own thought: "She was absorbed into the sum of beings; it was the God of Lucretius, *impotent* and *lost in his immensity.*"[60]

But if, on the other hand, wishing to escape this dissolution of beings in their abstract sum, the Nervalian mind tries to retain their individual traits, it saves their variety only at the expense of their essential unity. In the interior universe nothing remains distinct except by seeming sadly to be torn from the ensemble. It is "sparse fragments," the "divided sections of the serpent that surrounds the world."[61] The dream-circle seems to decompose, like "the body of a gigantic woman of whom the diverse parts have been hacked by a sword."[62] A decomposition that does not only destroy space and nature, but also time. This becomes "the renewing of a bloody scene of orgy and carnage."[63] The renewing of a division but not of a continuation. It would seem that the mind no longer has the power to hold together the elements of a fragmenting universe, nor the disparate moments of time. No longer from one or the other flows the continuous current of an homogeneous duration:

> Art thou sure of transmitting an immortal breath
> Between a dying and a renascent world?[64]

The great anguish of this God is not to feel Himself impotent to cause time to be reborn; it is perhaps to be too feeble to sustain it. If there is a new time, will this new time continue the old time and the cycle of the hours? Such is Nerval's anguish in the Olive Garden. It is as though he saw in the round, hands loosening and figures becoming detached. They defile. A light still lights them individually. But time no longer makes a circle. It is now only a discontinuous succession of points of duration. In turn, every figure falls back into the night, "like the beads of a chaplet whose cord is broken."[65]

Thus, whether in their ensemble, or whether individually, the elements of the Nervalian universe lose themselves in the night.

No one has experienced more painfully than Nerval the disaggregation of the interior world:

> It is a painful impression, indeed, as one goes farther, to lose town by town and country by country, all the beautiful universe that one created for oneself when young, by reading, by pictures and by dreams.[66]

> I have already lost kingdom by kingdom and province by province the most beautiful half of the universe, and soon I shall no longer know where to give my dreams refuge.[67]

> And here is yet another illusion, another dream, another luminous vision that will disappear without recall from this beautiful magical universe that poetry created for us . . .[68]

> Illusions fall one after the other like the rinds of a fruit.[69]

The most beautiful flowers have lost their scent.[70]

By disappearance, dispersion, or by wasting away, Nerval sees accomplished little by little the destruction of his "divine synchronism" and of his "universal synthesis": "Power is lacking in the universe."[71] — "Pan is dead."[72] — "The green naiad, exhausted, is dead in her grotto."[73] — Everywhere at the tightening horizon appear the indications of the decline of the cosmic forces. But if life is withdrawing itself from the periphery, is there not still a recourse that consists precisely in leaving the surface regions that no longer receive the revivifying energy of the center, and in descending into this center oneself, as into the only place where life still resides? Such is Nerval's temptation. If "the saint of the abyss is more sainted to his eyes," it is because his hands are still "full of fires"—of fires that no doubt no longer reach the deserted sky but that spring from their hearth of energy. There is the source, there the truly divine state. If it is no longer permitted to us to be the God of the universe circularly deployed with our dreams, it is still "possible to be God in *concentrating* our rays."[74] — The ballet of the hours has disappeared in what Mallarmé called a sidereal catastrophe, but what still subsists of the magic circle is the center, the pivotal hour. "The rose Pearl lies at the Center."[75] Rose with a violet heart, a fire that burns at the center: "We had wished," Tubal-Cain said to Adoniram, "that the central fire might be drawn by the circumference and radiate beyond."[76] That is no longer possible. Nevertheless there remains the principle of life at the center.

The last hope of salvation is therefore in a descent, at the bottom of the self, toward this principle. But this descent leads no less surely to the catastrophe of the ascending movement corresponding to it in the spaces of the sky. The being descending to the depths of himself must abandon one after the other all the mental territories he had conquered. He must bid adieu to the variety of his imaginings. By a fatal process the impoverished elements of the Nervalian world tighten their circle around the hearth. We find the echo of it in the correspondence: "I work a great deal," Nerval writes, "but it turns somewhat in the same circle."[77] And a few days later: "I am turning in a tight circle."[78] In another letter of the same period (December, 1853), he comes back to the same image and the same terminology: "What I am writing at this time turns too much within a restricted circle. I am nourished by my own substance and am not renewing myself."[79]

The immense and graceful circle of the hours has sloughed into a narrow cycle of a recommenced activity, in which the mind is disquieted to be a prisoner. Inexorably the circle tightens, and the serpent surrounding its prey contracts its rings. Opposite to that of Dante, Nerval's thought does not go from hell to paradise but from paradise to hell. It passes through a purgatory: "There is, in those sorts of towns, something similar to the circles of Dante's Purgatory immobilised in a single remembrance, in which are remade in a narrower center, the acts of the past life."[80] — "The circle narrows more and more, drawing closer and closer to the hearth."[81] Finally, in another passage from the same text (Les nuits d'octobre), this hearth is reached, or at least discovered by thought: "You resemble Dante's golden Seraphim, which casts a final light of poetry on the tenebrous circles—of which the immense spiral continues to shrink to end at that somber well in which Lucifer is enchained."[82] The immense spiral no longer enwraps an ever vaster universe. Quite the contrary, it "engulfs the world and the days."[83] At the extreme point of its retroactive movement there is no source of life, nothing but a point in space, without duration, without light, where a paralyzed being lies.

IV

Losing itself, turn and turn about, in the immensity of the spaces of the sky and the exiguities of an infernal center, Nervalian thought therefore finally finds itself without recourse. All thought that lives only of itself cannot suffice to itself. It ends either at the periphery, in the greatest vagueness and indetermination, or at the center, haunted by a fixed idea. For human thought cannot bear to be substituted either for the totality of the real, or for its simplicity. On the one side, as on the other, there is the same defeat and the same impossibility of escaping a state which only the mind of a God would render supportable. The spiritual history of Nerval is the history of a being that has wished to do without the world, to exist in his world. His ballet of the hours is only a gesture by which he attempted to give himself the spectacle of a universe that would be his own creation. This is his offense, and this is his punishment. For, on all sides, from the circumference and the center, Nerval finds himself a captive in his enchanted circle. Neither above, nor below, neither excentrically nor concentrically, is it possible for him to

escape himself. Everywhere a single image is encountered, that of
the self, the double, the enemy brother. All issues are therefore
closed; the doors of Redemption are blocked. It is then that in the
final pages of *Aurelia,* "abandoned up to then by the *monotonous
circle of his sensations and of his thoughts,*" Nerval encounters a
being who, for the first time, is not his double or the eternal reflection of his thought, "an indefinable being, taciturn and patient,
seated like a Sphinx at the supreme doors of existence."[84] Supreme
doors since their guardian "is placed between death and life" and
these doors conduct from the dream life to the real life, thus opening to Redemption. For the first time in Nerval's universe a living
being appears, a being who does not belong to that universe. Nerval
describes himself as spending long hours in reflection, his head
leaning against his companion and holding his hand. As in the
magic round, a magnetic current passes from Nerval's hand to that
of his brother in suffering. But this time, the current passes from one
living being to another; he establishes a rapport with a fraternal
reality. From this moment a great hope invades Nerval. Issues are
no longer blocked, since between man and man and from God to
man hands touch, and grace communicates itself. The oneiric circle
is broken, or rather it is replaced by a vaster circle, surrounding the
earth and men. A divine circle, an apocalyptic circle, no less charged
with an extensive and contractive force than that in which the
solitary mind had enclosed itself: "A sigh, a shiver of love leaves the
breast swollen by the earth, and the choir of stars unrolls in the
infinite; it withdraws and returns to itself, shrinks and blossoms,
sowing afar the seeds of new creations."[85] The real world is no less
magical than the imaginary world. Like it, it is fashioned from an
enlarging circle. Last incarnation of the ballet of the hours, the
choir of stars begins again to unroll; and the serpent surrounding
the world relaxes—for a time—his rings.

XI

EDGAR POE

To Elliott Coleman

I

I had swooned; but still will not say that all of consciousness
was lost. What of it there remained, I will not attempt to define,
or even to describe; yet all was not lost. In the deepest slumber
—no! In delirium—no! In a swoon—no! In death—no! Even in
the grave all is not lost.[1]

THERE IS therefore for Edgar Allan Poe a period in human existence when, in sleep, in a swoon, in delirium, something of consciousness still survives. It appears, it appears to itself, in the depths
of the indefinable, as consciousness of the indefinable. It is there,
but at the bottom of a well. The being who has fainted and who
sees himself outstretched in gloom lit only by his thought, does not
discover himself as someone who awakes and lives again. His consciousness is not something new which will be given him all at once.
All is not lost and nothing has been regained; there is simply a
consciousness which subsists, and which subsists at the center of its
confused understanding. "Encompassed by massy walls,"[2] "Shut up,
as if forever, within a magic prison-house of grandeur and
glory . . . ,"[3] the existence of the dreamer is isolated from everything
except from his dream; turned back into itself, living from itself, "a
palace of imagination"[4] which admits to its precincts only those
sensations immediately idealized by the action of a "mental sorcery."[5]
The man who sleeps is like a playing child: "The teeming brain of
childhood requires no external world of incident to occupy or
amuse it . . . ."[6] Thus, in dreams, no external world appears, except
at distances so great or under such vague forms that it is undis-
tinguishable from the texture of dreams. Nothing exists outside the
psychical limits, within shelter of which ". . . the realities of the
world affect the dreamer as visions, and as visions only."[7] The only

hiverse which persists is, "a universe made of differing emotions
id the most passionate and intoxicating excitations."[8]
A place encompassed by cliffs, mists of walls, a place beyond which
iere are no places, Poe's thought forms first of all its own limbo.
othing and no one can broach its enclosure:

> No unguided footsteps ever came upon that vale; for it lay
> far away up among a range of giant hills that hung beetling
> around about it, shutting out the sunlight from its sweetest
> recesses. No path was trodden in its vicinity; and to reach our
> happy home, there was need of pushing back, with force, the
> foliage of many thousands of forest trees, and of crushing to
> death the glories of many millions of fragrant flowers. Thus it
> was that we lived all alone, knowing nothing of the world with-
> out the valley . . .[9]

> On all sides, save to the west, where the sun was about to sink,
> arose the verdant walls of the forest. The little river, which
> turned sharply in its course, and was thus immediately lost to
> sight, seemed to have no exit from the prison, but to be absorbed
> by the deep green foliage of the trees.[10]

> No rays from the holy heaven come down
> On the long night-time of that town;
> But light from out the lurid sea
> Steams up the turrets silently.[11]

Thus, no entrance or exit can be found. A vegetal or liquid pro-
usion impedes creatures and light from coming in, or rivers from
owing out. It seems that what stirs in these regions does not move
ike a current of living water, but oozes out from within by the
imple gyration of its captive elements. In such a way do the images
ise. But from where do they come? Not from elsewhere, since there
s no elsewhere, not from before since there is no before. In the
ontinuity of the "long nighttime" there is no place for any previous
ime. The same moment and place are repeated indefinitely:

> At every instant the vessel seemed imprisoned within an en-
> chanted circle, having insuperable and impenetrable walls of
> foliage . . .[12]

Prisoner of an "enchanted circle," thought is therefore content to
un along its monotonous limits. No outer event comes to interrupt
r diversify its circuit. Here or there, inside or outside, the mind
ncounters nothing but the same dream, enveloped in the same

images. They counterbalance one another; they are the habitu[al] inmates of an identical thought. Thus the gaze—prospective, retr[o]spective—sinks into the divers directions of lived duration, di[s]covering there but abstract lines where every point is always simil[ar] to every other, until they lose one another in a kind of absolu[te] past and future, original and terminal night bordering time as th[e] absence of other places borders space.

Such is the poetry of Edgar Allan Poe; at least, the poetry whic[h] he has not written, but which is constantly alluded to in his poem[s]. For despite the hope he placed in the power of words, these cann[ot] define what is indefinable. Words belong in the diurnal sphere [of] consciousness, as the dream to that of sleep. The dreamer who star[ts] to put his dreams into words is not a dreamer any more. He is onl[y] an awakened man. In the deepest sleep all is not lost, since it [is] accompanied by consciousness. But from the moment the latter [is] separated from sleep and dreams, all is lost, for consciousness r[e]mains alone, separate, capable of establishing only the most dista[nt] and imprecise rapports with sleep.

This is why the moment o[f] awaking is for Edgar Allan Poe o[f] paramount importance. It is the first moment of a new life. It [is] also the last of an old one. It is the moment when, a little less co[n]fusedly, one understands that one will cease to be; a sort of transito[ry] phase in which the dream has become almost intelligible, almo[st] capable of expression, where the surging lights of the spirit hav[e] not yet caused it to vanish.

It is true, though, that many times in the works of Poe one ca[n] see beings which "emerge from total unconsciousness into the firs[t] feeble and indefinite sense of existence."[13] He himself said one da[y] that between "intervals of horrible sanity" he went through period[s] of "absolute unconsciousness."[14] But what matters here is not tha[t] consciousness was able to cease to exist, nor that it finally arrived a[t] a horrible sanity; it is that between these two states, when it bega[n] again to be, this new beginning expresses itself, not as a resumptio[n] or a rebirth, but like the slow appearance of a thought which do[es] not yet distinguish itself from dream except that it can think it.

But from the very fact that it thinks it, it will soon be unable t[o] think it anymore. Awareness of any dream separates itself from th[e] dream. It is a breaking and a moving away:

Arousing from the most profound of slumbers we break the gossamer web of some dream. Yet in a second afterward (so frail may that web have been) we remember not that we have dreamed.[15]

It is at this point that one must take hold of the poetic thought, at this first and last point, in which, commencing to be aware of itself, it loses consciousness of the shadowy place in which it had lived. To come despite itself to light and to speech, it is obliged in spite of itself to destroy its sanctuary. Even the look, the last look it gives in its withdrawal, is a destructive look. If the House of Usher slides whole into the chasm, it is because the violences of awakening determine its fall. Light gapes through its crevice. The nocturnal world is going to perish in the waters of forgetfulness. But before it perishes, the being who is the author and the witness of its destruction casts on it a look of farewell. Such is the mission of the poet. It consists in taking cognizance of what he takes leave of, what he will no longer be:

> In the return to life from a swoon there are two stages: first, that of the sense of mental or spiritual, secondly, that of the sense of physical existence.[16]

Of these two degrees, it is the first only that for the moment is important. What matters now is not the becoming aware of one's actual life, but the consciousness of one's previous spiritual existence, " . . . impressions eloquent in memories of the gulf beyond."[17] Later, the instant after, it will be possible to consider other questions, important in their place, such as knowing if one is; where one is. Then pleasure or terror will give to these questions the most precise answers. Now it is a question of not waking too fast. In the tenuous space of an "instantaneous intuition,"[18] it may be possible to affix in our spirit the picture of the world whose web we tear. We tear it, but we had made it, we had been enveloped in it. It is this which is not lost, which is not as yet quite lost. Just before waking, just before the end of sleep, there is a point, an "inappreciable point of time."[19] "A *point* of blending between wakefulness and sleep."[20] Everything is still contained therein. To maintain it or to maintain oneself in it is impossible; but it is perhaps not forbidden to transform its passive richness into thought and words. For that one must place oneself at the median point, "not" says Poe, "that I can *continue* the condition—not that I can render the point more than a point—but that I can startle myself from the point into wakefulness; and thus *transfer the point itself into the Realm of Memory.*"[21]

But the moment he is transported into the realm of memory, the dream is no longer a dream; it has become simply the remembrance of it. In the whole of his life as wakeful man, Poe, like Nerval, wished to rediscover the conditions of dream. He goes on in life surrounded by remembrances. But these are just shadows:

> We walk about, amid the destinies of our world-existence, encompassed by dim but ever-present Memories of a Destiny more vast—very distant in the bygone time, and infinitely awful.
> We live a Youth peculiarly haunted by such shadows, yet never mistaking them for dreams. As Memories we *know them*.[22]

In short, the dream is no longer dream; it has become memory, that is to say the act of the mind by which images are placed at a distance in the past. It is thus with all thought which finds itself removed from the vicinity of what it thinks, and in very different conditions. It measures the interval. It no longer joins what it has experienced to what it experiences. It is disturbed by forgetfulness:

> I have since found that this species of partial oblivion is usually brought about by sudden transition, whether from joy to sorrow or from sorrow to joy—the degree of forgetfulness being proportioned to the degree of difference in the exchange.[23]

What Poe says here of the feelings of a drowning man saved from death, is equally true of the poet. Returning to the actual, he can no longer "realize" his dreams. He can no longer conceive of them except in the past. From which springs the unreal atmosphere of Poe's poetry. It is no longer able to express its object, not only because this object is inexpressible, but because it has withdrawn into the depths of memory so completely that it can no longer be either localized or actualized. It is true that after a long interval it can reappear, unbidden, in consciousness:

> He who has never swooned, is not he who finds strange palaces and wildly familiar faces in coals that glow; is not he who beholds floating in mid-air the sad visions that the many may not view . . .[24]

But he who contemplates the floating visions does not know why they appear to him at once strange and familiar, nor why they float in the atmosphere. An immense imprecise zone envelops them and prevents them from having any place in duration. They are separated from the being who glimpses them by indeterminate expanses. As it occurs in the phenomenon of paramnesia it is impossible to join

them or to place them in any known past. They have glided to the
extremity of the gaze into a region which is that of pure anteriority:

> There is a remembrance of aerial forms, of spiritual and
> speaking eyes, of sound musical yet sad; a remembrance which
> will not be excluded; a memory like a shadow—vague, in-
> definite, unsteady. . . .[25]

> . . . dim visions of my earliest infancy—wild, confused, and
> thronging memories of a time when memory herself was yet
> unborn.[26]

Memory of a time when memory had not yet been born, shadow
of a shadow, Poe's poetry becomes the most indefinite thing there is.
Around an empty thought, it is a defunct glory, obscure, peripheric:

> And round about his home the glory
> That blushed and bloomed
> Is but a dim-remembered story
> Of the old time entombed.[27]

This poetry of memory becomes finally a poetry of oblivion.
Nothing is more different from Lamartine's poetry, which, also
menaced by the vague, finds in it enough power to conjure up the
living forms whose presence will save the spirit from annihilation.
For with Lamartine, in the resuscitation of the past, there is neither
forgetfulness nor memory, nothing but the passionate reunion of
always-loved beings in an always-living love. But with Poe there is
no trace of an affective revivification. Memory does not unify. It
separates. As with Mallarmé, it consummates the absence and
acknowledges the exile. Or if sometimes it leads the being which
remembers itself to the brink of a remembrance, it abandons it on
this brink:

> . . . In our endeavors to recall to memory something long for-
> gotten, we often find ourselves upon the very verge of remem-
> brance, without being able, in the end, to remember.[28]

Left on the verge, separated from its dreams not only by their
initial imprecision, but by the lacunas, the confusions, the growing
deterioration of memory, Poe has not even the possibility, as Proust
has, to hope for a miraculous restitution of time past. For what
still vaguely welters in the past, could in no case serve as a foundation to existence. How can the present be sustained by a disintegrat-
ing past? How can imagination subsist when the action through

which it lives, slows and stops? As in all pre-symbolist and symbolist poetry, in Poe there is a draining of the creative source. It is as if thought, as soon as it has moved from the center of its inspiration, which is the dream, begins to lose force, warmth and form, and no longer circulates in the heavy air except with a trailing and heavy wing. Every image becomes vaguer, more exhausted. The spirit which puts them forth, conceives them less and less distinctly. He repeats what he has said, but it is always with less assurance. With Poe, there is always a despairing effort to convince himself and to convince us of the reality of what he says, by increasingly pressing affirmations; and on the other hand there is the confession, as with Verlaine, of the fundamental perplexity, which is a perplexity about duration: "A condition of shadow and doubt, appertaining to the present and to recollection."[29] He who speaks is obliged to stop after every word, to begin questioning again. The dream into which he plunges as into a mist, extends around him. It is a familiar countryside whose paths he no longer knows. He finds himself a stranger in the heart of his native land. Nevertheless, around him are the same fogs, protected by the same limits. Yet everything has become precarious; everything is threatened in a veiled way. Beyond the limits of the dream there is a pestiferous and contagious world which might not be kept at a distance and which might penetrate into the circle of dreams: death rages beyond the walls and the prince shuts himself up in the depths of one of his fortified abbeys:

> A strong and lofty wall girdled it in. This wall had gates of iron. The courtiers, having entered, brought furnaces and massy hammers, and welded the bolts. They resolved to leave means neither of ingress nor egress to the sudden impulses of despair or of frenzy from within. . . . Security was within. Without was the *Red Death*.[30]

But despite the precautions and the walls, death penetrates within and stills the frenetic circle. There is the same process with the shadow of the closed room, within the ravaged city:

> To our chamber there was no entrance save by a lofty door of brass; and the door . . . was fastened from within. Black draperies, likewise, in the gloomy room, shut out from view the moon, the lurid stars, and the peopleless streets—but the boding and the memory of Evil, they would not be so excluded. There were things around us and about of which I can render no distinct account . . .[31]

Thus the dream is disquieted and contracts itself under the pressure of exterior forces. But there is worse still, "a heaviness in the atmosphere, a sense of suffocation." The air grows stale. Water no longer runs, or if it still flows, it is, so to speak, marking time, by a circular movement or a kind of palpitation:

> The waters of the river have a saffron and sickly hue; and they flow not onward toward the sea, but palpitate forever and forever beneath the red eye of the sun with a tumultuous and convulsive motion . . .[32]

Soon however, under the curse of silence, their last movement comes to an end. The "waters sink to their level and remain . . . ."[33] They will grow foul like the waters of the tarn into which the House of Usher falls. The weighted air is charged with miasmas. Things disintegrate, become mist within mist. One might compare them to circles of smoke following one another in the circumscribed space. But far from losing their density, they condense themselves into a greyish matter which clings to the contours of objects and buries them. It is "the sheeted Memories of the past,"[34] the "circle that ever returneth into the self-same spot,"[35] "the Memories that hang upon and cling around as a garment."[36]

The past disposes its heavy folds around thought, forming layer after layer of confused remembrances:

> . . . There will occasionally flash across my mind a sensation of familiar things, and there is always mixed up with such indistinct shadows of recollection an unaccountable memory of old foreign chronicles and ages long ago.[37]

Limited though this mental universe has become, it now appears too ponderous for the poet to be able to bear its pressures, too exhausting for him to lift its dead weight and quicken its motion. Fundamentally, as Gaston Bachelard says, "the rêverie of Edgar Poe is a rêverie about weight." Thus, like the world of Mallarmé, and for the same reasons, Poe's universe cannot subsist. It must perish, whether by the inner collapse of its own forces or whether by the incapacity or refusal to dredge up others from the outside. But where with Mallarmé this agony comes under the heading of frost or void, in an increasingly clear perception of an inward nothingness, with Poe, on the contrary, the death of the poem is horribly material. The vegetal universe which like subterranean flora has spread everywhere, a victim of its own profusion, or the lack of air and the source of life, perishes almost without resistance in the slow disaggregation of its elements. One might call it consciousness condemned to live through the nauseous liquefaction of what has been its existence, forced to see transformed into putrefaction everything it had imagined and loved. In spite of itself and in itself, Poe's poetry lets fall bit by bit its multifarious ingredients. Instead of composing itself it decomposes; everything vaguely alive that it had held being finally reduced to the impalpable, nothing is left but the consciousness of a duration emptied of its happenings, and that of a space reduced to the dimensions of a corpse. As intense as all the negative poetry of Victor Hugo and the *Igitur* of Mallarmé, in the poetry and prose of Edgar Allan Poe there is the extraordinary *Colloquy between Monos and Una,* in which the dream thought, step by step describing the progress of its own destruction, comes at long last to the greater abstraction, that of time and space:

> And now from the wreck and chaos of the usual senses, there appeared to have risen within me a sixth, all perfect. In its exercise I found a wild delight: yet a delight still physical, inasmuch as the understanding had in it no part. Motion in the animal frame had fully ceased. No muscle quivered; no nerve thrilled; no artery throbbed. But there seemed to have sprung up, in the brain, *that* of which no words could convey to the merely human intelligence even an indistinct conception. Let me term it a mental pendulous pulsation. It was the moral embodiment of man's abstract idea of *Time.* . . . And this sentiment *existing* . . . independently of any succession of events—this idea, —this sixth sense, upspringing from the ashes of the rest, was the first obvious and certain step of the intemporal soul upon the threshold of the temporal Eternity.[38]

This is the first decisive step toward final abstraction. All facts having vanished, all images being decomposed, nothing remains but a time empty of all content, reduced to the status of a vibrating pendulum.

But the abstraction is not truly total unless to the reduction of time there is added that of space:

> A year passed. The consciousness of *being* had grown hourly more indistinct, and that of mere *locality* had in great measure usurped its position. The idea of entity was becoming merged in that of *place.* The narrow space immediately surrounding what had been my body was now growing to be the body itself. . . .
> The worm had food no more. The sense of being had at

length utterly departed, and there reigned in its stead—instead of all things,—dominant and perpetual, the autocrats, *Place* and *Time*.[39]

Poe's poetry elects, for its last home, death but not unconsciousness. Beyond the decomposition of all thinkable entity, there still remains the double form according to which thought constitutes itself. And this double form is a container which does not contain anything any longer. The universe of Poe's poetry has become an empty hull. The inside having vanished, consciousness closes down upon its own inner emptiness.

II

Such is the universe of the dream, as it finally appears to him who dreamed it. Nothing of it subsists. It has entirely perished, and in contemplating its destruction, the contemplator, in a sense, witnesses also his own destruction. He is dead, yet he is still alive. As Maurice Blanchot says, "Literature is that experience by which consciousness discovers its being in its inability to lose consciousness." Like the knight in the Ariosto story, who not perceiving that he was dead continued to fight, the poet contines to live in spite of the fact that, like Mr. Valdemar, he can say "I am dead."[40] Even in the grave all is not lost. And indeed, nothing is lost, since what is lost is a mere nothing, merely a dream. In living the death of his dream, the awakening dreamer gets ready for the task of living. He takes off a shroud. An astonished Lazarus, he emerges into a second existence.

It little matters, therefore, if the consciousness of the life and the death of dreams has lasted the span of an instant or of a lifetime. And it is not inexact to say that Poe, all his life, tried to not quite awaken. But it is no less true that the continuity of this somnolence was often broken by repeated awakenings. From the consciousness of dream Poe passed to the consciousness of living. And it is this second consciousness which it is now necessary to consider.

Let us recall the phrase cited earlier:

In the return to life from a swoon, there are two stages: first, that of the sense of the mental or spiritual, *secondly, that of the sense of physical existence.*

There is nothing more striking in Poe than this succession of two consciousnesses. They correspond, more or less exactly, to the division of his work into poems and short stories. On the other hand, there is a spiritual awareness of an interior universe which the gyrations of images fills up; until, when these have disappeared, nothing remains in thought but space. But on the other, which is the side of awakening and soon, full consciousness, there is a thought first, without universe and without space, wholly concentrated in the moment and the place of its physical awakening.

> Very suddenly there came back to my soul motion and sound —the tumultuous motion of the heart, and, in my ears, the sound of its beating. Then a pause in which all is blank. Then again sound, and motion, and touch—a tingling sensation pervading my frame.[41]
>
> Slowly,—with a tortoise gradation—approached the faint grey dawn of the psychal day. A torpid uneasiness. An apathetic endurance of dull pain. No care—no hope—no effort. Then, after a long interval, a ringing in the ears; then, after a lapse still longer, a prickling or tingling sensation in the extremities; then a seemingly eternal period of pleasurable quiescence, during which the awakening feelings are struggling into thought; then a brief re-sinking into nonentity; then a sudden recovery.[42]

Longer here, quicker there, the movement described in these two passages is extraordinarily different from anything seen earlier. For what is uncovered here is not the dissolution of the contents of a thought, but the emergence in the latter of a certain nucleus of sensitivity. A little while ago what subsisted was the envelopment, by thought, of a shadow more and more unsubstantial; now what appears exists in a determined place and moment. A body manifests its presence, coming by degrees out of a swoon. To it, and to it only, attention attaches itself. For the first time in Poe's universe, something which does not melt into shadow shows itself, which is, and which remains, an *object*. Object of an almost animal attention: the spirit spies upon what happens in the body to which it is attached. Even before the appearance of ideas, in the sort of hollow left by the retreat of dreams, there surges a consciousness which ignores the past, which knows nothing of the future, but which is attentive only to the *actual*. The intrusion of physical watchfulness consummates the destruction of the dream-world; it substitutes for it a new reality of such intensity that from the moment of its approach, however feebly it may at first be perceived, it appears as the only thing that matters. This is just a throbbing of the heart, a tingling of the limbs, a haphazard return to life which occurs, not even in the fading of images but in their absence, as though everything were reduced to being only this tingling, this beating. Consciousness no longer envelops a world, a duration. It has constricted to an infinitely narrow place and moment. Hence it is necessary to stress the unusually acute aspect of this physical feeling of existence held by Poe. In a sense one could perhaps liken it to the experience of the self with Rousseau. No doubt, in a way, Poe continues the distinct sensationalist tradition of the eighteenth century. But in another sense he separates himself radically from it. There is not, there, as with Rousseau, a delightful and spontaneous blending of awareness and sensation. With Poe the first sensation is a strange and scandalous resuscitation. It is less a return to life than a reluctant arising from death. No doubt, what Poe wished to express here, in his description of physical awareness, is its quality of incredible newness. In a universe in which all the elements mingled in the same homogeneous mass, now appears, inassimilable, heterogeneous, blindly affirming its existence through repeated sensations, a self attached to its one body and which only exists in the present. Thus, the time in which one feels one's heartbeat, the place in which one situates tinglings and pins and needles, forever rejects into the depths of the mind the shadows of the past. Nothing exists anymore but the close and exclusive presence of a body from which the self draws all sensations.

From the moment he awakes, the sentient being finds new objects of experience. He transfers to each the exclusive attention he devotes to his body. This activity becomes his unique occupation for minutes, days, and even years. Poe minutely describes the indefinitely continued moment of the sensible awakening, in which, without thinking or reasoning, the mind lets itself be absorbed in the perception of objects:

> . . . that terrible state of existence which the nervous experience when the senses are keenly living and awake, and meanwhile the powers of thought lie dormant.[43]

> . . . that nervous *intensity of interest* with which, in my case, the powers of meditation . . . busied or buried themselves in the contemplation of even the most ordinary objects in the universe.
> To muse for long unwearied hours, with my attention riveted to some frivolous device on the margin or in the typography of a book; to become absorbed, for the better part of a summer day, in a quaint shadow falling aslant upon the tapestry or upon the floor; to lose myself, for an entire night, in watching the steady flame of a lamp, or the embers of a fire; to dream away whole

days over the perfume of a flower . . . such were a few of the most common and least pernicious vagaries induced by a condition of the mental faculties . . .[44]

No doubt the being who thus prolongs the half-wakefulness of his faculties, is not very different from the dreamer; but his dream is a day-dream and not the dream of sleep. There is a watchfulness within his dream; at the core of his absorption an object stands out sharply. Thus the shadowy universe, which once more sits itself at the periphery, is no longer a universe deprived of a center. This center, astonishingly intense, is clearly distinguishable from everything which surrounds it. It is the median point of the circle of perception. A new world takes shape, whose component elements no longer move indiscriminately in the void, but whose structure precisely consists in a rapport between the distinct and the indistinct. Its lighting is that of certain of Rembrandt's pictures, in which the light, far from being diffused everywhere, appears to emanate from a heart of interior light, to then lose itself in the shadows, but where the shadows also seem to group themselves around the center to draw from it a peripheric reality. Shadow throws back to light, as light to shadow. The attention gathers strength from all distractions:

> In my case the primary object was *invariably frivolous*, although assuming, through the medium of my distempered vision, a refracted and unreal importance. Few deductions, if any, were made; and those few pertinaciously returning in upon the original object as a center.[45]

By the power of attention directed to the main object, around this object is remade a kind of mental world. Yet it is but a mental world. Between the latter and the object which serves it as a center, there can only be a transitory and unhealthy relationship. These constitute a new sort of dream, similar to that which, so as not to awake, the dreamers imagine around an actual happening, the ringing of an alarm-clock, a noise in the street. With this difference, however, that the sleeper tries to stifle reality under the mass of the dream, and that here, on the contrary, the dream retires in the background and disposes itself peripherically around the mysterious central vigilance.

But in the normal awakening the being cannot be bound to passive perception. The wakening of the senses engenders that of thought. Now it is not by a futile love of the horrible that Poe so often placed this awakening in external conditions which are generative of fear. The being who returns to thought would be struck by the same terror if he did not awake in a tomb or in a torture-chamber. For to come back to thought is to awake into terror. As long as the attention is directed to the flame of a lamp, to a shadow falling aslant, to a tingling in the body, only the existence of this object matters, and the mind fully concentrates upon it with an intensity of interest which yet has nothing personal in it. It feels, it perceives, it is a watchful but detached spectator. But as soon as contemplation becomes thought, this thought becomes full of terror:

> At length the slight quivering of an eyelid, and immediately thereupon, an electric shock of a terror, deadly and indefinite, which sends the blood in torrents from the temple to the heart. And now the first positive effort to think. And now the first endeavor to remember.[46]

> Then the mere consciousness of existence without thought— a condition which lasted long. Then, very suddenly, *thought,* and a shuddering terror, and earnest endeavor to comprehend my true state.[47]

At this particular stage in his development, the human being such as described by Poe is no different from the awakening sleeper so noticeable in the world of Pascal or Proust. Like them, and for the same reasons—or absence of reasons—he awakes in the midst of anguish. Terror precedes all reasons for being terrified. He who is entombed is afraid before he knows why he is afraid or that he is entombed; not because he awakes in a tomb or a dungeon, but in such a way that *afterward* he would have to discover that he was in a tomb or a dungeon. Thus the terror is first the terror of thinking. But when, with Pascal or Proust, this terror comes first and must be identified with the general feeling of existence, with Poe it opposes itself to *sensation* and to *dream*. Instead of abandoning oneself to the dream state or to sense experiences, one must make an immense and strenuous effort. One must "try to live"—granted that here, to live, is also to understand where one is in one's life, to "understand one's real state." Hence it is not without reason that Poe's awakening is perpetually retarded by relapses and reversals. Subconsciously, the awakened sleeper fights against the conditions of conscious life. He clings to the security of passive perception.

He clings to it, he wants to stay in the narrow fixity of his luminous field. But he cannot, he must understand his true state, not simply to feel it but to understand it: i.e., he must place the present moment in rapport with the rest of his existence. To think, is no longer simply to perceive the place where one is, but to join it to those which surround one; and to join the moment in which one lives with those that precede or follow. Such is for the thinking mind the knowledge of its true state. What matters now is not any more the perception of an object at the center of vision. Neither is it the exclusive awareness of one's own existence. It is a clear apprehension of the combination of circumstances which determine the central position of the mind in the present moment. Thus, once again, the disposition of the mental universe changes, without in any way losing its double aspect of center and periphery. In the sphere of intellectual consciousness, as opposed to sensuous awareness, it is the central area which appears doubtful and obscure; the light comes from the peripheral. There are numerous passages in which Poe describes the difficulty experienced by the mind in order to link the moment and place in which it discovers itself with the past and the outside world. At first, to think is to grope, to feel blindly for truth, to encounter the obstruction of walls and shadows; or it is to emerge from a core of darkness into the outer light:

> Upon awakening from slumber, I could never gain at once thorough possession of my senses, and always remained, for many minutes, in much bewilderment and perplexity;—the mental faculties in general, but the memory in especial, being in a condition of absolute abeyance.[48]

> Upon awakening I felt strangely confused in mind, and some time elapsed before I could bring to recollection all the various circumstances of my situation. By degree, however, I remember all.[49]

> As in a former occasion, my conceptions were in a state of the greatest indistinctness and confusion. . . . For a long time I found it nearly impossible to connect any ideas; but by very slow degrees, my thinking faculties returned, and I again called to memory the general incidents of my condition.[50]

From narrow, obscure knowledge the mind tries to pass on to a larger and clearer understanding. It hesitates, it gropes about, finally it remembers everything. But as soon as it succeeds in doing so, it exchanges one terror for another. For to the horror of not knowing where one is, when one is, succeeds the horror of knowing. In passing from the cognizance of the present moment to that of the times preceding it, it passes also from the perception of effects to the perception of causes. It knows now what forces determine what it is and what it will be. The return of memory brings with it fore-knowledge. Poe's entire work is filled with these supreme illumina-tions, in which the knowledge of causes ineluctably *points* toward fatal consequences:

> I could no longer doubt the doom prepared for me by monkish ingenuity in torture.[51]

> No one will ever know what my feelings were at that moment. I shook from head to foot as if I had had the most violent fit of ague. . . . With the wind that now drove us on, we were bound for the whirl of the Storm, and nothing could save us.[52]

> "I shall perish," said he, "I *must* perish in this deplorable folly. Thus, thus, and not otherwise, shall I be lost."[53]

In enlarging the circle of its understanding, the spirit has there-fore only ascertained the reasons of its terror. The wider the knowl-edge of its doom becomes, the narrower appears the span of its doomed life. Once again, the mind discovers itself surrounded by a circle; a circle whose limits, formed by a fatal combination of circumstances, leaves no possibility of egress. These are walls which close upon themselves, a line of cataracts which barricade the hor-izon. He who embraces the whole distinguishes "stupendous ram-parts of ice, towering away into the desolate sky, and looking like the walls of the universe."[54] They form an amphitheater, around whose edges one "whirls dizzily, in immense concentric circles."[55] These shrink. And in a sort of lucid folly, the doomed creature dis-covers itself "upon the interior surface of a funnel vast in circum-ference, prodigious in depth, and whose perfectly smooth sides might have been mistaken for ebony, but for the gleaming and ghastly radiance they shot forth, as the rays of the full moon, from a circular rift amid the clouds, streamed in a flood of golden glory along the black walls."[56]

Thus, to a mind stripped of all hopes and doubts, fate appears as the inexorable circularity of a world without a shadow and without an outlet, illuminated by a ghostly radiance. It is characterized by the most rigorous concatenation of causes and effects, working toward a single end. This concatenation is represented by the image of a whirlpool, the sides of which sink down gradually toward the lowest point of their gyrations. It would be difficult to find a more elaborate symbol of the dizzy whirl of time and space. *Dizzy* whirl, since of all forms of madness, dizziness is the only one which is completely lucid, and which not only understands and foresees, but also creates, reality:

> And now I found these fancies creating their own realities, and all imagined horrors crowding upon me in fact.[57]

Lucid madness is the counterpart of the madness of dreams. In the one case, the gyration ends at a circular ceiling; in the other, at the center of a whirlpool.

III

In the dream as in the awakening, in stupor as in full consciousness, the mind always finds itself encircled. It is in a sphere whose walls recede or draw together, but never cease to enclose the spectator. Pleasure and terror, extreme passivity and extreme watchfulness, hyperacuity of the senses and of the intellect, are the means by which the mind recognizes the insuperable continuity of its limits. No one before Poe has shown with as much precision the essentially circumscribed character of thought. For him, that which is limitless is inconceivable. In this, he is opposed to the romantics, which in other ways he follows. He does not go beyond limits. He never stretches beyond his reach. If he likes to analyze paroxysms and frenzies, it is because they lead to an end, which is the bottom of a well or the ceiling of a tomb. If for him, man is buried alive, then man's mission is to explore the interior surfaces of his dwelling. He must learn his way about the place. It may be that this place is surrounded by death, but within it contains life. All, therefore, is not lost. In spite of its morbidity, Poe's work is saved by its intellectual power. It measures the span of the human enclosure.

Enclosure whose walls sometimes close in in the most frightful manner, but sometimes also spread out so far that they encompass the whole cosmos. Then they recede to immeasurable distances. Yet they never cease to enclose the mind:

> Even the spiritual vision, is it not at all points arrested by the continuous golden walls of the universe?—the walls of the myriads of the shining bodies that mere number has appeared to blend into unity?[58]

The stars therefore form a final screen for the eye; in the same way sheer distance creates a supreme limit for the mind:

> . . . Having once passed the limits of absolutely practical ad-measurement, by means of intervening objects, our ideas of distances are *one:* they have no variation . . .[59]

So, too, are the cosmic spaces circumscribed; and being circum-scribed, they form a whole and a sphere; or rather, an ensemble of spheres, encased concentrically one within the other:

> I love to regard these (things) as themselves but the colossal members of one vast animate and sentient whole: a whole whose form (that of the sphere) is the most perfect and most inclusive of all . . .[60]

> . . . We find cycle within cycle without end . . .[61]

Endlessly, circles spread out in space. Space is not only the expanse enveloping them, it is the milieu in which they circulate and undulate. The circles, Poe says, "revolve around one far-distant center, which is the Godhead."[62] They, and the creation which they contain, are "a radiation from a center."[63] Taking up certain Pythagorean notions, mixing with them Stoic and Platonic sources, Edgar Allan Poe writes in *Eureka* a kind of cosmic novel which simultaneously fascinated, in their youth, both Claudel and Valéry. Here there is no infinite sphere of which the center would be every-where and the circumference nowhere. Poe expressly rejects this Pascalian definition of nature, or admits it only for a universe actually infinite, to which he pays no attention. What absorbs him is the "limited sphere"[64] of the sidereal universe. Let us suppose absolute Unity as a divisible particle from which there is "radiated spherically—in all directions—to immeasurable but still definite distances . . . a certain inexpressibly great yet limited number of atoms."[65] At the extremity of their expansion, the atoms disposed in concentric layers, combine with each another "according to a de-terminate law of which the complexity, even considered by itself solely, is utterly beyond the grasp of the imagination."[66]

But if they go beyond, it is by the unimaginable complexity of these possible combinations, not by their nature, which appears strikingly similar to the working of Poe's imagination. Like it, alternatively, it diffuses and tightens: for in its immense but limited sphere the activity of the Godhead proceeds by dilations and con-tractions:

Just as it is in your power to expand or to concentrate your
pleasures (the absolute amount of happiness remaining always
the same), so did and does a similar capability appertain to this
Divine Being, who thus passes His Eternity in perpetual variation of concentrated Self and almost Infinite Self-Diffusion.[67]

Baudelaire was to say the same: "Of the vaporization and the
centralization of the *Self*. All is there."

The *self* concentrated and the *self* vaporized, the *self* of the sleeper
waking in the confines of his sealed chamber, and the cosmic *self*,
diffused to infinity, are always the same *self* within the same circle.
From the central points to the extreme there is always the same
motion, varied only by such differences as are produced by the
diversity of distances and the combination of elements whose place
may change, but never their number. To this number nothing is
added, nothing subtracted. An undulating movement covers all
space, prolongs itself throughout all duration, expands or contracts
the same consciousness. Space and time are a field filling thought:

As no thought can perish, so no act is without infinite result.
We moved our hands, for example, when we were dwellers of the
earth, and, in so doing, we gave vibration to the atmosphere
which engirdled it. This vibration was indefinitely extended, till
it gave impulse to every particle of the earth's air, which hence-
forward, *and forever,* was actuated by the one movement of the
hand.[68]

Thus the same vibrating principle pervades the same span. And
what is true of the universe of God is also true of the universe of
the poet. As God creates the world by diffusion and combinations
of His "primordial particle" in the atoms of the spheric universe,
in the same way the poet diffuses and combines the elements of his
spiritual life into a tale or a poem. He becomes the mental, and yet
universal, milieu, where, dilating himself, contracting himself,
multiplying the interaction of inner forces, a sphere is formed,
which is the "sphere of action."[69] One passes from cosmology to
poetic. It is a poetic of limitation:

If, indeed, there be any one *circle* of thought distinctly and
palpably marked out from amid the jarring and tumultuous
chaos of human intelligence, it is that ever green and radiant
Paradise which the true poet knows, and knows alone, as the
limited realm of his authority—as the *circumscribed* Eden of
his dreams.[70]

No long poem, therefore, is thoroughly beautiful because it goes beyond the inner frontiers of the mind. No long vista is constantly pleasant because the mind is lost in its vastness: "The most objectionable phase of grandeur is that of extent; the worst phase of extent, that of distance. It is at war with the sentiment and with the sense of seclusion."[71] Like the domain of Arnheim, the space of the poem should be enclosed. It should also be spherical: "It has always appeared to me that a close *circumscription of space* is absolutely necessary to the effect of insulated incident."[72] The more space is circumscribed, the more it satisfies Poe. This is why he loves *Marginalia:* "The circumscription of space, in these pencilings, has in it something more of advantage than inconvenience."[73] Surrounded, therefore, by a circumference, reduced to the exact space it occupies, the poem or the tale exists only in itself. It concentrates or dilates within the interior surface of its sphere; it is significant only in "the reciprocity of its causes and effects."[74] In the poem every element depends upon every other. Nothing is lost, nothing is added. No atom is displaced without causing everything to be affected. "Let the poet press his finger steadily upon each key, keeping it down and imagine each prolonged series of undulations."[75] "[The plot] is that from which no component atom can be removed, and in which none of the component atoms can be displaced, without ruin to the whole."[76]

No better application of this statement can be found than in *The Fall of the House of Usher:*

> . . . I had so worked upon my imagination as really to believe that about the whole mansion and domain there hung an atmosphere peculiar to themselves and their immediate vicinity— an atmosphere which had no affinity with the air of heaven, but which had reeked up from the decayed trees, and the grey wall, and the silent tarn . . .[77]

This atmosphere is a sphere. Without affinity to the air of heaven, reflected in the waters of its own tarn, the House of Usher exists only in the dense vapor issued from its ground. It has, so to speak, created its own space. It has also created its own particular duration. Not only does it exist in the spherical continuity of its own surroundings, but also in the linear continuity of the family it shelters. This "has perpetuated itself in direct lineage." So to the absence of connection with the air of heaven there must be added the "absence of the collateral branch." In the same way in which the house is enclosed in its own singular atmosphere, so too, its inhabitants are the prisoners of their own time, which cannot be mingled with that of the outside world. The temporal circumscription is no less rigorous than the spatial one. The two are united to "mould the destinies." "Man," says Leo Spitzer, "is now embedded in a milieu which may enclose him protectively, but may also represent his doom."[78] This doom is brought about, not by an external crisis, but by the condensation of a whirlwind whose origin stems from the particular atmosphere. When sinking into its own pool, the House of Usher disappears into itself. It reabsorbs its space and its duration. It completes, from cause to effects, the closed cycle of its existence and of the existence of its hero.

We have therefore here an exact symbol of the "totality of effect" which is the aim of Poe's art. As in the compact volume of a sphere, everything is in rapport with everything else, and with nothing but this all. And once again, as in the sphere, everything comes back to a central point.

XII

AMIEL

To Maurice Blanchot

I

As in the case of other children on whom the weight of the
Calvinist educational yoke has fallen, what is immediately perceptible in the young Amiel is submission to constraint. A constraint submitted to without the least desire of revolt. The child
docilely accepts living in the narrow limits of the family rules. Yet
never had a prisoner in his cell dreamed with a more total freedom
of a flight of spirit in the freest space:

> What I wanted, from my earliest childhood, was to defend
> myself, to remain free, to hide. . . . The *contraction* and the
> moral terror in childhood engendered in me *excessive effusion*
> and intellectual abnegation in youth. Not having learned to
> have a goal and to dare to be myself in the earlier years, I threw
> myself heart and soul into the ocean of curiosity.[1]

There is therefore first a contracted Amiel, enclosed in a restricted space, and yet, in the interior of this space, mysteriously
free. In a household where the mother, in dying, left a place that was
to remain vacant, and in which the father permitted no limitation to
his authority, Henri-Frederic kept quiet, anxious not to oppose the
will of anyone. Why resist, in any event? Always giving in, holding
back from acting, the child discovers the possibility of guarding by
the abnegation of his own will what was most precious within himself. In the depths of his refuge, silent, abstaining, he is nothing,
and if he is nothing, he is not vulnerable. In any case this is still
only an initial state, purely negative. At the first opportunity the
adolescent will hurry to change this condition for another. The
occasion will be furnished him by his studies. For Amiel, to go to
school, to study at the university, is at first to submit to the family

tyranny; then it is to see open vastly before him the field of the sciences. In invading this field, he thought to realize the exigence of liberty that he had conceived of in silence. One cannot stress it enough, study for Amiel was the very opposite of work. It was the means by which the spirit acceded to a world in which there are no tasks, nor constraints, nor any predetermined goal, nothing but the possibility to hurl oneself in all directions, like an animal newly let out of the stable. Returning later in thought to this essentially free period of his existence, Amiel cried: "It was joy that took possession of me at that moment, the feeling of independence, of enthusiasm, of the escaped colt; *every corner of the horizon called me.*"[2]

Study for Amiel, therefore, is the equivalent of woods and fields for a truant. Discovering the sciences, he experienced the same pleasures as others in sowing their wild oats or in being foolish. It is true that the profligacies of the young Amiel remained the simple profligacies of work. They are nevertheless profligacies. It is with frenzy that he gives himself over to the orgy of reading that he calls his cosmophagy.[3] In his avidity one must see a flight out of oneself. A flight rendered even easier since nothing held him to his home. Not one mental bond, not one natural inclination or acquisition forms for him the preliminary sketch of a character or the beginning debut of an orientation. Amiel begins by being only a human entity without characteristic, a species of internal void, to which a certain wresting into possession of the exterior world was to give the chance of fulfillment: "I want," he said, "to encompass all the facets of creation."[4] These are nearly the words of another young conquerer, the *Tête d'or*. But who cannot sense the difference between the furiously concrete appetite of Claudel and the simple desire for knowledge that the future professor of the Academy of Geneva attempts to quench? Golden Head is like the child that squeezes an object in its hand to carry it to his mouth. It is the whole world that he wants, and that he wishes to devour. For Amiel, on the contrary, cosmophagy is rather the means to let himself be devoured by the world. The acquisition of knowledge has for correlative the absorption of the being into that which he acquires. The more Amiel studies, the less he is himself and the less he is anyone. Everything happens as though the accumulation of knowledge corresponds to the disappearance of him who accumulates it. This curious combination of the annulment of the self with the acquisition of the non-self, is called by Amiel *objectivity:* "At twenty-five," he says, "I was an *objective,* that is to say an expansive and impersonal talent that found its joy in confounding itself with its radiance, to forget itself in things."[5]

What is it, to forget oneself in things? It is to turn one's curiosity toward the outside. The consciousness becomes pure consciousness of the external reality, the consciousness of objects without the intervention of the subject. It is surprising to discover that the human being who was later to manifest so much interest toward himself, he who was to consecrate all his thought to the elucidation of himself, begins by turning his back upon himself, by being entirely uninterested in himself. From this point of view, the young Amiel does not differ greatly from those other minds of his genera tion who chose to obey the scientific disciplines: a Claude Bernard, a Taine, a Renan. Like them, he dreams of a total science, of a simultaneous presence of the mind at every point of knowledge. To know is a form of ubiquity. It has to do with being at one and the same time in the entirety of the knowable world. Not for an instant does Amiel consider limiting his researches. These must totalize the real. And one sees Amiel, not only doing an immense amount of reading, but trying to go beyond all specializations by absorbing all specializations. A prodigious culture deploying in all directions appears like a spherical radiation of universal curiosities. To cultivate his nature in every sense, this was his unique preoccupation. Amiel notes in 1854, after a long meditation into which the study of the tables of contents of certain scientific journals had thrust him: "The attraction of the world outside awakens so energetically in me the *expansive force* that I *dilate without limit.*" And, in the same passage, he describes himself as being "absorbed, lost in multiple curiosity, in the infinity of erudition and the *inexhaustible details of the peripheral world.*"[6]

To carry oneself toward the outside world, is therefore to dilate oneself in a world at once so rich in its detail and so vast in its ensemble, that the mind has not enough time to embrace it and detail it. How was he to find the leisure to occupy himself with himself, to take stock of his minuscule central reality? Amiel has reason to say that with him thought transforms itself into pure expansive force. But this expansion is less that of the mind itself than of its contents. What ceaselessly grows is the number of objects englobed in the sphere of knowledge. Compare the expansive force of the Amielian thought with that of Rousseau's thought, for example. With Rousseau, it is no sooner sprung from the soul than one sees the spiritual energy spreading itself over the universe, carrying with it everywhere its particular way of feeling; in such a manner that the movement of expansion is by no means an acquisitive movement, but on the contrary a sort of gift made by the soul to the world, a generous identification of the central subjectivity with the peripheral universe. But, with Amiel, nothing spreads, unless it be the area comprising knowledge. Nothing is brought to the world by the mind, except the purely cognitive activity of the mind. At the periphery, there are objects, and there is the mind exclusively occupied in perceiving these objects. At the center, there is nothing. One would say that Amiel's exploration of the peripheral world has for corollary the total abandonment of the center. To cultivate his nature in every sense, is to cultivate intelligence, memory, the acquisitive faculties, that is to say that part of one's being which is orientated toward the exterior. As to the depths, as to the center, it is reduced to being a simple producer of expansive energy. The moment it is withdrawn from its point of origin, thought forgets it to begin the vast enveloping movement by which it attempts to capture the real. There is no other course for the mind. All spiritual energy has as its goal to encompass in its domain the greatest number of knowledges; it is only when the totality of reality is found to be included, that it becomes again possible to leave the periphery and to redescend toward the center:

> The same intellectual need to envelop things, *to go by way of the circumference to the center,* to exhaust all surroundings in order to arrive at a comprehensive and certain inner wholeness, to travel all around before going within, in order to leave nothing outside or behind; in brief this need of *totality* is the power and the weakness of my thought.[7]

Thus there is dangerously affirmed in Amiel the primacy of an activity properly centrifugal and peripheral. Before knowing oneself one must know the world; before apprehending himself as a unity, he must embrace the entire totality. However, the totality is, so to speak, strewn all about. To know the universe, even to know any single isolated object in the universe, is to "exhaust the surroundings," long before being able to "arrive at a comprehensive and certain inner wholeness." Far from apprehending everything at once by a synthetic intuition, one must go from fact to fact, from thing to thing, from knowledge to knowledge, by a movement akin to that by which one goes from one point to another along a circumferential line. Amiel's vast reading, his infinite curiosity, the greatly varied branches of knowledge which he explores, all this gives him a vision of the world which of course is not at all *total*, but simply *multiple*. It goes without saying that this is precisely the situation in which every mind aspiring to encyclopedic knowledge finds itself. But, with Amiel, the incompletion and discontinuity of the objects of knowledge almost at once take on a grave and almost a catastrophic turn. This is because for a person who has not taken the time to form himself, who has no will of his own, nor even that sort of preference for self held by the majority of other people, the impossibility of completing the totality eliminates the only chance he may have of finally coming to know himself in making converge on the center the experience acquired at the periphery. At this period of his life, which is that of the German years and of the first years of his instruction at Geneva one sees Amiel desperately working. Nothing comes of it, however. The science of the real is never achieved, and as fast as it develops it seems more than ever incomplete. Also, the acquisitive activity of the spirit becomes more and more centrifugal. To know, is to sink into the vastness of the unknown, to enlarge the perimeter of a science whose surface cracks in every direction. It is like Pascal, trying to hold in one glance in its entirety a circumference whose amplitude inexorably overflows the visual field.

To know is, therefore, in the final analysis, to witness the flight of the object of knowledge. But there is also another disappearance of another kind. At the very least, if it is impossible to know the world in its ensemble, it is not forbidden to fix the mind on such and such a point of this world. The exceptional disinterest of Amielian thought permits him, almost without effort, to "abolish himself" in the contemplation of particular objects. To contemplate, is to become that which one contemplates, not in transposing to it one's own characteristics (Amiel has none), but in bringing into oneself the characteristics of the contemplated object. Amiel's knowledge necessitates a transformation of the knowing subject into the known object. No one has had as great a flexibility, such a capacity to metamorphose himself into the things he has under his attention. And as those things belong to the external world, in the metamorphosing of himself into them, the result is he begins to exist, himself, in a purely external existence; which is to live not at the center, but at some point of the periphery.

But at no matter what point thought begins to live, it cannot establish itself there. No matter what form it may espouse, it must leave this form to espouse another. It goes from point to point, from thing to thing. It exhausts itself in passing through being after being. From this series of metamorphoses, how can one determine what still truly belongs to himself? No central life, no roots, nothing that persists, except the will to become other. And thus conscious-ness goes from form to form, scattering along the periphery a thought that remains void at the center:

> What an immense conglomeration of impressions of all kinds, and how many lives, individualities, spheres of existence have passed before me today! Of what use is this alchemy? *to multiply the living points of the soul,* to phosphorize the monad, to reillumine the sense of universal life. But this objectivation expiates itself by a momentary syncope of the personality, by the *dispersion of self.*[8]

> . . . *Always a stranger to my own antecedents, losing myself* and *scattered by objectivity throughout all the forms* of human nature.[9]

II

Perhaps my nature is like the nature of gases, antipathetic to all compression, limitation, captivity, and, of itself, like only an *indefinite expansion,* a *dilation in all directions,* a *mad dis-persion?*[10]

At the extreme, dilation becomes a vaporization. With Amiel, as with Lamartine, there is a final fading of the self and the world, both the one and the other volatilized by the contemplative force of the mind; "Two intensities of contemplation: at the first stage, it is the world that is volatilized and becomes pure dream; in the second stage, it is our self . . . ."[11] With Lamartine the vaporization of the world is always a semi-physical phenomenon. It consists in a pro-gressive diminution of the density of matter, thanks to which there is substituted a spiritual equivalent. With Amiel, this occurs in a rather different way. For him, from the beginning, no matter, no concrete objects, nothing but their ideal representation is projected in thought. In short, Amiel, a disciple of German idealism, remains close to Hegel. It is because he is aware only of ideas, that he identifies without any trouble, turn and turn about, with all ideas.

But this constant exchange of one idea for another, as a consequence, lifts from them all the little semblance and force that they held. Therefore it is by their intervention alone that the mind has the opportunity of verifying the reality of the objects they represented. As soon, therefore, as the ideas became dubious, the things also became dubious. There is a rapid decline in Amiel of faith in the reality of the external world. Everything he thinks tends to become unreal, in direct proportion to the facility with which he thinks. Even more, moving incessantly from one idea to another, he ends by no longer being sensitive to the movement by which every idea effaces itself to give place to another. Thus, in two ways, the void appears. It appears, as though in transparency, in the progressive diaphanousness of every idea, and manifests itself even more, and almost everywhere, in the troughs between ideas. Beyond what one thinks, there is always a space overflowing what one thinks: "Every stone thrown into my wave surrounds itself with concentric circles larger than the stone thrown in."[12]

Space is the place where ideas grow and fade. It is also the place in which the self vanishes:

> While continuing to be Proteus, you lose your substance, you volatilize your self, you are nothing. . . .[13]

> I am evaporated in dreams, into smoke and the flights of pure imagination.[14]

> It seems to me that all details evaporate, that I know nothing any more, want nothing, nothing in particular, I am as though on a summit *enveloped by boundless space*.[15]

At the very end of the movement that draws Amiel with it from detail to detail and particular object to particular object, there is no longer any detail at all, nothing except the universal. Thought therefore finds itself face to face with space. Space that one should not take here for a positive expanse. Amiel knows nothing of the transports of a Rousseau discovering the splendor of the spatial infinite. He does not recognize the presence of immensity. He only knows the immensity of absence. The phenomenon of evaporization has caused the individual character of all forms to vanish so that nothing subsists in the eyes of the spectator but a generality so uniform that everything in it is impartially mingled and annulled. And in the face of this vast anonymous objectivity is a consciousness just as impersonal and indifferent, distributing its attention on a completely levelled world, all of whose points seem reduced to the same insignificance. Such, in fact, is precisely the question here. When all detail evaporates, there is nothing but a universal reality so indefinable that it confounds itself and mingles with space. But not with a *real* space; only with the void. The void is what is discovered at the extremity of thought, when the movement of expansion becomes a movement of annulment. It is what lies beyond the farthest circle. Certainly, before Amiel's thought comes to this ultimate region, it has already explored a kind of space, since it has voyaged from discovery to discovery. But running from one to the other, how would it have had the time and the perspective necessary to understand the extent of the way travelled? No, before the final revelation, Amiel knows nothing of space; and it is only at the end of his expansive movement that space appears to him, like a plain that one sees unfolding before one, when one comes out from a region made up of deep and dense thickets. Space is that which surges up when the universe and the self fade and, the phantasmagory of appearances having dissipated, there is nothing left but the place left empty by their absence. Space is the replacement of an illusory plenitude by the insolvency following its evaporation.

Among the various symbols used by Amiel to represent the final substitution of the empty for the filled, there is one he preferred more than any other; it is that of the *soap bubble*. An old Baroque symbol of the ephemeral vanity of appearances, the soap bubble pleases Amiel because everything in it, its form, its reflections, its course and destiny, permits philosophizing on the void in which it is reabsorbed. One knows that during almost all his life, at least in an intermittent way, and up to a few months before his death, Amiel amused himself making soap bubbles. He called them, not without pedantry, *pompholyx:* "I am," he said, "a pompholyx suspended over the gulf of the infinite . . . ."[16] And on another occasion: "I am a balloon, detached from everything, wandering, a plaything of gusts of wind, surrounded by the emptiness of the atmosphere and even emptier in itself, waiting for the rain to flatten it or the lightning to crack it: before, I should have said I was a soap bubble, reflecting all the iridescent colors and all the graces of nature."[17]

He was not insensible to the beauty of these "miniature aerostats":

> What an admirable thing it is, these globes of such a fragile
> splendor, that make one dream, with their swirling prismatic
> colors, in which are countrysides, and clouds, that swim like

flotillas, go up into the sky like souls, and so perfectly represent life. Seeing them swell from one's breath, one is assailed by thoughts and images: "Birds of paradise, jewel-case of stones, oriental dyes, kaleidoscope, magic lantern, etc. the sphere, the global state, the welding, the divorce, the encasing, etc. — The relative rarity of successes, all conditions being equal, the unequal duration and vitality of walls, the magnificent cell, the resistance of the perfect form, the transformation of a drop of impure water into a diamond palace;—chimeras, creation, the suns that extinguish themselves in the empyrean;—a closed kiss. A pompholyx blown by Satan would die releasing a flame, glass blowers, alchemists, etc., etc. Miniature aerostat, aspiration toward the sky; subject of the wind. Beyond Aeolus.[18]

What strikes Amiel's imagination more than anything else, is the "global state" of the bubbles. Do they not thus realize in miniature the dream of totality that has haunted him since his youth? In the bubble's perfect form is shown, reduced, the image of the spherical development he would have liked to have given the encyclopedia of his mind. The bubble is a microcosm. The world is reflected in it. The diversity of colors is prismatically spread in it. Shortly before his death, Amiel composed a poem of a Marinist turn, that celebrated the *totum simul* enclosed in the soap bubble:

> Your conch shell with fragile walls
> In its refulgent movement reflects
> *All* the colors of the palette,
> Both earth and sky *at once.*

The poem finally ends with the foreseen catastrophe:

> One sees shine in the expanse
> The quivering meteor,
> Then that light of an instant
> Dies away, lost.[19]

The death of the bubble is the death of a double illusion. Prismatic colors, reflections of the other world, "spherical spirit" that, along its surfaces, reproduces the diversities of reality: it is a void returning to the void. In bursting, the bubble causes the whole system it mirrors and reproduces to evaporate. But in bursting it also vaporizes at the same time the self it pretends to embrace. In losing the world, Amiel's thought loses itself. It is lost in a scattering and a bursting.

III

> Dispersion, distraction,
> This is what annuls and exhausts you.
> May the experience instruct you;
> Distraction, dispersion,
> There is the evil! Where to find help?
> Do you know the name of the remedy?
> Here it is: concentration.[20]

Everywhere, in his journal, in his verse, in his doctoral thesis, even on the covers of his notebooks and on loose pages, Amiel, hundreds of times, denounces the evil and proposes the remedy. The evil is dispersion, evaporation. The remedy: "Make concentration follow dispersion."[21]

Here is what one finds in a notebook of maxims and directions:

> Infinite curiosity is infinite dispersion.
> Dispersion is the loss of force.
> All regret not being circumscribed, limited, held to one thing; or if they do not regret it themselves, it is regretted for them.
> To produce, is to reassemble, condense, concentrate forces, effort, life.[22]

One must therefore reassemble. But where and how reassemble? The most scattered being at the periphery, lowers its eyes to itself and verifies its lamentable deficiency of center:

> I do not really have a center, a calm, a plenitude.[23]

> In short, there is no central point, axis, pole, dominant interest, fixed will, general design, or decided goal.[24]

The incapacity to find the center of oneself is not a simple fault of youth; it is an illness that even worsens in maturity:

> The forties approach and I take on no firmness. Nothing centers and enriches itself; nothing reinforces and fixes itself in me.[25]

If the self has no center, one must then attempt to give it one. But how to give it one? — By an express act of the will. Amiel preaches a sort of practical voluntarism to himself: "Concentrate all one's forces on a point and take for this point what one can best do and consequently that which is most useful: this is the way to follow and the regulating maxim to lay down."[26] — Briefly, what Amiel would like is to compensate his lack of interior centrality by the action of a body in motion, that is to say, by an external center. Certain circumstances, in any case, can furnish the motion and serve as tutor to the act of will. For example, Amiel was delighted to be named professor of philosophy: will he not by this fact assume an obligation of concentration in some professional manner? Addressing to himself, following one of his habits, a series of remonstrances and objurations, he writes in his journal:

> Of course you were a philosopher, but an amateur philosopher, fragmentary, undisciplined; you are constrained to go up in grade, to cross a degree of initiation, to concentrate, to reassemble yourself, to meditate. The providential pressure brings back your intractable and expansive gaseousness to a more stable liquidity, more spherical, more tenacious, and yet susceptible of all forms and enclosing all seeds.[27]

Alas! the hoped for pressure of the craft seems only to have had the effect on the professor of making him draft small transactions and a few outlines of courses. The weeks pass, the months, the years. Amiel vainly tries to write a work that would be, for him, a center of attraction and action: "My duty is clearly laid out and warnings from outside take it on themselves from time to time to remind me of it. I should work, to reassemble in one place the results of my studies and my life . . . ."[28] The exhortations of a drunkard! Amiel writes nothing, except his journal, and continues to send his thought diverging toward a thousand peripheral points: "I decenter myself ceaselessly, employing all my strength to rid myself of the force of action. To act is to make oneself into an axe, a dart, a sword, it is to condense oneself in oneself and resolutely to thrust one's point against the world. You, on the contrary, you put the void in yourself, you make of your axe a hollow space."[29]

To make, and in making to make oneself was what Lequier said at almost the same time. But to make one must will, and the real centrality is not the end that one assigns oneself, but the energy with which one pursues its realization. What permits us to make of the work that we pursue a center of activity and interest is the preliminary concentration of our will. He, therefore, who does not possess the voluntary principle of unity in himself cannot exteriorly impose a principle of unity on himself: "Now," Amiel said, "I have very few habits, of character or of will. It is therefore inevitable that I dissolve myself like a fluid, that I expand myself, volatilize myself and vanish like smoke."[30]

It would therefore seem that there is no exterior concentration. Nevertheless there is a hope left. If one has no will, is there not a way of placing oneself in such exterior conditions as germinate and develop will? The cause of the dispersion of our ideas is in the conditions of dispersion. Let us therefore suppress these conditions, replacing them with others more favorable. If we find a hearth, we shall have a center of life.

Amiel is therefore considering marriage. In reading Michelet's book on Love, he came on the following phrase: *Concentrate thyself, or die.* He never forgot it. It ceaselessly reappeared in his journal. Now if it impressed his mind, this is not only by reason of its general sense. Michelet had placed this phrase at the very end of a book consecrated to love, as though to serve as a conclusion to it: "The whole of this book has its goal therein," he wrote: "Either concentrate yourself, or die." And he added, "The concentration of the vital forces presupposes before anything else the durability of the home." This met Amiel's most cherished ideas. The principal reason he always hoped to marry was that he thought the conjugal life would allow him to finally reach concentration:

> I have not found a love sufficient to hold my love while stimulating it, a determined goal, circumscribed, the domestic hearth of my soul and my thoughts, that would save me from the necessity to travel and change, that would give me a base of operations, a definite base, a *positive and precise center. . . .*[31]

> What are you searching for in marriage? . . . Answer: concentration. My existence is disseminated, lacking a *fixed point,* an axis, and this axis is the domestic hearth.[32]

But even less than he was to dedicate himself to a masterwork, Amiel was never to found a domestic hearth. The reason is the same. A work, like a home, implies a choice, a voluntary decision. To take a wife, to undertake a work, things that would permit us to concentrate ourselves, one must first know how to concentrate. Turning around the center, Amiel remains at the periphery. It is useless to long for the foundation of a point of exterior convergence without having already discovered the interior center. It is not in becoming a husband and a writer that Amiel is to become a man. It is in sinking into his own intimacy. The center of existence is not the exterior world. It lies in subjectivity.

IV

Until now, Amiel has not appeared to us as himself, but as always being engaged in a search that took him far off. In any event, questing after a total science, he attempts to situate himself at the periphery of things; even though he tries, on the contrary, to make some particular object the center of his thought and of his active life, in one case as in the other we discover only one Amiel masked by the objective that he gives himself. And one might even imagine that it will always be like this. There is no reason why Amiel should cease, in whatever moment it might be in an existence given over to things, to metamorphose himself by thought into the objects he proposes to this thought. There is nothing easier than to imagine an Amiel a slave forever of *objectivity*. Yet the singular faculty of metamorphosis that is his, functions in two different ways. In one sense, it is the positive force, thanks to which thought transforms itself into whatever object there may be. In another, it is the negative force, by aid of which the mind liberates itself from the form it has provisionally assumed. Amiel belongs to this category of beings who never long remain prisoners of their own thought. As with Gide, all that is necessary is to wait a little to find the force available. But to say that it easily eludes the objective forms of his thought is not to go far enough; one must also add that this subtraction proceeds by successive levels, in such a way that one can see in it a continuous denuding operation, in the course of which Amiel gets rid, one by one, of the different ways of being he has adopted. As a flux and a reflux that cause the tides alternatively to move inversely, there are in Amiel, besides periods of expansion and dissipation, contrary periods which are periods of withdrawal. Now for Amiel to withdraw is to strip himself. In the same way the movement of expansion is, with him, in the highest degree, a movement of acquisition, in which objects are added and juxtaposed, in the same manner in which the withdrawal of thought is the movement by which it strips itself, turn and turn about, of all the layers of objects with which it was, so to speak, clothed . . . . One could speak here of *strip tease,* if it weren't that the operation in question had, for goal, the revelation of the ultimate absence of form, in place of the vulgar exhibition that has, as its goal, on the contrary, the revelation of the form:

How we change! And how many metamorphoses I have already passed through since I have had consciousness of my being and memory of my former life. *How many envelopes, successively used,* of vanished whims, abandoned intuitions, neglected opportunities, repented emotions, how many personages there are in my Proteus, and how many individuals in me have died one after the other![33]

To the progressive metamorphosis by which his thought had surrounded itself by superimposed envelopes, similar to a series of concentric circles, is opposed a movement of "retrogressive metamorphosis,"[34] by which, rejecting the "used" envelopes one after the other, thought descends circle by circle to the center. There is a gradual penetration of the consciousness to its interior. One may compare it, in its initial stages, to that descent of the neophytes in the wells, down a magic ladder, of which each rung detaches itself and falls as soon as the foot ceases to put weight on it. Thus, strangely, the knowledge of the self is impoverished even as it deepens: "Every sphere of the being spiritualizes itself as it interiorizes itself by decreasing concentric spheres," notes Amiel in a memory aid in an anthropological course.[35] Successively abandoning the objective forms with which, in going over the same road but in the reverse sense, it had identified itself by turns, the mind makes its way toward a nonobjective knowledge, toward a knowledge that would not need to establish itself with any object. To do this, the consciousness becomes centripetal "and proceeds more and more by interior loops, like the skins of bulbs."[36] Exactly as in the Cabbala, the progress in the knowledge of the self is described by Amiel as the stripping off of onion-skins:

> In intimacy, my real *me* reappears. In ordinary life, everyone sees only one of the *concentric envelopes* of my interior *being,* one of my numberless *cases,* which resemble me like a series of superimposed costumes as, in undressing, certain comic actors resemble the person who lies beneath. The only difference is that the envelopes are not loaned, are a part of my individuality, as the *layers of a pebble* or of a crystal are the very crystal or the pebble and are in me without my wanting them to be.[37]

Such is the "descent into Hell" that Amiel makes in the intimacy of his self. Nevertheless, nothing less recalls Nerval's descent into a dubious region, in which the being presents images of himself that are more and more mythical. Here, on the contrary, one sees the thought eliminate the successive coverings of appearances. It is a search of the *being* that lies behind the series of *appearances*. Nevertheless it would be erroneous to believe that the Amielian descent "to the bottom of the interior chasm," implies on the part of him who proceeds there, any contention of spirit whatsoever. With Amiel, penetration is by no means an asceticism, it is as spontaneous as the antithetical movement by which his thought lifts and expands itself. If Amiel, in effect, by reason of his lack of will, finds voluntary concentration impossible, nothing is easier than for him to attain the center of his being by a descent into self which implies no intervention of the will. He has only to let go of everything, follow the slope and let gravity take over. Certain beings, it is true, are incapable of separating themselves from the least of their possessions. They hold onto them with the same energy with which a different action attaches shells to the hulls of ships. There are others for whom, on the contrary, there is no simpler gesture than that by which they unloose themselves from what they possess. The sacrifice for them is so much a part of their nature, that in sacrificing everything, they even sacrifice their own being. Not their goods, not their lives, but their very being.

Where to stop in the sacrifice? Where to stop in the descent into oneself? Rung by rung, degree by degree, advancing toward the bottom of the pit, which is the goal of the journey, Amiel has only to lift his eyes, like a falling man, to see spread out above him the successive images of his own being, abandoned in the course of this type of fall. While he progresses toward the extreme point of a spiral that tightens against itself, he can see, above, behind, the fan of exterior forms with which he had wished to identify himself and from which he now is separating himself more and more. But the spectacle of this withdrawal contains nothing distressing. It is as though the spirit, during a dream, saw dissipating itself in the distance the phantasmagoric forms that, for an instant, had troubled him. A strange drunkenness, one whose pleasure consists in the consciousness, not in the growth of the being, but in a diminution; less comparable to wakening than to the inverse movement by which the consciousness, in losing its objects, glides from agitation to rest.

Already, in a youthful letter, Amiel had written:

> There is an indefinable charm to feel oneself live while all else rests; one becomes transparent in oneself, the tumult of the exterior life and of thought quietens, and across its smoothing and hushing waves, one perceives the silent and peaceful depths of the heart. It is the hour of interior meditation.[38]

It is impossible, here, not to think of Rousseau's meditations in the previous epoch. As with the dreamer of the island of Saint-Pierre, there is in Amiel's contemplation a forgetfulness of the exterior world, a slowing down of the *tempo* of existence, a quieting of the being that corresponds to the silence of nature, and, in the feeling of internal and external calm, a transparence of the self to the self, which is true repose. It is the same with Amiel as with Rousseau: the return to the center is, before all else, a return to the profound unity of the soul, a *simplification*. But perhaps, in Amiel, this refound simplicity may have an even more real and absorbing power of unification. From this point of view, the successive disappearance of all the peripheric aspects of the being should appear here, no longer like an abandonment of these aspects on the way, but like their return to, and reabsorption in, the center. The central repose is not determined by the cessation of tumult. Let us rather say the clamour, coming as far as the center, is there transformed into silence. This magic metamorphosis is comparable to the reflux of a series of concentric circles and their radiation toward the common center from which they had emanated, a flowing back the effect of which is to cause to re-enter into the interiority of the center the properties that it had deployed outside. In another youthful letter Amiel sketches the description of this essential falling away:

> In proportion as the gaze extends itself, the penetration sharpens, the need for particular forms diminishes, and the limit of the aesthetic education is to see everything in nothing, all movement in response, all colors in light, all chords in a tone. Give me a movement, a tiny, a particular sound, and you have stolen all the others from me; rest, is the infinite substance, *in which all possibilities are held as pigeons in a dove-cote,* all the movements in their knot of equilibrium, all colors in the luminous *point,* all sounds in the vibrating *point.*[39]

Of all the metamorphoses that Amiel's soul submitted to, there is none more important than that of the reduction to the *punctual state.* It is found minutely described in a page of the journal, to which Amiel probably particularly held, since, after having corrected it with a great deal of care, he placed it among the chosen pieces that formed the second part of *Grains de mil.* Here is the page almost in its entirety. In it, Amiel opposes the punctual state to that of dispersion:

> If the mind is essentially mobile, and, so to speak, fluid, if the mental life is submissive to a continual movement of rotation,

like its prototype the planet, I can understand the almost irresistible tendency of the consciousness to disperse. *Except in the unique point of the center, except in its punctual condensation on its very life,* the consciousness perpetually tends to become a stranger to itself, to lose itself in the exterior, to evaporate in the peripheral region. Carried away as it is by centrifugal force, its dispersion is proportionate to the radius of its activity. *Brought back to its state of mathematical point* and centered on its axis of revolution, it offers the minimum of grasp to the destructive force; the more it augments in volume, the more it is endangered. *The contraction of contemplation, the return to the interior atom, to the monad* is therefore the law of personal conservation.[40]

It would be difficult to find in the whole of French literature (I say "French" precisely because the thought expressed here is evidently of Germanic inspiration) an equivalent text. No doubt with Rousseau, especially with the Rousseau of his last years, the need to "offer the minimum of grasp to the destructive force" often manifests itself by an analogous returning movement. But the destructive force before which Jean-Jacques beats a retreat is composed of a crowd of miscreants. He withdraws into himself, as into a citadel laid siege to from without by the enemy. What, on the contrary, is striking with Amiel, is that there is no enemy outside. If he withdraws, it is to no longer incur the danger caused by the extreme dispersion for which he himself is responsible. He offsets by a retracting movement from what is perilous, inversely, in his expansive energy. In sum, he gives in to a mistrustful movement within himself. It is not only to Rousseau that one must go to find equivalents, but rather to Maurice de Guérin, the anxious Guérin, conscious of his weakness, whose soul "sinks voluptuously in its flight" and "withdraws toward the places unknown by all and by themselves."

It is therefore in order first to find at the base of itself a fulcrum, that the soul sketches a movement of withdrawal which brings it back to its source. For, at the center of the series of concentric circles that hedge it in, the central point is the source, and it is really from this source that the circles have proceeded. To come back to the point, to return to the center, is to bring oneself back to the initial state from which the expansive movement had begun. It is to rediscover the origin. It is to replace oneself in the first locality, in which there is no loss of force, no weakening of being. An unimpaired force resides in the punctual state, which is the force of the

elemental. Except for Guérin (and Guérin himself ignored the
metaphysical depth of a leap as spontaneous in him as that of a
child running to hide its face in its mother's skirts), no one in France
has felt with an intensity as great as Amiel's this truly genetic feeling
which, from all the peripheral points of his dispersed thought,
brings him back to a point entirely different from all other points,
since it is a centered point, a point that, chronologically, logically,
and hierarchically, holds precedence over the others. Amiel's return
to the center therefore truly obeys, as he has said, the law of personal
conservation, that is to say the need to protect the insensate dispersion of the self that was literally destroying his being. But if the
law of the conservation of the being willed Amiel should withdraw
into the center, it is precisely because in the center, and only in the
center, is the being conserved: as though, while the excentric part of
oneself wasted itself on the surface, in the depths of oneself the
being that is really oneself, remains intact.

To describe this movement of return, important beyond all others,
Amiel makes use of a word that he made his own and to which he
gave especial significance. This is the word *reimplication*. One finds
it, among other places, in a long passage in *Grains de mil,* that
matches the one which has just been cited:

> There is a faculty very few men know, and that almost no one
> makes use of; I will call it the faculty of *reimplication.* — The
> ability to be able to simplify oneself gradually and without
> limit; the ability really to relive the vanished forms of con-
> sciousness and of existence; for example, to rid oneself of one's
> epoch and to retrace one's race in oneself to the point of becom-
> ing one's ancestor; even more, to disengage oneself from one's
> individuality until one positively feels oneself to be another;—
> even better, to disentangle oneself from one's actual organiza-
> tion by forgetting and quenching by degrees the divers senses
> and *entering* sympathetically by a sort of marvelous *reabsorp-
> tion* into that psychic state that is anterior to sight and hearing;
> —even more, to *redescend into this envelopment as far as the
> elemental state of the animal and even the plant;*—and even
> more deeply, *by a growing simplification, to reduce oneself to
> the state of the seed, the point, latent existence;* that is to say,
> to free oneself from space, from time, from the body and from
> life by replunging *from circle to circle* as far as the shadows of
> one's primitive being, by reproving, by infinite metamorphoses,
> the *emotion of one's own genesis* and by withdrawing oneself
> and by condensing oneself in oneself to the virtuality of limbo:

—a precious and all too rare faculty, supreme privilege of the intelligence, spiritual youth and will.[41]

In 1854, the rare readers of this extraordinary passage were no doubt not without surprise. One finds an echo, here and there, in the Journal, as when Amiel tells of a certain conversation with his friends Heim and Scherer, during a walk around little Salève, which had turned, at least in part, on reimplication. Also, a few days after that, Amiel held a conversation with a woman friend: "They have tripped up over my reimplication; that they find too bold for a public of dolts and mockers."[42]

One can imagine what scoffing the Genevois of that epoch let fly over an idea that in reality was so original and so profound that today one is barely able to understand it. Nevertheless at least one person, reading *Grains de mil,* was able to have an intimation of its importance. Thirty years later, writing the Introduction to *Fragments of an Intimate Journal,* Edmond Scherer still retains the spirit of the feeling of stupefaction he experienced in 1854 on reading the passage cited above: "I remember my curiosity when I read for the first time the process by which our friend had come to reduce himself to the state of a seed . . . I remember that I questioned the author on this passage, and the clarity of his affirmation augmented my surprise."

Actually, what Amiel describes in this text and elsewhere, could be described by the term *involution,* that is to say the same thing as *evolution,* but perceived or conceived in a reversed perspective. In an epoch when transformism triumphed, when Charles Darwin was soon to publish *The Origin of Species,* not only has Amiel conceived the processus of evolution as though he lived it from the inside, but he even imagines it, so to speak, turned inside out, seized by the thought in a series of retrograde stages. It is thus that by following, level by level, the itinerary of unfoldment, at once biological and intellectual, with which this has to do, that Amiel visualizes himself traversing the animal kingdom, then that of the vegetable, coming back at last to the elementary. And not content with this, he is able to place himself at the very birth of life, and of a life of which he is the subject. There lies the truly unique quality of the Amielian intuition. The genesis which is spoken of here is not achieved thanks to a correlation of objective experiences and logical inductions; for then it would merely be a certain group of facts and hypotheses, seen as the object of scientific knowledge. On the contrary, it is in the very terms of him who makes of it an intimate experience, the genesis of the being that one is, such as one discovers in a "refelt" emotion.

In going back in thought over the course of the development of the race, Amiel remakes in the same way, that is to say in reverse, the way followed in existence by the germ of life that was himself. To go back toward his own genesis or toward the general genesis of others, is to return to the same end, while traversing at least partially, the same road. Everything occurs as though the different biological evolutions, those of races, species, individuals, were coiled one within the other in the manner of concentric circles. No matter how large the circle in which one places oneself, no matter how far one is situated from the point of departure, it is toward the same center that one progresses, and, before attaining it, it is the same restriction of space, the same convergence of lines and the same simplification of life that one perceives. In this regressive movement always associated, in Amiel, with a profound need to seek protection at the center of the being, it is not difficult to see the manifestation of a Freudian complex. The goal of reimplication, Amiel himself says, is to "bring back the state of joint-tenancy, as nearly as possible to the foetal state."[43] Elsewhere, he expresses the identical vow "to return through the course of the years,—to go back into his mother's womb."[44]

But in the desire for reimplication there is far more than the expression of a "maternal complex." There is, as one has just read, the need to return to the state of joint possession of the being, to the absolute absence of determination. Whereas in the movement of the expansion of consciousness there was sown the pursuit of multiple objects, without ever mistaking oneself for the object itself, in the state of reimplication, on the contrary, thought, having detached itself from every object, now rediscovers itself as thought without an object, as radically indeterminate thought. Such, no doubt, is the "tenebrous depth"[45] of which Amiel speaks, "the tenebrous gulf of virtuality,"[46] that he situates at the origin and the center of the being: "The center of our consciousness is unconsciousness, just as the kernel of the sun is obscure."[47] Pure subjectivity, existing in itself, withdrawn, unfathomable, unrepresentable, which, like the Kingdom of Mothers in the Second Faust, exists at the base of everything, surrounded by everything, but without being anything, exactly in the manner of the center of the circle:

> The mind *objectivizes* all the rest.
> But *one cannot objectivize one's own center.*

There is in him an obscure point: the "I am mind."

This point is the *central abyss,* the tenebrous depth, the pledge of infinite development.

The latent self.[48]

Thus, turned exclusively toward itself, sinking into the opaque profundity of the minuscule place it occupies, consciousness become center is nothing more than an unloosed center of the circle, a point without dimension, absorbing itself in its vertical flight. It is certainly the "black point" of which Amiel speaks, the obscurity residing precisely in the center of light. In fact, consciousness without an object is a thought which forbids itself to think, at least to think explicitly, and which consequently ceaselessly searches and flies from itself in an endless movement, of which Maurice Blanchot many times has given an unforgettable description. Nevertheless the "subject" that reveals itself at the extreme point of the reimplication is not always the obscure kernel of the luminous consciousness: more often it is consciousness itself, not as a "black point," but on the contrary as a hearth of clarity. Of all the thinkers of the nineteenth century Amiel is, perhaps, with Maine de Biran, he who has best succeeded in situating himself at the most extreme point of lucidity from which one not only perceives the world, but one perceives oneself perceiving the world. And as with Biran, there is with Amiel the double feeling of a world perceived in the whirlwind of his peripheral life, and of a thought which, removed from external agitation, contemplates itself without cease: "My soul comes back to the pure consciousness of the self, immobile center of our perpetual mobility."[49]

From this point of view, the Amielian reimplication is nothing more than the consciousness of self, dear to the French philosophic tradition. Nevertheless Amiel himself finds it more Germanic than French: "The Latin world," he writes, "by its mental form, is condemned to petrify its abstractions and never to penetrate into the intimate sanctuary of life, into the central hall . . . . The Germanic spirit lives in itself and in the consciousness of the self to the very center."[50]

Here, Amiel shows himself to be profoundly unjust. For there is a certain consciousness of self, purely French, that for example illumines the Cartesian *Cogito. I think, therefore I am,* means: I think myself, and in thinking myself, I discover my existence and my substance both at once. And over and above the Cartesian consciousness, there is that other consciousness, more unsettled, more charged with confused elements, but no less French, which notably manifests itself in the feeling of the self with Malebranche, Lignac, Rousseau, and so many other writers of the seventeenth and the eighteenth centuries. But is it the rational consciousness of Descartes or the feeling of the existence of a Roussellian type with which one has to do here? Or again with the feeling of effort, such as is defined by Maine de Biran? Now one sees at once that the Amielian consciousness would not be able to identify itself with Biran's wilful consciousness, nor with Rousseau's feeling, and even less with the thinking substance of Descartes. In fact, with Amiel, in the expression "consciousness of the self," the accent leans with all its weight on the word consciousness, and the self holds almost a negative significance, that of a subject without a single internal characteristic: "My self," says Amiel, "is only naked consciousness, that is to say the perception of my metamorphoses, not the possession of an ensemble of forms, of faculties and of results."[51] There is therefore nothing more abstract than the self of Amiel. It is a self from which has been eliminated precisely everything that is not a part of consciousness: "I should like to suppress in myself that individuality which is a narrowness and a prison, and to be no more than simple lucid consciousness, no more than pure mind, disencumbered of the insupportable tolls of the individual role."[52]

To put it briefly, the denuded self's having become pure consciousness results in the consciousness of this self-consciousness becoming a "consciousness of consciousness." This expression (which Valéry was to take up later and make celebrated) is found in the Journal; and what is striking about it is that Amiel presents it as exactly synonymous with the word *reimplication:*

> Reimplication: it is the true name of the transcendent criticism, otherwise called: interior freedom, consciousness of consciousness.[53]

Reimplication equals consciousness: consciousness equals freedom. At the very end of oneself, when there have been found successively annihilated the thousand adventitious determinations of the objective person, there appears a self, a naked consciousness, which is at the same time infinite freedom. Nothing constrains it any longer, nothing determines it any more. On the contrary, having reduced the world to an ensemble of ideas, it contains these ideas in its mind; and having reduced that same mind to being in the face of consciousness no more than one more abstraction among others, consciousness, detached from the self, detached from all those ideas, which it adopts or rejects at will, finds itself standing over against itself and everything else in the most total freedom. At this point, which is the center of the center and the reimplication of the re-implication, nothing more than a thought exists (but is this existing?) in its pure virtuality.

This is what the following note seems to express, in which is re-traced the process by which the reduction of nature to mind and mind to bare consciousness, finally permits only one entity to remain, the freedom of virtuality:

Indefinite condensation: measure of freedom.
One is free only by what one dominates.
One dominates only what one comprehends.
One comprehends only what one possesses.
One possesses only what one contains.
One contains only what one has reduced, condensed, returned to the atom, to the idea.
Mind must therefore contain nature to be free of it and it is free of mind itself only in proportion to its spiritual condensation.
The point only contains all of space: virtually first, and finally truly.[54]

V

An extremely curious Amiel notebook exists, published, owing to the pains of Leon Bopp, under the title: *Délibérations sur les femmes*.[55] In it one finds Amiel keeping a critical account of the women he might marry. Let us forget the comical side of such a situation, due above all to the fact that we know (which Amiel did not) that he would marry no one, and thus that the moment of deliberation was to be inordinately prolonged for the whole of his life. Do not let us retain this moment only, necessarily brief in itself, even though repeated thousands of times. A being deliberates over the choice he is to make. It is a moment filled with anticipations and with retractions, with calculations and routs, of different destinies linked to different choices; a moment swollen, in a way, by the thought of the different existences possible that, like divergent rays, could come forth from it. But, on the other hand, a moment in which nothing happens, in which there is nothing, in which no decision is made. One can therefore scarcely imagine a moment at once more greatly filled and yet more empty. A whole series of lives are therein found *condensed,* without there being any life-principle therein.

A void containing everything, this is what fascinated Amiel. In this sense, he was similar to a miser:

> Like the miser who, while not spending his gold, loves it as the embodiment of possible joys, I attach myself passionately to this same freedom with which I do nothing.[56]

Just as hoarded gold or the flock of wives that were no wives constitute an *embodiment* of all possible joys, thus the central point of a circle not yet traced is the embodiment of all the rays that have not yet come forth from it. The point contains space, since it contains the totality of the rays which, in their development, embrace space; and yet it is without space, since it *decides not* to send forth its rays. The point is at one and the same time filled by the totality of space and destitute of all space. It is at once an all and a nothing.

This all-nothing, is reimplication. At the extreme of the movement which Amiel designates by this term, everything condenses itself, but at the same time everything draws away from the actual. Everything moves to virtuality, that is to say, in a sense, to unreality.

Such is the way Amiel travels to come to the idea of a secret, prodigiously rich "nothing." There resides the mathematical center of the self and the world, the place wherein possibles cohabit. Already, in certain fragments, Novalis had spoken of the self as the point in which we are freed: "The self," he affirms, "is the absolute place, the central point."[57] But it was one of Novalis' disciples, very well liked by Amiel, Lorenz Oken, who had pushed the farthest the speculations on the point and the nothing. For him, the original being, affranchised of all resolution, could not be confounded with the one first distinct and individual object, the first differentiation introduced by the mind. No, the ultimate term of reimplication, identical in geometry with the central point of the circle, could only be the zero of arithmetic, which, under the form of pure intensity, contains enfolded what the numbers develop in their extensive series. In reimplicating himself, in reducing himself to the point of nothing, Amiel feels himself coincide with the zero:

> I have been many things consecutively; but stripping myself of all these vaguer and vaguer incarnations, I have laboriously drawn near to the nothing, to this famous zero, from which

Oken causes nature to come forth, and into which I cause my exiguity to enter.[58]

All ideas, maxims, perceptions, habits, efface themselves in me like the wrinkles of a wave, like the folds of a cloud. The zero is the second number of all equation; my soul is no doubt a living equation, for it feels itself constantly taking up the pure worth of the zero, said otherwise, of indifference and of omnipossibility. . . . I am a virtual, latent being, which has not yet manifested itself.[59]

It is in the zero that I have sought my freedom.[60]

Vertiginous virtuality of the spirit, freedom, self, consciousness, germ of life, how many things (and how many absences of things) does not Amiel find in the zero! The zero has been proved to be inexhaustible. Now beyond the self, beyond consciousness, which is the foundation of the self, beyond even freedom, which is the foundation of consciousness, there is disclosed, always in the interior of the zero-point, an entity even more remote and esoteric still: "To enter into one's centrality, to contemplate within oneself, is to enter into God."[61]

No doubt, under one of its aspects, nothing is less Christian than a God assimilated to the zero. It is a God-abyss. The self and the world are consumed in it, annulled: "The zero is the infinite, is God. Brahma is an abyss from which comes forth or into which enters a succession of universes . . . ."[62] But the point contains space, and the nothing, the infinity of numbers, even as the negative aspect of God, masks His infinite positivity. In returning toward the center, the soul returns to a God whose vivid plenitude hides itself in the center and radiates from the center. A great reader of mysticism, Amiel discovers the analogy between reimplication and the method by which devout thought endeavors to reascend to God, divine spark, inhabiting the depths of the soul, in the *apex mentis:* "My *most central* life, the most secret, the most contemplative," Amiel notes cryptically on the cover of one of the first of his Journals. And he adds: "Relations with the *eternal sphere*."[63]

The eternal sphere is therefore where the central point of existence is situated. As in Neo-Platonic thought, center and circumference coincide. The infinite sphere is contained in its opposite, the point without dimension. But linked to this faith, that is the related faith in the coincidence of contraries, there is a belief in a personal God,

residing in the depths of the soul, from which emanate all the graces
of the Christian life. No more a God-abyss, but rather a God-seed.
The reimplication is a reintegration: "This reintegration is what
Christianity calls the Renaissance, the return to God, the *punctum
saliens* of the new life, the gateway of Salvation, the reconciliation
with the Father, conversion."[64]

At the moment when he tried most despairingly to fly from dispersion, and to hold himself in his punctual condensation, Amiel
had written: "What throws man most beyond himself? The life of
the senses. Which concentrates him most? Prayer."[65]

Twelve years later, Amiel wrote the same thing: "We lose ourselves in our own forest. It is only in God that we rediscover ourselves, and prayer is the only rendezvous where we once again take
cognizance of our true being. Therefore for the individual to withdraw from God is to become once more a stranger to one's own soul,
to one's own originality, one's most profound nature, and what is
best, most serious, and greatest at the *center* of one's spiritual life."[66]

One thinks of Baudelaire, who also thought to escape from dispersion by the concentration of prayer. But, in Baudelaire, to pray
was, before anything else, to obtain, in the place of his own faltering
will, a supernatural will. With Amiel, on the contrary, prayer is not
at all willful. It follows the natural inclination of the creature, it
gives way to the force of gravity which brings back the spiritual life,
like the rest, to the most exiguous and intimate point. It is true that
from this point the centripetal force changes into a centrifugal force,
and having reconquered centrality, the being begins a new period
of expansion.

VI

It will be time to make for myself a body, a bulk, a mass, a
true existence, coming out of the vague, cold and gloomy world
that isolated thought creates. It will be good to *ascend the spiral
that has coiled around me even to my center.*[67]

After the coiling, the uncoiling. After the reimplication, the "de-
implication."[68] Amiel, tired of an interiorization which brings him
"back to the point, to nothingness, an unhealthy state, for it sup-
presses us,"[69] dreams of extending his life once more in enlarging
circles: "Far from reducing one's life to the minimum, to the
mathematical point, one must dilate it, pour it out, enlarge it, com-

municate it in every sense."[70] Amiel also blames Maine de Biran, for example, who, placing himself in the center of philosophy, "Does not know that the self must enlarge itself to the very confines of the being, for the philosophic consciousness to have fulfilled its mission."[71] — Biran's fault is not that of having found a center, but of being unable to get out of it. Amiel on the contrary conceives the life of the mind as a series of alternate movements that sometimes recall the being, drawing it to its original depth, and then projecting it, dilating it, into the exterior world: "Eternal life (depth), particular life (activity), universal life (extent) . . . . This is the regular rhythm of the journey between two sleeps."[72]

The particular activities are here only a middle term between the unextended depth of a life seized in the eternity of its principle and, on the other hand, the expansion of an existence dilating itself by thought to the dimensions of the universe. From one to the other of the two poles, mind is the shuttle. Arriving at one extreme, off it goes in the opposite direction: "Universal life, my old dream, wakes again in my bosom. I want to place myself again in the great current, to come out of my Egyptian bondage . . . ."[73] Everything therefore recommences as before. Expansion succeeds concentration, as expansion had succeeded concentration.

Still, at the precise moment when life awakes, something truly new takes place; therefore it is difficult to find the equivalent in the first dilation. Nothing had been less precise, in fact, than the place and the instant from which the primitive expansion of the being had manifested itself in Amiel. Did it date from a day in country childhood, from some reading, from some plan of work? The liberation of a soul up to then submissive to childish restraints, Amiel's first expansion had been less the development of a subject taking cognizance of his nature and his progress, than the surging up in himself of a universal object, too vast to leave any room for the consciousness of self. From that time, how had the young Amiel been able to link the peripheral enlarging to a me-center, to an initial place and an original moment, in which the mind perceived itself about to depart and from which time, as soon as it had taken flight, the measure of its unfoldment could be gauged? At the onset Amiel's thought found itself thrown into full flight, absorbed in its distant objects and without any veritable point of departure. So that it is not absurd to say that, with Amiel, everything began, not from the beginning, but in some way in the middle, and he was obliged to await the swing of a long pendulum movement, so that the thought could come back to itself, and find, accordingly, though very tardily, an authentic point of departure:

> In these sublime moments, the body has disappeared, the mind has simplified and unified itself; passion, sufferings, whims, ideas, have been reabsorbed into the being, as drops of rain into the ocean which has engendered them. The soul has re-entered itself, returned to indetermination, it has *reimplicated* itself beyond its own life; it ascends into its mother's womb, becomes once more a divine embryo. Days which have been lived, habits which have been formed, folds formed, individuality, everything effaces itself, relaxes, dissolves, takes on again the primitive state, plunges once more into the original fluidity, without a face, without an angle, without suspended design. It is *the spheroid state, the undivided and homogeneous unity, the state of the egg in which life will germinate.* . . . This return to the seeding is a momentary renewal, and, as well, it is a means of measuring the road along which life has passed, since it will *bring it back to the point of departure.*[74]

A quarter of a century later, a few weeks before his death, Amiel was to take up once more his meditation on punctuality, considered, no longer as a point of issue and result, but as a point of departure for a fresh expansion of the being. He calls it "the indivisible and punctual state, a state of power, a fecund zero." And finding this last expression more apt than any other, he exclaims:

> Is not this the definition of the mind? The mind lifted up to space and to time, isn't this it? Its development, past or future, is in it as a graphic curve is in its algebraic formula. This nothing is an all. This *punctum* without dimension is a *punctum saliens.*[75]

As a graphic curve is contained in a formula, time and space are contained in the point. But from this moment time and space begin to spread out. Living place and moment where life abounds and where it emanates, the *punctum saliens* is the seed of an existence to come and of an extent defined by its future field of action. It is a center of energy. Also, in Amiel's system, only the masculine principle merits the name of *punctum saliens:* "Woman is a loving passivity which receives the idea and the spark; she is not electrified alone. Virility alone begins something spontaneous, is an origin, a *punctum saliens.*"[76]

The *punctum saliens* is the center of an organic circle, since it is the original point, the cause, the spouting-place. Far more than a concentration of riches, it is a concentration of forces, forces that only require to pour out. Differing from the first expansion, the new expansion explicitly proceeds from this point which guides it, and which, in the course of its development, never ceases to propel it. In retiring into himself, in causing to succeed to the first dissemination of his thought a concentration perhaps more rigorous than any other in the history of the mind, Amiel finally assigns an indubitable beginning to his thought. This now possesses a real initial point:

At the start, to the *punctum saliens* of the individuality is a spontaneous force, an act of will obscure but energetic.[77]

The individual is first of all a localized will, a continued principle of appropriation, a center of radiation and domination, a spontaneity which brings under subjugation everything it can attain in the world, as energetic activity, absorbing, conquering, which influences things beyond itself attracts, subjugates, moulds, assimilates, transubstantiates objects, and suborns beings, in brief, it incessantly swells its monad by the invasion and the annexation practised in the surrounding milieu.[78]

In sum, the individual is "a point which becomes a circle,"[79] an energy which radiates from a "center of will."[80]

There is also nothing surprising in seeing Amiel take up the ideas of Swedenborg and Balzac, and consider all willing beings as being enveloped in an *aura* and living at the center of a sphere of energy penetrating its environment:

Intellectually and spiritually every man is spherical and thinks spherically.[81]

How actions come forth from thee, as a consequence comes forth from a principle, as the rays come from the sun, naturally, freely, necessarily. Every being should radiate, projecting around himself his own atmosphere.[82]

Every energetic person surrounds himself without knowing or wishing it with this atmosphere which reacts on others without their knowledge.[83]

Thus, the energetic being par excellence, he from whom willed thought pours beyond himself with the greatest force, is the man of genius: "The genius is radiating concentration,"[84] writes Amiel.

In default of genius there is also the expansive power of love. If Amiel feels himself deprived of genius, he wishes to benefit from the effusive force which he distills in the feeling of love. Refinding, perhaps very conscientiously, for he is a great reader of Rousseau, the theme of "sympathy," dear to the eighteenth century, he dreams of a "sympathetic dilation," and of a "loving confidence:" "To have a home, a wife, a congenial circle, a life consonant to one's own. Marry thyself."[85] The beloved wife, the dreamed-of spouse, no longer appears to him as the center toward which he would tend. It is the first step in the movement by which the being escapes from its absolute centrality, the nearest circle, that which the point encounters as soon as, in space, it begins to dilate itself.

VII

A circle is but a dilated point, the center point,
To come from the point is to be born; to go into it
is [to die].[86]

The surging of the being beyond the extreme contraction in which it confined itself, is therefore equivalent to a birth. Let us say, more precisely, to a renaissance. Here and there in the Journal, more often at great distances one from another, one distinguishes exceptional moments in which animation and light are rendered to existence. Certainly, they are rare. But by the very reason of their rarity, they are welcomed with a fervor whose equal is not found except in a Guérin or a Gide. For they are the moments in which the soul again rediscovers strength, or recommences a vital movement, interrupted for many a day.

Sometimes the soul is so watchful for the reappearance of these fugitive states, that it provokes in itself, their premature arrival. Or else it perceives their arrival in advance, by anticipation. Before the soul moves, it feels itself ready to move. Before it leaves the point, it begins to exist: "In attentive and meditative inaction, our soul effaces its folds, dilates itself, unrolls, is reborn like the crushed grass or the trimmed hedge . . . ."[87] In such a phrase the resemblance to Guérin is striking. They are, in fact, similar beings, with the same nature. Their existence restores itself in the depths of the lair, from which, thanks to penetrating senses, they already hear the murmur of the event that will curtail their stay.

More often, this event is simply the return of light. When dawn is not the last point of a long watch for Amiel, that moment in which one most heavily senses approaching decrepitude, it is the sign of a rejuvenation of the being: "Dawn is the hour of projects, of wishes, of nascent action. The sap of nature pours out in the soul and pushes it to life."[88] And elsewhere: "What a benediction to return into vigor and again take possession of oneself! It is a new lease on life. Old things seem to have disappeared and to be replaced by fresh patterns . . . . One would like to start with a white page, begin entirely new habits, move into a newly renovated and clean house, in brief, to be renewed in all ways and to give oneself the vivid, biting feeling of rebirth."[89]

To begin to love again is to be reborn. And if to love is to say too much, at least the most precarious, the most humble feeling of sympathy can make the human being come out of its solitude and procure for it a fugitive dilation of the heart:

> When I rediscover sympathy, beauty, the power of admiration, it seems to me that I have refound my country, my element. In the instant, I feel myself reborn, my being dilates, awakes, re-animates itself. My *true self* surges forth, resuscitates, appears to me, and I see that I had gone to sleep with sadness and bore-dom.[90]

But no matter what the variable which carries the being to expand itself, it knows that it is in the whole extent of the future that this expansion will occur. Before it extends the future: "Freshness of the senses, vigor of health, plenitude of forces, elasticity of life, posses-sion of one's being, joyous spring toward the future, you shine be-fore me like the golden apples of Eden."[91]

Not an anterior and retrospective Eden, but one essentially prospective. There is therefore an epoch in Amiel's youth in which, like other men, he had abandoned himself with joy to the transport which threw him toward the future: "I sacrifice the present to the future,"[92] he wrote at this time. This is because the future is infinitely more *vast* than the present. Like a cone which widens outward from its point, the anticipating thought advances into a space which will enlarge. The future is the place, in fact, which nourishes and augments the thousand possible aspects of the becoming of the being. He who, at the most restricted point of him-self, had perceived, pressed one against the other, the numberless virtualities of his true nature, now sees them all deploy, so to speak, simultaneously, in future space. He sees them by a sight that goes ahead of time in the haste to arrive. Amiel is one of the most marvelously endowed beings there could be to be prescient of the splendor of the expansions that things dissemble in their sowing. Speaking of himself, he says: "In the seed he sees the tree, in the egg he sees the bird, in the pellucid molecule he sees the entire crystal."[93] And a few lines further on, he finds this admirable phrase, which applies better to him than to anyone else: "Every soul at the indiscernible state possesses the rough draft or the possibility of all human conditions."[94] Thus it is the future which gives to the possibilities the occasion to be realized. How is it possible not to transport oneself there in thought, to dream of things barely begun as being already accomplished, and even to experience this accomplishment as if one were oneself the subject and the cause? "My only goal," Amiel writes, " . . . is to take consciousness of my virtualities." — And a line further on he finds the decisive formula: "To experience in myself all the possibilities of human nature."[95]

Rarely has the future *spread out,* before the mind contemplating it, such a profusion of virtual riches:

> What there would be to say, to do, to write is without end and without number. I suffocate from unpublished ideas, half-seen possibilities, interesting works which will never see the light of day. I feel the fountains spring at every sweep of my baton, and all these jets of water deafen me.[96]

Nevertheless the very luxuriance of the future draws consequences after it whose gravity is progressively revealed.

First of all, he who lives in thought in the future, ends by being satisfied with a future of thought only. Why try to realize it in the present since it already exists, in an ideal form, in the future? That, for example, is Fontenelle's attitude. It was also to be Amiel's. Why act, he said to himself, why manage it so that the virtualities of my self actualize themselves, since they are already mentally realized somewhere in my mind? From this time on, Amiel abstained from doing anything. From the moment in the present when he conceived a certain future, up to that future itself, there is no longer extended the zone of continued activities, of progressive realizations, while, for most men human time is a concrete projection of the being toward a term which has been assigned to it. In the place of this essential zone of realizable duration, which joins the present to the future, with Amiel, there is now a veritable hole in time. The present no longer has the mission of causing the future to be. It is there, quite simply, to wait for it. A present which prolongs itself, immobile, inactive, in the expectation of a future which appears less and less imminent. The sterile situation of the early Mallarmé in the presence of a distant azure, from which the void separates him, is already Amiel's situation: "I remain virtual, and I continue to wait."[97]

I continue to wait . . . . This means, I wait, but I have almost renounced any anticipation of the arrival or the accomplishment of what I continue to wait for. More and more, the transformation of the virtual into the real appears to Amiel's eyes as a distant phenomenon, contingent, non-necessary, and perhaps even absolutely illusory. Far from being on the point of realizing itself, the forms of the possible lose proximity and imminence. They no longer have the slightest urgency. They withdraw into such a doubtful and distant future that they become confused with the mythical past: a sort of vague region of duration, which is the time of limbo and latency. Nothing happens. No event comes to disturb the passive waiting which reigns. There, everything which could have happened, everything which could yet take place, finds—one cannot say an existence, but a manner of residence.

Amiel has described this sort of *dead time* in the following passage from *Grains de mil:*

> Above the visible and manifest universe, where real beings accomplish, in joy and in sorrow, the exploding drama of their destinies, confusedly moves another universe, which no sun lights or warms, a somber, forlorn, interior abyss, where innumerable larvae swarm, blind and uneasy substances which ardently aspire to form and manifestation, but cannot, it being their law, cross the doorway of their black kingdom, see the wished-for light and live, after having subsisted so long, in the obscure womb of chaos. This funereal and subterranean region, this *kingdom of hope* and of sighs, this is the limbo of nature, and this stage of limbo, a noviciate imposed on all who would be born, is the *foetal period* of every being. Thus the first cradle of all existence is the night.[98]

By a singular metamorphosis, of which it is difficult without seeing the cause to comprehend in the force of substitution and remodelling, Amiel replaces in himself the lucid feeling of an accomplishment in daylight by the consciousness of a slow nocturnal gestation. This, immeasurably prolonged, becomes the normal climate of existence; as if the being evaded the necessity, imperious nevertheless, of being *born* and of *doing,* while indefinitely continuing a prenatal existence.

Such is the first manner in which there is corrupted in Amiel the experience of the future.

There is a second, perhaps even more grave.

He who so lucidly foresees the future, sees all possible futures. Now, among them, there are some alarming ones, even terrible ones.

Amiel ended by foreseeing only these. Every action, however innocent it might be, seems to him susceptible of engendering ills which detail themselves in advance with a prophetic anguish. The future is the space in which the consequences—almost always disastrous—of our acts, propagate themselves:

> Each thing, comprising evil and negation, *tends to dilate itself, to augment its being.* . . . A spark becomes a conflagration. A scratch becomes a wound, a negligence becomes a ruin. Bad humor can become exasperation. From this, comes the importance of the infinitely small and the imperious necessity of sustained vigilance. All misfortunes *begin by a point.* . . .[99]

> A *black point* is the beginning of a gangrene, from which a hurricane, a revolution can come, no more than a point. . . . It is in origins that the principal secret of destiny lies.[100]

The clouding over—the word is not strong enough—the progressive adumbration of the future therefore gravely affects the sense of space. Space was the field opening to the expanded soul, the magical transformation of the point into the circle and of condensation into expansion. All the fecund virtualities of the being tended to radiate therein.

Now, without changing its nature, space reverses its affective signification. It is still an opening field, but one which opens to danger or misfortune; and the center of the circle becomes the "black point" which, in growing, will wrap in darkness the totality of the expanse. As by concentric circles, the slightest error unchains a series of deplorable effects, whose perimeter continues to grow.

Here reappears the image of the stone thrown into water:

> Every fault, as a stone in water, agitates around itself a circle of moral life . . .; and the gravity of the fault measures itself by the *extension,* by the agitation and the alteration of the sphere of consciousness which it compromises.[101]

The most venal fault can therefore change the entirety of our spatial existence. Now how can we know in advance which of our actions will reveal themselves as being funereal? Whatever we do, no matter how slightly we disarrange the surface of the present moment, we determine an undulatory movement whose waves will extend as far as the least discernible future. Our distant happiness depends on our immediate act. Therefore, no immediate act! Let us not act, or let us act as little as possible. Let us apprehend that today's least little fillip may one day cause the heavens to fall upon us.

Of this terror for what the future reserves for us, let us give an example. After long hesitations to do with the choice of a fiancée, Amiel decides to propose marriage. He writes a letter to this effect. He mails it. Barely has he heard it fall in the letter box, than he is thunderstruck: it seems to him that his gesture has let loose a whole fatality:

> *Alea est jacta!* It seems to me I dream, and in letting fall the fold in the metallic box, I experienced a strange impression, no longer being able to distinguish if I was committing a good or a bad action, an heroic temerity or an unpardonable stupidity. The noise of the falling cover made me think of the inexorable doors of Hell. There is something inflexible in the halt that things declare on us. This scratched sheet, once escaped from my hands, becomes the prey of Destiny. Will it open the inferno or heaven to me? When I think that *the rest of my life will undergo the effect of this minute,* I cannot contemplate it without a certain terror. The future is always so obscure, duty is sometimes so uncertain and interests so doubtful, that one must believe absolutely in Providence in default of *doing nothing.*[102]

Needless to say, Amiel, trembling at the idea of the consequences of his act, knows no peace until he has annulled it. He takes back his offer,—proving that his faith in Providence is not as strong as his mistrust in Destiny. A mistrust which only deepens as the years advance, which, in advancing, draw him closer to that disaster which encloses all of Destiny. If the future is the place of possibilities, it is the place of funereal and frightening possibles. A multitude of perils wait for us, converge on us from all directions.

> Who has not had, at least once, the terrifying feeling of the multitude of possibilities, and the infinite menaces which enclose all the points of the horizon and of space?[103]

So, in the presence of the conspiracy of the future, Amiel feels himself to be vulnerable and feeble. One could not, in fact, imagine a more complete reversal than that of the situation in which he found himself. Instead of pouring himself out toward all the points of the world, now Amiel feels himself to be hedged in by perils which assemble against him. Why had he come out of himself, to adventure, as Rousseau says, on the "great surface?" Why had he not remained crouched down in that place which offers precisely the least amount of surface, which is to say the point? "I have not been able to maintain myself," he regrets, "in stoical impassivity, in the *invulnerability of the mathematical point.*"[104]

VIII

Little by little Amiel's existence strips itself of what little positive relationship it could have with the future. Distrust of the future is a connection, certainly, but a negative one. Of all the feelings, that which holds man the closest to the future is hope. Now from his youth Amiel had seen this dissipated in himself without leaving a trace. Not, properly speaking, that he had fallen into despair. More exactly, he had allowed himself to go into what he termed *inexpectation,* or *non-expectation:* "I am destitute of expectation," he writes, "because I feel myself to be too alone before the innumerable possibilities of the future, that is to say, of the unknown enemy."[105] The proof of the disappearance of expectation is a leitmotif of the *Journal.* It not only underlines the loss of a virtue, indispensable, it seems to him, for man. It also scores the straitening which is in process of once more being accomplished in Amiel's existence: "My faculties diminish, my horizon *withdraws,* hope dies . . . ."[106] — Or once more: "My life is defensive; it is not offensive. I have turned to the *contracted* stoicism instead of the leap of conquests."[107] — Without a doubt what appears in these texts is a new form, and infinitely graver than the preceding one, of the contraction of the being. It is no longer a question of coming back to oneself, to find in oneself truth, or power, or freedom. In spite of the vague pretension of following stoical wisdom, there is only one thing of importance here, and that is the movement of retreat, not to say, flight, of a being who feels itself dangerously menaced. Amiel has reached the place where he can no longer look the future in the face. There remains the past, which he contemplates with the attitude which was to be Proust's, which is to say turning his back to that which frightens him:

> But why is it that every day at waking seems to me to be a drudgery and a bore, while later on I see it under a less somber aspect? perhaps exactly by suspicion. You expect nothing good, and when nothing bad has happened, you have the satisfaction of surprise. You have gratitude, but no hope. Thus *you walk backward toward your future.*[108]

> My instinct is to moderate and *only to advance backward* in a life that promises only sorrow, vexations, and grief.[109]

> . . . There is hope only toward the past. I therefore *advance backward, without provision or prudence.*[110]

There is hope only toward the past. This means that the other side of the horizon closes, and that thought finds itself narrowed in a universe increasingly circumscribed. Nevertheless, toward the past, there is still hope. The past is, for Amiel as for Proust, the unique issue possible, the place one dreams of, the seat of happy and perhaps recapturable hours.

"I have retrospective sensibility,"[111] he notes one day. From time to time, with intoxication, he gives way to brusque retrospections. Sometimes an especially limpid quality of the light is responsible. One finds this in the two subsequent passages. One must read them one after the other, even though they were written with nearly a two month interval:

> It was the birds singing that awoke me, and I found in going into our streets, youthful sensations, due to the brilliant limpidity of the light that bathed and caressed all architectural projections and indentations: an Italian effect, Elysian, which brought my twentieth year back to me together with the delicious feeling of being alive.[112]

> It is true that the youth of the eyes and of desire, the leap of admiration, the freshness of being, have diminished in me and that consequently nature touches and speaks to me less than before; still, I recall that only a few weeks ago all my sensations of adolescence and Italy awoke again in me on the occasion of a sky truly limpid and a sun really gilded. The chimney-tops seemed triumphant to me, and the walls drunk with held-in happiness. I am therefore not quite old.[113]

Let us not search for anything original in these intermittent manifestations of affective memory. Amiel is subject to them, like more or less all the minds of his time. Still, with Amiel, to the resuscitation of the past is often allied another feeling, which is that of the preservation of the past, above all, the most profound past. For him who has experienced to the highest degree, the impression of the genesis of things, nothing is more moving than to rediscover things, so that in the long run, in expanding, and even in declining, they have become the germinal being which had been theirs at the beginning of their existence and perhaps of ours. Amiel often has this form of remembrance; he would like to constitute himself the faithful guardian of the first epochs of life, and if he should not become so himself, he admires those beings who by nature are gifted by an ineffaceable memory of the beginnings.

These beings are women:

> Woman goes over all her impressions in her remembrance. She ruminates, in some manner, her sorrows and joys, she rejuvenates them, rebegins them and re-experiences them. This plastic constancy, this eternal circuit around the loved object, always retains that feminine marvel, maternity, incubation. Every seed is surrounded, warmed, protected, in the heart as in the womb of woman, in such a way that it develops, dilates, organizes and lives like the embryo of an immortal being.[114]

Thus, with Amiel, or in any event with these beings with whom he sympathizes, remembrance can have the same diffusive force as the other activities of the self. The image of the past, that too, from a first kernel of emotions, has the ability to dilate itself across a mental expanse, of which one of its dimensions is the course of existence. One thinks of the fine remarks of Joubert on the maturation of certain forms of the past, which, thanks to the preserving attentions with which thought surrounds them, are able to perfect themselves in time. Everything that is feminine in Amiel's soul incites him to practise this "religion of remembrances."[115]

And yet, with him, the completion of remembrances is a rare phenomenon. Whether they never have the time to mature, or whether they are affected by a rapid putrefaction, Amiel's remembrances more often manifest an imperfect and abortive character. Either they are vague reminiscences, to which it is impossible to give a requisite precision; or else the memory appears as though shrouded under layers of forgetfulness which the gaze cannot pierce. More often the remembrance is not an entire image, but a fragmentary one, which, by reason of its incompletion, one would not know how to recognize: "Blind man's bluff in the void, hide and seek of a malicious destiny, how to name the unseizable sensation which persecuted me this morning at my waking? It was a charming reminiscence, but vague, without a name, without a contour, like a woman's figure half-seen by an invalid in the obscurity of his room and the uncertainty of delirium."[116] One thinks of certain episodes in *A la recherche du temps perdu*. Old imprecise scenes surge up, soliciting the spirit while it is not ready to lead them to the daylight and give them the perfection of a recognized and blossomed memory. But if in Proust's novel there are a quantity of missed memories, this is because, by contrast, we give our attention and our belief to those which are marvelously successful. How different it is for Amiel, in whom successful remembrance brings only a contradictory joy, while the failure of missed, abortive memories is a cause of constant regret!

Finally, moreover, with Amiel, all remembrances reveal themselves as being condemned to failure. It is because they are corroded by forgetfulness. Even more, they rapidly lose their power of rejuvenation. Soon they are content to give evidence of the death of what had been. With Amiel, as with Flaubert, memory often seems a sort of cemetery. Or else it is an abyss at whose base one perceives a being that is ourself, who is dead, and who now inspires in us a kind of revulsion:

> Yesterday, as I walked with my sister under the scented linden trees, I experienced that melancholy of dead years, of vanished months, of lost days, of time vanished beyond recall.[117]

> Do these reminiscences give me joy? No. The effect is more that of an odd melancholy. It is a fantasmagoria, and I say to myself: This is past, this is dead, this is the cemetery of what has been.[118]

> A visit to my apartment on the Rue Etienne Dumont. I returned with a secret horror. . . . I have an aversion against touching my dead past, of moving this lugubrious dust.[119]

> I felt that I was stifling among old papers, written or printed, that I was drowning in the dust of the past. I experienced the anguish of the Pompeians under the rain of Vesuvius's ashes or that of the walker who sinks into the sands of Mont Saint Michel.[120]

Being engulfed in forgetfulness, the pulverization of existence, the kind of horror experienced at contact with a mental terrain which, instead of serving as the support to thought, gives way under its weight, all this causes Amiel to experience something akin to the torment of engulfment. It is because remembrance has become an ambiguous substance, neither solid nor liquid, neither real nor unreal, neither positive nor negative, neither living nor dead, but a little of all this at one and the same time. In other words, memory no longer has sufficient consistency to support a human being. On the other hand, he appears to himself as used up, empty and incapable of holding the contents of memory. Life is slippery. Thought is a sieve that retains nothing. And Amiel compares his memory to a dry cistern, to a Danaides cask: "I forget everything," he writes, "and I never have with me more than the millionth part of my acquired capital, of my intellectual past. I am as empty as the Danaides cask, and if everything goes through it, nothing remains in it. Sainte-Beuve calls himself a mind broken by metamorphoses; I doubt that he could be more than I, in principle if not in reality. All my acquisitions return to the latent state, disappear in their virtuality, are absorbed in me without leaving any trace other than a more flexible aptitude to understand the thing or to recommence its study. I resemble the water filling all moulds, which retains no one of their forms."[121]

It is striking that to describe his fundamental fluidity Amiel makes use of the same image employed by Fénelon. Fénelon, too, found himself colorless, insipid, absolutely as formless as water, but such nevertheless that by the very absence of sensible qualities, he thought himself ready to take on the forms which grace wished to give him. Amiel, inversely, is a quietist singularly lacking in grace, whose flexibility ends by becoming purely negative: the negativity of him who resigns himself without resistance to lose bit by bit all that he has acquired. Never, with Amiel, is there the slightest velleity to oppose himself by his own effort to the dissolving force of forgetfulness. Or, in any case, such an effort never seems, with him, to have the slightest chance of success. Most of the time, like the stream of a waterfall, he is satisfied to watch his experiences slide into the void, or, if not the void, at least into that obscure center of the being where what has been, in ceasing to be, returns to indetermination. Also, with him, is not the phenomenon of forgetfulness different, in principle, from that by which the mind, in *reinvolving* itself, returns to its fundamental virtuality, except, it is true, on one essential point: that is to say, in the phenomenon of forgetfulness, the mind does not accompany things in their descent toward the virtual. Everything occurs as though it watched them sink in the direction of the center, while remaining, itself, on the rim.

From this point of view, the being abandoned by its remembrances feels itself forsaken somewhere on the periphery of existence. It is without memory, as it is without hope. It has neither past nor future. Having rid itself of everything which could exist beyond that point at which it lives, from one side or the other of its line of life, it has reduced itself to the most petty actuality, to the punctuality of the present moment. Amiel, perpetually, holds the sense of the extreme constriction of the scope of his duration:

> . . . extreme weakness to foresee and to recall reduction of my being to the mathematical point of the present.[122]

> . . . remarked how little I lived in the past or the present, forgetting one and the other and concentrating myself in the *impression* of the present.[123]

> The future and the past are effaced and I occupy myself but with the present.[124]

If nothing remains but the present, let us resign ourselves to occupy ourselves but with the present. Sometimes Amiel tries to adapt himself, as well as he can, to the situation in which he finds himself. Perhaps forgetfulness is not a bad thing, he says to himself. Thanks to it, one has made a clean sweep. Freed from all duties toward the past or the present, one is in a better posture to *rebuild the possible*. — On the other hand, it is indubitable that only the present is real. It is the place of our joys, better still, of our existence. Let us concentrate ourselves upon it. — But Amiel is neither a Horace nor a Gide. The *carpe diem* of the voluptuaries is not in his style, nor the rapid and passionate seizure of occasions. Not agile enough to disengage himself with grace, not substantial enough to give stability to the voluptuousness of the moment. — Incidentally, the very substance of the moment is, in a way, mined from the interior: "I no longer exist," Amiel states, "but in the present moment."[125] But he who exists in the present moment, barely exists even there: "I live in the present, I do not even live, I dream."[126] — Here, therefore, is a present in which already one no longer lives, in which one can, at the very most, dream. It is a present without either past or future, it is nothing much, if it is anything: "I can no longer take the present moment seriously,"[127] Amiel admits. And elsewhere: "Between the future that I reserve, and the past on which I ruminate, I have allowed the present to disappear."[128]

This last disappearance is far more grave than those which have preceded it. The effacement of the future, the swallowing up of the past appear like those great military disasters undergone in distant provinces, in which, finally, empires perish, but whose consequences make themselves felt only in the proportionate tardiness commensurate with the distance separating the capital from its frontiers. But it is an entirely different matter in the disappearance of the present, for it is at the very center of life that the disappearance of life takes place. Every instant it digs its own pit, and it is in this pit that a new instant eagerly throws itself, to perish in its turn. In such a way it is useless to hope to maintain oneself in any instant, and one must run from one to the other, as one would try to follow the current of a river by jumping from stone to stone.

Such is the reiterated movement of thought now disclosing itself in the act of accomplishment. This seems at first as an incessant to-ing and fro-ing of moments and hours:

> The hours come without bringing me, and leave without leaving me anything as worthwhile as what they take from me, my best years, my youth and my strength. I live from day to day...[129]

Time is therefore the heterogeneous continuity of which Bergson speaks. But this continuity has nothing of the melodic. It is, so to speak, a discontinued continuity, a procession of detached and undone parts: "All my thoughts and wishes crumble, scatter themselves, are unstrung, without being able to make a pyramid or even a necklace. Trifles devour me. I live only from day to day . . . ."[130] — The only activity which imbues a little steadfastness, or, at least, persistence against the crumbling of time, is the daily recording in the *Journal*. But, unlike the book in which Montaigne consigns his moods, Amiel's notebooks never record the slightest progress, either in the art of judging, or in that of living: "Discontinuity, non-perseverance, slackness, irregularity, intermittence in thought, have become ties in me. I live in the present, in the provisional, in the impression, and nothing stays put in my intellectual life."[131]

"My days," Amiel writes elsewhere, "are heterogeneous unities."[132] Heterogeneous, without a doubt, and to the highest degree.

But the extreme heterogeneity here achieves the same result as extreme homogeneity. Absolute difference confounds itself with absolute resemblance. Nothing is more monotonous than the *variations* of the *Journal*. One might say that they follow a way which infallibly brings them back to the same place. From this springs an impression of repetition pushed to an unimaginable degree. Here is the anguish of writing, described by Blanchot. It is pure repetition. Amiel recognizes this in saying: "I always begin again. Living, pondering, repeating, drivelling."[133] — Or elsewhere: "Twenty times have I noted this: I forget it and rediscover it; repeat it, tiresome repetitive rigamarole."[134]

As if to underscore his bad memory, he employs the mythical appellation of the Danaides cask; Amiel calls his life the perpetual recommencement of Sisyphus' torture: "Infinite circle, fatal rotation, the work of Sisyphus."[135] But there are many other terms with which to characterize it: "old ritornello," "squirrel spinning in its cage," "cat chasing its own tail," "spinning top," "whirling dervish," "great Buddhist wheel," such are a few of the images he makes use of to describe the reiteration. Yet all these images are images of a *circle*. Now, in fact, is revealed, in all the futility of its perpetual labor, the circular movement of the soul made captive by repetition. This movement is evidently at the opposite extreme from that tranquillity reigning in the center of the reimplicated soul. One might say that this latter finds itself as if divided into two absolutely irreconcilable parts. On one side, that of expansion, it is engaged in a displacement leaving it neither rest nor any opportunity to escape by the tangent; it is a victim of its automatic activity; it traces by its very agitation a circuit from which it is unable to withdraw. But on the other hand, thought rests in itself, stable, incapable of moving, incapable of doing anything other than coinciding with its lack of being. Objectively, thought is in the movement which traverses the cycle of its objects; but *subjectively* thought is in no object, it is nowhere, unless in itself; exactly as though it were borne into a furious whirlwind and never moved a finger. This is what Amiel states many, many times: "Only the center is fixed," he says. "Everything else, carried away by the centrifugal force, is a part of the nonself, of the exterior swirl."[136] — And in an admirable phrase which, better than any other, resumes the paradoxical relationship between the central immobility and the peripheral mobility: "To myself I am the immobile space in which whirls my sun and my stars."[137]

IX

A strangely immobile consciousness, reabsorbed in itself, around which the external activities of the mind pivot, drawn along in the great whirling movement of duration, here therefore is Amiel's final situation. Curiously enough, it does not greatly differ in appearance from the situation of divinity in the medieval cosmos. For a Boethius or a Saint Thomas, in fact, the divine eternity is comparable to a central immobile point, around which moves the entirety of duration, and it is exactly to this central point that all other points of duration have reference, so that they are all simultaneously present in the center, even though they succeed one another along the circumferential line of time. "Heal thyself of the successive by the simultaneous,"[138] Amiel writes in a phrase which has the very tone of scholastic language. To heal oneself of the successive, what is that unless it be to place oneself in eternity? And Amiel's spirit, harassed by the "unquiet stirring of the periphery,"[139] tries to withdraw entirely into the fixity of "the punctual state." "To escape the whirling of time by interior ecstasy," he writes, "to perceive oneself *sub specie aeterni,* is the ordering word of all the great religions of the superior races."[140] Now, has he not attained more than once to this degree of ecstasy by reimplication? Is this not the way by which, breaking its ties with the temporal life of the periphery, thought fixes itself in itself in the eternity of the central place? "As soon as time reduces itself to a point for us, we have entered into eternity."[141]

But the relationship which has just been made with medieval thought is superficial and illusory. As Brunschvicg clearly saw it,[142] in Amiel the reduction of time is equivalent to a suppression, pure and simple. As fast as things are reimplicated for him, they are detemporalized. Nothing is further removed from the Thomist eternity, which, in its plenitude, *contains* the reality of all durations. With Amiel, on the contrary, there is, as we have seen, a constant subtraction from the mind of the different realities of duration:

> I do not live in the future and barely in the present, nor in the past. Rather, I exist beyond time. The state of consciousness has nothing to do with the three dimensions of duration or extent. It is the *point,* the *eternal point,* the negation of detail and change.[143]

A capital passage, since it discloses for us the character of the Amielian eternity. An issue of subtraction and negation, it is not a filled eternity, it is an empty eternity. In any case, it is an eternity *in which everything dissolves itself:*

> All my activities, all my beliefs, all my ideas, seem to me dissolved in a limitless eternity.[144]

In the center, therefore, of the whirlwind of existence is consummated the definitive dissolution of existence. Eternity is nonexistence. A nonexistence which is situated at the heart of everything that lives, moves, and revolves, to desolidarize and oppose itself to its confusion. From which comes the extraordinary detachment of a consciousness which, *from afar,* judges the peripheral movement of life: "I take part, help, am present, so to speak, at the molecular whirling which one terms individual life."[145] — "I assist at the projecting of my own magic lantern."[146] — "I am a mummy, in the procession of time."[147] — "Like the somnambulists, I have a consciousness divided into two parts, and I hear myself walk as if it were the steps of another."[148] — Such are some of the forms Amiel uses to depict his doubling: a doubling so radical that it would be difficult to find an analogy. What is, for example, the famous Constantinian doubling, by comparison to this consciousness which "observes itself from beyond the tomb?"[149] The expression is from Amiel himself and perfectly expresses his final situation. It is that of a consciousness which, having entirely withdrawn from life, turns its glance onto the stirring of that which is not yet dead:

> I thought I was in the secret workshops of the soul, and saw life more or less as do those who are buried, who if they had a consciousness, would see the trees of the graveyard, that is to say, the roots.[150]

Like Charles the Fifth, Amiel ends therefore by assisting at his own obsequies. His adventure differs in no way from that of Edgar Poe, allowing himself, as he does, to be enclosed in thought in the sepulcher of him who is buried alive. Even worse, Amiel is a deceased one in whom consciousness continues to function. After a long work of elimination, thought presents itself to him as a center entirely liberated from all the forms of life which surrounded it. An extraordinarily *naked* center, without rays and without circles, a center become again a simple point, that is to say, nothing. Just as the Kabbala imagined the creation as a point from which the world came forth, Amiel imagines a creation which would re-engulf itself in the point.

The progress of this re-engulfment could not be better indicated than by these last citations:

The self withdraws from enclosure to enclosure . . .[151]

. . . The grandiose apparatus of life goes back piece by piece into the box.[152]

I feel the walls of my prison drawing in, and the stifling which will follow.[153]

. . . I have been content to breathe the flowers which were to hand and to reduce all my ambitions to a tight circle, a ray as close as possible to the grandeur of zero.[154]

Death reduces us to the mathematical point; the destruction which precedes it sends us back by increasingly narrowing concentric circles toward that final and inexpugnable refuge. In anticipation I savor that zero in which are extinguished all forms and all modes.[155]

Thus all is ended by a veritably final point.

XIII

FLAUBERT

To Leo Spitzer

In his book *Mimesis,* for almost a decade the standard study of the concept of reality in Western literature[1] and recently translated into English for the first time, Professor Erich Auerbach quotes the following passage from *Madame Bovary:*

> But it was above all at mealtimes that she could bear it no longer, in that little room on the ground floor, with the smoking stove, the creaking door, the oozing walls, the damp floor-tiles; *all the bitterness of life seemed to be served to her on her plate,* and, with the steam from the boiled beef, there rose from the depths of her soul other exhalations as it were of disgust. Charles was a slow eater; she would nibble a few hazel-nuts, or else leaning on her elbow, would amuse herself making marks on the oilcloth with the point of her table-knife.[2]

This passage, Auerbach declares, forms the climax of a presentation whose subject is Emma Bovary's dissatisfaction with her life at Tostes. In several cumulative pictures Flaubert describes the cheerlessness, drabness, unvaryingness, narrowness of Emma's world. This paragraph is therefore the climax of the portrayal of her despair. In itself it presents a picture: man and wife together at mealtime. But the picture is not represented in and for itself; it is subordinated to the dominant subject, Emma's despair. We are first given Emma, and then the situation through her. It is not, however, Mr. Auerbach continues, a matter of a simple representation of the content of Emma's consciousness, of what she feels, as she feels it. Though the light which illuminates the picture proceeds from her, she is yet herself part of the picture, she is situated within it.

It may be useful to reflect upon these enlightening, yet not completely satisfying remarks. No doubt, Flaubert's method consists in presenting, as an object for our contemplation, a subjective being which, in its stead, has for its own object of contemplation the surrounding reality of things. Emma, as Mr. Auerbach points out, "does not simply see, but is herself as one seeing." If Flaubert had simply decided to paint her from the outside, she would be merely an object among objects. With the room, the stove, the walls, the plate and the husband, she would be part and parcel of the plurality of things. If, on the other hand, Flaubert had wanted to make of her somebody like Bloom in *Ulysses*, or Clarissa Dalloway in *Mrs. Dalloway*, i.e., a purely subjective being, then there would have been no husband, plate, walls, stove or room. Nothing would have been left, except the sensations and emotions caused in Emma by these objects; and there would have been no Emma, or at least in us no consciousness of her as a person standing against a background of things, since she would have been reduced to the status of a stream of thoughts and feelings. In both cases something essential in Flaubert's novel would have been lost, in one case the objective world, in the other the subjective mind, and in both, the extremely delicate relationship between objective and subjective, which is the very substance of the novel. It is this constant relation which not only links together the dual aspects of the novel, but which also keeps each of these two realities from fragmenting itself into a sheer multiplicity, here of thoughts and emotions, there of objects. There is in *Madame Bovary* an inner coherence, and this coherence is due to the fact that things, simultaneous or successive, are constantly fused together in the unity of a single perceptive mind, and that conversely this mind is kept from disappearing in the flux of its own consciousness by the objectivity of a world with which it is in constant touch. This essential interrelation is excellently commented upon by Mr. Auerbach in his examination of the paragraph of *Madame Bovary* quoted above. But it seems to me that there is still something to be done. For in this paragraph there is not only a theoretical representation of reality; there is also a concrete medium through which this representation has been achieved. It is the business of the critic to examine, within the text, by what action Flaubert accomplished his purpose, i.e., to show vividly the interrelation of a consciousness and its environment.

Let us therefore go back to the text. First we read: *Mais c'était surtout aux heures des repas . . . .* What is given to us at first, is time. This time is not a continuity. It is a moment which repeats itself

again and again, but which is also, when it happens, the present
moment of Emma's life; the moment, above all moments, when
actually she cannot bear her existence any more. Thus what we
have at first, is something purely and intensely subjective, an awareness of time, an awareness of despair. But as soon as this awareness
is revealed, it is immediately located within a place, *la petite salle,*
and surrounded with a long enumeration of details, all objective in
themselves, but all endowed with affective powers: a stove that
smokes, a door that creaks, walls oozing, floor-tiles which are damp.
To these details there must be added all the other particulars, which
the author does not mention in this paragraph, but which were
described at great length in the preceding pages, and which are
present in the memory of the reader, as they are indeed in the
memory of Emma herself. Thus what is given here is greatly swollen
by what was given before. Details have an enormous cumulative
power. This is the power of number, or, to use an Aristotelian distinction, this is a numbering and not a numbered number. The
multiplicity — in itself meaningless — of all these details, takes force
and meaning from the fact that they all affect in the same way the
same person. Therefore, from their outside location around Emma,
they combine their force and their weight, in order to come down
and bring pressure upon her. To express this coming down and in,
of the outside reality, crowding on consciousness, Flaubert writes
this sentence: "All the bitterness of life seemed to be served to her
on her plate, and with the steam from the boiled beef, there rose
from the depths of her soul other exhalations as it were of disgust."

Let us consider successively the two balanced parts of this sentence. The first one is straight and to the point. One can feel in the
directness with which it rushes toward its goal, the very motion by
which the influx of despair, emanating from the surrounding
objects, passes through a sort of tangible space, in order to reach the
subject. To give this effect, Flaubert has purposely inverted the
objective and the subjective. Instead of a room, a stove, a door, a
tiled floor, there is now a "bitterness of life." The multiple objects
have been transformed into their subjective equivalents; just as, conversely, the soul of Emma, which is the goal of the combined
offensive carried out by things, has been symbolically represented
by the narrow objective circumference of her plate. Thus a deliberate confusion has been created between the subjective and the
objective; as if, by penetrating into Emma's soul, the images of
things had lost their objectivity and been transformed into feelings,

or as if Emma, by becoming affected by material things, had become also somehow material.

But there are still more discoveries to be made in this wonderful sentence. Its beauty consists in rendering exactly by the physical motion of the words, the psychic motion of the meaning. First the general expression, all the bitterness of life, substitutes for the manifold of things a subjective totality encompassing the whole of existence. Then, through the rapid flow of the following words, "seemed to be served to her on her plate," this peripheral reality shrinks down from all sides to lodge itself within the narrowest place, the plate of Emma. So the psychic motion, which in itself is invisible, has become a local and therefore a perceptible motion, through the figure of a space crossed over by the bitterness of existence finding its final home in the object on which is concentrated the attention of Emma. We are witnessing here an extraordinary narrowing of space, a rush of all causal forces, gathering from the depth of the past and from the three dimensions of external space, to converge on a central point, Emma's consciousness. But as soon as Flaubert has created this motion from the periphery to the center, he gives us a reverse motion from the center toward the periphery: "and, with the steam from the boiled beef, there rose from the depths of her soul other exhalations as it were of disgust." After the contraction the dilation. We do not doubt but that these exhalations go upward and outward, to join the outer regions wherefrom the condensed bitterness of existence came downward into Emma's plate. Thus, crossed over in both directions, the Flaubertian *milieu* appears as a vast surrounding space which spreads from Emma to an indeterminate circumference, and from the circumference to the consciousness of Emma.

This circular character of Flaubert's representation of reality is not a mere metaphor; or, if it is one, it is not one invented for the sake of the argument. On the contrary this metaphor occurs so often, and, when it occurs, fits so well and plays such an important part in the context, that we must consider it as the essential image by which Flaubert expresses the interrelation of objective world and subjective being. My purpose is to examine the different aspects and meanings presented by this metaphor in the work of Flaubert.

Let us take another passage from *Madame Bovary*. It can be found in a first draft of the novel, published in 1936 by Mlle Leleu. The moment of Emma's life here described belongs to a period slightly antecedent to the passage examined previously. Here she is shown during a walk she takes with her dog, a little Italian greyhound, in the country near Tostes:

> She began by *looking round her mechanically* to see if nothing had changed, since last she had been there. She found the same wall flowers on the stones, on the slab of the wall the same patches of dried up lichen, the same pebbles in the beds of nettles, and the three windows, always closed, which were rotting away . . . Her thoughts, aimless at first, were wandering at random, like the handsome greyhound who, unleashed, was *running round and round in the field,* chasing a rat in a furrow, or bringing himself to a stop in order to nibble the poppies . . . But when she had thus let her eyes roam over the horizon whereas her *diffused* attention had barely skimmed a thousand ideas following each other, then, *as two concentric circles at once contracting their circumferences,* her thoughts retired within herself, her wavering glances became transfixed, and sitting on the ground under the beeches, prodding the grass with the ivory tip of sunshade, she kept always coming back to this question: "Why, my God, did I marry?"[3]

Here, beyond question, the metaphor of the circle cannot be overlooked. It plays a conspicuous part. At first everything tends to become peripheral. Emma's thoughts wander at random, her eyes roam over the horizon, her attention is spread on a thousand ideas. The things that she perceives, the thoughts that she thinks, get farther and farther in the distance, and finally they distribute themselves in such a way that they form two concentric circles whose central point is Emma's consciousness. To give the right emphasis to this general impression of circularity, Flaubert has taken care to prefigure it by another circle, the one physically described by the dog running round and round in the field. But this is not all. Let us read again the beginning of the long sentence which constitutes the second half of the paragraph: "But when she had thus let her eyes roam over the horizon, whereas her diffused attention had barely skimmed a thousand ideas following each other. . . ." No doubt, these long undulating clauses, progressively opening, are shaped in this particular form, so as to give a physical impression of the corresponding widening of Emma's thoughts and feelings. But if we read the second part of the sentence, we detect a striking difference of rhythm. The clauses are shorter, straighter and faster; "her thoughts retired within herself, her wavering glances became transfixed . . . . she was always coming back to this question." Here, manifestly, diffusion has been replaced by contraction. The circles are shrinking, the thoughts from all sides are coming back, the words are running, as if impatient to reach their goal and to come to a full stop. This final fixation of all motion is represented in two, or even in three distinct ways. Just as the dog, who was running round in the field, comes to a full stop in order to nibble the poppies, so Emma's mind, which was wandering far away in circles among her memories and dreams, comes back to an idea on which it concentrates. And, in a way, this idea is different from all preceding ones, since it is not diffuse, remote and infinitely varied, but precise, intimate and absolutely unique. It is not circumferential, it is central. However this one central thought is closely connected with the previous multiplicity. It is out of this multiplicity that it was issued. It was this very multiplicity which, by fusion, contraction and inward motion, produced finally the central thought, as the result and summing up. Thus the center contains the circumference. And this center is represented once more, symbolically, by a single dimensionless object, which has replaced in the picture the whole landscape: the pointed tip of a sunshade, digging the ground. The circular horizon has shrunk to a mere point.

This infinite contraction of the mental and external spaces is in no way mysterious, either in itself or in its occurrence. It is the most natural motion of the human mind. We know that it is because the diffused attention of Emma, wandering aimlessly, has touched many ideas, that these ideas have awakened, echoed in her mind, evoked the picture of her whole existence, and given expression finally to the question which was at the core of her consciousness. Nothing was more genuine than this moving inward from the circumference to the center. And, on the other hand, nothing was less instantaneous. From extreme excentricity to extreme concentricity, it is step by step, by a slow and repeated process, that the thought goes back to the self. From the circumference to the center of the psychic circle, we see a gradual progress, we feel the time, we measure the distance.

We have seen space gradually contracting. Let us now see space completely contracted, space which cannot expand. All his life, Flaubert was intensely conscious of the narrowness of existence. Already in one of his earlier books, *Smarh,* he had spoken of "his sickly thought, *running in an iron circle.*"[4] In *Novembre* we find the following sentence: "Returning ceaselessly to my starting-point, I was *going round and round in an impassable circle.*[5] In August 1847, he wrote to Louise Colet: "I am attached to a patch of land, to a *circumscribed point* in the world, and the more I feel myself attached to it, the more I turn again and again furiously toward the sun and sky."[6] Nor was this feeling in Flaubert confined to his youth. On April 6, 1858, in his full maturity, he wrote to Mlle Leroyer de Chantepie:

> For the fourth time I am going to find myself again in Marseilles, and, this time, I shall be alone, absolutely alone. *The circle has shrunk.* The reflections I was making in 1849 when about to embark for Egypt, I am going to make again in a few days, when tramping the same streets. Thus our life *goes round* continually in the same train of miseries, like a squirrel in a cage, and each new step makes us gasp.[7]

Similarly all the works of Flaubert's old age have for their main theme circumscribed existence. For instance *Un Coeur Simple,* the story of Félicité, the maid-servant, from which I quote this passage:

> *The small circle of her ideas shrank even more,* and the chiming of bells, the bellowing of cattle did not exist any more. All living things now were moving as silently as ghosts. Only one sound still reached her ears: the voice of her parrot.[8]

This parrot, first as a pet, then as a stuffed bird, becomes gradually the central object in the old maid's circle of existence. At the end there is no more circle. There is only the stuffed bird, which is the unique point on which the old maid's look is fixed at the moment of her death. Another story from that period is the legend of St. Julian the Hospitaller. Julian is a great hunter, pursuing his quarry in many countries, until, in a culminating scene, the animals at bay turn upon him, *"making around him a narrow circle."*[9] The same feeling of suffocation can be found in *Salammbo,* where a whole army is shut in, to perish by starvation, in a narrow mountain pass. And the same picture of narrow activity, running blindly around in a small circle, is to be found in *Bouvard et Pécuchet.* Everywhere in the work of Flaubert there is the obsession of narrow, endless circularity. But nowhere does it appear more strikingly than in the story of Emma Bovary. Emma is essentially a person who feels herself enclosed and stifled within the bounds of the place where she lives and of the moment in which she thinks. Her whole existence at Tostes or at Yonville seems to her a shutting up within walls, a grouping around inside narrow limits; limits so narrow that sometimes they seem to join each other, to condense into a point, the point of time and space where she is constrained to live. She is here, here only, in the dimensionless *here;* she is forbidden forever to escape outside, into the infinite *elsewhere.* Nevertheless this *elsewhere* exists, it exists everywhere else, it is spreading on every side, and it is toward that *elsewhere* that her longing irradiates incessantly. The extraordinary constriction of Emma's existence, reduced to a mere punctum, is described by Flaubert in this passage, taken from the first version of *Madame Bovary:*

> Then the train of the same days started again. They were going to follow each other in the same manner, in Indian file, always similar, innumerable, bringing nothing. And they were before her, hundreds and thousands of them, enough for ten or twenty years! It will never finish, it will last until her death. The other lives, constricted, flat, cramped as they were, had at least some chance of an adventure, of a broadening *of their limits.* Sometimes there dropped an accident which shook their surface. An unexpected happening could *create peripeties ad infinitum.* . . . But, for her, nothing would happen.[10]

First of all, the beauty of this passage is due to the intense feeling of duration which impregnates it: Then the train of the same days started again. Duration appears here as a mere prolongation of the past into the present. But it appears also as a prolongation of the present into the future: They were going to follow each other in the same manner, in Indian file. The three dimensions of time, past, present and future, identify themselves with one another, in such a way, that they become a uniform and continuous texture. As far as the eye can reach, duration extends, forward, backward, always the same, forming a homogeneous bulk of temporal matter. But by a process which, in his famous sonnet *Le Cygne,*[11] Mallarmé will repeat, this vast extent of duration, spread uniformly on all sides, is also experienced by Emma as the narrowest possible span of time. The very uniformity of all past, present and future moments of existence, transforms and contracts all of them into a single moment; and this moment, incessantly rediscovered along the retrospective and prospective expanse of time, is never discovered but as the same narrow span infinitely repeated. So time is just an endless void of duration, in the middle of which life appears constricted, identical to itself, bringing nothing. However, this life is compared by Emma to others. These other lives, "constricted, flat, cramped as they were, had at least some chance of an adventure, of a broaden-

ing of their limits." Adventure, considered as a widening of existence, is described by a symbol well-known since the Stoics: "Sometimes there dropped an accident which shook their surface. An unexpected happening could *create peripeties ad infinitum.*" No doubt
the image suggested here is the one of a stone dropped in a pool.
From the point where it strikes the surface, concentric waves go
out in all directions. The circles widen, multiply, get farther from
the center. So an adventure, an accident, something unprovoked,
uncalled for, may fall suddenly into the pool of life, burst into its
stillness, produce circles of events going outward. The accident in
itself is nothing; just a piece of gravel thrown in the water. But
the small whirlpool it creates breaks the limits of the still narrow
circle of existence, to replace them by an infinite circumference.[12]
The most insignificant event may be the starting point of an immense future.

Everything, therefore, depends on these occurrences. But, thinks
Emma, they only happen to other people, they will never happen
to me. Now, in spite of Emma's forebodings, it is precisely Flaubert's purpose to make things happen to her. Not many happenings,
just three or four. Emma's life is a pool in which, occasionally,
stones are thrown. Or, more exactly, it is a series of pools, each one
a little bigger than the preceding one, first the father's farm, then
Tostes, then Yonville, finally Yonville plus Rouen. In the stillness
of each of these pools, at a particular time, a stone is thrown. This
throwing of the stone is invariably the appearance of a new lover.
From the moment he comes out, there start waves of emotion,
which for a time broaden Emma's life; up to the moment when, the
lover having gone, the emotion being spent, Emma is brought back
by a retrogressive process to her starting point.

Let us examine this starting point in the first and most fugitive
of Emma's love affairs.

Invited with her husband to a ball in an aristocratic country
house, *le château de la Vaubyessard,* Emma has been deeply moved
by this incidental excursion in a *milieu* so different from hers. She
has danced in the arms of a Parisian Viscount, whose elegance has
made on her a profound impression: "All things turning around
them, the lamps, the furniture, the wainscoting, the floor like a disc
on a pivot."[13] Let us keep in mind these physical gyrations in which
we must see a prefiguration of the mental gyrations which, later on,
will proceed in Emma's mind. The day after, Emma leaves the
château and the Viscount, to come back to the narrow circle of her

ordinary life. The only keepsake she has brought back from that memorable event is a cigar case which may, or may not, have belonged to the Viscount. Now this fortuitous dancing partner, whom Emma will not see any more, is a very small pebble in her life. Nevertheless we shall see, starting from the point of its falling, waves and waves of dreams irradiating in Emma's imagination. To follow this phenomenon, we have not only the final version of the novel, but also some preliminary drafts, and even in the primitive scenario referring to Emma's life after her return, we find this sentence: "The Viscount is a center, he disappears, but the surroundings stay and widen."[14] Another version, more elaborated, gives the explanation of this cryptic statement. First we are informed that sometimes Emma looks at the cigar case, which makes her dream of the Viscount. She wants to imagine his life in Paris, and she reads books about life in the capital. These books are mostly novels. Then comes the important passage:

> The memory of the Viscount was always passing, like a ghost, into what she was reading. She found his picture on every page. Examining the imaginary personages, she was always making parallels and comparisons with him. Thus he was enhanced by their poetry and he reflected his reality upon their fiction. Then *the circle of which he was the center, where all rays converged, gradually widened round him,* and, spreading equally in this expanse, the Viscount's personality become more and more diluted, like a drop of red wine that one lets fall in a glass of water.[15]

The image of the drop of wine corresponds closely to the one of the pebble. In both instances a fallen object, by dilation or dilution, becomes the center and generating point of a circular motion. In the final version the image changes once again, but still represents the figure of a circle:

> The memory of the Viscount always returned as she read. Between him and the imaginary personages she made comparisons. But *the circle of which he was the center gradually widened round him,* and the *halo* that he bore, drawing away from his head, broadened out beyond, lighting up other dreams.[16]

Here, instead of the pebble, or the drop of wine, we have the halo. The circle, narrow at first, becomes progressively so wide that it loses touch with the center, and, identifying itself with other dreams, irradiates confusedly in the distance toward a sort of peripheral happiness:

At the far end of life's vista, high above, she thus saw happiness lying in a marvellous abode.[17]

Here again we have a fundamental process of the Flaubertian mind, just the opposite of the one which makes the mind contract within narrow limits. It is the process of expansion, which generates innumerable reveries, leading from a central thought to a profusion of eddying images. As often as not, the starting point is a recollection. For instance, in a letter from Flaubert to Louise Colet, dated August 22, 1853, from Trouville, we find the following passage:

All the memories of my youth are crying out under my feet, like shells on the beach. Each wave that I see breaking on the seashore awakens in me distant *resounding echoes.*[18]

As in Proust, we can often find in Flaubert a whole world of reminiscences, "sortant d'une tasse de thé." But in Flaubert, contrarily to Proust, this springing forth of the past is never directed toward the recapture of any distinct reality. It is a spreading outward, a processus of indetermination. Thus, at the tinkling of a bell, stirring memories of Emma's youth, "Gentle vibrations made her thoughts quiver and *go widening in the infinite vagueness of retrospections.*"[19] The distinctness of each recollection is thus progressively replaced by their multiplicity, their vibratility, and, finally by the vastness of the place they have indistinctly filled up by their resonances. In *Smarh,* as in the three *Tentations,* we experience at a cosmic scale this feeling of expansion:

How vast is creation! I see the planets rising and the stars running, carried away with their lights. *The dome of the sky* is *widening as I go upward with it,* the worlds are rolling around me. So I am *the center* of this moving creation.[20]

And in the 1849 version of the *Tentation:*

The Devil: — Diffuse, expand, spread out.
Anthony: — I see the *circle widening,* I hear the rumbling sound of the spheres.[21]

Or:

Thy joy will grow unceasingly, according to the increases of thy love, like the vibrations of seraphic harps, which *widening from sphere to sphere,* unfold in the Infinite the praise of God.[22]

Thus, independently of any religious or philosophical belief, by the essential trend of his imagination, Flaubert's soul, like the soul

of St. Anthony, tends to become "diffuse, universal, stretched out."[23]
In a letter written by Flaubert to Louise Colet on the 3rd of March,
1852, we read:

> I have come across some old drawings that I colored when I
> was seven or eight years old, and that I have not seen since.
> There are rocks painted in blue and trees in green. Looking at
> them (at a wintering in an ice-field especially) I relived some of
> the terrors I experienced when I was a child. . . . My journeys,
> the recollections of my childhood, all these things reflect their
> colors on one another, they fall into line, dance in a prodigious
> blaze and *rise in a spiral*.[24]

The theme of the spiral is frequent in Flaubert. It may have come
from his friend Le Poittevin, whose novel, *Bélial,* is summed up in
these words by Flaubert: "The general idea is the whirl, the *infinite
spiral*."[25] Already in the youthful *Mémoires d'un fou* Flaubert writes
these curious words: "Oh! the infinite! the infinite! immense gulf,
spiral which rises from the abyss to the higher regions of the unknown, old idea within which *we go round, taken with giddiness*."[26]
The first two *Tentations* are full of spirals. Thus the Ophits say,
speaking of their snake-god: "His *spirals* are the *circles* of worlds
spread out concentrically."[27] And the Gnostics: "The mysterious
Gnosis raises up endlessly its *spiral,* and, driven by us, thou shalt
ascend ceaselessly toward the irradiating Syzygia, which will carry
thee high above in the bosom of the perennial Bythos, in the im-
movable *circle* of the perfect Plerom."[28] Moreover, we know that, on
more than one occasion, Flaubert planned to write a novel precisely
entitled *La spirale,* which would have had for subject the trans-
figuration of reality through dream, and of which nothing remains
except a few unprinted notes known through a German scholar,
E. W. Fischer. Quoting from these notes the phrase "comme une
spirale qui monte à l'infini," Mr. Fischer wonders about the meaning of the title: "Is it intended to mean that the thoughts of the
hero are moving along circles which rise infinitely, fantastic circles
around the reality, from which they fly, and to which, however,
they are attached as to their starting-point?"[29] It would be difficult
to get closer to the spirit of the author. Very likely, through the symbol of an ever-rising spiral, Flaubert wanted once more to illustrate
the circular widening of horizons, that we found already in *Madame
Bovary*. If we want further proof, let us recall this other sentence
from the *Correspondance:* "The heart in its affections, like mankind
in its ideas, *spreads endlessly in widening circles*."[30] Elsewhere Flau-

bert writes: "All feeling is an extension."[31] But in the whole of the
Correspondance there is nothing nearer *Madame Bovary* than the
following passage: "My existence, like a stagnant swamp, is so still
that *the least event dropping in it, causes innumerable circles. . .*"[32]

Yet in spreading outward the mind runs risks of which Flaubert
was well aware. The first one, which we have already seen, is the
risk of losing touch with the center of one's thoughts, and therefore
with all order and precision. In their famous discussion with Flaubert after the reading of *La tentation,* Bouilhet and Du Camp were
not entirely in the wrong when they told Flaubert: "You made an
angle from which *diverging* figures spread out so far that one loses
sight of them. . . . You proceed through expansion."[33] Perhaps when
using this particular metaphor, Bouilhet and Du Camp had in mind
the words said, precisely in *La tentation,* by the Heresies to Anthony: "We are the *diverging rays* which multiply the light, and all
converging toward its base to increase its span."[34] No doubt, in his
desire of extending immensely the scope of his work, Flaubert, in
the 1849 version, had developed divergency at the expense of con-
vergency. But out of this multiplicity of directions and desegrega-
tion of all images in the void of space, a new danger appears, which
is the danger of giddiness, madness, mental hemorrhage that nothing
can stem. Flaubert writes: "I have often felt madness coming in
for me. In my poor head there was a whirl of ideas and images, and
it seemed to me that my consciousness, my very self, was sinking
like a ship in the tempest."[35] The ship sinks at the center of the
whirl, while at the periphery there is a maddening circular motion.
This is just such a psychic catastrophe as we witness in *Madame
Bovary,* when Emma, rejected by Rodolphe, goes back through the
fields. There is no center left in her, or, more exactly the mental
center of her self is a bursting point, exploding and projecting itself
in countless fragments in all directions:

> She remained lost in stupor, and having no more consciousness
> of herself than through the beating of her arteries, that she
> seemed to hear bursting forth like a deafening music filling all
> the fields. The earth beneath her feet was more yielding than the
> sea, and the furrows seemed to be immense brown waves break-
> ing into foam. Everything in her head, of memories, ideas, went
> off at once like a thousand fireworks . . .
> Suddenly it seemed to her that fiery *spheres* were exploding
> in the air like detonating *balls* when they strike, and were
> whirling, whirling to melt at last upon the snow between the

branches of the trees. In the midst of each of them appeared the face of Rodolphe. They multiplied and drew near her, penetrating her. Then all disappeared.[36]

But at the opposite extreme of this ultimate state of mind, where there is no longer any circle, or center, or any existential coherence whatsoever, there are in *Madame Bovary* all the passages where the excentric and concentric motions balance each other, and the circumference does not lose its relation to the center. In *Par les champs et par les grèves,* Flaubert writes: "A reverie can be great and give birth at least to fruitful melancholies, when, *starting from a fixed point and never losing touch with it,* the imagination hovers within its luminous *circle.*"[37] This hovering of the dreams within a luminous circle, to the center of which they are closely related, is expressed in the first *Education sentimentale,* at the moment when the hero discovers that he is loved:

> The universe appeared to him, through a luminous vista, full of glory and love, and his own life *surrounded by a halo,* like the face of a God; happiness spread over him; it was *coming out* of everything, it exuded even from the walls.[38]

In a preceding passage, the halo, "drawing away from his head, broadened out beyond, lighting up other dreams." Here, instead of disappearing into the distance, the halo irradiated by love seems to reach a limit, from which its reflected light comes back toward the center of emanation. In our first example, we have seen all the surrounding bitterness of existence concentrate into Emma's plate. Here, through the same concentric approach, we see all the surrounding sweetness of the world reaching the soul.

The same process is repeated again and again in *Madame Bovary.* For instance, this description of the motion by which the image of Emma comes from the depths of the past into the center of Léon's consciousness:

> It seemed to him that the face of this woman was *sending from far away on his present life a kind of reverberation,* like these setting suns, which, close to the ground, cast out as far as us their luminous undulations.[39]

Or this admirable passage, which unfortunately Flaubert did not retain in the final version, where through the happiness of her present love, Emma not only unfolds herself to the external reality, but also experiences in the apex of actual love the fulfillment of past desires, kept at the periphery of her mind:

Besides, in loving him, not only did she fulfill her need of love, but she also satisfied all her old desires, which had been inhibited. . . . All the feelings of her soul *converged* in this love, as the spokes of a wheel around the axle which supports them.[40]

Thus, what Flaubert intended to show in *Madame Bovary* is a life which at one moment contracts and at another unfolds; a life which sometimes is reduced to a moment without duration and a point without dimension; and which sometimes, from that moment and from that point, extends to a circular consciousness of all its duration, of all the depths of its dreams, of all the spatiality of its environment:

All these reminiscences were *widening her existence.* They seemed to form immensities of feeling, *to which she turned.*[41]

The relation, here, is from a dimensionless present to the vastness of peripheral life. But it may also happen conversely that from the breadth of a present existence, now peripheral, all the activities of the soul converge on a single central object.

Thus in the *Correspondance:*

It is to you that my thought *flows back,* when I have been through the *circle* of my reveries; *I cast myself on this thought at full length,* like a weary traveller on the grass alongside the road.[42]

But, above all, this admirable passage of the first *Madame Bovary,* where we find the same image:

She concentrated on this recollection; it became *the center* of her spleen; all her thoughts *converged upon it.* . . . The humblest details, the past, the future, memories of simple words, fancies, comparisons, disgusts, she piled everything into this recollection, *her soul stretched at full length toward this center of heat.*[43]

All these texts prove clearly that what Flaubert conceived and succeeded in devising, is a new way of presenting the relations between the mind and all surrounding reality, a more convincing way than the one used by his predecessors. While eighteenth-century novelists, and Stendhal himself, were satisfied to go with the hero along the narrow track of successive time, and while Balzac constructed most of his plots as a line of force projected very straight in time and space, Flaubert is the first who builds his novels around a series of centers encompassed by their environments. For the first time in the history of the novel, human consciousness shows itself as it is, as a sort of core, around which sensations, thoughts and memories move in a perceptible space. Thus it becomes possible to discover and express the depth of the human mind; a depth which can be conceived as an expanse through which radiations diverge, or, conversely, as the convergence of all peripheral life upon the sentient being.

But there is yet a last form of circularity that must be examined. It is the *ordering* of all activities around an image which dwells permanently in the center of the soul. The whole novel becomes then the continuous reshaping of a reality in itself disordered, taking form, meaning and motion from the living center to which it is related. Such is, it seems to me, the true structure of *l'Education sentimentale*. Critics often consider it as a formless novel, a novel which has precisely for its subject-matter the formlessness of existence. Charles Du Bos has written some beautiful pages on the "milieu intérieur" of this novel, in which, for him, "Nothing takes hold, everything is oozing, and it seems that we are inside the *flowing* motion of time."[44] But in insisting on this flowing *away*, Du Bos failed to see that in the *Education sentimentale* there is also a constant flowing *in* and *around*. Here, clearly there is no progression of water going downstream. As Flaubert said himself of his novel, "There is no progression of effect."[45] Thus it would be more exact to compare its motion to the one of a *circular* river. Again and again, in the works of Flaubert, the word *circulation* appears, weighted with meaning. For instance, in *La Tentation:*

> The blood of man pulses in his heart and swells the veins of his feet. The breath of God *circulates* among the worlds and the contingencies of these worlds.[46]
> Dost thou see, like blood in an enormous body, the universal Haensoph *circulating* in the hidden veins of all the worlds?[47]

Thus, in *l'Education sentimentale,* Frédéric Moreau is constantly perceiving, around him, currents of life quickening the circumambient world:

> He stayed to contemplate the quadrille, blinking his eyes to see better, breathing the soft perfumes of women, which were *circulating* like a kiss endlessly diffused.[48]
> The ceiling, rounded in the form of a cupola, gave to the

boudoir the shape of a basket; and a scented draught was *circulating* under the fluttering of fans.[49]

When he came up again to his study, he looked at the armchair where she had been seated and at all the objects she had touched. Something of her was *circulating around*. The caress of her presence was still enduring.[50]

But this incessant motion of peripheral life would have no meaning, and the novel no form, if, at the center there were not a coordinating element. This element is the love of the hero. If Frédéric had not loved Madame Arnoux, the novel would have been formless and meaningless. But this is not the case. As Jean-Pierre Richard says in his study on *La création de la forme chez Flaubert,* in *l'Education sentimentale* "All objects are disposed around an oriented axle."[51] It is because, from the first page of the novel, Mme. Arnoux draws Frédéric's love, that whatever amorphous elements exist in Frédéric's life, begin to gravitate around her image, taking light from her:

And as a traveller lost in the midst of a wood, whom all paths lead *back to the same spot,* continually, at the end of every idea, he was finding again the memory of Mme. Arnoux.[52]

All the streets were leading toward her house; all carriages were standing in the squares to bring him there more quickly; Paris was related to her person, and the great city, with its thousand voices, was murmuring like an immense orchestra, *round her.*[53]

Thus the main purpose of Flaubert's novel is to create relation and order. This order is formal. From the center to the circumference, from the circumference to the center, there are constant relations. These are the relations set by the sentient subject between each moment of its consciousness and its total environment. Flaubert's novel belongs to a region explored, in a famous article, by Professor Leo Spitzer: the region of *milieu* and *ambiance.*[54] Sensible and emotive elements form a tangible circle, at the core of which there is, to quote the most perfect expression of Flaubert, *"A luminous center, toward which the entirety of things converge."*[55]

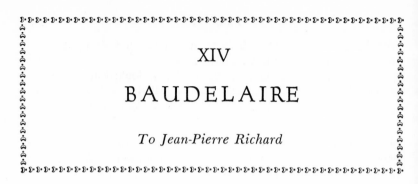

XIV

BAUDELAIRE

To Jean-Pierre Richard

I

"Nature . . . quivers with a supernatural and galvanic quivering."[1] It is by this quivering that everything in Baudelaire begins. At certain hours, "admirable hours, veritable festivals of the brain,"[2] objects suddenly find themselves decked with more vivid colors, endowed with a strange setting off, with a keen resonance: "Sounds ring musically, colors speak."[3] An exceptional energy makes everything tremulous. They sparkle, resound, trepidate. To be is no longer enough with them, they come alive. To this intensity bursting everywhere outside, there corresponds a similar intensity within. It is the time when "the more vigilant senses perceive more reverberating sensations,"[4] in which "all sublime thought is accompanied by a nervous shaking."[5] Things vibrate, thought vibrates. A vibration which is in every contour, noise, or color without, in every idea within. Or rather, there is neither within nor without, simply the sudden and multiple apparition, somewhere, in the perceptive field, of the same vibrating intensity. All things are touched and exalted by a translating, nay, a transfiguring power, metamorphosing them; so to speak, on the spot!

This is the first unforgettable experience of Baudelaire's imagination. It is equivalent to a birth. The birth of the world, the birth of the being who apprehends the world. Everything happens as though, in a moment of such intensity that no previous or later moment could be likened to it, the world of exterior objects attests its exclusive presence, if by nothing more than the violence by which it manifests its sensible qualities. And at first this profusion seems absolutely satisfying. It inspires an immediate happiness, a feeling of physical ecstasy. Nothing is lacking in a world which is content

266

with living and affirming its existence by the intensity of its lines, its colors, and its sounds. But the existence of this world is without duration, and even without space. The moment in which it springs forth is not linked with other moments. The place in which it rises is less a place than a multiplicity of places in each one of which the sound resounds, the line is traced, the color marks. Everything being on the same level, nothing is set out relative to other plans. It is an extent riddled with places, but in which there is no space, for space is the relation between places, and there is no relation. In every place every object vibrates, but it is only the trembling of a particular existence. The universe is an aggregation of shudders, a plurality of vacillating flames.

But by the very reason of the violence by which it exerts itself, this vibration of things cannot limit itself to the instants or the places where, each one for itself, they quiver. The movement animating them prolongs itself beyond their contours and their momentary reality. They begin by being there, there where they live and resound, excluded, it would seem, from everything else by the very violence which attaches them to frontiers which they define as they take life. And then, without transition, like a pollen detaching itself from the plant, the vibration begins to travel in space.

Space without obstruction and without opacity, free space. An intense luminosity is equally distributed there: "One might say that a never growing light makes objects glitter more and more; that the stimulated flowers yearn to rival the blue of the sky with the vividness of their colors, and that heat, causing perfumes to become visible, makes them rise into the heavens like smoke."[6] To the expanding energy of colors and scents there corresponds the enticing influence of space. To the passive intensity with which the senses "absorb form and color,"[7] there corresponds the active intensity with which the spirit lures them into its transparent field. Space opens out, crystal-like, without mist and without obstacle. Everything soars into it, everything begins to unfold within it, to fly or to swim:

> I see joyous shores *unroll*
> Dazzled by the fires of a monotonous sun.[8]

> Beautiful isle of green myrtles, filled with blooming
>   flowers . . .
> Where the sighs of adoring hearts
> *Roll* like an incense over a garden of roses . . .[9]

My soul, you nimbly move,
And, like a good *swimmer* who swoons with ecstasy in the
    wave,
You gaily furrow the profound immensity . . .[10]

. . . We will *fly* in the infinite, like birds,
butterflies, gossamer threads, perfumes, and
all winged things.[11]

To roll, to swim, to fly, to sail, are the almost equivalent terms by
which Baudelaire expresses the movement of the senses protracting
itself in free space. Free but not empty, for if the flight of images is
similar to a flying bird, to a swimmer who breasts the waves, it
resembles also, the element, ethereal or liquid which, in unrolling
itself, upholds this swim or this flight. It is a flood, but a flood which
spreads out, which not only overruns places, but occupies them, an
energy which in dilating itself actually creates the milieu, aqueous
or aerial, in which its vibratory thrust is pursued. And this mobile
milieu, pouring itself out on all sides, sweeps along the thought it
envelops in such a manner that, simultaneously, two phenomena
are accomplished, that by which the wave of sensation invades space,
and that by which, situated at the crest of the wave, thought progressively occupies the same expanses. Thus objective space and subjective space, that which is *covered over* by the vibration of things,
and that which is *discovered* by the vibration of thought, are but
one. It little matters yet that these two movements are condemned
to get separated, because of the limitation of one and the infinity of
the other. For the moment, they are conjoined. One follows the
other; one supports the other:

And we go, *following the rhythm of the wave,*
Rocking our infinity on the finite of the seas.[12]

The sea is thy mirror; thou contemplatest thy soul
In the infinite *unrolling* of its wave.[13]

Infinite unrolling of the sentient wave; vibratory progression of
colors and forms; sonority of sounds; and above all, dilation of
scents:

Of the antique Venus the superb phantom
Planes over your seas like an aroma.[14]

As other souls scud along on the music,
Mine, O my love, swims on your perfume.[15]

If indeed, Baudelaire is more the bard of perfumes, than of any other sense-data there is no reason to believe that it is because of an abnormally developed olfactory faculty. It is not with Baudelaire, but with others, Colette, for example, that one finds the manifestation of a hypersensitive sense, rare with men and frequent with animals, which is called flair. More than sound and even more than color, odor seems to Baudelaire the primary sense power, that which is most capable of occupying space and of being able to reveal its amplitude. Odors have "the expansion of infinite things."[16] He who has the agility of the mind and of the olfactory sense necessary to breathe them, not alone where they are wafted to him, but wherever they diffuse themselves, "travels on perfume,"[17] diffuses himself with it, and finds himself swimming on an effluvious flood. Smelling is a sea, not liquid but aerial, whose waves are lighter but also as universal as those of the ocean. Moreover, contrary to sound, light, and color, odor when spreading itself out, seems to lose nothing of its primitive energy. "A grain of incense fills a church."[18] Odor is as strong at the circumference of the circle as in the emanating center. In brief, it manifests itself as the most perfect of all the movements by which the sentient activity takes possession of space. It spreads out without loss. Finally, without changing the configurations of the expanses that it occupies, without modifying, either, anything of its own nature, or of the nature of the objects which it impregnates, it infiltrates everywhere, it leaves no interstice. In itself, space is something invisible; odor, in spreading itself in it, becomes its soul and, at the same time, the act thanks to which it becomes visible: "An infinitesimal and perfectly chosen scent, with which there is mingled a slight moisture, floats in this atmosphere . . . ."[19] As the perfume diffuses itself, space becomes atmosphere, as a liquid or a gas reveals itself when one mixes with it a coloring. All the energies of feelings, but odor, to the highest degree, impregnate, and in impregnating, make space apparent.

It also makes time apparent. To swim, to fly, to roll, to sail, all these terms of Baudelaire, far from implying a sort of instantaneous irradiation, express a continuous movement, which, at the same time, consumes and realizes duration. As in Aristotle's universe, we are here in the presence of an operation which, to be fulfilled, needs a certain becoming. But becoming for Baudelaire is not the passing from potentiality to act. No substantial form guides here the movement toward its end. Or rather, there is no end. The only action that is required of things is that they should vibrate, and that their vibration should prolong itself. To become means simply to continue to act, and as, in spatial reality, to continue to act signifies to progress, to occupy more and more of space, so in the temporal reality it signifies to vibrate unceasingly, to occupy more and more of duration.

Hence, from the point of view of time, the expansion of all feelings with Baudelaire first appears as a movement toward the future. But this future differs only from the present, by the fact that it extends indefinitely into the distance:

> My dreaming soul gets under sail
> For a distant heaven.[20]

> We will fly without truce or rest
> Toward the paradise of my dreams.[21]

What is here uncovered to the gaze is not a distinct eschatological future, toward which the soul progresses as toward the termination of its pilgrimage. There is nothing less celestial than Baudelaire's paradise. There is nothing less different from the "paradisical" states experienced on earth in the actuality of perception. The dream is simply a continued sensation. The future, even the eternal future, even the terminal paradise, is, on a far vaster scale, the sheer repetition of what vibrates in the senses, of what is already present in the mind. In the same way that the spatial expanse is, little by little, filled by the effusion of a perfume, so the temporal space is, little by little, filled with the diffusion of a dream. Thanks to this, time seems like a swelling instant which by this swelling extends on all sides its own fixed quality. "In the depths of her adorable eyes, distinctly, I always see the hour, always the same, a vast hour, solemn, as big as space, without divisions of minutes or of seconds;—an immobile hour."[22]

But sound, color, scent, do not only grow in the direction of the future. The moment they begin to vibrate, that is to say to project their resonances toward the future, they instigate in the depths of the soul the echo of an analogous movement accomplished in the past. When the colors flame, when sounds resound, and perfumes become fragrant, corresponding forces make echo to them in the depth of memory. It is as though sensations had the faculty of extending their vibrations in the direction, not only of the future, but of the past; or, more exactly, as if the present was, at one time, both the point of departure of a movement orientated toward the future, and the point of arrival of a different and yet identical movement, coming from the past; so that, prolonging itself ahead, the present finds itself, at one and the same time, and without changing its substance, the prolongation of an anterior life which, like a wave coming up from behind, pours over it its undulation and its murmuring:

> . . . Sometimes one finds an ancient scent bottle that remembers,
> From which springs, alive, a returning soul.
> A thousand thoughts slept there, funereal chrysalis,
> Softly trembling in the heavy shadows,
> Loosening their wings to take flight . . .
> Behold, here comes the intoxicating memory, flying
> In the troubled air . . .[23]

. . . Fugacious and striking impressions, even more striking in their repetition since they are more fugacious, which sometimes follow an exterior symptom, a kind of warning like the sound of a bell, a musical note or a forgotten perfume, which are themselves followed by an event similar to an event already known and which occupied the same place in a chain of events previously perceived . . .[24]

Exactly as Baudelaire anticipates Proust in the description of the phenomenon of affective memory (and its analogy with paramnesia), the intention guiding him is quite different. Baudelaire does not in the least wish to establish, outside of time, an identity of essences between the separated moments, but, on the contrary, to suggest that in the interval between the moments, time has never ceased to reign, an always-identical time. Repetition proves the identity of duration; a duration constituted by the continuity of a resonance, sometimes so feeble that it is imperceptible, and sometimes given its original strength by the action of a sensorial event of the same nature. All the sensations of the past continue to last and to quiver in our depths, sometimes so faintly that we no longer perceive them. But let the same toll of the bell, the same musical note, make itself heard once more, let the same perfume fill our nostrils, then remembrance again takes up the pristine sensation, and, crossing the intermediary temporal expanses, "comes back" in us, bringing us as well as its particular quivering, the consciousness of the field of duration which it has never ceased to traverse.

In time as in space the phenomenon of vibration therefore appears as a double extension: extension of the vibrating object, and of the place where it is vibrating. On the one hand, Baudelaire, in imagination, follows the dilation of all that he perceives, so that any object becomes susceptible, to his eyes, of an immense development, to the point that he imagines his mistress in the form of a giant who "grows freely in her terrifying games."[25] But on the other hand, and this is the more frequent, to the dilation of beings there is added the dilation of the expanse in which these beings inflate themselves, and this second dilation can coincide with the first, but can also differ from it in two ways. Sometimes the movement by which the resonances invade the expanses of space and of duration is less rapid than the elongation of the expanse itself. The wave of images is as though outstripped by the expansion of the field in which they unfold. They propagate themselves within a field whose limits are fleeing away. And sometimes, too, the movement of expansion appears as if realized in the interior of a space and a time already extended, so that beyond this space and time which have already been invaded there are still a space and a duration infinitely to be invaded, and in spite of their effort to fill up these expanses, the images constantly find before them an unoccupied zone. It little matters that this impression in Baudelaire is due—as with De Quincey—to a narcotic. It is not the cause that is important here, but the effect. The "monstrous growth of time and space"[26] of which Baudelaire speaks, has as an outcome, not as with Balzac or Gautier, in the constitution of a filled world, filled with forms, but on the contrary, around these forms, of an empty world, or at least vacant, that is to say of a world not yet filled by them, in which, nevertheless, the gaze, continuing the trajectory followed by their movement of expansion, can go down. Such is "depth" in Baudelaire. When the poet writes:

> How beautiful are the suns in the warm evenings!
> How deep is space! how forceful, the heart![27]

He is not expressing the same thing three times, but causing thought to pass through three different and successive stages. In the first, the local and momentary beauty of the suns spreads out into the evenings and the regions they warm; in the second, beyond the evenings and these places, yet containing them, there is revealed the depth of space; finally, human emotion, more powerful than solar heat, goes from the nearby places, warmed by the sun, to that profound and remote expanse. Baudelaire's thought needs the support of concrete things to expand, but it expands beyond things. Now alone and without their support, it conquers space and duration:

> Involuntarily, I depicted for myself the delicious state of a man seized by a great reverie in absolute solitude, but in a solitude with an immense horizon and a vast diffused light; an immensity without other decoration than itself.[28]

> My soul seemed to me as vast and pure as the vault of the sky (with which I was enveloped); the remembrance of terrestrial things came only to my heart in a faint and diminished form . . .[29]

> . . . The sensation of space extended to the final conceivable limits.[30]

To have the sensation of space is not only to feel space, it is, thanks to the sensation of space, to feel oneself as vast as space. And what is true for space, is even more valid for duration. If for Baudelaire, the profundity of space is an "allegory of the profundity of time."[31] it is because time here is, so to speak, spread out so that its parts are placed side by side in the manner of parts of space; but it is also because Baudelaire's time, in ridding itself of almost all its specifically temporal characteristics—succession, change, discontinuity, irreversibility—and in substituting specifically spatial qualities, nevertheless never loses, in Baudelaire's eyes, its most authentically temporal characteristic, which is to be lived by a human being, to have as substance, a human experience. So that time being spatialized, it is all of lived experience which also shows itself as spatialized, and consequently, as identical to space. In rendering space sensible, Baudelaire's thought makes time visible, that is to say, renders the extent of existence visible. An existence not any longer confined to the narrow place and moment in which the primitive sensation arose; not even limited by the circumference of the spreading field of this sensation; but an entirely developed existence, without limits, immense, in which there is no completed past, nor future in suspense, since all is simultaneously present along the whole of its course.

In being able to experience the sensation of space, Baudelaire is able to experience as the same sensation, the sensation of duration; a duration which one must understand in the Bergsonian sense, which is to say a *lived duration,* with only this difference, but it is an essential one, that for Baudelaire the experienced duration is, not the opposite, but the same thing as space. In Baudelaire's experience, experienced duration and experienced space are exactly analogous one to the other. When Baudelaire speaks of the profundity of space and of the profundity of time, nothing is farther from his thinking than scientific or cosmic time and space. Profound space, profound time, are the same things as the profound milieu, or the "profound years." They are the time and space of Baudelaire's individual existence:

> There are moments in life when time and extent are more profound, and the feeling of existence immensely augmented.[32]

> In certain almost supernatural states of soul, the profundity of life is entirely revealed.[33]

> Hashish then extends itself, over all of life like a magic varnish, it solemnly colors it, and enlightens all its profundity.[34]

In the same profundity, time, space, and the feeling of existence coalesce. At the utmost of their limits, if they have limits, time and space appear as identical to life. To contemplate the exterior spectacle of space, or the interior spectacle of the "profound years," is always, directly or allegorically, to contemplate oneself, and by this contemplation, to possess oneself. As I possess the sky and the stars by lifting my gaze to them, I possess myself and all the instants in which I have been myself, in looking at them in my memories. Memory is, first of all, an amplitude. Nothing is more different from Proust's retrospective vision, always limited, intermittent, and fragmentary. In his happiest, most forceful moments, Baudelaire's vision hovers far above existence.

This continuity of existence has the smooth amplitude of a plain or a sea. It has the marvelous simplicity of free space. But this simplicity engenders a complication. For I am at the same time he who contemplates, and the object of this contemplation. On the one hand, I exist in the place and the moment in which I am looking, and on the other hand, I see my own look traversing and possessing an expanse and a duration that are still myself. So that the feeling of my existence doubles and even triples itself. I am he whom I see; I am he who is seen, sometimes at the extremity of the line of my look; and I am he who, by the movement of the vision, is able, in some way, to rejoin and see myself. When Baudelaire writes a phrase like this one: "He looks with a certain melancholy delight across the profound years and audaciously plunges into infinite perspectives,"[35] in this apparently simple phrase, three different states of the same being are, in the most complex fashion, evoked and linked: Baudelaire as a melancholy spectator, placed in a certain moment, as though on a shore; Baudelaire as a distant object identified with the profound years, and a third Baudelaire who, by an audacious movement, links the Baudelaire of the shore and the Baudelaire of the distance and the horizon. This movement is very exactly a movement of *perspective,* an act by which, to reach profundity, one opens an avenue in the visual field across which the gaze travels. The magical perspective which Baudelaire disposes in his landscapes, exactly corresponds to the perspectives which he arranges in the "pictures" of his own existence. As in Baudelaire's descriptions "one sees in the depths oriental towns and architectures,"[36] thus in Baudelaire's reminiscences "the profundity of life" seems to be "bristling with multiple problems."[37] In the depths of space, in the depths of time, the same "serrated scenes" are limned.[38]

The amplification of life therefore becomes a complication, a multiplication. Life is not only an infinite expanse, but also an infinity of possible rapports between the various points included in this expanse. Even more, these infinite rapports are not fixed rapports, but changing rapports. At every moment, the new sensation which I experience, the new place in which I find myself, the movement, sensorial or intellectual, to which I lend myself, modify all the relations which I maintain with my entire life. Space, time, life are not therefore the simple continuity I thought myself able to embrace with a glance and possess once and for all. I am now aware of the infinite variations which all the aspects of my existence can offer. I discover myself, not only in my profundity, but in my multiplicity. I am not only an extent of existence, but a number.

As time lived, finally identified itself for Baudelaire with space lived, so, for him, space lived became identified, in the end, with a multiplication of the self, with, so to speak, a *number lived.* "Number," Baudelaire said, "is a translation of space."[39] And elsewhere: "The proportions of the being and of time are disarranged by the innumerable multitude and intensity of feelings and ideas."[40] Wine, hashish, sensation, excited imagination, all are "a way of multiplying the individuality."[41] In the same way that the total spread of existence is enlarged by the vibrating expansion of the sensations unfolding in it, so every moment and every place of existence are multiplied by the number of vibrations whose seat they are. It is not

only the whole which is extended, it is also every individual particle
at the interior of the whole. Baudelaire says that one must "lengthen
the hours by the multiplication of sensations."[42] They must also be
lengthened by their reverberation. As has been seen with respect to
the resonance of the past, sensations not only have the power of prolonging the vibrations into the future, they also have the capacity
of awaking at a distance, in the profundity of the past, analogous
resonances. The multiplication of existence is therefore due to the
fact that, like a ricocheting stone, the sensation repeats its bound
along the whole surface of the being. But, differently from the stone,
sensation can simultaneously multiply its ricochet in all the spatial
and temporal dimensions of living. The moment it vibrates, it
vibrates here and there, near and far, in the future as in the past.
It is a particular happening, and yet a universal one, since it manifests itself simultaneously in the most diverse points of existence.
Such is for Baudelaire the phenomenon of *echo,* or reverberation.
It is only possible because, on the one hand, thanks to the continual
spreading of the vibration, the poet takes cognizance of the totality
of the vibrating extent; but also because, on the other hand, against
this background, he perceives particular notes, which are emitted or
sent back by different points. Every one of them sends out a call to
which from another point, from all points, there replies the same
sonorous appeal:

Like long echoes which mingled from afar . . .[43]
It is a cry repeated by a million sentinels . . .[44]

Baudelaire's greatest verses are those which express reverberation.
Reverberation of sounds, colors, light, reverberation of various happenings in life, which, at a distance one from another, send to one
another a strange, and yet familiar call, since it is always the characteristic call of the same being. So much so, that of all the diversities
of tone, shades, forms, and feelings, which cross and meet one another, only the better accentuate by their diversity the "shadowy and
profound unity" of the mental space. Distance separates them, but
unites them too, since it is a traversed distance. And this distance
crossed and recrossed and rendered visible, by the thousand movements which are accomplished in it, is not an anonymous space, it is
the very space of the being, the whole of its spatial and temporal
dimensions. "Intensity, sonority, limpidity, vibrativity, profundity
and reverberation in space and in time,"[45] all these different qualities which Baudelaire enumerates in the famous passage of the

Fusées, and which are the qualities by means of which images of the tangible world, and, carried by these, the intelligence of man, take possession of the exterior world, these are also the qualities thanks to which he takes possession of himself, of all of himself, i.e., of the whole of his existence, recognizing at one and the same time its diversity and its unity:

> Let us suppose a beautiful expanse of nature in which everything becomes verdant, lurid, freely sparkled with dust and light. . . . Shadows slowly change, chasing before them or extinguishing tones, as the moving light makes others to stand out. These reflect back and forth to one another, and, modifying their qualities by glazing them with transparent and borrowed qualities, *multiply to infinity their melodious marriages.* . . . This great symphony of today, which is the eternal variation of the symphony of yesterday, this succession of melodies, in which variety always comes out from infinity, this complicated hymn is called color.[46]

This complicated hymn may be called also life. Desperate though its elements may be, numerous as may be the play of their reflections and echoes, a same *accent,* a same *general color* forms "a concert agreeable or dolorous, yet logical and without dissonances."[47] The infinite multiplication of sensations, of images, of thoughts along the whole of a life, far from hiding its harmony, reveals and even accomplishes it.

II

> From these luminous pictures an intoxicating *vapor* arises which soon *condenses itself* into desires and regrets.[48]

What Baudelaire says here of Delacroix's pictures, applies equally to his own life. For he who represents his own life to himself as the ascension and expansion of an ensemble of images, finally sees these dissipate themselves into vapor at the zenith of their motion. Then thought, deserted, falls back on itself and is consumed with regrets: "A *vaporization* and a *centralization* (or condensation) of the Self. All is there."[49]

All is there, and nothing is there, for everything has vanished into the distance. Nothing is left but an impoverished center, deprived of its irradiating power. The vaporization of existence is, indeed, the extreme limit of the movement by which Baudelaire tries to match space. A spatialized existence is a vaporized existence. It becomes diluted in magnitude and in number. It pulverizes itself into such dust that it no longer has either forms, or dimensions, nor any recognizable characteristics. It is at one and the same time immense and imperceptible. In one sense it is everything, since it is disseminated everywhere; in another, it is nothing, since it is nothing more than dust and smoke. Or if, in some corner of space there still survives an image, this image is no longer a growing force, but a diminishing one. Its movement of expansion has become a movement of separation. As in Lamartine, Nerval, or Poe, in Baudelaire there is a general phenomenon of the dissolution of living forces. They vanish at the horizon in a mist of light. The sound, even the scent of things, and the echoes and reflections which generally last more than they, soon are no more than shadows. Through propagating themselves in space, they lose in it, degree by degree, the power of their vibration and their reverberation. In the expanse which they filled, which they animated, there is nothing left but a whirlwind of volatile essences. Dissolving themselves into vapor, they dissipate themselves into space. Everything empties itself out into windings, becoming fainter and more attenuated. Such is the phenomenon which Baudelaire describes at the beginning of *Harmonie du soir:*

> Here now is the time when, vibrating on its stem,
> Every flower *evaporates* like the fume of incense;
> Sounds and perfumes *turn* in the evening air,
> As in the dizzy langour of a melancholy waltz . . .[50]

Vaporization is therefore the decomposition and the disappearance of the mental world, at the extreme limit of its excentric development. In the final analysis, everything is dissolved in space. Everything, too, is dissolved in forgetfulness. How many times has Baudelaire described this last image, trembling in itself, which things project, before vanishing in the abyss of time?

> The traveller . . . turns back in the evening toward the country crossed in the morning, and remembers, with tenderness and sadness, the thousand fantasies which filled his head while he was traversing these lands, *now evaporated into horizons.*[51]

The vaporized lands are the expanses of time and space. They constitute a horizon, that is to say, a distant limit, beyond which the gaze may not diffuse itself and from which he who gazes is separated. Very far away a sort of circular barrier forms itself which the eye barely reaches, and which it cannot pierce. And yet it is beyond this barrier, in the distance, in the past, that happiness and life have withdrawn:

> I think of the Negress, thin and consumptive,
> Trampling in the mud, searching, with a haggard eye,
> *Behind the immense wall of the fog,*
> The *missing* coco palms of superb Africa.[52]

Baudelaire's poetry is no longer a poetry of presence: the presence of things, the presence of oneself in the vibration of things, the presence of space. Behind the immense wall of the fog a universal retreat has occurred. The immensity is now only the immensity of an absence. Instead of being a joy, the dilation of time and space becomes a void, a loss and a suffering:

> Space inflated itself, so to speak, to infinity. But the expansion of time became an even more vivid anguish.[53]

> I feel enlarging in my self
> A yawning chasm; this chasm is my heart![54]

Here the chasm is absolute distance. The enlarging expanse is fleeing space; which flies, carrying with it everything one had distributed in it, that is to say, the contents of the mind. Behind the wall of the horizon, no doubt the luminous circle of spiritual life continues to enlarge, but on this side of that barrier remains a shrunken world to whose center one is nailed. To the immensity of what is far, is opposed the narrowness of what is near-by. To the plenitude of what existed and no longer exists is opposed the poverty of what now is:

> How big the world is by the light of the lamps!
> In the eyes of memory, how small it is![55]

The sad beauty of these lines depends on the reversal of terms. For if the cramped circle of the lamp had in the old times been equal to the vast circumference of an appetite which alone the universe could satisfy, the immensity of this universe is now reduced to the periphery of a remembrance which can no longer dilate itself.

Baudelaire's impotence is the impotence of the being who cannot extend himself, because he has extended himself too far, because all his imagination and even will power have evaporated all around, in the distance, in peripheric space:

Suppose you are seated and smoking. Your attention will linger a little too long on the clouds of blue smoke coming from your pipe. The idea of a *slow, successive and eternal evaporation* will take possession of your spirit, and soon you will apply this idea to your thoughts, to your way of thinking. By a singular equivocation, by a kind of transposition or intellectual quid pro quo, *you will feel yourself evaporating* . . .[56]

Tobacco, wine, opium, dreams, all vivid sensation, all effort of the expansive imagination ends, in the long run, in the exhaustion of the will. All that "is atomized, so to speak, and *disperses* individual energy."[57] — "You have *thrown your personality to the four winds of heaven,* and now you have difficulty in reassembling and *concentrating* it."[58]

Fallen back on himself, Baudelaire tries to reassemble himself. He meditates on Emerson's words, which later on will also fascinate Rilke: *"The hero is he who is immovably* centered."[59] — "The inclination toward productive *concentration,"* Baudelaire writes, "should replace, in a matured man, the love of wastage."[60] Yet if he seeks to concentrate himself, it is to find again, thanks to concentration, the faculty of amplifying himself, and, consequently, of volatilizing himself once more: "The more man concentrates himself," he again writes, "the more he is apt to dream *amply, profoundly."*[61]

Now, we have seen that, to dream amply, profoundly, is precisely to disperse, in the long run, one's energy in amplitude and in profundity. From concentration to dispersion, and so on, by an infinitely renewed processus, the soul exhausts itself, like a fish which the fisherman maneuvers at the end of his line. This fisherman is Satan. His prey is the soul; and to "lead" it, all he needs to do is to "tire" it. Or, to use another image which expresses the same process of dissolution of the will:

> On the pillow of evil there is Satan Trismegist
> Who for long rocks our charmed mind
> And the rich metal of our will
> Gets all vaporized by this expert chemist.[62]

Dissolution, vaporization, are indeed also terms for chemistry and alchemy. In any case, the soul is the captive of a fatal movement. In place of the free world in which the imagination joyously moves, a prison space stands out. It is the same space, but inverted, a travesty, hideously transformed.

As in the space of the dream, vibrations propagate themselves there by successive undulations, going from the center to the circumference:

> For who can calculate the force of reflection and of repercussion of any incident in the life of a dreamer? Who can think, without trembling, *of the infinite enlarging of circles in the spiritual waves agitated by a stone of chance?*[63]
> . . . All action, hurled into the whirlwind of universal action, is irrevocable and irreparable in itself . . .[64]

Thus errors and vices have the same diffusive and reverberating force as dreams of beauty and of paradise. They project, into the spaces of the spirit, no less faithful and unalterable images of ourselves than those of our purest feelings. The expansion of our dreams ends not only in the volatilization of our will, but also, at the same time, to our incapacity to direct our dreams, and consequently to the horrible metamorphosis of these, beyond our reach, in a mental universe over which we have no influence except by the ugliness of phantoms which, despite ourselves, we project into it. In the interior of the circle circumscribed by the "immense wall of fog," everything which remains of expansion is the expansion of an unwholesome and even demoniac force, the swelling of a carrion, the multiplication of the worm and of the evil:

> One would have said that the corpse *puffed* by a vague
>   breathing,
> Lived by *multiplying* upon *itself*.[65]

The bloating of the carrion exactly corresponds to the amplification of the paradisical dream. It reveals the frightening mutation of the happy circle into a "tragic circle."[66] The "divine essence of the vicious circle"[67] has now become an infernal essence. And this circle itself, like its analogous circle of paradise, is made up of a plurality of vibrating, whirling images. They draw the spirit into their whirling:

> We imitate, horror! the spinning top and the ball
> In their waltz and their bounds; even in our sleep
> Curiosity torments and rolls us over . . .[68]

> Doubt environs him, and ridiculous Fear,
> Hideous and multiform, circles around him.[69]

Turning around themselves and turning around ourselves, curiosity, passions, evil ideas, form a circular movement which not only encloses us in its vertigo, but which also constitutes a sort of mobile screen beyond which our gaze and our will cannot go. The sky lowers. The horizon shrinks. To the universal movement of expansion which opened and uncovered the surrounding expanses, an inverse movement of constriction and obstruction succeeds. No one has more often or more tirelessly described the closing of the horizons than Baudelaire: "Impermeable horizon,"[70] "black lid of the great stew-pot,"[71] "splenetic cupola of the sky,"[72] "blood-red horizon walled in on all sides,"[73] these are some of the terms by which he has described the circumscription of space of which, like Poe, he has experienced a horror, but whose tragic conditions he has been incapable of utilizing. For, differently from Poe, Baudelaire cannot resign himself to forgetting the blue horizon and free space. Or, if he accepts or even calls for forgetfulness, it is not the better to accommodate himself to the "narrow" life, which is the only one possible in the monstrously reduced circle in which he is forced to live. Behind the wall of fog he *knows* that the coco palms of superb Africa are balancing, and if he is trampling in the mud, it is because he is searching, with eyes that no longer see, a vanished transcendence:

> When the heavy lowering sky presses down like a lid
> On the moaning spirit, the prey of long despair,
> And when from the horizon *embracing the whole circle*
> It pours out a black light more sad than all nights;
> When the earth is changed into a humid dungeon,
> Where Hope, like a bat,
> Brushes the walls with its timid wing
> Knocking its head on the rotting ceilings . . .[74]

Like a blind man whose gaze searches the sky, or a bat knocking itself on the vault of a dungeon, an obstinate hope prevents Baudelaire from renouncing the very act which is, for him, creator of beauty and joy, the act of expansion. The bat is no different from the other symbolic beings, birds, swimmers, ships, by which Baudelaire expresses the movement of the mind in surrounding space; unless it is that, knocking its head and brushing the walls, it struggles against an insurmountable limitation. If it continues to fly, it is not to explore the interior surfaces of its hovel, but to escape at any price, since a life without space, without expansion, is not a life, but a death.

A last method of evasion is left. If expansion is no longer possible, if, all around the being, the blood-red horizon is walled in on all sides, if the circle is well closed, and the shadows black, if "in the mirey and leaden Styx no eye of Heaven ever penetrates,"[75] and if the eye of the damned never pierces, around and above the Styx, the leaden cover of Heaven, there is still a possible solution, that which consists no longer in extending oneself but in digging down, not in diffusing oneself but in thrusting down. For Baudelaire as for Nerval, the last possible movement is the descent, a movement, too, that is circular, made up of increasingly narrow circles, approaching more and more closely to the center:

> It seemed to him, every night, that he was going down indefinitely into abysses without light, beyond all known profundities, without the hope of being able to go back.[76]

If Baudelaire chooses hell's direction, it is, without any doubt, and as he has often explained, in part because of the fascination exerted on him by evil. But the beauty of evil, quite simply, is the beauty of movement, the final possible movement. At the extremity of this narrowing movement there is, as Baudelaire knows, the terminal fixity, the absolute paralysis of the being which, like Dante's great damned, finds himself situated in the center, because the center is the dead point. But the descent of the "dizzy stairway"[77] is still one more kind of dizziness. It is the final turning movement, the last whirling possession of space which is permissible: the final stage before the *point* at which one stops and at which one immobilizes oneself forever.

III

The failure is therefore double and total. Imagination has evaporated, the will is paralyzed. Baudelaire is the twice-defeated being, twice wounded:

> ... The wounded one who is forgotten
> On the shores of a lake of blood, under a great
> pile of dead,
> And who dies without moving, in immense efforts.[78]

Who dies without moving! Rather, who dies from not being able to move! The supreme effort made by Baudelaire is an effort to get up, to walk once more, to move in space once again.

For Baudelaire can renounce neither movement nor space. He cannot renounce the possession, by movement, of space. If it is indeed impossible to live in infinite space because, through an infinite series of motions, one disseminates there one's life, and if it is no less impossible to live in constricted space, because at the extremity of this constriction there is no longer any movement, nor, consequently, life, is there no way of conceiving a space in which one could move without losing oneself, and concentrate oneself without becoming immobilized in it? A space which would no longer be the immense expanse, in which the imagination exhausts itself because nothing there upholds the will; and which would no longer be the interior profundity in which the will sinks as in quicksand, because it lacks the expansive force and elevating force of the imagination. A space neither immense nor narrow, in which there would be neither dissemination, nor immobilization, in which expansion and concentration, instead of being movements going in opposite directions, would be conjugal and harmonized movements.

But how to conjugate these contrary movements? For it is not a case here, of finding the middle way between two contraries. One must be at once both concentrated and expansive, concentrated without having ceased to be expansive, and expansive without having ceased to be concentrated. Even more, in simultaneously accomplishing this, the two movements must mingle, they must have a common ground, a common space, yet this community should not imply some restriction in their own actions. In other terms, and paradoxical though this may be, the diffusion of the spirit must become a directed diffusion, and its concentration must become, equally and inversely, a diffused concentration.

Thus Baudelaire conceives a double movement, all of whose characteristics would always be associated with opposite traits: a movement at once both sinuous and rectilinear, diverse and simple, intentional and imaginative, in a space at once infinite and finite, vast and narrow, distant and near. This double space, possessed by a double movement, is not inconceivable if one considers the elements which compose it.

First, the point. The point is center. It is without dimensions, without imagination. It is pure will. It is fixed. The point is the final place, absolute concentration, the extremity of the movement of profundity, the eternal stop in a place without space.

But it is also the initial place, the line's starting point.

The straight line is infinitely superior to the point. It is the point which moves out of its inertia and directs itself. It is still concentration, since it has but one dimension, but a moving concentration which projects itself in space. Nevertheless it is "dry and naked."[79] It is like a stick. Going straight along its way, it disregards what is not on its way. It traverses space without possessing it. It is direction without diffusion.

The curved line is therefore preferable to the straight. It is, as Leonardo and Hogarth said, the line of beauty. Of all the curves, the most perfect is that of the circle. But first "there is no perfect circumference"[80] or, if there is one, it is in the world of the absolute ideal, in which pure beauty "hates the movement which displaces the lines."[81] For the circle is without movement. It is an achieved curve, a movement at its termination, the final point co-incident with the initial point. No more than the center, can the circumference satisfy Baudelaire, for in one case as in the other, there is not possession but only determination in space, not a movement but a fixation. Of all the thinkers and poets who have meditated on the figure of the center and the circle, Baudelaire is the only one who has refused to give in to the magic of a representation which is nevertheless the most adequate symbol of the ideal (divine or infernal). And if he rejects it, it is precisely because it is the symbol of the attained ideal, the ideal in oneself and not in its moving rapport with the spirit which approaches it. Baudelaire therefore detested the circle, he doesn't even want to think of it as the circle: "The circumference," he said, "which is the ideal of the curved line, is comparable to the analogous figure composed of an infinity of straight lines . . ."[82] The circle is therefore only a polygon. There is, therefore, no *real* circle. There are not even figures analogous to the circle, that is to say, made of simple contours, of a continued stroke enclosing a form: ". . . a good drawing is not a hard line, cruel, despotic, immobile, enclosing a shape like a straight-jacket; the drawing should be like nature, living and in motion . . ."[83]

The outlining line is therefore the deadest, the least natural of all. Like the straight line, it is the symbol of a will without imagination. Worse still, it is like the central point, a will without movement, stopped.

Hence the sinuous line, dear to the artists of the eighteenth century, is the only remaining one. It is more alive, more imaginative. Humanly speaking, it is the most beautiful of all. None better than Baudelaire has detailed the graces of the sinuous line. Capricious, undulating, varied, digressive and complicated, it is "a language in which you read the agitation and the desire of souls,"[84] "the undulations of reverie and the jolts of consciousness."[85] Made up of concavities and convexities which "complete and pursue one another,"[86] they never stop; always, and differently, they begin again and, by their arabesques and detours, reveal all the infinite possibilities of direction, which are the riches of space, and all the successive variability that is the substance of time. It is at once space and time; space, because it flows everywhere, puts everything in rapport with everything else, covers everything like a net; time, because, always being different from itself, it gives a part to all the successive points of its course. And finally, since it essentially is transitory and yet persists, and is discontinuously continuous, it is a number, it makes of space and of time the marvelous simultaneous and successive blossoming of a multiple life:

It is an immense joy to elect to live in plurality, in undulation, in movement, in the fugitive and the infinite.[87]

But to elect, thanks to the sinuosity of the imaginative movement, to live in number, in time, in space, isn't it, once again, to diffuse oneself, and consequently, to evaporate, in number, in time, in space? An absolutely sinuous line, a purely imaginative movement, is no longer, in the long run, a line, a continuous movement, an aggrandizement and an enriching of forms, just as an infinite multiplication of points of color is no longer color. Once more, everything runs the risk of evaporating and of leaving the mind in the middle of things, fallen, immobile and without communication with its vanished universe. Unless the expansive movement of the spirit can be tied in some manner to a voluntary movement; unless the essential erratic thrust of the sinuous imagination is sustained or contained by a rectilinear tension and intention. The only means of possessing space, time, number, is to link the sinuous movement to the rectilinear movement, the effusion of fancy to the voluntary effort, the curved line to the straight.

For the straight line, as has been seen, is not pure concentration. It is a point which moves, a stretched energy which projects itself, which attains and traverses space. And the sinuous line is not a completed line, a perfect circumference, but an always moving aggregate of incomplete circumferences, which move up toward perfection without ever fixing themselves in it and without ever renouncing attaining it. The straight and the curve, the straight which upholds the curve, the curve which interlaces itself with the straight, together form a movement at once voluntary and poetic, which traverses and possesses space.

A straight line around which is wound a sinuous line, such is therefore the form, even the formula, of the poetic activity, of the possession of space, of happiness, of the poem.

For Goethe, this took the form of the first plant, original, typical, that is to say, of nature; for Baudelaire, this was to be the form of art, that is to say, counter-nature.

This is already, in a slight way the form of the chandelier, suspending its crystalline complications at the end of a stem:

> What I have always found most beautiful in a theater, in my childhood, and even now, is the chandelier,—a beautiful luminous object, crystalline, complicated, circular and symmetrical.[88]

Above all, it is the symbol of woman:

> To see you walk in cadence,
>   Beautiful in your abandon,
> One would say a serpent dancing
>   At the end of a stick.[89]

> Even when she walks one would imagine
>   that she dances,
> Like those long serpents which the sacred jugglers
> Agitate in cadence at the end of their long sticks.[90]

Symbol of woman, but even more generally, of the human being, since the complete human being is at once man and woman, serpent and stick, will and laxity. For Baudelaire, the superior genius is the man-woman, the man "bathed in the gentle atmosphere of the woman,"[91] and who, surrounding his virility with this flowing, creates for himself, a universe that, too, is male and female, an androgynous universe.

A symbol, therefore, of the complete man, but the complete man is not the stationary man, on the contrary, it is man on the march, the wayfarer:

> To be away from home, and yet to feel at home everywhere; to see the world, *to be at the center of the world* and be hidden from the world. . . . The lover of the universal life is a kaleidoscope gifted with consciousness, which, with every one of its movements, represents multiple life and the moving grace of all the elements of life.[92]

The wayfaring man is a moving center which traverses and links the circumference, incessantly re-begun, caused by the eddies of the crowd. The association of the straight with the sinuous line is therefore, in general, the association of all moving objects in space, since—around the straight line depicted by a specific object—space, by an immense and eurhythmic process, varies and joins all its positions:

> . . . The infinite and mysterious charm which lies in the contemplation of a ship, especially a ship in motion, is held . . . in the successive multiplication and in the generation of all the imaginary curves and forms operated in space by the real elements of the object.[93]

Space possessed by the conjunction of the straight line and the sinuous line is therefore a rhythmic space, a musical space. With the rectitude of the motive are mingled "arabesques of sounds."[94] Thus in an episode of *Paradis artificiels* a guitar player begins to *improvise around* the music of a violin: "The guitar allowed itself to be *guided* by it, and it splendidly and maternally *dressed* the slender nudity of its sounds."[95]

Imagination clothes the nakedness of the will, and in dressing it, it endows it with a splendor which is made up of the possession and the joy of space; as the will guides the imagination, and in giving it a direction, prevents it from dissolving, by making of it a directed convolution, similar to the smoke coming from the poet's pipe which, like his poetry, unrolls and turns around a thought, giving it grace and depth:

> I am the pipe of an author . . .
> I interlace and lull his soul
> In the blue and mobile network
> Which mounts from my flaming mouth.[96]

The poetical act is therefore a spiral that is wound and unwound around a directed thought. It is a thyrsus:

> Around this staff, in capricious meanderings, stems and flowers play and frolic, some sinuous and transient, some bent like bells or over-turned goblets. And an astonishing glory springs from this complexity of tender or brilliant lines and colors. Would one not say that the curved and the spiral line court the straight line, dancing around it in mute adoration? . . . The staff is your will, straight, firm, and immovable; the flowers are the voyaging of your fancy around your will . . .[97]

A moving complexity of successive circumferences is sketched along the length of a center which, itself, moves. This is the symbol of poetry, and this is the symbol of life:

> . . . The thousand circumstances which envelop the human will are a circumference in which the will is enclosed; but this circumference is moving, alive, spinning, changing every day, every minute, every second in its circle and its center.[98]

In the symbol of the thyrsus, which Baudelaire has borrowed from De Quincey,[99] the author of the *Fleurs du mal* finds the most adequate expression of his enterprise. Not the symbol of the perfect circle, closed upon itself, because this form represents a divine beauty, inhuman, an achievement impossible for the double and imperfect beings which we are; not the symbol of the central point, the sign of a concentration no less inhuman and rightly satanic; but the symbol of the center and the circle both moving, a true representation of imperfect and human beauty which, by an effort of will and through forms always unfinished, lifts itself like an immense twisted column toward perfection, and, in so lifting itself, envelops and carries space in its ascending movement. For human beauty is of a double composition, made up of "an external element, invariable . . . and of a relative element, circumstantial."[100] The eternal, invariable element is the projection of the straight line of the will; the relative, circumstantial element is the sinuous expansion, yet maintained and sustained, of the imagination. Both lifting up together, these two lines give the poet his space.

MALLARMÉ'S

PROSE POUR DES ESSEINTES

I

Hyperbole! from my memory
Triumphantly unable art thou
To rise up, today a script of gramarye
In a book clothed with iron:

For I install by science
The hymn of spiritual hearts
In the work of my patience,
Atlases, herbals and rituals.

IF THE POEM is dedicated to Des Esseintes, i.e., to the hero of
Huysmans' famous novel, *A rebours* (published in 1884), it is because it is akin to the sort of poetry Des Esseintes professes to love
more than any other, the poetry of low Latinity and the Middle
Ages. It is a *prose,* or a sequence, in the sense of a Church prose,
such as the *Salutaris Hostia* or the *Dies Iræ;* hymns sung during
Mass, usually between the Epistle and the Gospel. Thus two of the
main characteristics of the poem are from the very first made apparent, its memorative quality, or the solemn recalling to the mind
of a great event of long ago, and, secondly, its ritualistic or even
magical aspect, the part it plays in the performing of rites through
which some supernatural deed is accomplished. Such is the precise
purpose of Mallarmé's poem: to create something equivalent to the
ancient religious hymn, to be tantamount to what Mallarmé calls
elsewhere "liturgical remembrances."[1] Like the medieval prose,
Mallarmé's poem will be an incantation directed toward a transcendence. Or, more exactly, its object will be to answer the question: Is such an incantation still possible?

Will a rite become exteriorized through being practiced . . .?
One needs, on certain evenings, to read, as I did, the exceptional

book of Huysmans, in order to understand that the old rite must be adapted or transferred to some personal hobby.[2]

Mallarmé's poem is thus an adaptation or a transference of the Christian rites to the poet's personal preoccupation. It simultaneously borrows its form from the mediaeval tradition, and turns its back to this tradition. Unlike the ecclesiastical hymn, which it closely imitates, it does not aim toward an already established transcendence in order to make it come down upon earth, but it raises itself toward a nonexistent transcendence, in order to make it come to existence by the very act of the poem's rising.[3]

The poem, therefore, will be a rising, the rising of the poet's mind toward a heaven of his own. In the etymological sense of the word *hyperbole (uper,* beyond; *ballein,* to project), it will be a projection upward and outward. This excentric motion of the mind will have its starting point in the hypothetical conception of some transcendence, and its terminal point in the achievement of this transcendence by the elevation and expansion of the mind. Thus, this transcendence is, at the same time, something past and something future. It is past, since history bears witness that at one time a hyperbole was raised by the faith of men; and it is future, since in a time to come the poet will again attempt to raise a hyperbole. But in the meantime the marvelous hyperbolical motion cannot yet be accomplished. The hyperbole is unable yet to raise itself. Having raised itself in the past, destined to rise again in the future, the hymn now does not raise itself, and the poem does not exist, except in the form of the sealed word and the ironclad book. When the word is sealed and the book locked, the poem cannot be sung and the song cannot rise up. It is deprived of its magical power of elation and expansion; it is inert and dead, comparable to the genie of the Arabian Nights who, bottled up in a vase, cannot free himself nor expand.

Before the rising of the hyperbole there must be the preparation of the hyperbole. Before singing the hymn, the poet must *install* the hymn. He must place it in a text, in order to start from the text. This text is no longer the old-fashioned text of religious hymns or of books of gramarye. It is its modern counterpart, the poem: *"I say that between the ancient processes and the magic with which poetry persists, there is a secret likeness."* The poem, then, is a work of magic, a work of patience and alchemy (the expression *work of patience* is used by the alchemists to mean the *grand oeuvre,* or the transmutation of a vile metal into gold). But before this transmutation and elevation, there must be a preparation. The text of the poem is not the hyperbole, but the place from which the hyperbole will raise itself. It is not the alchemical operation, but the gathering, the fixing and the arranging of all the elements with the help of which the operation will be performed. Like the atlas, the herbal, and the ritual, it contains all the ingredients by the composition of which the work of patience will be completed. When it is completed, there will be no need anymore for science, patience, and craft. The period of installation will be at an end. Suddenly the future will not be the future anymore, but the actual present; the poem will not be any longer a dead world; the countries of the atlas will cover the earth, the dry flowers in the herbals will bloom again, and new prayers will arise from the rituals. The hymn, then, will be not only installed, but sung. And the song will rise up and expand. It will be a hyperbole, spreading triumphantly in space.

It is to this triumphant spreading of the hymn that Mallarmé invites us. This hymn will be the hymn of the future, but it will be also in the future the equivalent of the hymn of the past. Thus, in order to imagine what it will be, it is right to let it first appear in the aspect of a vision of the past.

II

We caused our face to wander
(For I maintain that we were two)
On many charms of the landscape
O Sister, comparing thine own to them.

What we distinguish in this first unfolding of the hymn, is primal harmony. In the far away past, in a time which is likened to the time of Eden or to the Golden Age, and which will be called, further down, the summer midday, or zenith, of existence, two beings wander in a garden. They are distinct from one another, yet, in another sense, they are one. There is a talker and there is a listener, somebody who is making comparisons and somebody who is compared. Yet the one who is compared has a sister-like resemblance to the one who is making the comparisons. Both walk with the same step, cast the same glance, have the same face. The unity of the two members of the couple is still reinforced by the use of the first person of the plural, *we*. Thus, what is suggested here is the image of a single person, walking alone but with his thoughts, talking to himself and comparing what is in his mind with what exists in the outside world. The theme is the conversation one holds with oneself, with the particular metaphysical and semantic problems which are implied by such an ordinary, and yet such a complex, action. If I speak to myself, and if I also listen to myself, am I really identical to myself in these two distinct operations? Besides, granted that what I transmit to myself is a faithful image of myself, will not this transmitted image be altered in the act of transmission? This is what happens each time an old idea comes to my mind, because, between the remoteness of the idea and the actuality of my mind, there is a distance of time which may be the cause of a misunderstanding. "We shall try to discover," says Mallarmé in 1869, "what effects the words would produce in us when *pronounced by the interior voice of our mind,* disposed as it is by a familiarity with the writings of the past, *if these effects are a long way off from the daily ones.*"[4] There is in the interior dialogue the risk that he who listens may be too far away from him who speaks, and that possessed by the present sense of the word he no longer comprehends its past sense. It is as if there were two interlocutors, one who is my old self, the other who is my present self; they may not belong to the same epoch, they may converse without being contemporaries, and the result of this discrepancy is the consciousness, not of an identity, but of a difference. Such is the customary experience of all thought that would like to remain *actual.* It finds out that in order to think itself it is mysteriously obliged to lose its actuality, to withdraw itself from itself in order to realize itself in an anterior distance.

However, such is not the case in the conversation which is described in this stanza. For, precisely, this conversation is not happening now, it is simply presented as having happened, that is to say, as having taken place in the mythical past. The mythical past, the time of Eden or of the Golden Age, is the only time which was not divided, where there was no *before* and no *after,* but an eternal Now. In that time there was always a perfect coincidence between what was said and what was heard. The spoken word and the perceived word had exactly the same meaning and were not distorted by time and distance. The harmony was perfect, the certainty absolute.

This is, then, the time of unison, and this is also the place of unison. The perfect harmony which exists between the two interlocutors, is constituted, not only by the fact that they live in the same time, but also by the fact that, perceiving the same objects, they move in the same place. To the temporal identity there corresponds a spatial identity. *This* is only truly equal to *that*, if *this* and *that* are both demonstratively related in the same way to a third term. Such is the mathematical proof of identity—the only truly satisfactory one. If, as it is said in this stanza, "we were two," and yet we "had only one face," we are assured of the oneness of this face only by the fact that both representations of this single entity bear the same relation to a third term. This term is *place*. In the exteriority of place the one who is talking and the one who is listening find a common relation. Comparing their own charms to the charms of the garden, they discover that these charms are the same. Therefore, they themselves are also the same. A landscape which is identical to themselves, reveals to themselves their own inner identity.

Self-consciousness, then, or the inner dialogue of the self with the self, is achieved by an identification of the self with the outside world. The world and the mind do not differ in the least, except in the fact that the former expresses the latter. Thanks to the outside reality of things, the mind can know itself. The world is a language with the aid of which the mind can speak and listen to itself, and identify itself with itself. Between inner and outer realities there can be made a comparison, which is an equation: *"Man,"* Mallarmé says, *"and his sojourn upon earth make a reciprocal exchange of proofs."*[5]

Everything, thus, is perfectly simultaneous in time and place. Everything, inside and outside, is immediately discovered as being the same. But this primal and essential comparison is nevertheless a motion: the discursive motion by which the mind goes from object to object, comparing their external charms with its own inner beauty. Hence, in the perfect harmony of identification, there is introduced the possibility of discord and dissension. The oneness of the mind is discovered only through the multiplicity of the charms of the garden; and it can be expressed only by an equal multiplicity of words, an enumeration.

III

The era of authority is troubled
When, without motive, it is said
Of this midday that our double
Unconsciousness investigates,

That, ground of the hundred irises, its site
—They know whether it really was—
Bears no name that is proclaimed
By the gold of the summer bugle.

The era of authority is troubled. Before this trouble of authority, which is also a trouble of authorship or of the relation of the poet with nature, the former lived harmoniously with the latter, enjoying a perfect understanding and rectitude of language, which were given him by the constant adequacy between his mind and all the objects of the outside world. There was no discrepancy between his thoughts, his words, and the things designated by his words. Now this era of authority, certainty, and orderliness comes abruptly to an end. Without any motive or positive advantage, carried away subconsciously or thoughtlessly by the pleasure it takes at investigating things, the mind introduces in the general harmony a grave disorder. First of all, this disorder becomes patent in the disposition of space. The unity of the garden is troubled. It becomes obscured by the very number of plants which grow in it. Each one attracts the attention of the mind, and therefore also distracts it from the whole. Each particular plant, each individual part in the totality of the garden, has to receive a distinct name, and in order to be so named, has to be separated from all the other plants and parts of the garden. So, instead of having only one garden and a single name for the whole of the garden, the mind now has an infinity of names, each of which designates a part, and none of them designates the whole. The outside world as a whole bears no name any longer. It has become anonymous, and therefore unthinkable. And what happens for the outside world, happens also for the self. Instead of enjoying the consciousness of its own identity, the mind now is aware only of the confused multiplicity of its thoughts.

Through the dangerous growth of science and language, the mind has lost touch with the simplicity of truth. It does not see the forest for the trees. It has also lost touch with itself. Within and without the mind, there is no longer any simplicity, but an endless proliferation of things and names.

To this parcelling of space there corresponds parcelling of time. Instead of keeping simultaneously under its eye all the charms of the landscape, the mind proceeds now from one to the other, in an essentially transitive manner. Moving toward new prospects, it leaves behind the old ones. These old prospects become therefore retrospects. What they fill up, bit by bit, is the past. The more rapidly the mind progresses in its investigation of things, the more quickly these things are named, catalogued and finally ranged in memory. There, they constitute an ever expanding demesne of things which are known and named. On the one hand, the mind constantly progresses, on the other hand, whatever is acquired by the means of this progress is immediately pushed into the past. Thus a growing distance appears between the actuality of the mind and the non-actuality of everything that is, or has been, thought by the mind.

IV

> Yes, in an isle the air charges
> With sight and not with visions,
> Each flower was growing larger
> Without our discussing it.
> So much so, immense, that each flower
> Ordinarily adorned itself
> With a lucid contour, a hiatus
> Which separated it from the gardens.

Suddenly, after the negation, we hear again the affirmation. After the description of obscurity and disorder, there is again a picture of certainty and harmony. But the affirmation which, with a great energy, is introduced here by the *yes* at the beginning of the sixth stanza, does not proclaim the renewal of the Golden Age. It simply re-emphasizes its past existence. It cannot be denied, Mallarmé concedes, that now science and language proceed by successive visions and expressions. But it cannot be denied, either, that, once, science and language, far from proceeding successively, had the power of possessing truth instantaneously and intuitively; and that this intuition revealed the fundamental identity of the mind and the world. Today, it is true, this intuition is not possible any longer; it does not constitute any more an integrant part of the present experience. But it existed undeniably in the past, and therefore it still constitutes an integrant part of the past. The past is like an island, seen far-away in the great sea of existence, an island made of time and space, the midday of old, a place distinct and remote from the present moment, but in which it is still possible to find the perfect harmony between being and thought, and between thought and language. There, hyperbolically, everything that exists can be seen in a larger, clearer, and simpler form, without it being necessary to consider successively all its aspects or enumerate all its charms. Thus in the past, in the contemplation of the past by the means of memory, I can still rediscover and reconstitute the old harmony, I can detach myself from the actual and betake my mind into a spiritual island in which whatever is thought by me is named, and, by being named, becomes a reflection and an explanation of my own self. The past, or, at least, the ennobled and enlarged version of it which is given to me by memory, is the true and only place in which I can still find between me and nature a universal analogy. There the intelligibility of all the objects of the external world still provides me with a language by the means of which I can communicate with myself and understand myself. Therefore self-knowledge still depends on my relation with nature, but with a nature which does not belong to the present—a past nature. The language which I use in order to communicate with myself is borrowed from a world which, it is true, does not exist any longer, since it is past, but which necessarily still subsists in my mind. All around me, at an increasingly greater distance, in increasingly larger forms, there are flowers which do not grow in any garden of today. Indeed, they are separated from today and from any actual place by the hiatus of time, but they have continued to grow immensely in the immense site of my thought. These flowers are *thought* flowers, recollected flowers; they are essentially non-actual and such that they are absent from all present gardens or nosegays. But precisely because they are abstracted from the reality of today, and yet present to the mind which names them, they have become mental things, verbal entities, with the aid of which the mind can speak. Each object of this new world is susceptible to being detached and considered independently. Each thing is not a thing any more, it is not imprisoned, as things are, in the confused multiplicity of other things. It can be isolated, considered in itself, because it is not a thing, but simply the abstract notion of a thing. Thus it appears in the mind, miraculously separated from everything else, defined by a lucid contour. The universe in which I find the exact equivalent of my thought is a universe which is not different any more from my thought. It is not made up of existing objects, but of nonexistent objects, that is to say, of objects about which, when I realize that they have existed, I assume that they can exist again. They are past and future, but never present; therefore they are purely mental. Consequently the equivalence which I establish between nature and myself is not any longer an equivalence between what I think and what is existing, but an equivalence between what I think and what is no more or not yet, but, being no more or not yet, is still present in my thought. My thought is not to be identified any longer with an external world, but with a world which, having become entirely internal and ideal, is now simply the content of my mind. Everything else having been eliminated, I compare myself to my spiritual objects, i.e., to my Ideas.

V

Glory of the long desire, Ideas,
Everything in me was elated at seeing
The family of the Irideae
Rise up to this new duty . . .

The world in which I find the exact equivalent of my self is a world of ideas—a world made up exclusively of my ideas. In realizing this, I realize the most glorious progress of my mind. The long search, undertaken in order to find in things the exact equivalent of my thoughts, has brought me finally to the point of retaining only the reflection of these things in my mind. Born of my long desire, the ideas of things rise up to a new duty which does not consist any longer in being, but in being thought. Out of the very depth of my thoughts I see the ideas springing, surging, growing, and invading the field of my spiritual space. Their growing is my growing, their propagation is my propagation. I rise up with them; I participate in the enlarging of their forms. Everything in me is elated at seeing them multiply their stalks and occupy a space more and more vast, in which my transfigured mind progresses and expands at the same rate. I had denied nature; I had forgotten its name. I had reduced it to anonymity. Now, I find it again, idealized, identical to my rising song. *"The idea grows only by means of its own negation,"* says Villiers de l'Isle Adam, quoting Hegel. *"Is not the continuous motion in the growing of trees and blades of grass the same as the one which makes the suns projecting their rings oscillate and jump out of themselves?"*[6] By the same motion, the Mallarméan prose or hymn oscillates and jumps out of itself in the cosmos of the mind. It is as if a *"metaphorical heaven were propagating itself around the thunderbolt of the verse,"*[7] or indeed a "turning fire of hymns."[8] The poem, Mallarmé says, is *"the enlarging of space by vibrations up to the infinite."*[9] And elsewhere: "Around this center of myself I sit like a sacred spider connected with all the threads already issued from my mind." The mind is a web of ideas, a network of all the crossing points at which ideas are connected with other ideas and with the central point, which is myself. Thoughts and words spread outward, like *"the reflection of a circular flight, high up, of jewels or souls,"*[10] enveloping in its circumvoluted play of light all the mental activities of the central self.

Such is the exaltation, the ecstasy of Mallarmé's poetry. This exaltation is, at the same time, glorious and solitary, since the glory it aims at has nothing to do with external fame. It is the spectacle offered by the self to the self, when it projects itself, so to speak, circularly, at a cosmic distance, but always in itself, in such a way as to be always able to bring back to itself the reflection of its hyperbolical image: "The self, projected, absolute!"[11] It is as if, in a room made up of mirrors, a prince would treat himself to a gala performance of which he would be at once the author, the audience, and the infinitely multiplied hero. Or as if, to use another hyperbolical image, a God, intending to create a world, would content himself with the display of all the ideas of that world, without ever passing to the act of creation.

The Mallarméan exaltation is a spectacle. It is primarily commanded by *sight*. But the universal flowering and scintillating of forms, irises, and rainbows, which is thus seen, is seen only inside the mind, and this sight is nothing but an in-sight, an introspection. Mallarmé's poetry is a mirror, the facets of which are disposed in such a way as to send back to the poet a single image—his own. Not the image, of course, of Stephane Mallarmé in the flesh, but of the spiritual being, which, through the disappearance of all individual features, becomes the anonymous subject of an action which is an elevation and an elation. Each reader of Mallarmé's poetry, each "spiritual heart" can, indeed, repeat for his own sake the same experience and, to use the expression of Gérard de Nerval, become thus the God of the universe of his dreams; with the single reservation that, unlike Nerval's dream, the dream of Mallarmé manifests itself, not in the form of feelings, but in the form of the most severely abstracted notions. The flowers, roses or irises, the swans, the constellations, the jewels or the hair of women, which are the familiar objects of Mallarmé's world, have no more existence than the symbols of the world of geometry; that is to say, like points, triangles, circles, and spheres, they are purely fictitious. Invented by the mind, they are nothing but figments of the mind.

VI

But this sensible and tender sister
Carried her glance no farther
Than to smile and to understand her
I confine my ancient care.

Scattering in all directions its multitudinous and scintillating image, the Mallarméan mind has spread itself hyperbolically in a space of its own. This space is constantly crossed and recrossed. Not only are ideas thrown upward and outward in it, like rockets, but when they reach the outer limit of their journey, they flash back their reflection to the mind. "Through the convergence of the harmonic fragments to the center,"[12] everything flows back to its source. "I perceive myself," Mallarmé writes, "like the undulating motion of a tranquillizing opiate, the vibrating circles of which flowing in and out, constitute an infinite limit which never coincides with the stillness of the center."[13] Thus the mind is, simultaneously, the infinite limit of the spreading thoughts and the still point from which they proceed and to which they come back. Through this constant outflowing and inflowing, space is possessed by the mind, even more so, it is literally lived in all its parts.— More than once in the poem, up to now, we have seen space described in one way or another: as the closed book, as the place of the installation of the hymn, as the garden in which the hundred irises bloom, as the isle in which the flowers grow larger. But neither the simplicity of Edenic nature, nor the plurality of the external world, nor even memory—this space which is nearly entirely ideal—constituted for Mallarmé the perfect space, i.e., the perfect site for the mind. All these symbolical places were, more or less, vitiated by a grave defect: they were all exterior to the mind. They encompassed it, yet excluded it. Existing outwardly, when the mind existed inwardly, they formed, all around it, a reality which was essentially heterogeneous to it. They allowed it to situate itself in their center, to compare itself to them, not to spread itself within them. Space and mind seemed therefore to be two mutually exclusive entities. Now, by abolishing the external universe and replacing it by a combination of pure notions, Mallarmé eliminates this classical opposition of space and mind. Space is reduced to its mental equivalent. It becomes a purely notional extension. In the same way as the poet conceives his ideas, so he conceives the space in which they gravitate. He *"installs . . . a purely fictional milieu."*

Space, then, is not any longer heterogeneous, not exterior to the mind. It is the field which the mind gives itself in order to proceed freely, through its own expansion, toward its glorification.

Infinitely enlarging its own sphere, the Mallarméan mind works toward its "total expansion."[14] But this "enlargement of place through vibrations up to the infinite" cannot be achieved without a corresponding diffusion, in that place, of all the images by which the poet accomplishes this spiritual amplification. There is always in Mallarmé's poetry an excentric motion by which things get vaster and vaster, but by which also they disappear in their own vastness. This is, for instance, what happens in the Funereal Toast in honor of Théophile Gautier:

> . . . I want to see
> To it that he who vanished yesterday, in the ideal
> Duty which the gardens of this star exact of us,
> For the honor of the tranquil disaster
> Survives by a solemn agitation in the air
> Of words . . .

True, the vanishing which is alluded to here, is the vanishing, through death, of the person of Théophile Gautier, and what Mallarmé wants to see survive here, are the words of the dead poet; but these words are represented as an agitation and vibration of the air, which gets more and more remote. The waves of sound which they emit, get vaster and vaster, but also fainter and fainter. Hence we understand that the tranquil disaster, which is depicted in the Funereal Toast, does not consist only of the disappearance of the central figure, but also of the disappearance of all images which represented it. Poetry, like all the projections of the mind, evaporates in the same way as the smoke of a cigarette. It disappears upward, outward, in whirls of mist:

> All the breath summed up,
> When slowly we expire it,
> In several rings of smoke
> Is abolished in other rings . . .[15]

From ring to ring, from circle to circle, the breath of the mind diffuses itself in space; but, at the same time, it expires, all the circles disaggregate and vanish. Thought is like the spiral staircase of *Igitur;* it is *"a dizzying winding process, indefinitely flying away."*[16] At the extreme of its movement of expansion, when the mind sees its own image infinitely and gloriously dilated. "Vibratory vanishing,"[17] it does not see anything any longer. By dilating itself everywhere, the mind has abolished itself everywhere.

This catastrophe is cosmic. It is also ridiculous. For nothing is more ridiculous than attempting to become all, and ending by being nothing. The experience of what we may call peripheral nothingness, is for Mallarmé, as for Nerval or Baudelaire, a disaster on a colossal scale, but for Mallarmé it has also its funny side, it is quite a laughable matter. The consciousness of absolute failure always marks in Mallarmé a return to common sense. The vaporous and vibratory disappearance of all the objects of his mental universe, is, after all, for Mallarmé, of slight importance, since, from the beginning, he had perfectly understood that these objects were purely fictional. Therefore why be sorry about their loss? While there is in Mallarmé a part of himself, which, through ecstasy and hyperbole, gets monstrously inflated, there is also another part, lucid, tenderly skeptical, "a sensible and tender sister" of the ecstasy, who, observing this inflation, is perfectly aware of its exaggeration and silliness. Of these two dialoguing sisters, Irony is the sensible one. She is the wise virgin. Her mission, purely negative, consists in gently, but firmly, declining to accompany her foolish sister in the reckless imaginary excursion the latter makes. Mallarmé's irony applies to the expansive force of the ideal the most potent brake, which is the consciousness of the unreality of this ideal. If there is a ridiculously swollen-headed Mallarmé who disappears in the distance, there is a quite uninflated Mallarmé who "does not carry his glance farther than to smile." Denying the truth of the hyperbole, refusing to budge and to bulge, he sits still at the center of the deflated world.

VII

Oh! may the Spirit of litigation know
In this hour when we are silent,
That the stems of multiple lilies
Were growing too much for our reason

And not as the riverbank weeps
When its monotonous play lies
In wishing for the amplitude to come
Among my young amazement

At hearing all the sky and the map
Endlessly attested on my walk
By the very wave which recedes,
That this country did not exist.

To the affirmation there has succeeded again the negation. Ecstasy has been answered by irony. In the conversation which the mind holds with itself, we can thus see an alternate motion which causes it to lean sometimes toward the *yes,* and sometimes toward the *no.* The conversation is a dispute of the self with the self, a litigation. The issue is as follows: Must we allow our thoughts and words to multiply and grow vaster, so much so that they will become a lie and lose all contact with reason; is it necessary to say that only what is, is,[18] or must we bring ourselves back to the narrow rock of truth? Such is the Mallarméan dilemma. One alternative necessarily carries the mind toward the affirmation, the multiplication, the amplification of hyperbole; the other one brings it back to truth, constriction, negation, and therefore also to sterility, stillness, and silence. Irony is the negative act, through which, everything being reduced to nothing, it appears clearly that there is nothing more to say and that the business of the poet is to stop and be silent. All other alternatives are excluded, and especially the one which would consist in monotonously and plaintively wishing for the amplitude of the ideal to come, when it is very well known that, in spite of all the attestations of the imagination, it can never come and can never be. So the adult Mallarmé of the *Prose* specifically rejects the attitude adopted by the youthful Mallarmé of twenty years before. He does not want to maintain, with an unreachable ideal, purely negative relations, based only on one's incapacity to attain it and sing it. Mallarmé, now, says *no* to the kind of poetry which was his own at the time when he could only weep at the idea that the country of his dreams did not exist. Nay! if the country of dreams does not exist, if the poet was wrong in thinking that he could extract from his mind a universe authenticated only by his words, in this case, as Irony points out, the only solution is to keep silent, and in the absence of the dream world, to resign oneself to be, like a swan caught in the ice of a congealed pool, a motionless point all around which there is nothing but blankness and negation.

VIII

> The child abdicates her ecstasy
> And already wise in her ways
> She says the word: Anastasis!
> Born for eternal parchments,
>
> Before a sepulchre starts laughing
> Under some sky, her ancestor,
> At bearing this name: Pulcheria!
> Hidden by the too large gladiolus.

Thus ends the conversation Mallarmé holds with himself. It ends, like all conversations, in silence. Or, rather, it would so end, were it not for the fact that, just before ending their talk, the two interlocutors will utter, one a last word, the other a laugh, which is a last exclamation.

Just before this supreme moment, the difference which divides the two members of the couple, is as great as possible. One affirms the actual existence of the dream, and pretends hyperbolically to be diffused in all its vast extension. The other one, on the contrary, denies the existence of this dream, replaces expansion by a void, and substitutes for the hyperbolical discourse the silence of disillusion. No doubt, it was possible to stop the conversation at this precise moment, when the contradiction is most blatant and when the antithesis denies and dissolves the thesis: *"We will choose,"* Mallarmé writes elsewhere, *"the tone of conversation as the supreme limit . . . and stopping-point of the vibrating circles of our thought . . . ."*[19] Now, the tone of conversation is the tone of irony; and, indeed, it is Irony herself which, by the means of her antithetic smile, stops here—and definitely, it seems—the expanding circles described by the mind of her foolish sister. The principle of negation, then, has won. The dialectic of poetic consciousness ends with the defeat of poetry and the triumph of irony.

Yet, at this last moment, the defeated principle, Poetry, still finds the means of throwing at her opponent a supreme argument. Irony, she says, is right. Youth is made wiser by the ways of experience. One must abdicate ecstasy, and acknowledge that the multitudinous and immense world of dreams does not exist. Everything is conceded;

everything is given up and lost. Yet, abdicating her present experience, the Mallarméan child abdicates only the *presentness* of it.
Like a king who renounces his throne, but who still continues to be
called a king, poetry renounces her queenship, but does not forego
having been a queen. This royal quality, or virtue, reigning over a
spiritual kingdom, is not an existence, but an essence; not a reality,
but an ideality. I cannot say that I am the God or the King of the
universe of my dreams, but nothing and nobody can deny me the
right of saying that I *have* been God or King of these dreams; and
therefore, that I can be again, in some future time, God or King of
new dreams. Only the present moment is real. Only this moment can
compel me into being nothing but what I am. But if I am a prisoner
of the absolute principle, according to which *only what is, is,* the
validity of this principle is strictly confined to the present moment.
When, on the contrary, I imagine myself in the past or in the future,
I can always be ideally what I wish to be. Therefore I proclaim the
anastasis, that is to say, the renewal of my dreams, the perpetual
possibility of identifying myself anew with them, not in the present
moment, which is necessarily the moment of the death of my dreams,
but beyond the present moment, in a future in which the past is
resurrected ideally.

Thus, beyond the negation, there comes again the affirmation.
But by a processus which is closely similar to the one we find in
Hegelian philosophy, the new affirmation is not a mere repetition of
the first one. It has assimilated the negation and therefore changed
its own character. The new affirmation implies now the renunciation
of ecstasy, i.e., of the immediate expansion of the mind in its
dreams. To proclaim the *anastasis* of the dreams, is not to proclaim
their eternal actuality, but, on the contrary, their eternal non-
actuality. The dreams can never be actualized, they can never become real, except ideally,—not in the real world, but in the poem on
the eternal parchment.

The *anastasis,* then, is the affirmation of the eternal renewal of
the poem in the mind and in the book.

Everything was lost, everything now seems to be regained. For the
hyperbole of ecstasy there is substituted the hyperbole of true
poetry, the work of wisdom and patience. Through the practice of
these virtues, the poet will go back into the past and acquire there
the science of rites, thanks to which, in the future, the poem again
will spring to life and expand in space. Everything is regained, yet
everything is lost again, since, at this very moment, the old opponent,

Irony, starts laughing. She is no longer the tender sister of Poetry, but her grim ancestor. She does not smile, but utters a sarcastic laugh. For Irony is nothing ultimately but Death. Grim and senile shadow of the ghost that the child will become inevitably in time, narrow grave in which the inflated possessor of space finally will be entombed, Death throws to her enemy a last denial. True, everything is saved, since the object of the dream is outside the reach of Death. Death can only destroy the real and can never touch the ideal. But everything is also lost, everything *will be* lost, since the dreamer himself is not immortal. Death kills, not the dream, but, at least, the subject in whom the dream must be born. The dream is eternal, but the dreamer is mortal. Everything is thus lost, since the dreamer, the one upon whom everything depends, will be lost. *Pulcheria,* the name of Beauty will be engraved—but upon a grave.

This final negation is directed, not toward the existence of the dream, or of the poem, but toward the existence of the dreamer, the poet. It lays him in his sepulchre. It abolishes him. Irony, death, negation have the last word. But in the most unexpected way the argument contained in this last word can be reversed. By abolishing the poet, that is to say, the living subject in whose mind the poem must take shape, Death gives him unintentionally the last perfection he needed in order to identify himself completely with his poem. Being dead, having become a non-being, like the poem, the poet has become, like the poem again, a purely ideal entity. He is not any longer the author of the poem, but the ideal subject of an ideal object, which is the poem. The last word of Mallarmé is a word of death, but it is not a word of defeat. Taking away all actuality, first, from the poem, then, from the poet, Mallarmé places them, one after the other, in the only region where they are safe from death. This is the region, not of reality, but of virtuality. There, everything can grow freely and immensely; there, irises, lilies, gladioli, and all the rest of the family of Irideae get so much enlarged that they become celestial and produce another species of irises, the iridescent rainbow, the hyperbolical scarf of the goddess Iris. The poem is "a circular flight of images and words," an exuberant growth in an imaginary sky. And at the center of this flight there is also an imaginary being, a hero who does not exist, a mind which is a void. From the center to the periphery and from the periphery to the center, there is a constant play of words and light, but this play is only a play, nothing ever takes place there, except in a fictitious way. "Everything is magically illusion and disillusion."

XVI

HENRY JAMES

To Jean Rousset

I have to the last point
the instinct and the sense
for fusions and interrelations,
for framing and encircling . . .[1]

"Consciousness is an illimitable power . . . ."[2] The moment that
Henry James' thought begins to take cognizance of itself and of
the world, it recognizes the infinite character of its task. This consists of representing. Now, everything is to be represented. The
being who applies himself to reflect the objects of his experience,
perceives that nothing is excluded from his experience. "Experience
is never limited and it is never complete."[3] The universe is an immense spider web whose threads recross one another indefinitely and,
at the same time, prolong one another. How to distinguish, how to
choose in this multitude, vibrant, silken, iridescent, made up of
repeated contacts, of subtle contiguities, of ceaselessly renewed
relationships? Like the sea wave whose murmur, for Leibniz, is
made up of all the particular sounds produced by the droplets
composing it, for Henry James, experience, the total of consciousness, is at every moment formed by a vertiginous ensemble of
connected impressions, linked in a web of events so pressed together
that the spirit exhausts itself counting them.

The exterior world is therefore a vast living expanse along which,
from all sides, and lost to sight, a shiver runs and scatters. "Life is,
immensely, a matter of surface . . ."[4] But the inner world, that of
depth, reveals an equivalent immensity and complexity. From his
earliest youth, James found himself to be the ecstatic and overwhelmed victim of what he calls "the terrible fluidity of self-revelation . . .";[5] a fluidity the more torrential since it was without let-up,

added to by an inexhaustible reservoir of remembrances. In his family they "professed amazement, and even occasionally impatience, at my reach of reminiscence . . ."[6] One might have been even more surprised by its fertility. Far from being, as with Proust, a fortuitous time rarely rediscovered by the working of involuntary memory, the past, with James, is always present and goes on constantly, enlarging itself like a spot of oil in the consciousness; so much so that in the last analysis the great problem for James is not to remember, but quite the contrary, to clear his thought by forgetfulness. For in his consciousness, images of the past come in swarms.

Speaking of a book of reminiscences which he intended to write, James states:

(I found) discriminations among the parts of my subject again and again difficult—so inseparably and beautifully they seemed to hang together. . . . This meant that aspects began to multiply and images to swarm. . . . To knock at the door of the past was in a word to see it open to me quite wide . . .[7]

And further on he confesses:

I lose myself, of a truth, under the whole pressure of the spring of memory . . .[8]

Nothing is more significant in Henry James than this loss of self caused by the very abundance of memories. If thought is disturbed and gets lost, it is not through diminution, it is through plethora. The mass of remembered images obstructs and overwhelms him. It adds itself to that other mass, no less profuse, which is that of present perceptions. In this prodigiously rich universe, in which, without respite, the mind sinks down, without direction and without end, as in a virgin forest, it is submerged as much by the multitude of detail as by the enormity of the ensemble. An inextricable entanglement of associations impedes his vision and slows his step. Henry James feels himself to be lost within himself, as a disciple of Copernicus felt himself to be without a landmark in the vastness of cosmic space. As Pascal saw the universe measurelessly enlarging itself around him, so James, at the extremity of his gaze, sees himself ramify, subdivide, and finally burst the perimeter of his experience. To become aware of himself and of the world is to become aware of a double expanse the limits of which it is no more possible to attain, as it is not possible to separate the parts. Everything gets tied up together; everything goes on, and develops in "one mighty loom spreading many-colored figures."[9] It is in vain that one seeks to "isolate, to surround with the sharp black line, to frame in the square, the circle,"[10] some element which cannot be isolated. The first representation of the real which one finds in Henry James is thus an illimitable, inform, and unintelligible actuality. Never has a thought shown itself, at first, so embarrassed by its own luxury. Where shall one find a way out, an end, a remedy? One needs at all costs an act of mind to stop short this proliferation which is both marvelous and fatal. Henry James gives himself limits, as one becomes a convert, as one emigrates, as one decides radically to alter one's life. For him, the formal order is an almost despairing way to escape from what he calls *"to work in terror, fairly, of the vast expanse of the surface."*[11]

> Therefore it is that experience has to organize for convenience and cheer, some system of observation—for fear, in the admirable immensity, of losing its way.[12]

To the admirable immensity will be opposed the system of observation which will establish limits there. The important business for the writer is to place boundaries where, naturally, there are none. For James, as for the classics, literature is a limited representation, therefore formal, therefore artificial, of what for him, is illimitable: "Really, universally, relations stop nowhere, and the exquisite problem of the artist is eternally but *to draw, by a geometry of his own, the circle* within which they shall happily appear to do so."[13] Thus, with James, the circle in no way plays the part of a theological or a cosmic symbol; it has nothing to do with the *being* of things. It is pure representation of an appearance. An arbitrary cutting-out accomplished by the artist in the great fluid mass of experience, it creates a cloister in whose shelter reality can be isolated, contemplated, and represented, without running the risk of melting into the universal multiplicity of phenomena. The terror inspired in Henry James by the admirable immensity has, for him, as effect, the immediate desire to elevate barriers. So this thought, spontaneously and initially one of the most formless possible, almost from the very first adopts the most rigorous formalism.

It is therefore of the utmost importance to discern by what processes formalization in Henry James is accomplished. Already there is the simple fact that thought constituting itself into a "central" consciousness carries with it a kind of circular disposition of the environing world. The mind is a search-light moving in space.

On all sides it projects its rays. The universe builds itself concentrically from a central source of light.

Thus consciousness now does not appear any longer as an illimitable activity. It spreads out in the fields which it illumines, but in
the very manner in which it proceeds, one must note, says James,
"something that holds one in one's place, makes it a standpoint in
the universe."[14]

A whole series of novels by Henry James represents with precision
the modalities of a central point of view opening onto a peripheral
world. "The first thing we do," says James, "is cast about for some
center in our field."[15] And elsewhere, " 'Place the centre of the
object in the young woman's own consciousness,' I said to myself,
'and you get as interesting and as beautiful a difficulty as you could
wish.' "[16] From *Roderick Hudson* to *The Ambassadors,* it is easy to
point out in the works of Henry James those novels in which the
consciousness of a central character forms the *"middle light,"*[17]
around which all the other elements, driven back to second place,
must be content with playing the role of objects. Like Adolphe, like
Julian Sorel, or Emma Bovary, certain of James' characters (Row-
land Mallet, Newman, Caponsacchi, Isabel Archer, Maisy, Strether)
see themselves given the almost exclusive importance due those
beings by whose eyes what is to be is going to be perceived. The universe appears to be, if not an invention of their mind, at least the
frame filled by their interpretative fancy, or the ensemble of elements whose cohesion and even intelligibility depend on their
organizing power. With most of the French novelists of the
nineteenth century, the central consciousness is more often psychological than aesthetic. It is the starting point from which are
revealed, before anything else (except perhaps with Flaubert) the
inner depths of the conscious being. It is quite otherwise with Henry
James. If consciousness diffuses itself there, it is almost exclusively
outside itself, in zones which are those of external life. James' consciousness, a surprising fact at the time, turns away from interiority.
It is, so to speak, never the center of itself. It remains purely a point
of view. A point of view which, most of the time, is that of a character whose investigating look, different from all others, holds the
faculty of leaving on the objects which it contemplates, a nuance, a
specific coloration, which is the stamp of its contemplative activity.
Every look attests the entirely relative way of looking of a definite
being. And the novel of which it is the center has as its goal to make
this invariable individuality of point of view to appear in the

variety of objects on which he exerts it. Moreover, behind the centrality of the principal character, there is still, with Henry James, another centrality, if one can so phrase it, even more withdrawn; that of the author himself. Every central character is for James a means of perceiving things according to the angle of incidence which a creature of his choice gives him. At the back of the consciousness of the character, there is therefore the consciousness of the novelist. It is like the consciousness of a consciousness. Occult, dissimulated into the background, it reigns no less everywhere. It is the center of the center. From the commanding point of view which it occupies, it silently imposes on its universe the interpretations of its thought and the choices of its will.

Among the essential aspects of the work one must therefore note the supremacy manifested by the center on the sphere in which it exerts its action. Often James represents this superiority under the form of a radiating consciousness, more noble or more delicate or more innocent than those of the beings in whose milieu it is placed. Around the lofty-minded soul are grouped the ordinary ones. "My problem," Henry James writes, in speaking of a novel which he titled *The Spoils of Poynton*, "has decently to be met—that of establishing for the other persons the vividness of their appearance of comparative stupidity, that of exposing them to the full thick wash of the penumbra surrounding the central light . . . ."[18] "It isn't *centrally* a drama of fools or vulgarians," he says elsewhere, à propos of another novel, *The Ivory Tower*, "it's only circumferentially and surroundedly so."[19]

James therefore takes his delight in disposing around a certain central purity a more or less dense crowd of secondary characters, comic or tragic. To the central light are opposed the penumbras which it cannot always penetrate. If in itself it shines with an invariable brilliance, it does not bring the same intensity of light everywhere. There is nothing more striking in Henry James than this power's limitation at irradiating light. Certain of his works are like a bursting of sunrays, fan-shaped, through a ceiling of clouds trying to prevent their display. The resistance opposed by opaque peripheral objects to the illuminating power of central fire is one of the most certain means by which the novelist manifests the calculated limitation of his universe.

But if the Jamesian novel is most often the expression of a radiating look or thought, that is to say of a movement which goes from the center to the circumference, it can as easily be the reverse.

As in Flaubert's novels, so well-loved and criticized by Henry James, one sometimes finds with the latter the description of a peripheral milieu, which exerts pressure at the center of the action on the consciousness of the hero. Instead of being an essentially diffusive force, the central consciousness becomes then a simple receptive center. And the beauty of these tales consists then, exclusively, in the entirely passive relationship to which the mind submits relative to the environing world:

> That such an hour has its meaning, and that the meaning might be great for him, this of course *surged* softly in, more and more, *from every point of the circle that held him.*[20]

Sometimes the affluence of the peripheral element is so great that it covers over and submerges, at least temporarily, the central consciousness:

> The sense was constant for her that their relation was as if afloat, like some island of the south, in a great warm sea that made, for every conceivable chance, a margin, an outer sphere of general emotion; and the effect of the occurrence of anything in particular was to make the sea submerge the island, the margin flood the text. The great wave now for a moment swept over.[21]

A wave that now unfurls and now withdraws. Of whatever sort, however, the movements are which traverse Henry James' novels, they unroll between two limits. On one side, there is a thought placed in a center, on the other, a world having nothing any more of the illimitable. The choice of a consciousness, for James, is the choice of a *form*. Thanks to the point of view which it assumes, the consciousness, at the heart of the work, becomes an authentic *"principle of composition."*[22] A finite world finds itself linked with a thought which, itself, is finite. The universe no longer is a fleeing infinity. The novel's space is that which is enclosed in a visually and mentally determined field.

To the finite space, moreover, a *finite time* corresponds. We have already spoken of the diffluent character of memory with Henry James. It extends everywhere, submerges everything. To the overflowing activity of his memory, Henry James also opposes the same restrictions as to the illimitable multiplication of his actual experiences. Instead of allowing the influx of remembrances immeasurably to swell the temporal area of consciousness, he assigns extremely narrow limits to it. Like his brother William, Henry James reserves his attention to the "specious present," that is to say to the small circle of duration which, at every moment of existence, barely encloses the feeling of the immediate past and of the imminent future. In short, life is a matter of actuality, as it is a matter of outside interests. Let us put memory in the ante-room and leave it there. "The ragbag of memory hung on its nail in my closet, though I learned with time to control the habit of bringing it forth."[23]

The Jamesian novel therefore will frequently be divested of the past. Its characters find themselves in relationships which more often than not are the effect of present junctures. They take new positions because of events which are themselves just as new. A matter of the surface and not of depth, of a displacement in space and not in time. The Jamesian character has usually little duration; or rather, his duration unlike the one of Flaubert's or Tolstoy's characters, has no temporal thickness. Between his actual existence and the depth of his mind stretch no thick layers of memories. The duration of these characters is comparable to that of celestial bodies; not that it is particularly long—it is rather the contrary—but it consists, as the one of stars, in the successive localization of the selfsame entity in different points of space. In a certain minute and a certain year, it is here; in another moment and another year, it is there. Its nature does not change. What changes is the relationship all other points of space have with it. This makes for a complex calculus in which time is of great importance, yet less than space. To go from Europe to America, or from America to Europe implies, in this regard, a more significant mutation than to pass from adolescence to manhood. In any case it is more calculable. It is also more easily contained within the precise limits the mind sets.

There is still another way in which Henry James can prevent himself from becoming lost in profundity. This is to assign to his character a past which is close to the present, a duration which is least removed from the world of the surface:

I delight in a palpable imaginable *visitable* past—in the nearer distances and the clearer mysteries, the marks and signs of a world we may reach over to as by making a long arm we grasp an object at the other end of our own table.[24]

The near past is thus neither dangerous nor prolix. By reason of its shallowness it is almost flush with the present: it is without distance and without depth. Therefore it is not a true past. It is made one with places. It is within reach of the hand.—But then, what does one do with the real past? Ignore it? This is what, most often, James is content to do. But sometimes the demon of curiosity, and that other demon, more perverse still, which incites a novelist to choose as a subject what he fears most and in which he least delights, draws him down into the depths. This is what occurs in what is perhaps the most famous of Henry James' stories, *The Turn of the Screw*. But the fabulous past—impalpable, unimaginable, nonvisitable—which one finds in it is actually less perilous for James than the real past, the historic past. Despite the precautions he takes and the limitations which he gives himself, the desire persists in him "to remount the stream of time, really to bathe in its upper and more natural waters . . . ."[25] This is what he attempted to do in *The Sense of the Past,* an unfinished and posthumous novel, in which he gives his hero a disposition most different to his own, one which renders the mind "oddly indifferent to the actual and the possible."[26] But this past, far away as its upper range may be situated, also seems close to him for it does not in fact differ basically from the close past; it is also a distanceless past enclosed within precise limits: "It was when life was framed in death," James says of his character, "that the picture was really hung up."[27] Death here, therefore, is not a new, illimitable dimension, given to the person who disappears. It is, on the contrary, the definite stoppage of existence, its placing in a determined frame. The same perspective is found in another of James' stories, *The Altar of the Dead.* An old man creates a cult for his departed friends. He thinks of them before a symbolic arrangement of candles placed in a circle on an altar. Now that their lives are finished it becomes possible, so to speak, to make up their sum total and to enclose them in a circumference of retrospective meditations. The past is therefore not an infinity. Limited by death, it forms the subjacent frame of the present, hence, a limitation.

The limitation imposed by the circle is, for that matter, not single but double. In a circle there is not only an external rim, traced by the circumference, but at its interior, a point-limit, which is the center. For certain intellects, such as Plotinus, Cusa, Boehme, Amiel, or Blanchot, it is true that the center is not a limitation. It is a sort of interior infinity, a species of abyss. For Henry James, on the contrary, the center is a stopping-point, the place where convergences encounter each other and get immobilized. As has been noted, the circumferential limitation can be formed by the assemblage of the

exterior objects on which, by turns, is placed the attention issuing
from the center. Nevertheless, since there are two limits, it is simple
to invert them, and, reversing the perspective, to manage in such a
way that the object of attention becomes the point of arrival of a
movement of prospection and exploration (one would have to say
of *in-spection* and of im-ploration) coming from the periphery. So
everything changes, consciousness, from central, becoming peripheral, and the object contemplated, becoming the central objective.
Let us imagine, therefore, in the heart of a novel, a certain object—
animate or inanimate—a vase, a town, a woman, it doesn't matter
what. What does matter, is that there is a mind which bends over it,
envelops it, places it at the center of its attention. At first this watchful thought is still distant, or its attention is divided, or it is otherwise occupied. Little by little it becomes fixed and draws near. At
last, drawn into the circle, it concentrates itself upon the object. No
doubt Balzac earlier—and before him, Rousseau—had known how
to describe a world made up of convergent covetousnesses, at whose
center, held as between cross fires, a victim fought. But Henry James
is the first novelist to perceive that every one of these lusts has its
seat in an appropriately peripheric consciousness; he gave to
certain of his novels the structure of a central object reflected in such
a kind of consciousness. Perhaps, incidentally, there was no more
natural gesture for the author of *The Portrait of a Lady* than to
begin by withdrawing and give first place to that on which his attention was fixed. In his social and sentimental relationships one sees
him at first keeping his distance, only coming forward after some
time, and with a thousand precautions toward the interiority of
others. This is what is made very clear in the following lines, taken
from a letter of Henry James' to one of his women friends:

> I don't know—and how should I?—much about you in detail
> —but I think I have a kind of instinct of how the sidebrush of
> things that I do get in a general way a reverberation of, touches
> and affects you, and as in one way or another there seems to
> have been plenty of the stress and strain of life on the circum-
> ference (and even some of it at the center, as it were) of your
> circle I've not been without feeling (and responding to,) I boldly
> say, *some of* your vibrations.[28]

As this curious epistolary text shows us, James preferably places
himself at the tangential point of the circles projected by souls. It
is in this point that, in his opinion, he can more easily detect the

waves emanating from the lives of others. He it is who sympathizes from afar, who vibrates delicately at a distance. More than that, to add to the space which separates him from the object to which the most lively sympathy allies him, he deliberately places between himself and the object a kind of character-witness, whose double mission consists in observing the object in question, and dissimulating the presence of the author. "I have already betrayed my preference . . . for 'seeing my story,' through the opportunity and the sensibility of some more or less detached, but not strictly involved, though thoroughly interested and intelligent, witness or reporter, some person who contributes to the case mainly a certain amount of criticism and interpretation of it, . . . a convenient substitute or apologist for the creative power otherwise so veiled and disembodied."[29]

There are therefore in the exercise of the peripheral consciousness the same possibilities of *control* as in the functioning of the central consciousness. A certain spectator, behind whom the intentions of the author are hidden, does his job, which consists of observing and interpreting. He casts a more and more informed look toward some central mystery. It is he who spies, who foresees, who even explains and makes ready. The events take place as he had predicted, as though to show their submission toward an intelligence which has thought them, even before their accomplishment. Thus Jamesian thought gives itself over to a game of marvelous subtlety. At the center of action there is an object, and on this object an attention places itself. The attention observes the object in all the complexity of its relationships. Finally, it knows it, and from the moment it knows it, it is as if the object became its creature and began to obey its instructions.

But to come to this result, what inspections, what proceedings and preliminary conjectures! James' peripheral thought detests nothing so much as to *be abrupt* in the progressive knowledge of his object. Then, too, he does not go down to the object in a straight line, but on the contrary, multiplies around it circumvolutions of all kinds. In *The Wings of the Dove, The Golden Bowl,* and *The Sacred Fount,* which are among the most sinuous of his novels and those least in a hurry to come to the final and central termination of their career, the moment that Henry James succeeds in establishing his interpretive thought in the neighborhood of an object to be investigated, he makes it turn right around by a spiral movement which closes on its prey only with extreme slowness. A prey which can be, as in *The Spoils of Poynton,* an assemblage of inanimate things, but which can also be, as in *The Golden Bowl,* the image of a loved person, to which the mind constantly returns. It is this situation which is described in a passage in the latter novel, in which the love of a woman is compared to a garden in whose center an ivory tower is set:

> She had walked round and round it—that was what she felt; she had carried on her existence in the space left her for circulation, a space that sometimes seemed ample and sometimes narrow; looking up all the while at the fair structure that spread itself so amply and rose so high, but never quite making out as yet where she might have entered had she wished.[30]

In the final analysis, however, Maggy will arrive at the foot of the ivory tower and succeed in entering it. The Henry James novel advances by a movement often almost imperceptible, but it never marks time, and its progression is one of an understanding that wishes to be patient and meticulous. And in a sense, as it approaches the center, it is true to say of the investigative thought, that it turns in a narrower and narrower circle. But in another sense, since its inquiries ceaselessly grow in number, the circle containing them seems to become more and more vast; the more so as the mind is not content to perceive what is, but *supposes* what *could be,* so that reality thus discovered is engrossed in all kinds of possibilities. Thus, the inquiring motion which envelops the object can appear, turn by turn, immense and narrow, similar in this way to the circles which imagination follows in certain dreams. It is a movement of this kind that in *The Sacred Fount* is witnessed by the reader when, lost in the thousand suppositions which some mysterious happening arouses in him, the indiscrete, fanciful, and perplexed observer, who with James is always the typical representative of the peripheric consciousness, walks at sunset in a park whose capricious avenues, perpetually leading back one into the other, represent fairly well the meanderings of his cogitations. And it is then that, like a decisive answer to the complicated network of his interrogative approaches, at the bottom of the perspective, there appears the very person who holds the key to the problem and around whom the fantastic frame of hypotheses has been built:

> This was the light in which Mrs. Server, walking alone now, apparently, in the grey wood and pausing at sight of me, showed herself in her clear dress at the end of a vista. It was exactly as if she had been there by the operation of my intelligence.[31]

How many times in a Jamesian novel the reader does become a witness to this perfect coincidence of objective reality and of the mind which conceives it, as though, to employ James' expression, one was the effect of the sorcery of the other! A cry of triumph seems then to spring to the lips of him to whom, one might say, it has only been necessary to think of something to have it realized. Now the mind, finally ceasing to turn around its object, can rejoin at one leap, at the center of its investigations, truth confirmed.

A truth which, moreover, at the very instant in which it reveals itself, appears as the managing principle of all which surrounds it.

More than any other of James' novels, *The Sacred Fount* seems to have as its aim the description of the phenomenon by which things distribute themselves around a center, while this makes its presence felt at the very heart of peripheric consciousness. For instance, in this novel, there is a particularly notable scene in which a group of guests one evening are listening to a musician. "It was the infinite that, for the hour, the distinguished foreigner poured out to us, causing it to roll in wonderful waves of sound, almost of colour, over our receptive attitudes and faces."

Let us be wary however of believing that the infinity of which James speaks here is the same as the illimitable multiplication of sentient experience of which, there at the beginning, there was question. Here what is specifically considered is an infinity, if one may so phrase it, ordained and set in a frame. On the one hand, it would seem that the music should diffuse itself indefinitely into a sky where colors and sounds harmonize; but on the other, this great excentric current is as though dominated and directed by the same central presence which we have seen in the preceding passage, since James takes care to add: "The perfection of that, enjoyed as we enjoyed it, all made a margin, a series of concentric circles of rose-color (shimmering away into the pleasant vague of everything else that didn't matter), for the salient little figure of Mrs. Server, still the controlling image for me, the real principle of composition, in this affluence of fine things."[32]

Once more, center and principle of composition identify. But this principle no longer is the conscious subject surrounded by the objective world. On the contrary, it is an *objective principle* which is enveloped by the subjectivity of consciousness. Around the object, the mind gravitates, as a spectator turns around a statue which he wishes to admire from all angles. This is what James calls, "the planned rotation of aspects."[33] Instead of a plurality of environing things, there is a unique object on which the mind concentrates itself and whose essential simplicity is to some extent counterbalanced by the multiplicity of its aspects. From this point of view, the Jamesian novel is singularly like a poem by Mallarmé, it, too, being made of "circumvolutionary plays" and of "the exhibition of all its facets" by a mysterious entity in which one finally recognizes the center of all.

The Jamesian novel therefore tends, despite all the windings and arabesques which mask the center, to establish in this the simplicity of a unique object contemplated by a unique consciousness. It is in the simplicity of the central object that the principle of composition now wholly resides. But if this is so, it is not necessary that consciousness, where the object is reflected, should in itself be *one*. The unity of consciousness is only indispensable when the consciousness is the center, not when it is circumferential. With a kind of intellectual frenzy, Henry James explores the infinite possibilities open to the novel by the variation of successive points of view. A whole series of characters defile, in whose consciousness the author insinuates himself by turns, in order to contemplate with ever-differing eyes an object which, of itself, remains unalterably the same. This is what James calls "the law of successive aspects," of which a certain number of his novels are very precise examples. One can find in them the figuration of a new kind of time and space. Around an objective center is established a moving circle of points of view, from one to the other of which the novelist passes. Nothing changes, except the point of view. Time is therefore constituted by the substitution, not so much of one moment for another, as of one *point* for another. It is therefore as "local" a time as possible. The novel is a succession of localizations. One can compare it, as James does, to "the house of fiction (which) has in short not one window, but a million . . . . At each of them stands a figure . . .,"[34] or, again, to "a chest of drawers."[35]

Thus space in the Jamesian novel now appears as a circular field, divided into a multitude of adjoining compartments, in each of which exists a consciousness. The most perfect representation of this space is found in the Preface to *The Awkward Age*. Henry James tells us that, wishing to make the editors of a review understand the composition of this novel, he had drawn on a paper the following symbolic figuration: *"a circle consisting of a number of small rounds disposed at equal distance about a central object."* "The central object," James explains, "was my situation, my subject in itself, to which the thing would owe its title, and the small rounds presented so many distinct lamps, as I liked to call them, the function of each of which would be to light with all intensity one of its aspects."[36] A surprising image, but marvelously exact, of what the novelist wanted to accomplish: a novel constituted of a plurality of consciousnesses, all aimed at the same object. One could also compare this space to that of an auditorium. Everything there is directed to unify in a center a sheaf of peripheric interests. While, in the real theater, the watching consciousnesses, passively united, submit to the magic of a central object which alone holds the power to engender variety, in Henry James' novel, on the contrary, it is the witness-consciousnesses, which constantly come to bestow on the central object new virtues and even new possibilities of existence; so that the object thus contemplated appears to live a thousand lives, brought to it, and suggested, by a thousand different looks, by a thousand new interpretations of the real. The astonishing peripheral activity of multiple consciousnesses has the effect, with James, of dilating the real and loading it with all the possibilities which he implies. The real is a center surrounded by a luminous halo of possibilities, at once infinite and finite.

XVII

CLAUDEL

Nearly a year ago I finished a new book
which I will call *Five Great Odes.* . . .
They are great lyrical monologues
in which I take up again, poetically,
certain themes from my book on philosophy,
for example: of the inexhaustible in the
closing of things, the *circle* as the model
of all forms, finite and yet infinite,
egg, seed, open mouth, zero.[1]

I

AT THE very beginning, a "creative act"[2] is discovered. That this
act comes from God, that it ends in producing the world, matters
little at the moment. It is enough now that it becomes manifest, and
as a birth. "I am" first means: I am born, I unfold, I issue forth, I
come to light. "I am a source of light and energy."[3] No doubt this
light and this energy immediately diffuse themselves on all sides,
outside of myself, in space, but if they diffuse themselves, it is from
me; I am the source. I ceaselessly refer to it, toward it I return as
"the very source of sensation, the table of distribution, the control-
room."[4] In every instant I am born, in every instant I find my instant
and my place. Such is "the vital act, the essence of myself (which) is
the elaboration of a nervous vibration."[5] Every moment lived by
Claudel, every place in which he found himself, was therefore the
moment and the place in which Claudel took possession of his own
existence. Just the moment in which one draws a breath, just the
place in which one feels the beating of one's heart. It has neither
duration nor extent. But it is the starting point from which there

gets constituted duration and expanse: "Solely the *point* gives us the idea of initiation and of departure."[6]

This sole point is therefore nothing else than a point of departure. It is not a place in which one settles oneself, it is a place from which one starts out. Or rather, his gaze must necessarily travel from the fixed point—the tree, crossroads of branches in which the Claudelian being perches—so that he is at the same time he who remains immobile in the fork of the tree and he who, as prime mover, from the height of this branch, has his eye cross and recross the countryside. To be, is to be in a point, within it, at the most delicate point of the instant and the place, but it is also to be outside, as a system of rays and forces darted onto the exterior. No one is more capable than Claudel of staying just where he is, but no one is more incapable of refraining from radiating beyond that area. Thus for Claudel, the *sole point* is not a point of *arrival*. Grace, and in the first place, creative grace, is never for him, as for the puritan, the Jansenist or the quietist, that act of issuance from a transcendence so absolute that there is nothing else to do but to receive it at the extremity of a line whose initial point would be God. For Claudel, the unique point is, on the contrary, a point in which, indescribably, there are situated at one and the same time both the act of God and Claudel himself. Grace does not come, it moves, it raises up. The act of the Creator therefore cannot be distinguished from the birth and the activity of the creature. The power of one is thus the power of the other, as though, by an intussusception, immediate and without distance, or simply by the transmission of the *impetus* from one billiard ball to another, Claudel, created, became creator, and consequently felt in himself, the need not only to submit to the creative will, but actively to realize its intent. In the first surging of this being which is a source of light and energy, it would therefore be useless to try to separate God's share and the part of man. From the first moment, Claudel is entirely divine-made and entirely Claudel. But this totality and perfection of being is still in the virtual and punctual state. It is a divine germ, a possible God: an idea of self, of God and the world, searching blindly to free itself of its exiguity and to realize itself in a field of action.

Now as to this field, it must be filled up even before it is understood: "The being never ceases being born, it never ceases to fill up the form which has been attributed to it."[7] Before discovering what this form may be, it is necessary to render it visible, and, that through a process of dilation and in-filling, like a balloon, which, in order to know itself as a balloon, would by interior breathing, fill out its own form. The being is a sentient power, embryonic, overflowing its center from every side, finding in the four dimensions of space and of time a territory to occupy. It projects itself into it, spreading itself out in concentric circles, pursuing its obscure completion from stage to stage:

I must complete myself not only in space but in time.[8]

The being . . . continuously fills this circular territory . . . by a vibration which goes from the center to the periphery.[9]

With Claudel, the initial movement therefore goes from an initial point toward limits as yet unknown. It is a *"quest of space by the Point."*[10] This space is as yet without form, even though in the depths of itself the being is already an auto-creative force which unfolds itself spontaneously without knowing its future form. Hence, to it, the field which it invades seems illimitable. Soon, no doubt, nothing will seem more repugnant to Claudel's thought than the conception of a human or cosmic infinity. But before possessing his frontiers, the being for Claudel is first a movement without frontiers, an expansive force which as yet perceives no obstacle and spreads itself out everywhere to fill everything, and to touch everything:

In the period which one may call embryonic, thought is in possession of an illimitable field. It is always, so to speak, angling for fishes, a sensibility stretched out on all sides, an instrument for catching game, a sun of rays and of feelers . . .[11]

Claudel describes the first movement of his existence as like "the emission of a wave."[12] From all sides, from circle to circle, in a space as yet interior, the being propagates itself, a sun of rays and feelers which ceaselessly swells the area of its exploration and of its occupation. This latter is not necessarily either immediate or total. From the instant which is always first and in which it forms itself, the expansive force has all of space before it and all of future time. Duration, as space, is something which opens itself, the milieu through which the Claudelian being has precisely all of time in which to realize itself. Thus its development has, like that of the vegetable or the animal, an initial slowness. If the being progressively extends the field of its interior activity, it is essential too, for it to occupy all places, to link them solidly to the center, to distribute everywhere the plastic radiation of its presence. With Claudel there is (as with Sartre) a viscous state of thought and of body, in which, despite its enormous excentric energy, the being reveals "a laziness at withdrawing from a certain *thickening center*."[13] Then its heaviness slows it down, inciting it precociously to congeal its circular spreading, to secrete beyond its first lymphatic conquests the shell of an egg or of a snail: "Then the *round being* in the shelter of its calcium tunic questions itself on its own existence."[14] Or it may be compared with the pearl, which Claudel defines as "a desire slowly ripening and realizing itself in the form of a *sphere*."[15] This is the first stage, the first circumference of the being, in whose interior the latter takes a series of measures, which are to the advantage of its body, and establishes contact with the totality of its physical self. It is not difficult to imagine Claudel as a somnolent Buddha, torpid in its armored carapace but lending an ear to the circular vibration filling it, and gazing attentively upon its navel: "The umbilical, . . . is the indication of our milieu. It is from this as from a center that all the co-ordinates of the human body radiate."[16] But beyond the thick roundness of the body, space continues to extend itself, and Claudel's appetite forces him to shake off his lassitude. He must erupt on the other side. One can imagine the Claudelian senses as antennae, or even better, as tentacles. They agitate themselves all around the corporeal sphere, stretching further and further their "sun of rays and feelers."—"So, let it be a *circle* of which the luminous source is the center."[17] This center is the eye. It is a sort of navel from which there radiate also co-ordinates, but co-ordinates which this time no longer inform us on our bodies but on the world of space and of objects: "A long ray coming from the *center* of our eye leans us against the envisaged object."[18] The eye is "a portable sun,"[19] thanks to which there is established at the end of the line, made up by our eyesight, a physical contact with exterior things. We are at one and the same time in the center, at the initial point *from where* we see, and at the circumferential point *to where* we see, to where we project our vision. External space, with everything it encloses, is therefore susceptible of being possessed. Our movement of expansion does not stop at our corporeal surfaces, we are able to seize hold of that which is beyond ourselves, that is to say, the world. Like the devilfish or the octopus, we are an animal of suction and of prey.

But upon what to prey, or rather, upon what not to prey? A being which defines itself as an expansive force cannot accept frontiers before this force is exhausted or stopped. And for the moment it seems to be free and inexhaustible. From the image of the preying animal it is necessary to pass to that of the conqueror. A Mongolian conqueror of a universe of steppes. Nothing makes it stop for breath. Its intolerance equates its exigence. Both are total: "It is of the whole that I have need."[20]—"Do not deny me what I claim, which is All."[21] Among Claudel's characters the first in order of importance is Tête d'or. He will metamorphose himself into Turelure. He is a beggar who wills himself to be a millionaire, an adventurer who makes himself emperor. Piling up territories or riches, he always starves for more. If he has not everything, he has nothing. Even after his conversion, Claudel will be nothing but a poorly repentant conqueror. Like Isaiah, he always longs to say: "This place is too small for me, make room for me."[22] Too narrow a place, unless it becomes universal. In his circular spreading out the Claudelian being is "always searching for new shores."[23] He knows that "all that is of the earth, earthy, belongs to him to walk on, and it is inadmissible that he could be deprived of any particle of it."[24] He has a right to the universe. He is not "whole, if he is not wholly one with the world surrounding him."[25]

In its universal expansion, the Claudelian force therefore continues to be circular. For the physical roundness of the body there is now substituted the no less physical roundness of the world. Like Christopher Columbus, Claudel "discovers . . . that he can no longer do without the integrality of the sphere."[26] This is "a globe, an apple that one can hold in the hand."[27] But what it is important to remark is that this need of possession is not satisfied with trying the surface weight, and it is the thickness and the concentric organization of all layers which the possessive will wishes to penetrate. It is "the agglomeration of the rapports to the center"[28] which makes the globe. And Claudel, placing himself in the center, in the strategic place, from there, like a Lucifer, not paralyzed but galvanized by God's thunder, perpetually projects the possessive waves as far as the circumference of the earth. His touch not only fondles the surfaces it comes from the depths to finger all points of the mass. The tentacles of the senses spread themselves out everywhere.

Nothing, therefore, at first glimpse, distinguishes Claudel from the great *expansive* poets of the nineteenth century, whom he unremittingly detested. Like the Faust of Goethe, like Byron, Hugo, or Lamartine, he is at first someone who takes no limit into consideration. He brutalizes space, he treats it as conquered territory. His exigence is total. Total not only in the field it pretends to occupy but also in the character of this universal occupation. For it is not only for him a question of devouring, but of absorbing, everything, to cause everything to go into his own substance. Claudel is the frog who, to make itself as big as the bull, installs itself inside the latter and by dilation occupies the whole mass. One of the literary perils which the twentieth century has escaped is the spectacle of a more and more voluminous Claudel, obstructing imaginary spaces. Outside, he would have emptied things, inside he would have filled up the void, and this, as far as the eye could reach; so that in the final analysis there would have been nothing left in the universe except an enormous spherical Claudel, which, like Leviathan, would have "possessed the eternal sea."[29] However, this picture, at once laughable and tragic, was not realized. It was not improbable, though Claudel's temptation is not that of Saint Anthony. It does not consist in seeing unfold before him the infinite variety of forms; for Claudel, all forms are good. It simply consists in seeing space open before it. At this sight the desire to engulf it and be engulfed in it seizes the poet in his very entrails. Now space seems infinite, and Claudel could have passed his whole existence in wishing to absorb it.

Hence, from the *Tête d'or*, to all subsequent works, Claudel's evolution is not only characterized by his conversion to God (he was already a mystic, though, no doubt, as he said of Rimbaud, a wild one) but also by his conversion to limitation and measure. In attaining God, Claudel at the same time attains the boundaries of his expansion. He reaches his limit. He finds himself on this side of infinity. From that time, the space in which he dilates himself circularly changes character. It is a finite space which is surrounded, as in the Middle Ages, by an infinite space—God or the Empyrean: "The true image of the infinite is the circle, the zero . . . . So the circle is at the same time the perfect image of the finite, of creation realized."[30] At the interior of this finite space all is finite, beginning with myself. I am a wave which lengthens, an excentric and centrifugal force; but I am also a force which stops at its own limit, which refuses to go farther. I am characterized not only by my power of expansion but also by my power of obstinacy. The objects around me which I discover to be penetrable and assimilable, become external forces with which I enter into struggle and conflict. They resist me, I resist them. Around me they form a circle and make pressure. Against them, I make a circle. I am their limit, and they are mine. I exclude them; they exclude me. From this mutual incompatibility I draw information and knowledge. Beyond the circular world, which concentrically extends the sphere of its multiple pressures around me, I am a sphere on the surface of which they produce indentations. By this I know the outside, as by my resistance I know the within. Claudel makes of his being an image no different from that of a battered mass of arms. "Experience circumscribes man."[31] And indents it also:

> If we schematically represent the domain of the animal vibration as *a circle whose ultimate wave is the circumference,* we can imagine all impression, all sensation, coming from outside, by an indentation, which affects not only the exterior form, but the whole extent of the area that it encloses. Every wave coming from the center is bent by this obstacle.[32]

I am therefore simultaneously limited, from within and without, by my own power of resistance and by the resistance of things. Closingness is on both sides. A closing which not only implies the impossibility of my continuing my excentric expansion but also the possibility of knowing myself through knowing limits. The refusal, which Claudel opposes to so many thoughts or people, does not come from ignorance, arrogance, from a lack of curiosity, or of charity. Simply, he resists. And in resisting he apprehends. The principal object of the Claudelian theater is the discovery the characters make of themselves by opposing others. If, to make use of his famous pun, co-gnizance is co-nascency, it is as in politics, through the discovery of the reciprocal pressures exerted on each other by the different spheres of influence. A power takes consciousness of itself when it takes shape. And it takes shape when it sets one back against a wall: *"Every living being is a circle,* more or less modified, but always limited by a contour."[33]—"Every thing is defined and defining."[34]

The force of expansion thus becomes a force of formation. Starting from a point, the Claudelian being extends itself in space and in time in successive waves up to a definite limit: "Every year a circle around a circle comes to mean something, to register a span of time, to transform the homogenous flux into a numerical unity."[35] From this fact the time of a tree or of man cannot be confused with the Newtonian flux, no less human space with an infinite expanse. Like the Aristotelian becoming, time consists of the developing and the gradual completing of a form. Now all form is a variation of the circle. The human being is a continued act by which there is formed and fixed an undulatory energy which moves from the center to the circumference.

II

Schematically the wave can be defined as a movement which, starting from a center, reaches all the points of an area circumscribed by the limit which it traces in stopping. It creates on all points a total displacement, followed by a *reaction, or a tendency to return to the first position* . . .[36]

Come to the extremity of its excentric movement, the Claudelian being, by an inverse movement, flows back to its first position. Double time of human activity, made, like breath, of inspiration and respiration. But if the Claudelian being finds itself back at its starting point, it is to find itself there in an altogether different state. Having crossed and recrossed its field of action, filled its place, delimited its circumference, it knows itself in the ensemble of its form, just as from his post of command, the head of a firm knows himself in the activities of his workshops. Beside, having made contact with things, having measured its strength on all sides, with external bodies, having perceived behind their immediate pressures, other pressures and other forms, he knows that its existence and its own self are also defined from outside by the cosmic totality. Co-gnizance and co-nascency do not only require a pushing in all senses from one's own irradiating force but a converging on one's own from all sides by the forces of the universe. Such is the sense of the famous *co-naissance:*

We do not cease co-naissance into the world, that is to say that our knowledge is the work of the *circular unfoldment* of our being, constantly in a state of vibration, to which, to insert themselves, there come the various touches which are the objects of this special co-naissance.[37]

But these touches and these insertions do not now appear as simple indentations on the surface of the being. In the same way as there is a reflux of the being toward its sources, there is a confluent movement of the universe toward the central point of the self: "Everything comes to meet us."[38] Everything is outlined around us like "a contour of souls and places."[39] The being which is co-naissant in the world, therefore finds itself situated at a point from which not only can it leap toward this world, but from which, too, it can see coming to meet it the world toward which it is going. It is a "center of convergence,"[40] the "key-point of the construction."[41] Man "constitutes, wherever he is, a center":[42]

I espouse the world! I see interlaced around myself every kind of relationship whose essential condition is this central and dominating position which I see attributed to me.[43]

This is the same situation which Proust perpetually tried to reach and which he never attained, except at the end of *Time Rediscovered,* in which he permits the glimpse that a being perched on stilts or having clambered up all the steps of Combray's church tower, could simultaneously see: Guermantes and Méséglise and the four corners of the horizon. The strange thing is how difficult it is for Proust to realize what Claudel achieves with such ease. For the latter, human space is what distributes itself around a center. And the center can only be Claudel himself. Everything opens, spreads out, sets itself in order into a single landscape in which the gaze finds and creates unity. "Everything depends on everything; everything is homogenous."[44] To settle himself in his central position Claudel has no need to make the successive aspects of his experience alternate in his thought. This is always circular and always total. It does not distinguish opposing directions in the divergence of which Proust's thought is torn and lost. For Claudel, all directions are given at the same time to the perceptive and organizing center. The Claudelian being is a meeting of roads, a crossing of glances. How could he become lost or lonely in space, since space is a homogeneous simultaneity, from every side and from one end to the other, in which everything finds a place, a move, gets linked and crossed, like a countryside around a "crossroad."[45] The world is a "ceilinged universe."[46] No matter how far it stretches, it is always within limits recognized by the "specialist of the horizon."[47] Thus the object of poetry is nothing else but the universe, "sacred reality, given once for all, *at whose center we are placed.*"[48] Is not the poet that "geometric point in which the surrounding place, composing itself harmoniously, takes, so to speak, existence and consciousness of itself?"[49] Like Anne Vercors, "around himself he ceaselessly sees the earth as a fixed heaven all painted with changing colors."[50]

Yet these colors are changing, so much so that on the immobility of the fixed circle of space, the mobility of time makes another circle go round and round, composed, it would seem, of shifting colors. But may there not be a danger for Claudel to see undone here the profound harmony which he experiences between his central position and the peripheral reality? From the moment that it manifests itself as the rapport of a center to a circumference in a fixed space, the spatial simultaneity is absolute; from the fork of the tree in which I climb to the extremity of the landscape, I discover that everything I see—developing at the same time the ensemble of its planes and of its lines—is simultaneously present to me. But the moment, for example, that I perceive a moving vehicle, I discover a universe in which what existed exists no longer, and in which what now exists is going to be replaced by what yet does not exist. Among all ideas, that of time was that which was to menace in the most mortal fashion Claudel's poetical summa. Hence this is the idea which constrained the poet to the hardest effort. Time, for Claudel, is not pure successivity. Far from being a point, endlessly proceeding along the imaginary line of duration, it is for Claudel similar to space, but to a turning space. Claudelian time is clock time, a clock on which the hour is always shown, not by the movement of a hand moving from number to number around a motionless dial, but by the very movement of this dial, pivoting around its center. So that, in a sense, it is all the hours at once. It little matters that time goes from instant to instant; from the most distant past to the remote future, all the instants are always simultaneously placed all along the curve of duration. And all instants, past, present, future, refer also simultaneously to their center which is my present consciousness. No one ever affirmed more energetically the reality of the human *Totum Simul* than Claudel: "It is not the future (or the past) which I envisage, it is the present which a god urges us to decipher . . . . An immense, a total, hour is calculated at every moment."[51] This total hour: "at the center of horizons, the astronomer, upright on the moving Earth like a sailor on his boat,"[52] calculates it. Also, the newspaper reader who, glancing at the meteorological bulletin, with its concentric curves, discovers there a true dial of the world. This is "an implicit summary of the total daily situation, the bearings, if I may put it thus, of our instant in the midst of its coordinates."[53]

In brief, time does not differ from space. It is a turning space which in turning does not refer itself less universally than fixed space to the human center. Space and duration are "circumferential reporters:"[54]

> Everything comes to be measured by this double diameter of an invisible circle which distinguishes right and left and up and down. Everything passing by comes to ask the time of this super-meridian gnomon.[55]

In short, everywhere, at every moment, everything is present for
Claudel. Around him, everything forms a peripheral reality with
which he feels a profound sentiment of solidarity. No matter what
the universal hour, no matter from what place it is perceived, the
total hour always reveals itself in a total universe. A universe made
up of time, made up of space. But this totality is neither spatially
nor temporally abstract. The very web and woof of the spatio-
temporal universe for Claudel is a homogeneous spherical continuity, in which everywhere and always an inexhaustible variety of
concrete objects is discerned. The cosmic sphere is not infinite, but
it is inexhaustibly rich. In every place and at every instant individual
forms are singled out. Their contours are reciprocally delimited. So
that to understand the universe is not only to be co-naissant with its
whole, but to be co-naissant with every one of the entities composing
it. There is nothing more striking in Claudel than the displacement
which he brings about from subjective to objective knowledge. His
thought and his vision remain no less rigorously central, but this
centrality now becomes that of the object. To describe the latter,
Claudel does not contemplate it from a distance, but from the interior. As every painting includes a "luminous point" which is "the
pivot of the composition,"[56] so every object appears as a center
"encircled by the radiation of its signs."[57]—"Every body constitutes
the final sum of an ensemble of convergent series. It is the point of
intersection of the thread with the web."[58]—"I understand that
every thing does not subsist in itself alone, but in an infinite rapport with all the others."[59] To understand something one must
therefore dispose the universe all around one: "When I speak of the
pine, of the banyan, when I speak of Chinese towns, it always begins
with a kind of mental definition involving consequences, and with
the place which the object occupies from the point of view of the
composition as a whole . . ."[60] The Claudelian description is therefore a definition. It necessarily includes, as always, a central point
and a converging or irradiating roundness. Thus the apple, "this
round thing in our fingers, . . . the fruit of an issuance of valleys . . .,
of a convergence of slopes."[61] Thus the lily: "On this lengthened
stem, which serves it to delve to the bottom, to pull up life through
the moment and accident, there *blossoms in a circumference* made
up of petals geometrically disposed, the flower, or essential and
synthetic cup, hilum of cover, which brings the perfect meaning
and the supreme *center* to the calculated arrangements of a *concentric universe.*"[62]

To define the flower—lily or rose—Claudel, differently from Mallarmé, evokes, not an absence, but a universal circular presence.

But it is not only objects easily definable—flowers or fruits—which are thus surrounded by a kind of cosmic ring. The countryside, the sea, rivers, towns, everything is a pretext for the same arrangement:

> The earth propagates vast waves around itself, which bring with them the most various disturbance.[63]

> Understanding the general direction, the essential arteries and confluences, the detours created by an obstacle, the points of convergence, and these soundings, which are the blind alleys in the middle of a refractory isle.[64]

> I think of these Roman streets, deliciously shady, . . . which come out, all of a sudden, on a fairy-like fountain, on some marvelous palace, the color of gold, the color of the day. And these squares, these crossroads cherished by Wisdom, these are the Points of convergence which permit the Ecclesiast, at once, to dilate and to unite again.[65]

> The town . . . is born of an ending and a departure, of an encounter and a crossing.[66]

In Claudel's universe every object and every being can therefore become the center of the circle. From the circumference to the center, and from the center to the circumference "there is a constant coming and going."[67] "Even for the simple flight of a butterfly, the whole of the sky is necessary."[68] Reciprocally, the flight of the butterfly is necessary to the sky. Thus, everything is center, every center refers to the circumference, and vice versa. All creatures do not exist only in themselves, in their center, but in the double undulatory movement by which they receive everything and transmit themselves everywhere. Beyond the rose, from all sides, to the limit of the summer, there is sent the fragrance of the rose. Now this movement, by which the being effaces itself and its action is prolonged, is a movement of dedication and of glory. It seems that if everything is a center it is to carry to the periphery, not its own existence, but its portion of energy and reality, to make the circle more complete and the total reality more perfect:

> No rose! But this perfect word in an ineffable circumstance.
> In which everything finally, for a moment in this hour, is born![69]

Everything propagates and lifts itself up, carrying the spirit:

I work within and from all sides see everything lifting up at once![70]

As by degrees we go up . . ., the eye looking behind creates peace and harmony on an ever-enlarged circle of nature.[71]

As I go up, as this sublime body of the Church of which I am a part and from whose strength I am a communicant, helps me to mount, the vision of which its stem constitutes the center, and to which the circumferential horizon refers, becomes larger. I serve as a point of departure and arrival for a radiation of lines, ever more extended.[72]

There is an ascensional movement in Claudel which is not contradictory with the image of the center and the circle. For it is from its own center, and without leaving it, that the being, so to speak, lifts himself up vertically on the spot, in order to contemplate a horizon always limited yet always enlarged. The Claudelian tree grows up without ceasing to project around it, its spherical foliage. But as it lifts up and discovers a vaster field, the sphere of its expression also dilates and becomes simpler. Like the fragrance of the rose which, in propagating itself, causes the rose to be forgotten and is no more than a perfect word or an ineffable circumference, so the human word becomes a circumferential murmur, an immense O, outlined by the mouth. What are set forth by the mouth, are the self and the world, the beings and the things, and the universe containing them. To convey their roundness, the poet "produces around the emotive center a kind of tremulous lip, the crest of a wave, the liquid surrection of a sort of vocal organ."[73] The lips are "the definite round around the word, around the vocal ejaculation."[74] But the word itself, which is the cosmic word, the word which encircles the world, does not finally express the world except to direct it beyond, to a transcendent Being. Therefore, Claudel's last word is a word deprived, not of sense, but of all particular meaning, a word-limit, an anonymous circle of dilation, a *zero:* "O, is a mirror, unless it is the perfect void and the roundness of the soul dilated toward the real spirit."[75]—"What does he need, God asks Himself, speaking of praying man, if not from the whole of the universe to say to Me, O, to open toward the sun with his tongue at the center, a catholic abyss?"[76]

"A call to the circumferential horizon,"[77] "a peripheral feeling,"[78] the Claudelian word finally divests itself of all form. From beginning to end it is no more than an impersonal thrust toward a transcendent reality. It searches for the horizon, the end, the supreme limit. The world and the self have become a sort of nothingness, a desert consumed by a torrid light:

> ... a place removed from all direction, all profane destination, a platform without slope in which no particular horizon predominates and becomes detrimental to *this perfect circle which is the transcription of the Infinite on its surface.*[79]

III

"One found his God at the center, the other sorrowfully asked for his at the horizon."[80] One and the other of these pilgrims represent Claudel; one and the other in their quests have the same objective but a different direction and have felt the same joys, the same sorrows, and sung the same song. He who, in his search for God, goes from the center to the circumference, in the final analysis comes out on all sides, on the world's surface. Like Tête d'or, he has the sun in his arms. Claudel dreams of "taking God's measure, which leaves nothing outside, like someone who in order to describe encircles the object to be described."[81] The circle which he strives to delineate is "a ribbon which, in turning about the surrounded object without emitting anything, allows us to attain by means of the finite the form and the possession of the infinite."[82] Claudel attempts to trace a circle around God; he tries to cause the finite circumference of the finite world to coincide with the infinite circumference of God. Hence he extends to the limits of cosmic space, not only the excentric thrust of his thought, but the inexhaustible enumeration of the encircled and encircling world. Nevertheless, the center and the circle of God are not man's center and circle. The divine transcendence goes beyond all human circularity and centrality. On the one hand it withdraws in uncircumscribed space, so that the exploration of the horizon ends in defeat and sorrow. But on the other hand, too, it retracts and draws back into the inverse direction which is the one of the center so that in one sense as in another, interiorly as exteriorly, God cannot be seized. Nevertheless, it seems that failing the circumferential God, at least the central God will be found. From the periphery of the world every object, every living being, every intimate thought cannot do otherwise than designate Him.

Just as for Dante and Denis the Areopagite, both the suffering Church and the triumphant Church are, for Claudel, a disposition and a movement around the center, an orientation toward Him. From all sides the universe leans toward this central reality. In a celebrated passage which he himself has recalled three times, Claudel describes every drop of water as obeying its circumferential slope, *"escaping toward the deeper center of a more enlarged circle."*[83] Creation is a Church, and this Church, like that of Pierre de Craon, is arranged in such a manner that "from all the points in endlessly changing frames, one never ceases to envisage the sacred Center in the flames."[84] Around the center, creation makes a circle. We must obey "like the circle to the center"[85]—the circle existing only in the impossibility of its escaping from the center[86] and being elsewhere than with it.[87] A divine, yet human, center, since it is God and Christ. Hub of the wheel, point of intersection of the diameters which form the circle and which form the cross, the Christ and only the Christ is the crossroads of all roads. Only He, as one now sees, can claim the title of the unique Point which gives the idea of initiation and departure. Around Him the universe converges, and from Him, it diverges. God is initial and final.

And from this it seems possible to place oneself once again in the central point of all life. If there is a time to act from within to without, there is also a time to act from without to within. There is, on Claudel's part, a sort of final withdrawal of the whole being toward the mysterious Point which is that of all of birth and all of death: "We are *taken back* to the authentication of our limit. We *abandon the periphery for the center."*[88] Now, the limit which thought establishes here is no longer the peripheric limit but that which mind discovers in the retrograde movement which it realizes toward its source and toward God. There is a transcendence of the center to which the human spirit must submit and which it may not transgress. An original God, a profound God, retracts Itself inaccessibly into Its central unity. The creature, no matter where it is, no matter how close to the center it may be, even placed *on* the source, is not *at* the source; it is always outside God. "Excluded principle, foreclosed origin,"[89] man, in this life, is always kept at a distance from the center. He "endures his source."[90]

Final sorrow, constant sorrow, until, like space, eyes and time are closed: "Then Time shall be closed upon us and the Present shall be its eternal center."[91]

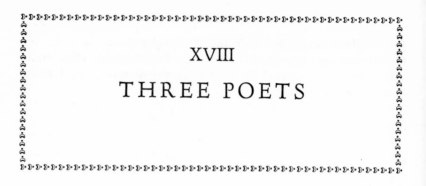

XVIII

THREE POETS

I

Rilke

FROM THE FIRST, space is manifest in Rilke. "We live under the sign of the plain and the sky." The plain, the sky, are what is found everywhere and all around, what is beyond and immensely at a distance: such are the expanses in which the trees of Worpswede and the villages of Russia stand out. A naked space, a virgin and flat territory. One goes across it endlessly, without an obstacle. One pours into it freely the objects of one's thought.

From every object, from every thought, space extends. And every object of thought slides and plunges in space. To feel, to think, is from every object and in the space surrounding it, to prolong everywhere, indefinitely, the lines of its progression toward its distant perfection:

> Souls of children as yet mute
> Which, gently, *in greater circles,*
> Move toward life . . .[1]

Space is therefore a sheet of still water, on which, in circles, is written the undulatory and excentric progress of things. All irradiates from it, all grows from it. It is the hollow which will overflow, the nothingness which will be filled, the absence which will become presence. Space is God, it is the future, it is the ideal, it is the field of becoming.

Little by little, nevertheless, time covers space. Time is a slow inundation. Everything one feels, everything that one is, forms the crest of a circular wave which enlarges as it goes, progressing without respite in its invasion of space. Space is *vastness;* but time is *the more and more vast:*

> To live is senseless except with reference to many
> Circles of space growing and developing . . . .[2]

> I live my life in excentric orbs
> Spread out onto things . . . .[3]

Time is therefore like a series of peripheral ripples which extend themselves further and further and less and less perceptibly into the indefiniteness of the universe, so that everything grows there, but also everything dissolves and loses itself, so that, in this temporal irradiation of things across the expanse, each one, to take up again Nerval's expression, "vanishes in its own grandeur."

In brief, time is the perpetual vanishing of things and of being in space: "I feel as though I were crushed," Rilke writes, "by the continual experience of a too-rapid change."[4] In vague, immense places in which everything alters, the being "wears itself out in metamorphoses," renouncing its own characteristics and changing them for others and finally, for none: "Every one of us presents himself as a collective being whose innumerable elements constantly regroup themselves, renew themselves or die, help one another or deny each other by turns."[5]

So time which carries us along and changes us, constantly removes us from him who we were at our starting point. How can we, if not stop the march of time, at least slow it down? How can we, above all, keep in countercurrent some link with our origins? In the vast forward movement which draws our thought toward the future, it becomes more and more uncomfortable to maintain, in the background with the past, the relationships one holds with a being in whose proximity one has never ceased to live. The counterpart of the expansion into space and into the future is an inevitable weakening, the retreat—soon, the total disappearance—of the past, the principle, nevertheless, of expansion itself. Absorbed in the progressive dilation of the circle constituting it, the consciousness tends more and more to neglect the original center in its movement of expansion. One sees a striking example of this in a letter from Rilke to his wife, in which, assuring her that, at the center of his existence, now become nomadic and excentric, there remains the remembrance of their mutual life and of the place where their daughter was born, he lets slip the following confession: "I cannot limit my attention to that center, when the periphery extends in all directions to the infinite."[6]

The center fades away because of the amplitude of the circle. Worse still, the diffusion of the latter brings about its destruction. Later on, in a poem on Narcissus, was Rilke not to write these revealing lines:

> Even in sleep nothing holds us sufficiently together,
> O center giving way in myself, O kernel full of weakness . . .[7]

With Rilke, the expansion of thought therefore takes on a clearly negative aspect. It establishes itself less as the unfolding of a conquering force, than as the inability of the spirit to hold together the different parts of itself in one center. Thought is too feeble to firmly tie up its own clustering. Now of itself it is loosened and scattered. Rilke is perhaps the only poet in whom the pouring out of thought into space seems to be owed, not to the tension of tightened energies, but to the slackening of the ties of the being. Everything occurs as though, in Rilke's cosmos, the centripetal force being nonexistent, the result is that things, given over from the beginning to the sole *impetus* of the centrifugal force, flee spontaneously in every direction far from their point of departure.

With Rilke, such is the fundamental movement: it is a rushing out or a soaring which is immediately revealed as being a pure movement of flight. Existence is an attempt to escape. Life escapes into death. And, as with Lamartine and others, it appears that, with Rilke, the intervention of death can have no other effect than to accentuate and complete the general movement of dissolution, which is precisely the effect of life. Therefore, in the first Duino Elegy, speaking of the state of the soul which immediately succeeds the loss of life, Rilke writes: "It is strange to see floating, dispersed in space, all those things which had been joined."[8] It is therefore clear that death does nothing more than life: it disperses. If the thoughts of the newly dead become scattered, it is not because they are dead, but rather because they are still living a little, and because there is still, in them, something left to dissolve, to unloosen, to drive further away like a dust. As long as there remains in us any vestige of a conglomerated form, there is life, and consequently too, the dissolution of life: "To feel, is to volatilize ourselves." It is only beyond all form, at the end of all movement, in the dispersion of the last vestiges of life, that the formless is attained—that immobile profundity without characteristic or substance in which the being finds itself yielded up to non-being, "vanished without leaving a trace."

It is therefore confirmed that time is at once both the great destructor of the being and the great creator of space. It is the unceasing work of disintegration by which what was, now being no more, leaves a vacant place which is space. Space is the void which, just by ceasing to exist, that which sinks into inexistence manages to produce. Far from being, as it at first appeared, a future becoming the present, space is now a present becoming the past. It is that immense Nothing which shuts irrevocably over engulfed actualities. Space is death finally swept of all life, naked death.

And now space spreads itself out like the profundity of a submarine tomb, like an interior ocean into which all dead existences have glided. No sooner are beings no more, than there they are again, there, far in the depths, continuing a detached life beyond their death, floating, unprecedented. Rilke's whole thought pivots around this unbelievable transmutation by which, in the consummation of their death, beings go beyond their mortality and reappear, intact, beyond, endowed with a spontaneously immortal existence. For if the actuality of things and of beings is that of corruption, and if corruption is a perpetual and tragic metamorphosis, there is always a more absolute defeat than all the others, by which the being tears itself from its destiny, breaks away from its temporal condition and reappears, not as it was, but as death altered it, "removed from every accident, disengaged from all penumbra, withdrawn from time and delivered to space."[9] Then too, there is no permanence, beyond the most mortal experience of time, except through the "absolute consenting to change, and to the transformation of our states."[10] Every past instant becomes an absolute instant. Now it is separated forever from all the others to come. In place of an equivocal becoming in which the instants glide one after another, and in which their continued flowing never ceases to determine the alteration of beings and things, in place of a time which never stops losing itself and losing everything, now a strange absence of time comes which surges and spreads out between all times, between all the isles of time which it surrounds with emptiness. Nothing, any longer, is attached to anything else, nothing draws anything into the same destructive flux. Nothing exists any longer except the same profundity of space, at whose interior, far away, freely, there float no longer things, no longer beings, but the equivalent images which their disappearance evokes in the mind.

Consequently, everything which reappears beyond time, reappears in a space which is the "reverse of time," which is "the other side of Nature." There things no longer proceed one from another. They are content to be. They *are*. They occur. Forever, they take on the character of a "pure event." Instead of existing in the flowing and fleeing continuity of duration and of the exterior spaces, they exist singly, innocently, without cause and without fate, without past and without future, having no other justification than their presence alone. "Alone in space," as a hand sculpted by Rodin. There is the presence, for instance, of a tree, of a rose, of a woman, of a grief. A presence underlined by a stroke which isolates it. Of all the objects thus continually surrounded and drawn by Rilke's words, one can say what he said of Rodin's bronzes or stones: "No matter how ample may be the movement of a sculpture, no matter from what infinitely remote place it may spring, even though it be from the depths of the sky, this movement must close upon itself, so that *the great circle is completed,* the *circle of solitude* which *encloses* all works of art."[11]

A circle which encloses, which distinguishes and limits. How different a circle from those which, in the first manner of Rilke's poetry, ran, like a shiver along the skin, one after another, finally to vanish where all limits are confounded. Every object is now surrounded by translucent and distinct partitions, like a ship built inside a bottle. There it occupies a circumscribed place, which is its own space. And the rapport between this space and the object which it envelops is so exact, that there is no need to notice anything else, the simple conjunction of a space and an object is enough to support a perfect kernel of thought:

> Alone O opulent flower
> you *create* your own space . . .
> Your fragrance *surrounds,* like other petals
> your numberless calix . . .[12]

From the center from which its stem springs, to the final ring of scents which surround it, the flower therefore exists in itself, and one must even affirm that nothing exists here except the flower. One might say that the entire creation has *gone into seclusion* so that in its stead and in its place the rose might be created. A purely mental creation, furthermore, and close to Mallarmé's roses. The Rilkean rose, it too, is the absent one—more, the defunct one—of any bouquet. To think or to feel something, for Rilke, is, in fact, to withdraw it from the confused and crumbling conglomeration which is the temporal world. Nothing surrenders its intimacy, nothing reveals its essence, nothing *is* and *is* understood, unless it is no longer in touch with anything, unless it no longer is motivated by anything; briefly, unless, irrevocably detached from everything and placed in nothingness, it offers its simple existence there to the mind.

An existence which can be defined, either as a curtailment from the world of the living, or perhaps more exactly, as that from which the world of the living gets curtailed. An existence environed by the circle of solitude: "We need only to *be there,* like the earth, absolutely, in space."[13]

In the vacancy of thought there is nothing else but this, a little drop of reality which forms itself, which swells and detaches itself to become, at the heart of an expanse emptied of any other image, an extraordinarily distinct shape, and the only one one may see in the whole field of the mind.

Yet, nevertheless, a shape surrounded by all the span of the mind. That which is, is in a space. In the Rilkean poem, the object never appears complete, compact, opaque, ignoring and repelling the space which borders it, as in a Parnassian poem. If it is not bound to others, it is no more bound to itself. To exist, it must be at ease in space. Rilke's space is therefore not only the silent retreat of all that is not an object distinct from the mind. Around this object it is something open and free, something which is exactly the contrary to the flowing and changing confusion in which, ordinarily, there are found engulfed the objects of our exterior experience. Here, from the object, everything opens and everything makes room. If for Joubert space is a freedom to think, for Rilke it is freedom to be. It is a pure spaciosity, the power of all existence freely, indefinitely, and solitarily to become perfect.

But this perfection holds nothing of the temporal, or, in any case, of the successive. For "how to call time that which is rather a new state of freedom, as truly tangible as space, a more open kind of environment, without evanescence?"[14] Instead of being the place in which objects disappear, space is now the place where, like jewels in a case, things are set in a hollow form. Moreover, isolated from all happenings, every perfected thing no longer inscribes itself here in a historic continuity. Its existence is the independent existence of an instant which, separately, apart from every other moment, locates itself where it wishes, as it wishes, in the floating manner of a reminiscence or a premonition. It belongs to no past, to no determinable future. Or rather, endowed, so to speak, with an intemporal actuality, lifted above time by a kind of vertical aspiration, now all these moments become "creatures of space," and distribute themselves in it in the manner of stars, continuing to live, every one with its own distinct brilliance, in a permanent and simultaneous life.

Thus space becomes the counterpoise of time:[15] "To adapt those things subject to time to a less menaced world, calmer, more eternal, which is pure space,"[16] such is the unique, the total, function of poetry.

II

T. S. Eliot

Like a wayfarer robbed, stripped, and thrown at night into a river, whose chill water brings him back to consciousness, the thought of Eliot finds itself plunged into duration. A swift current carries along and stupefies the mind. If only it were possible to cling to the present moment as to a fixed point! But there is no fixed point. The moments pass. They pass so swiftly, so completely, that the sole image which survives them is that of "flickering intervals of light and darkness."[17] Far from having the slightest continuity, duration is entirely composed of the multiplicity of intervals and the successive disappearance of the images they separate. A time comparable to a woof perpetually torn to pieces, or to "a heap of broken images,"[18] whose pieces fall over backwards. The sole concern is with the incessant and, so to speak, frantic passage from before to after:

> Only a flicker
> Over the strained time-ridden faces
> Distracted from distraction by distraction
> Filled with fancies and empty of meaning
> Tumid apathy with no concentration
> Men and bits of paper, whirled by the cold wind
> That blows before and after time . . . .[19]

A blinking, a distracting, a whirling time is an insensate motion that carries people no matter where, anywhere except where they find themselves, and which, being aimless, returns in the end to its beginning: "In and out, in an endless drift of shrieking forms in a circular desert."[20]

There is nothing to hope, it seems, from this time or this world. But now and again the song of a bird arrests the step of the hurried traveler; or it may be "the leap of one fish, at a particular place and time, the scent of one flower, an old woman on a German mountain path, six ruffians seen through an open window playing cards at night at a small French railway junction where there was a water-mill . . . ."[21] These images mysteriously affix the mind to their momentary reality. They are profoundly different from the time just described. They subsist in themselves. They are outside of motion, outside of time perhaps. Each one constitutes a "sudden illumination."[22] Nontemporal and yet situated in a moment and in a place, these visions possess a sort of peculiar plenitude. Like certain Proustian images, they seem to be set down at the point of intersection of duration with a nontemporal reality.

Driven by forces of which he has a horror, jostled by the crowd, delivered over to the violent mobility of the epoch, Eliot occasionally finds the means of halting, at countercurrent, at countertime, and listening, as to the song of a bird, to the prelude of another time: "There is a first, or an early moment which is unique, of shock and surprise, even of terror *(ego dominus tuus);* a moment which can never be forgotten . . . ."[23] In this "partial ecstasy"[24] it seems that one has a presentiment, not of the secret of one instant, but of all instants; for "the pattern is new each moment."[25]

But the ecstasy is only a partial ecstasy. "The glory of the positive hour" is "infirm."[26] The sense of it escapes us. The moments fly, and their meaning with them. Later, a long time after, one will be able to fathom their message: "Only in time can the moment in the rose garden . . . be remembered."[27] Never will the moments be repeated; they will be content to "survive in a larger whole of experience."[28] Far from us, far from the present, in our memory, having become past, they will become attached to all the traditions which constitute that past.

From the fugitive seizure of the present, thought thus passes to the permanent seizure of the past. That cannot happen without a primary and grievous sacrifice. To renounce the present in order to contemplate the past is not only to renounce joy, since that exists only in the actual, but also to renounce the direct apprehension of truth by "sudden illumination:" "What happens is a continual surrender of the poet as he is at the moment to something which is more valuable."[29] Everything will depend now on a precarious contact with a precious and remote truth which memory badly preserves, and which is corroded by the brutal indifference of present time toward all traditions. And yet, says Eliot, it is necessary to accustom oneself to "depend upon tradition and the accumulated wisdom of time."[30] This dependence, or this "historical sense," implies a "perception, not only of the pastness of the past, but of its presence."[31] It is necessary to consider the past as a "simultaneous order," to live "in what is not merely the present, but the present moment of the past."[32]

The search for lost time in Eliot is therefore totally different from what one finds in Proust, but no less important. It depends on a voluntary memory, on a continuous abnegation, on a patient effort to recover, to reassemble, to readapt under new conditions, what was lost. Far from being restored at one stroke by the affective memory, the past is regained only by the exercise of all the mental and physical powers. It is less a memory than a reacquired habit, the effect of a vow of fealty. A new time is revealed which is no longer the furious movement by which, in order more easily to possess the future, the present disencumbered itself of the past, but the reflective motion by which, resigning itself to not existing by itself, the present concentrates upon the actions necessary to assure the preservation and the transmission of the past:

> Not the intense moment
> Isolated, with no before and after,
> But a lifetime burning in every moment . . . .[33]

But from this fact a new character of the past is also revealed. It is its integrality. To decide to transmit the past to the future is to decide to transmit to the future all of the past. For a long time Eliot thought that present duty consisted simply in choosing what was best in the past. But he had to recognize that he could not be dispensed from accepting the worst also. Acceptance of the past does not solely imply the acceptance of its virtues, but also its sins. There is no discrimination, no prescription, no liberation by rejecting or forgetting. "Time is no healer."[34] To accept the past is to accept the burden of its sins and the necessity for their expiation. It is to accept time with all its consequences.

Thus the new time takes on a significance no less tragic than the former time. For the tragedy of discontinuous moments there is substituted the tragedy of a time that is ineluctably continuous. In the former view, nothing seemed linked to anything; everything appeared to escape and elude itself. Now all seems linked together in so dense a fashion that no moment can escape any other, and each appears to have to assume the responsibility for the whole duration: "How can we be concerned with the past and not with the future? Or with the future and not with the past?"[35] All our past actions and thoughts look to all our future actions and thoughts as to acts of justification or expiation. From the beginning to the end of time, our actions depend one upon another. They adhere to each other, and so very closely that between the beginning and the end of the series which they constitute, there is no break and, it would seem, very little difference. Like a reverberating echo whose sound returns to the same place, all the beings we have been and shall be, form one uninterrupted being that unceasingly receives its heritage from its own hands: "In my beginning is my end, and in my end is my beginning." When we accept the burden of our past, we also accept our future. They have the same face, the same being, the same time. This time of absolute responsibility, like that of radical irresponsibility, is circular.

In neither case can one escape the motion of the wheel. There is not a moment of our existence, nor of the history of the world, which does not turn with all the other moments around the same pivot.

But epochs and moments do not exist simply in the process of their circular mutation. And if they follow one another in an order which is that of the rotation of duration, each one of them, fixed to the circumference, remains in constant relationship with the pivot which precisely determines that constancy. At the center of general mobility there always appears, and always at a distance, an immobile reality that continuously keeps the mobility from losing itself in the unlimited and the moments from falling into the most indescribable incoherence. It is because this point never ceases to exist and to act, that all the other points are aligned in a circle, and that by reason of the rigorous solidarity which is imposed on them, there is not a simple anarchy of moments but a duration. And it is also because this point continues to exist and to act that the circular continuity of the moments does not become a meaningless and fatal concatenation of causes and consequences. Each moment is in relation with all other moments; but each moment is also in relation with a moment that is outside of all the others, because, contrary to what they are, it itself is fixed and eternal. As the fleeting experience of "partial ecstasies" had indicated, each circumferential moment of duration is immediately traversed by a ray that issued from that transcendence. Each moment is, therefore, in time, and yet outside of time, animated as it is by a nontemporal power. Horizontally, so to speak, it receives from the past an impulsion which it will transmit to the future; but vertically, shall we say, it still receives its own peculiar efficacy. Along the length of a supernatural road there travels to it a force that permits it not, to be sure, to escape from time, but to give it a supratemporal significance and value: "It is out of time that my decision is taken."[36] Thus, each decision we take, each action we begin, each sacrifice we make, is not necessarily the exclusive effect of antecedent causes and the cause of subsequent effects. At every moment it is possible for us to give time a new and permanent inflection. It is in our power to "redeem the time,"[37] but not to annihilate it.

But we can accomplish this redemption of time, in and through time, only by resigning ourselves to time—that is to say to our human condition: "Only through time is time conquered."[38] Christian time is the time of sacrifice. The sacrifice that we make of our passions, our joys, our own person, in order to accept, first, the order of the past, next the duties imposed by the future, and finally the total submission to the central authority of The Being; "still point of the turning world," that point which we left in order to undertake our peripheral and dolorous Odyssey in duration,

> And the end of our exploring
> Will be to arrive where we started
> And know the place for the first time.[39]

Thus, the thought of Eliot rediscovers and relives all the stages of the experience of time, as it is revealed in, among others, American literature. Like Melville and like Poe he undergoes the terrors of gyratory time. Like Emerson and like Thoreau he perceives the importance of the isolated moments that are the revealers of transcendence. Like Hawthorne he comprehends the profound solidarity of the present and the past. But this retrospective solidarity leads him to discover, like Whitman, a solidarity more vast, which links to past and present the prospective reality of the future, and makes him understand finally, with James, that if all times adhere to one another, each moment contains also an infinite virtuality. It is in the power of man, not to change time, but to change the meaning of time. And of all the ways in which this power is exercised, there is none more efficacious, as Emily Dickinson understood, than abnegation, Thus Eliot remains faithful to tradition in expressing his own thought, which is precisely a reflection upon fidelity and tradition. In expressing himself he preserves a heritage. All the times of his predecessors are found once again in his time.

III

Jorge Guillén

Not the self, nothing but the outside. Here, everything begins by the presence of a purely objective reality. There is no being except in the exterior. Yet, without a doubt, there, there is a being. The presence of the being is evident. It is like a flood of light filling the void. The light is what is, which, in being itself, shows itself. To be is to light up and be lighted. It is to carry, hold the testimony of its own reality. What is, is there, exact, intact. No part of it stays hidden in the shadow. Everything is in the light, and all is light. Being and appearing are one, and this *one* is a true total. The world is complete. Nothing is missing.

Always supposing that there would be an eye to see it, the plenitude of the universe is therefore, in its entirety, immediately perceptible. So the world presents itself to the gaze, and the world is the gaze. There is a universal consciousness whose splendor is itself universal. Not only does the world exist in itself, but it delights in itself. Parmenides, earlier, had compared it to a sphere. Guillén compares it to a cupola, that is to say, again to a sphere, but seen from the inside. For if it is true that the only reality is outside; in reflection, the outside becomes an inverted outside, turned inside-out like a glove, an outside which *interiorizes* itself. The world is an immense concave surface, whose inner side, made up of light and of the sky, offers itself simultaneously and in all points, to the gaze. Even more, since nothing is lacking, it is necessary that there should be no hiatus anywhere; on the contrary, that the smoothest continuity should distinguish it in every direction. The better to make itself seen, the world everywhere disposes itself in curves:

> Curved, the firmament rests,
> Compact azure, on the day.
> It is the rounding
> Of the splendor: noon.
> All is cupola . . .[40]

Space is a cupola. Duration too. In the same way in which different parts of the expanse range themselves one beside another in a whole, whose coherence is at once apparent, in the same way the different events of the historic past juxtapose themselves into an ensemble whose continuity is immediately intelligible. Guillén's time is therefore as little Bergsonian as possible. The revolving moments come to take their place, every one in its turn, in a sort of edifice in which they occupy a quantity of contiguous compartments, similar to the frescoes succeeding one another on the walls of certain Italian churches. Time is an increasing space or, more exactly, one whose content never ceases to grow. Even though an indeterminate number of compartments, as yet unfilled, still wait for the artist's hand, the temporal whole is achieved and presents the same roundness as space.

Such is the spectacle that Guillén's poetry offers. From the outset, perfection is attained, and from the outset too, it is revealed. Here, there is therefore neither progress, nor opposition, nothing but the recording of objective splendor. From this point of view, Guillén's poetry separates itself distinctly from the rest of European poetry. It does not begin from the interior but from the exterior. It places that which is, not in the central hollow of the consciousness, but in the peripheral manifestation of a tangible reality. Everything is there, and everything begins from there. It is nevertheless true that the exterior perfection of the being having been immediately verified, the poet runs the risk of having nothing left to say. Everything has been said once, and for all. But Guillén's attitude is not to be confounded with that of the Eleatics. It is not satisfied to recognize the splendor of the external being. It seizes and describes its efficacy. Yes, without a doubt the being is that which is placed outside. It develops itself on all sides in curves which close in on themselves; but, in closing, these curves enclose the point at which their action converges. The perfection is not static. It is an organization of the cosmos directed toward a center:

> And to the evident rays of the sun,
> There is brought back
> The essential city.[41]

Like the circle, the center can itself be objective: an object placed in the middle of a universe of objects. This object can be a tree, a town, a rose. Just as there is a Rilkean rose, so there is a Guillénian rose:

> All is cupola. There is resting,
> Central, not searching for it, the rose
> To a sun at its zenith subjected.[42]

A flower is presented in the extreme condensation of an object on which the world gently closes; yet how real, and how different, in consequence, to Rilke's purely mental flowers! A physical sun imposes its benefits on it. It is from its environment that it obtains that which is necessary to it to live. It is a center which entirely depends on the action of the periphery.—There is nothing here, either, which recalls the static combinations of Mallarmé's poems. No inaccessible azure and no nostalgia of the azure. The whole of the sky, on the contrary, conspires to give its most precious favors to the rose. And the rose is at one and the same time, both desirous and satiated, confident in the repetition of the gifts which have been given to it, and which, as well as existence, bring it satiety and rest.

A singular relationship which seems to reverse the habitual direction of thought. What? Everything no longer springs forth from the interior? What? It is no longer *from the center* that life is born and is propagated? Coming from within the soul, as with Rilke, or from the divine center, as with Eliot, will not a whole series of rays or of excentric circles issue forth and cover space? On the contrary, with Guillén, it is concentrically that space is traversed and that the beneficent forces converge to pour out their influence on the object on which their rays finally meet and coincide. So Guillén, counter to all the poetry preceding him, rediscovers not only the sense of ambient fecundity, of the cosmic generosity, but also, by a corollary movement, the feeling of the receptivity, the happy humility of the being which finds itself overwhelmed by a luminous and dispensing nature. To the simple presentation of an objective center there is now substituted the revelation of a median consciousness. Not a flower, a tree, a town, but myself. Myself at the center of the world, I who receive all from the world:

> From its creation, the air
> Encircles me. Divine circle!
> To a continuous creation
> Created by the air, I yield myself.[43]

> I perfect myself by the light
> I am, thanks to this beautiful
> Revelation which is the globe.
> An avidity without eclipse
> Rounds itself in me . . . .[44]

> It was I,
> In that instant, center
> Of so many environs,
> Who saw all
> Complete, as for a god.[45]

There is nothing of more importance with Guillén than this tardy apparition of the consciousness of the being. The consciousness, here, has in no sense the pretension of manifesting the supremacy of thought on space and of interiority on exteriority. It is content with placing the conscious subject at the very point where it is best situated to benefit by the munificences which a peripheral universe pours out in profusion into its interior space. Now, this point is evidently the center. The center is, par excellence, the concluding place. Not as the Aristotelians had imagined it, the lowest and most vile place in the universe; not as the Platonists had thought it to be, the most elevated, and most spiritual, but simply that around which the richness of the world is apportioned. Now every situation of space is that of the center of space, as every moment of time there is the center of duration. No especial privilege assigns an advantageous position to the human consciousness; no especial duty constrains it to see the world from any determined point. In no matter what place it finds itself, consciousness has no other mission than to render visible to the spirit the extraordinary concentration of temporal and spatial realities which abound. This is what one might call the *Cogito* of Jorge Guillén: I am, but I am by grace of the air and the light, by the revelation of a world whose admirable sphericity concentrates itself in me, as there spreads around me my desire to embrace the sphere. I find myself to be the median point of things. They end in me, as I dilate myself in them:

> O prodigious concentration! . . .[46]
> The present occupies the center
> Of so much concrete immensity.[47]

If the history of the circle begins with Parmenides, one can end it with Guillén. With one as with the other, the circle is the form of the perfection of the being.

NOTES TO TEXT

INTRODUCTION—NOTES

1. *Liber XXIV Philosophorum*, éd. Clemens Baeumker, Beiträge zur Geschichte der Philosophie des Mittelalters, 1928, pp. 207–214; cf. sur toute l'histoire du cercle infini le livre capital de Dietrich MAHNKE, *Unendlich Sphaere und Allmittelpunct*, Halle, 1937; cf. aussi E. JOVY, *Études pascaliennes*, t. VII et Marjorie HOPE NICOLSON, *The Breaking of the Circle*, Northwestern University Press, 1950.

2. *De Consolatione*, Lib. V, Prosa 6; cf. aussi Lib. IV, Prosa V. où Boèce oppose à la fixité centrale de la Providence la mobilité périphérique du Destin: *"Igitur (fatum) uti est ad intellectum ratiocinatio; ad id quod est, id quod gignitur, ad æternitatem tempus, ad puncti medium circulus."*—Tous les commentaires du Moyen Age sur ces textes sont importants, et, en particulier, celui de Scot Érigène (*Sæculi noni auctoris in Boetii Consolationem Philosophiæ Commentarius*, éd. E. T. Silk, American Academy in Rome, 1935). Voir surtout la phrase suivante: *"Nam, ut a centro circulus sic ab ævo deducitur tempus; et idem est in tempore ævum quod est in circulo centrum ... Nihil est enim aliud ævum quam contractio totius temporis præsentialiter habita in conspectu omnia videntis."*

3. νῦν ἔστιν ὁμοῦ πᾶν.

4. *Ennéades*, III, 7.

5. *Quæstiones Disputatæ, De Mysterio Trinitatis*, q. 5, art. I, 7–8, *Opera Omnia*, éd. Quaracchi, t. V, p. 91.

6. *Paradiso*, XIV, 1–3.—Sur les mouvements excentrique et concentrique dans le *Paradiso*, et la conversion de l'un dans l'autre, cf. Karl WITTE, Dante-Forschungen, 1879, t. II, p. 181, H. FLANDERS DUNBAR, *Symbolism in Medieval Thought*, Yale University Press, 1929, p. 88, Herbert D. AUSTIN, *Dante Notes*, Modern Languages Notes, 38, 1923, p. 140 et Allen TATE, *The Symbolic Imagination*, Kenyon *Review*, Spring 1952, pp. 257–277.

7. *Paradiso*, XVII, 18.

8. *Paradiso*, XXIX, 12.

9. *Vita Nova*, XII: *"Ego tanquam centrum circuli, cui simili modo se habent circumferentiæ partes; tu autem non sic."*—Cf. sur ce passage G. BOFFITO, *Bollettino della Societa Dantesca*, N. S., 10, 1902, p. 266 et Charles SINGLETON, *Romanic Review*, avril 1945; contra, Enrico PROTO, *Rassegna critica della*

Letteratura Italiana, 1902, pp. 192–200, et J. E. SHAW, *Italica*, juin 1947, pp. 113–118.

10. *Summa contra Gentiles*, Lib. I, cap. LXVI: "... *Cuilibet tempori vel instanti temporis præsentialiter adest æternitas. Cuius exemplum utcumque in circulo est videre: punctum enim in circumferentia signatum, etsi indivisibile sit, non tamen cuilibet puncto alii secundum situm coexistit simul, ordo enim situs continuitatem circumferentiæ facit; centrum vero, quod est extra circumferentiam, ad quodlibet punctum in circumferentia signatum directe oppositionem habet."*

11. *Declaratio quorundam Articulorum*, op. 2: "... *Centro similatur æternitas; quæ cum sit simplex et indivisibilis totum decursum temporis comprehendit et quælibet pars temporis est ei æqualiter præsens* ..."

12. *Commentarii in Primum Librum Sententiarum Pars prima*, Rome, 1596, p. 829: "*Exemplum illorum extitit de centro per respectum ad quemlibet punctum circumferentiæ, cui dixerunt simile esse de nunc æternitatis, per respectum ad quamlibet partem temporis. Unde æternum dixerunt coexistere præsentaliter toti tempori.*"—Cf. aussi Gilles DE ROME, *Defensorium sive Correctorium Corruptorii Operum Divin Thomæ*, Cordoue, 1702, p. 10.— Contra, cf. Duns SCOT, *Lib. I. Sententiarum*, Dist. 39, qu. unica.

13. *De Decem Dubitationibus*, éd. Cousin, t. VI, p. 82: "*Sicut igitur si centrum haberet cognitionem circuli, centralem utique haberet cognitionem* ... *Sic et Providentiæ unialis cognitio in eodem impartibili est omnium partitorum cognitio; et uniuscujusque individuissimorum et totalissimorum* ..."—Le texte grec de Proclus est perdu; cette traduction est de Guillaume de Moorbeke.—Cf. Pierre COURCELLE, *Les Lettres grecques en Occident*, p. 289.

14. Jean GERSON, *Tractatus super Magnificat*, *Opera Omnia*, éd. Ellis du Pin, La Haye, 1728, t. IV, p. 438.

15. *De Divinis Nominibus*, cap. v: "*Et in centro omnes circuli lineæ secundum primam unitatem consubstitutæ sunt.*" (traduction de Scot Érigène) —Cf. tous les commentaires de ce passage, en particulier saint Maxime, George Pachymère, saint Dorothée l'Archimandrite et l'abbé de Verceil.—Maurice de Gandillac a très bien vu l'importance du thème du cercle chez Denys. Cf. son édition des *Œuvres de Denys*, Aubier, p. 40.

16. *Paradiso*, XXVIII, 16: "*Un punto vidi che raggiava lume*"; id., 41–42:
    "*De quel punto*
    "*Depende il cielo, e tutta la natura.*"

17. *Paradiso*, XXX, 103–105.

18. *Adversus Arium*, lib. I, 60; Pl. 8, c. 1085: "... *Summitates et medium est in unoquoque* ... *Magis autem simul existentia sine aliquo intervallo, sphæra est et prima, et perfecta, et ipsa sola sphæra; at vero alia juxta similitudinem sphæricam magis.*"

19. Cf. H. LEISEGANG, *Denkformen*, 1928; M. F. RAUHUT, *Revista de Filologia hispanica*, I, 235 seq., et Leo SPITZER, *Le Style circulaire*, Modern Language Notes, 55, 1940, pp. 495–499.

20. *Cristoforo Landino*, Commentaires sur la Divine Comédie.

21. *Vita*, éd. W. Œhl, Deutsche Mystiker, p. 151: "*Es sagt ein weiser Meister, Gott sei, seiner Gottheit nach, wie ein gar weiter Ring, dessen Mittelpunkt allenthalben sei und der Umschwung nirgends. Hier nimm dies in deine bildliche Betrachtung: wenn jemand mit einem schweren Stein fest in ein stillstehendes Wasser würfe, so entstünde ein Ring im Wasser. Und der Ring macht aus seiner Kraft einen anderen, und der abermals einen anderen* ... *Das bezeichnen die drei Kreise: Vater, Sohn, heiliger Geist. In diesem tiefen*

Abgrunde spricht und gebiert die göttliche Natur im Vater das Wort hervor . . . Diese geistige, überwesliche Geburt ist die vollkommene Ursache aller Dinge und Geister, sie in ihr natürliches Dasein hervorzubringen."— Dans ce passage Suso s'inspire d'Eckhart (*Predigten*, 50, éd. F. Pfeiffer, p. 165) : *"Ich habe etwenne gesprochen ein gellchnüsse. Der einen stein würfe in einen wiger, von dem èrsten valle entspringet ein kreiz, der ist kleine und doch sò kreftic, daz ander kreize von ime enspringent, und der ander kreiz der ist wïter denne der èrste und ist doch niht sò kreftic, der dritte ist noch wïter . . . Har üf merkent. Der èrste üzval daz ist der sun üzer dem vater; der ist sò kleinlich unde doch an gotlicher maht so kreftic, daz er sache ist aller üzbrüche . . ."*—Sur Eckhart-Suso et la mystique allemande du cercle, voir surtout l'excellent livre de Maria BINDSCHEDLER, *Der lateinische Kommentar zum Granum Sinapis*, Bâle, 1949.

22. *Commentaria Sententiarum*, l. I, dist. I, p. 1, art. I, q. 1; cf. aussi *Hexæmeron*, col. 6, 8.

23. *Itinerarium Mentis ad Deum*, cap. v, 8.

24. Texte donné par DENIFLE, *Archiv für Literatur-und-Kirchengeschichte des Mittelalters*, t. II, 1886, p. 571: *"In divinis quodlibet est in quolibet, et maximum in minimo, et sic fructus in flore. Ratio, quia Deus, ut ait sapiens, est sphæra intellectualis infinita, cujus centrum est ubique, cum circumferentia nusquam, et cujus tot sunt circumferentiæ, quot puncta . . . Sic Deus est totus in qualibet creatura, in una, sicut in omnibus."*

25. *Paradiso*, XXXIII, 94–96.

26. Henricus HARPHIUS, *Theologia mystica*, lib. II, pars 5, col. 2: *"Dicitur etiam quandoque mens, quæ scilicet ipsis viribus interior est et supereminet: quia vires in mente sicut in origine sua sunt counitæ, ex qua scilicet effluunt ut radii ex solari rota, et in quam refluunt. Et est illud centrum in anima, in quo vera Trinitatis imago relucet: et tam nobile, quod nullum illi nomen proprie convenit, licet in multis nominibus circumlocutive manifestatur."*

27. *A Discourse on the Freedom of the Will*, London, 1675, p. 93.

28. *Œconomie divine*, Amsterdam, 1687, t. VII, p. 387.

29. *De Triplici Vita Hominis*, cap. VI, 45: *"Das ewige Centrum des Lebens Geburt und der Wesenheit ist überall. Wenn du einen kleinen Cirkel schleusst als ein kleines Körnlein, so ist darinnen die ganze Geburt der Ewigen Natur . . ."*

30. *Paradiso*, XXXIII, 7.

31. Alanus DE INSULIS, *Opera*, Migne, Pl. 210, col. 578.

32. *Roman de la Rose*, éd. Langlois, Société des anciens Textes français, 1914, t. IV, pp. 254–256.

33. *Analecta Hymnica Medii Ævi*, Leipzig, 1886, t. XX, p. 88—L'analogie entre le cercle et le triangle divins se retrouve dans de nombreux textes et emblèmes du Moyen Age et de la Renaissance. Cf., par exemple, le cercle inscrit dans un triangle, avec aux coins de celui-ci les lettres du tétragramme JEVE, dans un texte de Garnier de Rochefort, cité par Clemens Baeumker, *Beiträge zur Geschichte der Philosophie des Mittelalters*, 24, 1926, p. 35. Garnier de Rochefort y mentionne la première définition de Dieu dans le *Livre des vingt-quatre philosophes: "Spiritus Sanctus es. ardor Patris et Filii; monas gignit monadem et in se suum reflectit ardorem."*—Rappelons aussi ce passage de Gerson, dans le *Tractatus super Magnificat*, qui relie les deux premières définitions du même livre: *"Unitatem Dei per unitatem centralis puncti posse manudici. Hinc est ex Philosophis Dei descriptio, quod est sphæra intelligibilis cujus centrum est ubique, circumferentia nusquam.—*

Unitatem divinam gignere unitatem, et in se suam reflectere unitatem per amorem spirativum, triangulo intelligibili perfecte circulato." (Opera, éd. Ellis du Pin, t. IV, pp. 443–444.

L'on trouve la même identification du cercle et du triangle dans un passage des *Prisons* de Marguerite DE NAVARRE, dont Abel Lefranc a montré l'importance *(Grands Écrivains de la Renaissance,* pp. 170 sq.) :

> D' extérieur en l'intérieur entre
> Qui va par moi, et au milieu du centre
> Me trouvera, qui suis le point unique,
> La fin, le but de la mathématique;
> Le cercle suis dont toute chose vient,
> Le point où tout retourne et se maintient.
> Je suis qui suis triangle très parfait
> Le tout-puissant, sage et bon en effet . . .

Enfin, dans son *Orbis Sensualium Pictus* (1658), Coménius reproduit la figure du cercle inscrit dans un triangle, avec, en marge, le mot *Deus.* Dans sa *Theologia naturalis* (Vérone, 1779, p. 34) Christian Wolf commente cet emblème de la façon suivante: *"Comenius pingit triangulum cum circulo inscripto . . . Circulus designat æternitatem, triangulum circumscriptum Trinitatem in unitatem . . ."*

34. *In Hexæmeron,* col. 1, 24, *Opera omnia,* éd. *Quaracchi,* t. V, p. 333: "... *Non solum venit ad superficiem terræ, sed in profundo centri, et, in ventre centri, in corde terræ', salutem operatus est: quia per crucifixionem anima sua ad infernum descendit, et restauravit cœlestium sedium vacationes. In hoc profundo medio salus est, quia recedens a medio humilitatis, damnatur."*—Cf. le très beau commentaire sur ce passage par M. Étienne GILSON, *La Philosophie de saint Bonaventure,* Vrin, 1924, p. 222.

35. Cardinal DE BÉRULLE, *Opuscules de piété,* éd. Rotureau, Aubier, 1944, p. 184.

36. Angelus SILESIUS, *Cherubinischer Wandersmann,* l. III, 28.

37. Richard CRASHAW, *In the glorious Epiphanie of Our Lord God, a Hymn sung as by the three Kings,* the Poems, éd. L. C. Martin, Oxford Clarendon Press, 1927, p. 255:

> To Thee, thou Day of night! thou east of west!
> To thee, the world's great universal east.
> The Generall and indifferent Day.
> All circling point. All centring sphear . . .
> O little all! in thy embrace
> The world lyes warm, and likes his place.
> Nor does his full Globe fail to be
> Kist on Both his cheek by Thee.

38. Alonso DE BONILLA, *Nuevo Jardin de Flores Divinas,* Baeza, 1617, Biblioteca de Autores Españoles, t. XXXV, p. 45:

> Es Dios la original circunferencia
> De todas las esféricas figuras,
> Pues cercos, orbes, circulos y alturas
> En el centro se incluyen de su esencia.
>   De este infinito centro de la ciencia
> Salen immensas lineas de criaturas,
> Centellas vivas de las luces puras
> De aquella inaccesible omnipotencia.
>   Virgen, si es Dios el centro y el abismo
> De donde salen lineas tan extrañas,

Y vuestro vientre á Dios incluye dentro,
  Vos sois centro del centro de Dios misma,
Y tanta, que al salir de esas entrañas,
  Se hizo linea Dios de vuestro centro.

39. *Ennéades*, VI, 8, 18.

40. *De Divisione Naturæ, Opera*, Migne, Pl., 122, c. 625: "*Est enim centrum universale linearum initium in quo omnes unum sunt.*"

41. Robert GROSSETESTE, *De Lineis angulis et figuris*, éd. L. Baur, *Beiträge zur Geshichte der Philosophie des Mittelalters*, 9, 1912, p. 64.

42. *Expositio Libri Exodi*, Die Lateinischen Werke, éd. Kohlhammer, t. II, p. 22: "*Ipsius esse quandam in se ipsum et super ipsum reflexivam conversionem et in se ipso mansionem sive fixionem; adhuc autem quandam bullitionem sive parturitionem sui . . . Vita enim quandam dicit exseritionem, qua res in se ipsa intumescens se profundit primo in se toto, quodlibet sui in quodlibet sui, antequam effundat et ebulliat extra.*"

43. *Mosaical Philosophy*, London, 1659, p. 133: "*So that from God all things did flow and spring, namely out of a secret and hidden nature to a revealed and manifest condition, from an unknown estate unto an evident and known existence; from a pure Archetypal simplicity into a real type or similitude; from a radical fountain into a Sea, and from a mere point into a circle or circumference; verifying that saying of the wise Philosopher: God is the centre of everything, whose circumference is nowhere to be found.*"

44. *L'Univers ou Discours des parties et de la nature du Monde, Second Curieux*, éd. John C. Lapp, Cornell University Press, 1950, p. 144: "*Car Dieu est substance, puissance et action, qui surpassent et de qui dépendent toutes autres substances, puissances et actions. D'où prit source l'opinion des poètes qui ont chanté tout être plein de Jupiter, c'est-à-dire Dieu être épanché partout et particulièrement et généralement.*"

45. *Le Chat* (1573).

46. Pierre RAMUS, *Commentarii de Religione Christiana*, Francfort, 1583, t. I, cap. III: "*Quapropter Deus omnibus et locis et temporibus adest, omniaque perpetua virtute implet, nec usquam vel unquam impletur. Recteque philosophus ille dixit, Deum sphæram esse, cuius centrum esset ubique, peripheria nusquam.*"

47. Lettre à Descartes du 5 mars 1649: "*Hanc autem repetitionem centri divini, quæ mundum occupat, ulterius productam, infinita par est extra cœlum visibile spatia secum expandere.*"

48. *Tractatus de Deo et Anima vulgaris* (1457), Supplementum Ficinianum, éd. Kristeller, Florence, 1937, t. II, p. 147: "*Il centro adunque divino è in ogni loco, cioè la virtù di Dio alle nature attribuita è in ogni minima particula dell'universo.*"

49. Ralph CUDWORTH, *A Treatise concerning eternal and immutable morality*, l. I, cap. III, 8: "*Wherefore although some novelists make a contracted idea of God, consisting of nothing else but will and power, yet his nature is better expressed by some in this mystical or enigmatic representation of an infinite circle, whose inmost centre is simple goodness, the radii, rays' and expanded area, plat' thereof, all comprehending and immutable wisdom, the exterior periphery or interminate circumference, omnipotent will or activity, by which every thing without God is brought forth into existence.*"

50. *Quæstiones in Genesim*, Paris, 1623, col. 57: "*Est ergo Deus indivisibile centrum, cuius irradiatio in omnium rerum peripheriam extenditur.*"

51. *Articuli adversus Mathematicos, Opera Latine Conscripta*, Florence, 1889, t. I, pars 3, p. 60: *"Considerate vim omnem circuli esse in centro ... Anima centrum quoddam est, quæ etiam est circulus se ipsum movens."*

52. *Explicitatio totius astronomiæ, Opera*, Genève, 1658, t. II, p. 649: *"Ad centrum omnia contendunt: et homo est centrum totius mundi."* Cf. aussi *Astronomia Magna, Opera*, t. II, p. 567: *"Homo a mundo cinctus est, sicut punctum obitur a suo circulo."*

53. *De Hominis Dignitate, Opera*, Bâle, 1601, t. I, p. 208: *"Medium te mundi posui, ut circumspiceres unde commodius quicquid est in mundo."*

54. *Theologia Platonica*, l. III, cap. II: *"Merito dici (anima) possit centrum naturæ, universorum medium, mundi series, vultus omnium, nodusque et copula mundi."*

55. Carollus BOVILLUS, *Liber de Sapiente*, éd. Klibansky, Leipzig, 1927, p. 353: *"Homo nichil est omnium et a natura extra omnia factus et creatus est: ut multividus fiat sitque omnium expressio et naturale speculum, abjunctum et separatum ab universorum ordine, eminus et e regione omnium collocatum, ut omnium centrum."*

56. Juan DE LOS ANGELES, *Conquista del Espiritual y Secreto Reino de Dios* (1595), Nueva Biblioteca de Autores Españoles, Madrid, 1912, t. I, p. 45: *"Deste espiritu, ó intimo, ó centro, ó ápice del ánima procedon todas las fuerzas della, no de otra manera que los rayos procedon del sol ..."*

57. *A Treatise of Freewill*, éd. Allen, London, 1838, p. 28: *"This is an ever bubling fountain in the centre of the soul, an elater, or spring of motion ..."*

58. Henry MORE, *Antimonopsychia*, strophe 34.—Parlant de l'âme, More dit: *"central depth it has, and free dilation."*—Un peu plus loin toujours à propos de l'âme, More se sert des expressions *"hidden centrality"* et *"central energy."*

59. *Poésie*, éd. Gentile, Scrittori d'Italia 70, 1915, p. 42:
> *L'anima si faria un'immensa spera,*
> *Che amar, saper e far tutto potrebbe*
> *in Dio, di maraviglie sempr'altera.*

60. Thomas TRAHERNE, *Centuries of Meditations*, éd. B. Dobell, London, 1908, p. 136: *"My Soul is an infinite Sphere in a Centre."*

CHAPTER I—NOTES

1. *Commentaire sur les Vers d'or des Pythagoriciens*, trad. M. Meunier, 1931, p. 261.

2. *De decem dubitationibus*, passage reproduit par P. Courcelles, *Les Lettres grecques en Occident*, p. 289. M. Courcelles pense avec raison, semble-t-il, que Boèce (Cons. IV, prose 6), a été influencé par ce passage. Le rôle de Boèce dans le développement du thème du cercle a été énorme.

3. Cf. RAVAISSON, *Essai sur la métaphysique d'Aristotle*, 1837, t. II, p. 532.

4. *De divinis nominibus*, cap. V, art. 6.

5. *L'Amour des Amours*, Lyon, 1555, p. 33.

6. Lyon, 1570, p. 13.

7. Paris, 1573, p. 9.

8. *Œuvres*, éd. U. T. Holmes, Un. of North Carolina Press, 1938, t. II, p. 104.

9. *Ibid.*, p. 262.

10. Paris, 1583, p. 45.

11. Paris, 1582, f° 110 v.

12. Anvers, s. d., p. 28.

13. P. 171.

14. P. 116.

15. *"Possiamo affirmare che l'universo è tutto centro, ò che il centro de l'universo è per tutto: e che la circonferenza non è in parte alchuna . . ." De la causa, principio et uno, Opere italiane,* éd. Paul de Lagarde, Güttingue, 1888, p. 278.

16. *Liber de Nichilo,* 1510, f° 75 v.

17. P. 103.

18.   *"Glory is like a circel in the water*
      Which never ceaseth to enlarge itself . . ."
        King Henry the Sixth, First Part, Act. 1, Sc. 2.

19.   *And as a pebble cast into a spring,*
     We see a sort of trembling circles rise,
     One forming other in their issuing,
     Till over all the fount they circulize;
     So this perpetual-motion-making kiss
     Is propagate through all my faculties,
     And makes my breast an endless fount of bliss . . .
       Ovid's Banquet of Sense, Poems and Minor translations,
        Chatto and Windus, 1875, p. 35.

20. *Alcime,* Paris, 1625, p. 116.

21. *A la Baronne de Chantal,* 7 mars 1608, cité par H. BREMOND, *Histoire du sentiment religieux,* t. I, p. 113.

22. *Œuvres,* t. II, p. 154.

23. *"Humanitatis extat virtus omnia ex se explicare intra regionis suæ circulum, omnia de potentia centri exerere."—De conjecturis,* Lib. II cap. XIII, *Opera,* éd. Lefèvre d'Étaples, t. I, f° LX r.

24. *". . . Ist der mensch ein kern und die welt der apfel . . ."—Astronomia magna, Sämtliche Werke,* München, 1929, Bd. 12, p. 164.

25. *"Minimum est virtute maximum . . ."—De triplici minimo et mensura,* Francfort, 1591, p. 55.

26. Ce livre devrait reprendre d'ailleurs bien des intuitions de Burckhardt.

27. *"Cum igitur spatium illud extra mundum imaginarium imagineris, non nihilum, sed divinæ substantiæ plenitudinem in infinitum distensa ut concipias oportet."—Iter exstaticum cœleste,* 1671, p. 436.

28. *"A liberal Man moves in a Sphere of Wonders . . ."—Christian Ethicks,* 1675, p. 473.

29. *Centuries of Meditations,* éd. Dobell, London, 1908, p. 136.

30.   *O Joy! O Wonder! and Delight!*
       O sacred Mystery!
     My soul a Spirit infinit!
     An image of the Deity!

     . . . .

     A strange extended Orb of Joy,
     Proceeding from within,

> *Which did on evry side convey*
> *Its self; and being nigh of Kin*
> *To God, did evry way*
> *Dilate its self even in an instant, and*
> *Like an indivisible centre stand,*
> *At once surrounding all Eternity.*

My Spirit, éd. H. M. Margoliouth, p. 54.—Sur Traherne, les poètes métaphysiques et le cercle, lire le très bel ouvrage de Marjory H. Nicholson, *The Breaking of the Circle,* Northwestern, 1949.

31. *Lettre à Champvallon,* s. d.

32. *Poésies,* éd. Boase- Ruchon, Genève, 1949.

33. *L'Astrée,* éd. Vaganay, Lyon, 1926, t. II, p. 262.

34. *Id.,* p. 301.

35. *Jeux rustiques:* Contre les Pétrarquistes.

36. *Œuvres spirituelles sur les Évangiles de Carême,* Paris, 1620, p. 5.

37. *Théorèmes,* t. II, Toulouse, 1622, p. 144.

38. *Œuvres, poétiques,* Paris, 1672, p. 173.

39. *Id.,* p. 240.

40. *"Oh llama de amor viva—Que tiernamente hieres—De mi alma en el mas profundo centro!—. . . Aquello llamamos centro mas profundo que es à lo que mas puede llegar su ser y virtud y la fuerza de su operacion y movimiento, y no puede pasar de alli; así como el fuego ó la piedra que tienen virtud y movimiento natural y fuerz para llegar al centro de su esfera, y no pueden pasar de alli ni dejar de estar alli sino es por algun impedimento contrario . . . El centro del alma dios es."—Llama de amor viva,* 1.

41. *Poésies spirituelles,* Paris, 1671, p. 41.

42. *Poésies et cantiques spirituels,* Paris, 1790, t. III, p. 3.

43. *Id.,* p. 79.

44. *Les Saintes Décades de Quatrains de piété chrétienne,* Amsterdam, 1671, p. 39.

45. *Id.,* p. 71.

46. *Œuvres,* éd. Ginguené, Paris, 1811, t. II, p. 290.

CHAPTER II—NOTES

1. *Adone,* Canto IX, stanza 108:

> *Meraviglia talor, mentre s'estolle,*
> *Arco stampa nel Ciel simile ad Iri.*
> *Traformarsi l'umor liquido a molle,*
> *Volto in raggi, in comete, in stelle il miri.*
> *Miri qui sgorgar globi, eruttar bolle,*
> *La girelle rotar con cento gizi,*
> *Spuntar rampolli e pullular zampilli,*
> *E guizzi e spruzzi e pispinelli e spilli.*

2. *Essai des merveilles de nature et des plus nobles artifices,* 9e éd., Lyon, 1636, p. 464.

3. *Adone,* Canto X, Stanza 174:

> *La gran rota del tutto in picciol tondo . . .*

4. Girolami PRETI, *L'Oriuolo*, in *Marino e I Marinisti*, a cura di Giuseppe Guido
   Ferrero, La letteratura italiana, Storia e Testi, vol. 37, p. 717:

   > Come sfera maggiore in ciel s'aggira,
   > che col suo cerchio i minor cerchi abbracia,
   > e le rotanti sfere al corso tira,
   > che del corso di lei seguon la traccia;
   > cosi ruota maggior qui seco gira
   > ruote minori, e col fuggir le caccia;
   > e, com' appunto i cieli, intorno ruota
   > corso a corso contraria e ruota a ruota.

5. Ciro DI PERS, *Bella Dipanatrice*, in *Marino e I Marinisti*, p. 943:

   > E se pria dilatossi in ampi giri,
   > Or la raccoglie in uno, e vuol ch'unita
   > solo nel suo bel volto e viva e spiri.

6. *Crashaw's Poems*, éd. L. C. Martin, Clarendon Press, p. 175:

   > Come then youth, Beauty, and Blood, all ye soft powers,
   > Whose silken flatteryes swell a few fond houres
   > Into a false eternity, come man,
   > (Hyperbolized nothing!) know thy span.
   > Take thy owne measure here, downe, downe, and bow
   > Before thy selfe in thy Idea, thou
   > Huge emptinesse contract thy bulke, and shrinke
   > All thy wild Circle to a point!

7. Cf. Jean ROUSSET, *La Littérature de l'âge baroque en France*, Corti, 1953,
   p. 138:

   > Sphæra, non vitrea quidem,
   > Ut quondam Siculus globus,
   > Sed vitro nitida magis,
   > Et vitro vitrea magis.
   > Sum venti ingenium breve
   > Flos sum, scilicet, aëris;
   > Sidus scilicit æquoris;
   > Naturæ jocus aureus,
   > Naturæ vaga fabula,
   > Naturæ breve somnium.
   >
   > . . . .
   >
   > Sum bladum, petulans, vagum,
   > Pulchrum, purpureum, et decens,
   > Comptum, floridulum, et recens,
   > Distinctum nivibus, rosis,
   > Undis, ignibus aëre,
   > Pictum, gemmeum et aureum,
   > O sum, scilicet, O nihil.

8. William DRUMMOND, *Madrigal*, cité par M. H. NICHOLSON, *The Breaking of
   the Circle*, U. of Michigan Press, 1940, p. 42:

   > This life which seems so fair
   > Is like a bubble blown up in the air
   > By sporting children's breath,
   > Who chase it everywhere,
   > And strive who can most it bequeath.
   > And though it seem sometime of its own might,
   > Like to an eye of gold, to be fixed there,
   > And firm to hover in that empty height,

> *That only is because it is too slight.*
> *But in that pomp it doth not long appear,*
> *For even when most admired, it is a thought*
> *As swelled from nothing, doth dissolve in nought.*

9. *Poésies et cantiques spirituels*, 4 vol., Paris, 1790, t. IV, p. 247.

10. *Laudate*, cité par H. BREMOND, *Histoire du sentiment religieux*, t. I, p. 203.

11. *Andrew Marvell's Poems*, éd. H. M. Margoliouth, Clarendon Press, p. 112.
(Il y aussi une version latine de ce poème) :

> *See, how the orient dew,*
> *Shed from the bosom of the morn*
> *Into the blowing roses,*
> *(Yet careless of its mansion new,*
> *For the clear region where 'twas born,)*
> *Round in itself incloses;*
> *And, in its little globe's extent,*
> *Frames, as it can, its native element.*
> *How it the purple flower does slight,*
> *Scarce touching where it lies;*
> *But gazing back upon the skies,*
> *Shines with a mournful light,*
> *Like its own tear,*
> *Because so long divided from the sphere.*
> *Restless it rolls, and unsecure,*
> *Trembling, lest it grow impure;*
> *Till the warm sun pity its pain,*
> *And to the skies exhale it back again.*
> *So the soul, that drop, that ray*
> *Of the clear fountain of eternal day,*
> *(Could it within the human flower be seen,)*
> *Remembering still its former height,*
> *Shuns the sweet leaves, and blossoms green,*
> *And, recollecting its own light,*
> *Does, in its pure and circling thoughts, express*
> *The greater heaven in an heaven less.*
> *In how coy a figure wound,*
> *Every way it turns away;*
> *So the world-excluding round,*
> *Yet receiving in the day;*
> *Dark beneath, but bright above,*
> *Here disdaining, there in love.*
> *How loose and easy hence to go;*
> *How girt and ready to ascend;*
> *Moving but on a point below,*
> *It all about does upwards bend.*
> *Such did the manna's sacred dew distil;*
> *White and entire, thou congealed and chill;*
> *Congealed on earth; but does, dissolving, run*
> *Into the glories of the almighty sun.*

12. *Œuvres poétiques*, Paris, 1672, p. 407.

13. *Andrew Marvell's Poems*, p. 26; Pierre LEGOUIS, *André Marvell*, Paris, 1928, p. 75:

> *Now therefore, while the youthful hue*
> *Sits on thy skin like morning dew,*
> *And while thy willing soul transpires*

At every pore with instant fires.
Now let us sport us while we may,
And now, like amorous birds of prey,
Rather at once our time devour,
Than languish in his slow-chapt power.
Let us roll all our strength and all
Our sweetness up into one ball,
And tear our pleasures with rough strife,
Through the iron gates of life.

14. *Cowley's Poems*, éd. A. R. Waller, Cambridge University Press, p. 186:

If Past, and Future Times do thee obey,
    Thou stopst this Current, and dost make
This running River settle like a Lake,
Thy certain hand holds fast this slippery Snake.
    The Fruit which does so quickly waste,
    Men scarce can see it, much less taste,
Thou Comfitest in Sweets to make it last.
    This shining piece of Ice
    Which melts so soon away,
    With the Sun's ray,
Thy Verse does solidate and crystallize,
    Till it a lasting Mirror be.
    Nay thy Immortal Rhyme.
    Makes this short Point of Time,
To fill up half the Orb of Round Eternity.

15. Guido CASONI, *La Lucciola, Opere scelte di Marinisti*, a cura di Giovanni Getto, Torino, 1954, p. 472:

Luciolatta gentile,
mentre scherzi e t'aggiri,
fai a l'ombre un monile
co'tuoi lucidi giri.

16. Giovan Francesco MAIA MATERDONA, *Giuoco di neve, Lirici Marinisti*, a cura di Benedetto Croce, Bari, 1910, p. 111:

Cilla di bianco umor massa gelata
coglie e preme e ne forma un globo breve;
n'arma poscia la mano, a fredda neve
calda neve aggiungendo ed animata.

17. *Il Gioco delle Carte*, in *Opere scelte di Marinisti*, a cura di Giovanni Getto, p. 456:

Fugace instante, indivisibil punto.

18. BERNIS, *Épître sur les mœurs*.

19. *Essay on Man*, Epistle 1:

And now a bubble burst, and now a world.

20. *Théorie des Tourbillons cartésiens, Œuvres*, Paris, 1761, t. IX, p. 244.

21. *Id.*, p. 281.

CHAPTER III—NOTES

1. *Pensées et Opuscules*, éd. Brunschvicg, Hachette, p. 567.

2. *Id.*

3. P. 646.

4. *Du côté de chez Swann*, I, p. 11.

5. P. 428.

6. P. 427.

7. P. 347.

8. P. 348.

9. P. 356.

10. P. 419.

11. P. 695.

12. P. 427.

13. P. 418.

14. P. 431.

15. P. 434.

16. *Expériences nouvelles touchant le vide.*

17. Cf. *Lettre de Pascal à Le Pailleur.*

18. P. 488.

19. *De Hominis Dignitate.*

20. *Theologicæ Conclusiones,* 1515, f. 15 v.

21. P. 352.

22. P. 347.

23. P. 174.

24. P. 519.

25. P. 519.

26. Cf. sur la "préhension sensible" chez Pascal l'excellent livre de Jean DE-MOREST, *Dans Pascal*, éd. de Minuit, 1953.

27. P. 560.

28. P. 491.

29. *Opus Oxoniense*, l. I, dist. 39.

30. P. 492.

31. P. 318.

32. P. 321.

33. P. 355; cf. variante.

34. P. 434.

35. 3ᵉ éd., Paris, 1640, t. I, p. 305.

36. En marge: *Cusa, excitatio*, l. X, cap. XII.

37. *De Docte Ignorantia*, l. I, cap. XXIII.

38. *De la causa, principio, et uno*, dial. 3.

39. P. 434.

40. *Theologicæ Conclusiones*, f. 50 r.

41. P. 442.

42. Cf. Jean DAGENS, *Bérulle et les origines de la restauration catholique*, Desclée, 1952, p. 54.

43. P. 352.

44. P. 351.

45. *Théologie naturelle*, Paris, 1635, t. II, p. 172.

46. P. 184.

47. P. 581.
48. P. 519.
49. P. 581.
50. *Pascal par lui-même*, éd. du Seuil, 1952, p. 51.

CHAPTER IV—NOTES

1. *Cavaliere che manda un pallone alla sua donna*, in *Marino e I Marinisti*, a cura di Giuseppe Guido Ferrero, p. 1015:
> *Questo globo, che spesso in aria avvento,*
> *ove de'miei sospiri i fiati ascondo,*
> *Nice, fia tuo: gradisci un sì bel pondo,*
> *e sia del donò il tuo desir contento.*
> *Questo rotava cento volte e cento,*
> *con Giacinto scherzando, il dio più biondo.*
> *Par del mondo un'idea, se non è il mondo,*
> *e prigione volubile del vento.*

2. *Le Cabinet du Philosophe*, 2ᵉ feuille, *Œuvres*, t. IX, p. 565.
3. *L'Ode de M. de La Faye mise en prose*, *Œuvres*, Paris, 1753, t. I, 2ᵉ partie, p. 503.
4. *The Analysis of Beauty* (1753), éd. J. Burke, Clarendon Press, 1955, p. 55:
> ". . . *The serpentine line, by its waving and winding at the same time different ways, leads the eye in a pleasing manner along the continuity of its variety, if I may be allowed the expression.*"

5. *Les Jardins*, *Œuvres*, Michaud, 1820, t. IX, p. 59.
6. *Id.*, p. 75.
7. *Geschichte der Kunst des Altertums*, Wiens, 1934, p. 151:
> "*In der schönen Jugend fanden die Künstler die Ursache der Schönheit in der Einheit, in der Mannigfaltigkeit und in der Übereinstimmung. Denn die Formen eines schönen Körpers sind durch Linien bestimmt, welche beständig ihren Mittelpunkt verändern und fortgeführt niemals einen Zirkel beschreiben, folglich einfacher, aber auch mannigfaltiger als ein Zirkel, welcher so gross und so klein derselbe immer ist, eben den Mittelpunkt hat und andere in sich schliesst oder eingeschlossen wird.*"

8. Tommaso GUADIOSI, *La Ragna*, in *Marino e I Marinisti*, p. 1026:
> *Delle viscere sue tesse e compone*
> *pargoletto animal tra ramo e ramo*
> *ingegnoso ricamo:*
> *di fila innumerabili dispone*
> *talor sferica mole,*
> *che distinta di rai rassembra un sole.*
> *E mentre al vago e fragile disegno,*
> *consumando se stesso, è tutto intento,*
> *ecco improviso vento,*
> *che, dibattendo il mobile sostegno,*
> *le molli fila infrante,*
> *dissipa la bell'opra in uno istante.*

9. *Essai sur les causes qui peuvent affecter les esprits et les caractères.*
10. *Essay on Man*, Epistle 1:
> *The spider's touch, how exquisitely fine!*
> *Feels at each thread, and lives along the line.*

11. *Œuvres,* Paris, 1844, t. II, p. 626.

12. *Histoire naturelle,* Imprimerie Royale, t. III, p. 8.

13. *Discours préliminaire du Nouveau Dictionnaire,* Hambourg, 1797, p. 146.

14. *Introduction à la connaissance de l'esprit humain, Œuvres,* éd. Gilbert t. I, p. 13.

15. *Über die Tugend-Volkommene Unvergleichlich-Schöne Aramena,* in Anton Ulrich VON BRAUNSCHWEIG'S, *Die Durchleuchtige Syrerin Aramena,* Nuremberg, 1679, Bd. 3, S. 1:
> "... *das künstliche Zerrütten*
> *voll schönster ordnung ist. Es gehet aus der mitten*
> *des klugen Absehens Punct: wan man die Striche zieht*
> *zum kunstbemerkten Dupf/das Fügungs-Bild man siht*
> *vollkommen klärlich stehn.*"

16. *Preface to Troilus and Cressida* (1679), *Essays,* éd. W. P. Ker, Clarendon Press, t. I, p. 208:
> "... *As in perspective, so in Tragedy, there must be a point of sight in which all the lines terminate.*"

17. *A Parallel of Poetry and Painting* (1695), *Essays,* t. II, p. 143:
> "... *The hero is the centre of the main action; all the lines from the circumference tend to him alone.*"

18. *Anklagung des verdehrten Gesmackes,* Frankfurt, 1728, p. 112, cité par René WELLEK, *History of Modern Criticism,* Yale, 1955, t. I, p. 148.

19. *Spectator,* n° 415, June 26, 1712:
> "*Among all the Figures in Architecture, there are none that have a greater Air than the Concave and the Convex, and we find in all the Ancient and Modern Architecture, as well in the remote Parts of China, as in Countries nearer home, that round Pillars and Vaulted Roofs make a great Part of those Buildings which are designed for Pomp and Magnificence. The Reason I take to be, because in these Figures we generally see more of the Body, than in those of other Kinds ... Look upon the Outside of a Dome, your Eye half surrounds it; look up into the Inside, and at one Glance you have all the Prospect of it; the entire Concavity falls into your Eye at once, the Sight being as the center that collects and gathers into it the Lines of the whole Circumference:*"

20. *Œuvres,* éd. L. Aimé-Martin, 1818, t. IV, p. 373.

21. *Id.,* p. 94.

22. *Id.,* t. IX, p. 120.

23. *Id.,* t. VIII, p. 9.

24. *Spectator,* n° 590, September 6, 1714:
> "*In our Speculations of infinite Space, we considered that particular Place in which we exist, as a Kind of Center to the whole Expansion.*"

25. N° 565, July 9, 1714.

26. *Traité des Sensations, Œuvres,* éd. Théry, t. III, p. 86.

27. *La Henriade,* Chant 7; passage cité dans l'*Encyclopédie* à l'article "Soleil".

28. *Œuvres,* éd. Pléiade, p. 403; c'est un fragment de l'*Hermès.*

29. *La Nature,* Chant 1 (1760), *Œuvres,* éd. Ginguené, Paris, 1811, t. II, p. 290.

30. Matthew PRIOR, *Poems on several Occasions,* éd. A. R. Waller, Cambridge University Press, 1905, p. 278:
> "*In vain We measure this amazing Sphere,*
> *And find and fix its Centre here or there;*

> *Whilst its Circumference, scorning to be brought*
> *Ev'n into fancied Space, eludes our vainquish'd Thought.*

31. *The Moralists, Characteristics,* éd. J. M. Robertson, London, 1910, t. II, p. 98.
    "*O glorious nature! . . . Thy being is boundless, unsearchable, impenetrable . . . Wearied imagination spends itself in vain, finding no coast nor limit of this ocean, nor, in the widest tract through which it soars, one point yet nearer the circumference than the first centre whence it parted.*"

32. *Allgemeine Naturgeschichte und Theorie des Himmels, Sämtliche Werke,* Leipzig, 1867, t. I, pp. 290–297:
    "*Es ist zwar an dem, dass in einem unendlichen Raume kein Punkt eigentlich das Vorrecht haben kann, der Mittelpunkt zu heissen: aber vermittelst einer gewissen Verhältniss, die sich auf die wesentlichen Grade der Dichtigkeit des Urstoffes gründet, nach welcher diese zugleich mit ihrer Schöpfung an einem gewissen Orte vorzüglich dichter, gehäuft, und mit den Weiten von demselben in der Zerstreuung zunimmt, kann ein solcher Punkt das Vorrecht haben, der Mittelpunkt zu heissen, und er wird es auch wirklich durch die Bildung der Centralmasse von der kräftigsten Anziehung in demselben, zu dem sich alle übrige, in Particularbildungen begriffene elementarische Materie senkt, und dadurch, soweit sich auch die Auswickelung der Natur erstrecken mag, in der unendlichen Sphäre der Schöpfung aus dem ganzen All nur ein einziges System macht.*"

33. Arthur Lovejoy, *The Great Chain of Being,* Harvard, 1936.

34. *Essai sur le goût* (1758).

35. *Œuvres,* éd. Gilbert, t. II, p. 28.

36. *Le Rêve de d'Alembert,* éd. J. Lough, Cambridge University Press, p. 126.

37. Diderot, *Œuvres,* éd. Assézat, t. II, p. 306.

38. *Id.,* t. XVIII, p. 224.

39. *Neveu de Rameau.*

40. *Le Rêve de d'Alembert,* p. 115.

41. *Eléments de physiologie, Œuvres,* t. IX, p. 275.

42. *Œuvres,* t. XVIII, p. 115.

43. *Le Rêve de d'Alembert,* p. 115.

44. *Traité de la lumière,* 1690, chap. 1.

45. *Le Rêve de d'Alembert,* p. 113.

46. *Dictionnaire philosophique,* art. *Chaîne ou Génération des événements.*

47. *Eléments de philosophie de Newton,* première partie.

48. *Institutions physiques,* Nlle éd., Amsterdam, 1742, pp. 150–152.

49. *Lettre à la Princesse Sophie de Hanovre,* du 6 février 1706, *Philosophischen Schriften,* éd. Gerhardt, Berlin, 1875, p. 566.

50. *The Temple of Fame,* v. 435–447; *Essay on Man,* Epistle IV, v. 361–372; *Dunciad,* liv. II, v. 383–418.

CHAPTER V—NOTES

1. *Traité élémentaire de sphère, Œuvres et corr.,* éd. Steickeissen-Moultou, Paris, 1861, p. 199.

2. *Émile,* éd. Garnier, p. 323.

3. *Id.,* p. 3.

4. *Id.*, p. 2.

5. *Id.*, p. 35.

6. *Id.*, p. 260.

7. *Id.*, p. 43.

8. *Id.*, p. 179.

9. *Id.*

10. *Confessions, Œuvres,* éd. Pléiade, p. 426.

11. *Id.*, p. 58.

12. *Émile,* p. 43.

13. *Huitième Rêverie,* éd. Pléiade, p. 1074.

14. *Id.*

15. *Nouvelle Héloïse,* I, l. 54.

16. *Id.*, Avertissement de la 2ᵉ éd.—Sur le thème de la jalousie et de la multi-
plicité de la douleur chez Rousseau, cf. l'admirable passage d'*Émile et
Sophie,* lettre 1: "Il n'est plus un, il est tout entier à chaque point de douleur, il semble se multiplier pour souffrir."

17. *La Philosophie de l'existence de Jean-Jacques Rousseau,* 1952, p. 151. Sur
tout le thème de l'expansion le livre de Burgelin est capital. Cf. surtout ch.
v, *passim.*

18. *Émile,* p. 62.

19. *Préface du Narcisse.*

20. *Émile,* p. 59.

21. *Id.*, p. 62.

22. *Lettres morales,* lettre 6, *Corr.,* t. III, p. 369.

23. *Émile,* p. 60.

24. *Lettres morales,* passage cité.

25. *Lettre à d'Alembert,* éd. Garnier, p. 183.

26. *Id.*, p. 184.

27. *Nouvelle Héloïse,* IV, l. 11.

28. *Id.*

29. *Émile,* p. 59.

30. *Id.*, p. 63.

31. *Huitième Rêverie,* p. 1074.

32. *Lettre à Henriette,* 4 nov. 1764, *Corr.,* t. XII, p. 29.

33. *Dixième Rêverie,* p. 1009.

34. *Essay on Man,* Ep. IV:
> *Self-love but serves the virtuous mind to wake,*
> *As the small pebble stirs the peaceful lake;*
> *The centre moved, a circle straight succeeds,*
> *Another still, and still another spreads;*
> *Friend, parent, neighbour, first it will embrace;*
> *His country next; and next all human race.*

35. *Émile,* p. 268, note.

36. *Id.*, p. 252.

37. *Nouvelle Héloïse,* I, l. 38.

38. *Id.*, V, l. 3.

39. *Id.*, IV, 1. 2.
40. *Id.*, II, l. 5.
41. *Id.*, VI, l. 8.
42. *Id.*, VI, l. 11.
43. *Neuvième Rêverie*, p. 1085.
44. *Id.*, p. 1093.
45. *Lettre à d'Alembert*, in fine.
46. *Dialogues*, éd. Pléiade, p. 805.
47. *Émile*, p. 252.
48. *Dialogues*, pp. 752 et 913.
49. *Id.*, p. 713.
50. *Id.*, p. 826.
51. *Id.*, p. 882.
52. *Ébauche des Rêveries*, fragm. 19, éd. Pléiade, p. 1170.
53. *Nouvelle Héloïse*, II, l. 14.
54. *Huitième Rêverie*, p. 1077.
55. *Sixième Rêverie*, p. 1056.
56. *Confessions*, p. 428.
57. *Dialogues*, p. 822.
58. *Troisième Lettre à Malesherbes*, 26 janv. 1762, éd. Pléiade, p. 1141.
59. *Huitième Rêverie*, p. 1075.
60. *Septième Rêverie*, p. 1962.
61. *Id.*, p. 1063.
62. *Id.*, p. 1066.

CHAPTER VI—NOTES

1. Ludwig Tieck, *Schriften*, Berlin, 1828–1854, Bd. 7, S. 188, *William Lovell:* "*Was mich in meinen Schmerzen am meisten niederschlug, war, dass die Natur und alle Gegenstände umher so kalt und empfindunglos schienen. In mir selbst war der Mittelpunkt aller Empfindungen, und je mehr ich aus mir hinausging, je weiter lagen die Empfindungen auseinander, die in meinem Herzen dicht neben einander wohnten.*"

2. *Notes sur l'Évangile de saint Jean*, éd. Naville, t. III, p. 306.

3.   *Ich bin der Mittelpunkt, der heilge Quell,*
      Aus welchem jede Sehnsucht stürmisch flieszt,
      Wohin sich jede Sehnsucht, mannigfach
      Gebrochen, wieder still zusammen zieht.

   Novalis, Schriften, éd. Kluckhon, Leipzig, 1929, Bd. 1, S. 221, *Heinrich von Ofterdingen.*

4. Saint-Martin, *L'Homme de désir*, Lyon, 1790, p. 78.

5. Saint-Martin, *Des erreurs et de la vérité*, Édimbourg, 1775, p. 411.

6. *Id.*, p. 410.

7. *Id.*

8.   *Thou perceivest the Flowers put forth their precious Odours,*

> *And none can tell how from so small a center comes such sweets,*
> *Forgetting that within that Center Eternity expands*
> *Its ever during doors . . .*
>
> William BLAKE, *Milton,* 2ᵉ livre, 34.

9. *To see a World in a Grain of Sand*
And a Heaven in a Wild Flower,
Hold Infinity in the palm of your hand
And Eternity in an hour.

William BLAKE, *Auguries of Innocence.*

10. *Adolphe,* chap. III.

11. Jean-Paul RICHTER, *Sämmtliche Werke,* Berlin, 1841, Bd. 10, S. 204, *Der Jubelsenior:* "*So viel hab'ich, ohne noch für die Presse darüber nachgedacht zu haben, heraus, dass in unserer Idee von der Totalität eines jeden Menschen ein Hauptzug, ein Brennpunkt, ein* Punctum Saliens, *vorglänze, um welches sich die Nebenpartien abstufend bilden.*"

12. F. W. J. SCHELLING, *Sämmtliche Werke,* Stuttgart, 1860, Bd. 1, 8, S. 326, *Die Weltalter:* "*Das ganze räumlich ausgedehnte Weltall ist nichts anderes als das schwellende Herz der Gottheit, das durch unsichtbare Kräfte gehalten in in beständigem Pulsschlag oder Wechsel von Ausdehnung und Zusammenziehung fortdauert.*"

13. LAMENNAIS, *Esquisse d'une philosophie,* Renouard, 1840, t. III, p. 23.

14. J. G. HERDER, *Sämmtliche Werke,* ed. Suphan, Bd. 13, S. 114, *Ideen* ". . . *den Mittelpunkt des Kreises, in welchem alle Radien zusammen zu laufen scheinen.*"

15. Johann GOTTLIEB FICHTE, *Sämmtliche Werke,* Berlin, 1845, Bd. 5, S. 493, *Religionslehre:* "*Alle innere geistige Energie erscheint im unmittelbaren Bewusstsein derselben, als ein sich Zusammennehmen, Erfassen und Contrahiren seines ausserdem zerstreuten Geistes in Einen Punkt, und als ein sich Festhalten in diesem Einheitspunkte gegen das stets fortdauernde natürliche Bestreben, diese Contraction aufzugeben, und sich wiederum auszudehnen . . . Kurz das ursprüngliche Bild der geistigen Selbständigkeit ist im Bewusstsein ein ewig sich machender und lebendigst sich haltender, geometrischer Punkt.*"

16. *Sämmtliche Werke,* Bd. 2, S. 37, *Darstellung der Wissenschaftlehre:* ". . . *Die formale Freiheit sich nur anschaue, als Zusammenziehen eines verfliessenden Mannigfaltigen* möglichen *Lichtes zu einem Centralpunkte, und Verbreiten dieses Lichtes aus diesem Centralpunkte über ein nur dadurch gehaltenes und factisch erleuchtetes Mannigfaltige.*"

17. *Sämmtliche Werke,* Bd. 1, S. 412–415, *Ueber die Würde des Menschen:* "*Die Philosophie lehrt uns alles im Ich aufsuchen. Erst durch das Ich kommt Ordnung und Harmonie in die todte, formlose Masse. Allein vom Menschen aus verbreitet sich Regelmässigkeit rund um ihn herum bis an die Grenze seiner Beobachtung . . . Durch sie halten sich die Weltkörper zusammen, und werden nur* Ein *organisirter Körper; durch sie drehen die Sonnen sich in ihren angewiesenen Bahnen. Durch das Ich steht die ungeheure Stufenfolge da von der Flechte bis zum Seraph; in ihm ist das System der ganzen Geisterwelt, und der Mensch erwartet mit Recht, dass das Gesetz, das er sich und ihr giebt, für sie gelten müsse; erwartet mit Recht die einstige allgemeine Anerkennung desselben. Im Ich liegt das sichere Unterpfand, das von ihm aus ins unendliche Ordnung und Harmonie sich verbreiten werde, wo jetzt noch keine ist; dass mit der fortrückenden Cultur des Menschen, zugleich die Cultur des Weltalls fortrücken werde . . . In jedem Momente seiner Existenz reisst er (der Mensch) etwas neues ausser sich in seinen Kreis*

mit fort, und er wird fortfahren an sich zu reissen, bis er alles in denselben verschlinge: bis alle Materie das Gepräg seiner Einwirkung trage, und alle Geister mit seinem Geiste Einen Geist ausmachen."

18. F. W. J. SCHELLING, *Sämmtliche Werke*, Bd. 1, 6, S. 167, *System der gesammten Philosophie und der Naturphilosophie insbesondere: "Der Mittelpunkt ist der ganze Kreis, nur in seiner Idealität oder in seiner Affirmation angeschaut, die Peripherie ist der ganze Kreis, nur in seiner Realität angeschaut."*

19. *Philosophische Vorlesungen aus den Jahren 1804 bis 1806*, Bonn, 1836, t. II, p. 417, cité par Alfred SCHLAGDENHAUFFEN, *Frédéric Schlegel et son groupe*, Paris, 1934, p. 162.

20. NOVALIS, *Schriften*, Bd. 1, S. 17, *Die Lehrlinge zu Sais: "Es ist ein geheimnisvoller Zug nach allen Seiten in unserm Innern, aus einem unendlich tiefen Mittelpunkt sich rings verbreitend."*—Sur Novalis et le thème du point il faut lire les excellentes remarques de Maurice Besset, dans son livre, *Novalis et la pensée mystique*, Aubier, 1947, pp. 97–102.

21. G. W. F. HEGEL, *Jenenser Logik*, hrsg. von Lasson, S. 161: *"Diejenigen, deren Unendlichkeit das Ich ist, sind selbst Unendliche, Reflexionen in sich selbst, nicht blosse Kreise, sondern welche selbst zu ihren Momenten Kreise haben und die Kreise dieser Kreise sind."*

22. *Essai sur les révolutions anciennes et modernes. Œuvres*, éd. Dufour, vol. II, p. 102.

23. *L'Humanité, Harmonies, Hachette*, p. 160.

24. SHELLEY, *Prose*, ed. D. L. Clark, University of Mexico Pr., 1954, p. 173, *Essay on Life: "Each is at once the centre and the circumference, the point to which all things are referred, and the line in which all things are contained."*

25. *Prose*, p. 293, *A Defense of Poetry: "Poetry . . . is at once the centre and circumference of knowledge."*

26. KEATS, *To B. Bailey*, 13 March 1818: *"It is an old maxim of mine that every point of thought is the centre of an intellectual world."*

27. *. . . Hither come and find a lodge
To which thou may'st resort for holier peace,—
From whose calm centre thou, through height or depth,
May'st penetrate, wherever truth shall lead.*
WORDSWORTH, *Excursion*, liv. III, v. 106–109.

28. COLERIDGE, *Poetical Works*, ed. E. H. Coleridge, Oxford, 1912, t. I, p. 296: *"On awaking, the author appeared to himself to have a distinct recollection of the whole."*

29. *Id.*

30. *Id.*, p. 370: *". . . A silent shade, as safe and sacred from the step of man as an invisible world."*

31. *Id.*, *And suddenly, as one that toys with time,
Scatters them on the pool! Then all the charm
Is broken—all that phantom-world so fair
Vanishes, and a thousand circlets spread,
And each mis-shapes the other.*

32. *Id.*, p. 115:
 *. . . by sacred sympathy . . . makes
The whole one self! self, that no alien knows!
Self, far-diffused as fancy's wing can travel!
Self, spreading still!*

33. *Ms. Logic,* in J. MUIRHEAD's, *Coleridge as a Philosopher,* London, 1930, p. 229: *"Personality is a circumference continually expanding through sympathy and understanding, rather than an exclusive centre of self-feeling."*

34. *Miscellanies æsthetic and literary,* Bell, 1911, p. 409: *"The progress of nature is more truly represented by the ladder, than by the suspended chain, and ... she expands as by concentric circles."*

35. *Anima Poetæ,* ed. E. H. Coleridge, Boston, 1895, p. 88: *"(I) go on from circle to circle till I break against the shore of my hearer's patience, or have my concentricals dashed to nothing by a snore. That is my ordinary mishap."*

36. *Biographia Literaria,* Bell, p. 53: *"One whole life would be divided between the despotism of outward impression, and that of senseless and passive memory."*

37. *Anima Poetæ,* p. 208: *"What a swarm of thoughts and feelings, endlessly minute fragments, and, as it were, representations of all preceding and embryos of all future thought, lie compact in any one moment!"*

38. *Aids to Reflections,* Bell, 1884, p. 346: *". . . a scudding cloudage of shapes."*

39. J. G. GREEN, *Spiritual Philosophy founded on the teaching of the late S. T. Coleridge,* Macmillan, 1865, t. II, p. 44: *"A succession of fragmentary and unconnected phases."*

40. *Miscellaneous Criticism,* ed. T. M. Raysor, London, Constable, 1936, p. 387: *". . . the arbitrary bringing together of things that lie remote."*

41. *Note on Tenneman's Geschichte der Philosophie:* *"The shifting current in the shoreless chaos of the fancy in which the streaming continuum of passive association is broken into zig-zag by sensations from within and without."*

42. *Anima Poetæ,* p. 257: *"Now the breeze through the stiff and brittle-becoming foliage of the trees counterfeits the sound for a rushing stream or waterflood suddenly sweeping by. The sigh, the modulated continuousness of the murmur is exchanged for the confusion of overtaking sounds—the self-evolution of the One, for the clash or stroke of ever-commencing contact of the multitudinous, without interspace, by confusion."*

43. *Treatise on method,* éd. Alice S. Snyder, London, Constable, 1934, p. 66: *". . . divided into innumerable fragments scattered over many volumes, like a broken mirror on the ground, presenting, instead of one, a thousand images, but none entire."*

44. *The Friend,* Bell, 1883, p. 342: *"Man is inevitably tempted . . . to break and scatter the one divine and indivisible life of nature into countless idole of the sense."*—Bien entendu, le mot "idole" est pris ici dans le sens où Bacon l'emploie.

45. *To Thalwell,* 16 octobre 1797: *". . . The universe itself! What an immense heap of little things! I can contemplate nothing but* parts, *and* parts *are all little. My mind feels as if it ached to behold and know something great, something* one *and* indivisible."

46.   *Stay awhile*
Poor youth, who scarcely dar'st lift up thine eyes!
The stream will soon renew its smoothness, soon
The visions will return!
                                       Poetical Works, p. 371.

47. *"A centre, as it were, a sort of nucleus in the reservoir of the soul";* cité par J. L. LOWES, *The Road to Xanadu,* Boston, 1927, p. 55.

48. *Miscellanies aesthetic and literary,* p. 20: *"An old coach-wheel lies in the coachmaker's yard . . . There is beauty in that wheel . . . See how the rays*

*proceed from the centre to the circumference, and how many different
images are distinctly comprehended at one glance, as forming one whole,
and each part in some harmonious relation to each and all."*

49. *The Philosophical Lectures,* ed. K. Coburn, London, 1949, p. 326: *"Organization is nothing but the consequence of life . . . ; it is, in truth, its effects,
formed by the infinity of radii which proceed from that as a centre, and
which taken collectively, form the circumference."*

50. *Ms. Logic. Coleridge as a Philosopher,* p. 122: *"(There is) a central Phaenomenon in Nature, and a central Phaenomenon in Nature requires and
supposes a central Thought in the Mind."*

51. *Miscellanies aesthetic and literary,* p. 47: *"Man's mind is the very focus of
all the rays of intellect which are scattered throughout the images of nature."*

52. *Id.,* p. 511: *"The principle of unity must always be present, so that in the
midst of the multeity the centripetal force be never suspended, nor the sense
be fatigued by the predominance of the centrifugal force."*

53. SCHOPENHAUER, *Sämmtliche Werke,* Leipzig, 1891, Bd. 6, S. 86, *Parerga und
Paralipomena: "Denn ihnen ist jede Geistesanstrengung, die nicht den
Zwecken des Willens dient, eine Thorheit, und die Neigung dazu nennen sie
Excentricität."*

54. *Id.,* Bd. 2, S. 371, *Die Welt als Wille und Vorstellung: "Sobald wir hingegen
uns von dieser (Oberfläche) ganz zurückziehen, verlässt uns das Bewusstseyn,
—im Schlaf, im Tode, gewissermaassen auch im magnetischen oder magis-
chen Wirken: denn diese alle führen durch das Centrum."*

55. *Id.: "Der Wille als Ding an sich ist ganz und ungetheilt in jedem Wesen wie
das Centrum ein integrirender Theil eines jeden Radius ist: während das
peripherische Ende dieses Radius mit der Oblerfläche, welche die Zeit und
ihren Inhalt vorstellt, im schnellsten Umschwunge ist, bleibt das andere
Ende, am Centro, als wo die Ewigkeit liegt . . ."*

56. *Also sprach Zarathustra,* 3° partie: *"In jedem Nu beginnt das Sein; um jedes
Hier rollt sich die Kugel Dort. Die Mitte ist überall."*

57. Friedrich GUNDOLF, *Gœthe,* Berlin, 1916, S. 115: *"Jeder Moment in Gœthes
Existenz besass die Eignung um Mitte und Träger zu sein für das Ganze
seines Lebens."*

58. *Id.: "Der Punkt auf dem der griechisch Gesinnte . . . steht, ist immer der
Mittelpunkt des Alls . . ."*

59.
> *Vermögt ihr mich auszudehnen,
> Zu erweitern zu einer Welt?*
> > *Prometheus,* Ier acte.

60.
> *Könnt ihr den weiten Raum
> Des Himmels und der Erde
> Mir ballen in meine Faust?*
> > *Id.*

61. *Sämmtliche Werke,* Jubiläums-Ausgabe, Bd. 30, S. 226, *Annalen* 1807: *"Der
Geist schieszt aus dem Zentrum seine Radien nach der Peripherie; stöszt er
dort an, so läszt er's auf sich beruhen und treibt wieder neue Versuchslinien
aus der Mitte, auf dass er, wenn ihm nicht gegeben ist, seinen Kreis zu über-
schreiten, er ihn doch möglichst erkennen und ausfüllen möge."*

62. *A Lavater,* 19 février 1777: *". . . mich kümmert ausser meinem Kreis nun
gar nichts.*

63. *A Knebel,* 16 février 1784: *"Persönlich bin ich glüchlich. Die Geschäffte, die
Wissenschaften, ein paar Freunde, das ist der ganze Kreis meines Daseins in
den ich mich klüglich verschanzt habe."*

64. *Sämmtliche Werke*, Bd. 38, S. 58: *"Man pflegt das Glück wegen seiner grossen Beweglichkeit kugelrund zu nennen, und zwar doppelt mit Recht: denn es gilt diese Vergleichung auch in einem andern Sinne. Ruhig vor Augen stehend, zeigt die Kugel sich dem Betrachtenden als ein befriedigtes, vollkommnes, in sich abgeschlossenes Wesen."*

65.
> *Sofort nun wende dich nach innen:*
> *Das Zentrum findest du la drinnen,*
> *Woran kein Edler zweifeln mag.*
> *Wirst keine Regel da vermissen,*
> *Denn das selbständige Gewissen*
> *Ist Sonne deinem Sittentag.*
> *Sämmtliche Werke*, Bd. 2, S. 245.

66. *A R. E. Schubarth, 8 juillet 1818: "Es ist ganz einerley, in welchem Kreise wir unsere Kultur beginnen, es ist ganz gleichgültig, von wo aus wir unsere Bildung in's fernere Leben richten, wenn es nur ein Kreis, wenn es nur ein wo ist."*

67. *Tagebuch*, 1780, passage cité par Werner Kraft, *Über Prosasätze von Goethe*, Die neue Rundschau, 1955, t. II, p. 243: *"Ich muss den Cirkel, der sich in mir umdreht von guten und bösen Tagen, nährer bemerken, Leidenschaftlichkeit, Anhänglichkeit, Trieb, dies oder jenes zu tun. Erfindung, Ausführung, Ordnung, alles wechselt und hält einen regelmässigen Kreis. Heiterkeit, Trübe, Stärke, Elasticität, Schwäche, Gelassenheit, Begier eben so. Da ich sehr diät lebe, wird der Gang nicht gestört, und ich muss noch heraus kriegen, in welcher Zeit und Ordnung ich mich um mich selbst bewege."*

68. *Sämmtliche Werke*, Bd. 19, S. 137, *Wilhelm Meisters Wanderjahre: "Wie kann sich der Mensch gegen das Unendliche stellen, als wenn er alle geistigen Kräfte, die nach vielen Seiten hingezogen werden, in seinem Innersten, Tiefsten versammelt, wenn er sich fragt: darfst du dich in der Mitte dieser ewig lebendigen Ordnung auch nur denken, sobald sich nicht gleichfalls in dir ein herrlich Bewegtes um einen reinen Mittelpunkt kreisend hervortut?"*

69. *Sämmtliche Werke*, Bd. 39, S. 343: *"Die Idee der Metamorphose ist eine höchst ehrwürdige, aber zugleich höchst gefährliche Gabe von oben. Sie führt ins Formlose, zerstört das Wissen, löst es auf. Sie ist gleich der* vis centrifuga *und würde sich ins Unendliche verlieren, wäre ihr nicht ein Gegengewicht zugegeben: ich meine den Spezifikationstrieb, das zähe Beharrlichkeitsvermögen dessen, was einmal zur Wirklichkeit gekommen, eine* vis centripeta, *welcher in ihrem tiefsten Grunde keine Ausserlichkeit etwas anhaben kann."*

70.
> *Blattlos aber und schnell erhebt sich der zärtere Stengel,*
> *Und ein Wundergebild zieht den Betrachtenden an.*
> *Rings im Kreise stellet sich nun, gezählet und ohne*
> *Zahl, das kleinere Blatt neben dem ähnlichen hin.*
> *Die Metamorphose der Pflanzen, Sämmtliche Werke,*
> Bd. 2, S. 248.

71.
> *Leicht bewegt, in mästiger Eile,*
> *Um dem Wagen, Kreis um Kreis,*
> *Bald verschlungen Zeil' an Zeile,*
> *Schlangenartig reihenweis,*
> *Naht euch, rüstige Nereiden.*
> *Second Faust*, v. 8379–8383.

72.
> *Komm! hebe dich zu höhern Sphären!*
> *Second Faust*, v. 12094.

73. *Zur Morphologie,* 1. IV: *"Das Höchste, was wir von Gott und der Natur erhalten haben, ist das Leben, die rotirende Bewegung der Monas um sich selbst, welche weder Rast noch Ruhe kennt; der Trieb, das Leben zu hegen und zu pflegen, ist einem jeden unverwüstlich eingeboren . . ."*

74. *Sämmtliche Werke,* Bd. 36, S. 6, *Zum Shakespears Tag:* ". . . *Seine Stücke drehen sich alle um den geheimen Punkt . . ."*

75. *Gespräch über die Poesie,* Athenaeum, Dritten Bandes Zweites Stück, 1800: *"Mir selbst bleibt der Meister der fasslichste Inbegriff, um den ganzen Umfang seiner Vielseitigkeit, wie in einem Mittelpunkte vereinigt, einigermassen zu überschauen."*

CHAPTER VII—NOTES

1. *Le Vallon,* "*Méditations,*" Hachette, p. 151.
2. *La Semaine Sainte,* "*Méditations,*" p. 271.
3. *Ischia,* "*Nouvelles Méditations,*" p. 26.
4. *L'Immortalité,* "*Méditations,*" p. 142.
5. *Ischia,* "*Nouvelles Méditations,*" p. 27.
6. *L'Occident,* "*Harmonies,*" p. 134.
7. *La Vallon,* "*Méditations,*" p. 151.
8. *Hymne du matin,* "*Harmonies,*" p. 55.
9. "*Méditations,*" Préface de 1849, p. 44.
10. *Voyage en Orient,* t. I, p. 339.
11. *Voyage en Orient,* t. II, p. 175.
12. *Ressouvenir du lac Léman,* "*Méditations,*" p. 204.
13. *Raphaël,* p. 62.
14. *Voyage en Orient,* t. II, p. 95.
15. *Voyage en Orient,* p. 36 et "*Méditations,*" Préface de 1834, p. 56.
16. *Voyage en Orient,* t. Ier, pp. 409–410 et "*Méditations,*" Préface de 1834, p. 44.
17. *La Vigne et la Maison,* "*Recueillements,*" p. 297.
18. *La Mort de Socrate,* "*Méditations,*" pp. 335–336.
19. *Invocation,* "*Harmonies,*" p. 40.
20. *Jocelyn,* p. 84.
21. *La Solitude,* "*Nouvelles Méditations,*" p. 84.
22. *La Prière,* "*Méditations,*" p. 215.
23. *Dieu,* "*Méditations,*" p. 287.
24. *La Solitude,* "*Nouvelles Méditations,*" p. 84.
25. *L'Humanité,* "*Harmonies,*" p. 160.
26. *Hymne du soir,* "*Harmonies,*" p. 87.
27. *Le Chrétien mourant,* "*Méditations,*" p. 277.
28. *Cours familier de littérature,* t. VI, p. 199.
29. *La Chute d'un Ange,* p. 224.
30. *L'Isolement,* "*Méditations,*" p. 117.
31. *Le Désert,* "*Voyage en Orient,*" t. II, p. 573.

32. *Philosophie,* "*Méditations,*" p. 237.

33. *L'Enthousiasme,* "*Méditations,*" p. 181.

34. *L'Homme,* "*Méditations,*" p. 123.

35. "*Méditations,*" Préface de 1834, p. 67.

36. *Jocelyn,* p. 127.

37. *Dieu,* "*Méditations,*" p. 278.

CHAPTER VIII—NOTES

1. *Des artistes,* "*Œuvres diverses,*" (O.D.) , Conard, I, 356.

2. Introduction aux Études philosophiques, par Davin.

3. *La Fille aux yeux d'or,* 1re édition.

4. *La Fille aux yeux d'or,* "*Œuvres,*" (O.) , Conard, 13, 321.

5. *Ursule Mirouet,* O., 8, 68.

6. *Catéchisme social,* O.D., 3, 691.

7. *Théorie de la démarche,* O.D., 2, 642.

8. *Séraphita,* O., 31, 184.

9. *Une Fille d'Ève,* O., 4, 92.

10. *Louis Lambert,* O., 31, 170.

11. *Ursule Mirouet,* O., 8, 67.

12. *Z. Marcas,* O., 21, 404.

13. *Les Proscrits,* O., 31, 24.

14. *Traité de la vie élégante,* O.D., 2, 170.

15. *Louis Lambert,* O., 31, 123.

16. *Compte-rendu du Traité de la lumière de Herschell,* O.D., 1, 366.

17. *Catéchisme social,* O.D., 3, 695.

18. *Une Ténébreuse Affaire,* O., 21, 246.

19. *Les Employés,* O., 19, 119.

20. *L'Envers de l'histoire contemporaine,* O., **20, 294.**

21. *Séraphita,* O., 31, 298.

22. *Les Martyrs ignorés,* O.D., 3, 136.

23. *Le Cousin Pons,* O., 18, 109.

24. *Les Paysans,* O., 21, 181.

25. *L'Envers de l'histoire contemporaine,* O., 20, 349.

26. *La Vieille Fille,* O., 10, 297.

27. *Louis Lambert,* 1re édition.

28. *Théorie de la démarche,* O.D., 2, 629.

29. *Les Martyrs ignorés,* O.D., 3, 137.

30. *La Peau de chagrin,* O., 27, 24.

31. *Les Martyrs ignorés,* O.D., 3, 137.

32. *Une heure de ma vie,* dans "*la Femme auteur,*" Grasset, 1950, p. 246.

33. *Maître Cornélius,* O., 29, 228.

34. *La Cousine Bette,* O., 17, 127.

35. *Louis Lambert,* O., 31, 97.

36. *Louis Lambert,* O., 31, 114.
37. *Le Lys dans la vallée,* O., 26, 57.
38. *Louis Lambert,* O., 31, 151.
39. *Sténie,* 132.
40. *Le Cousin Pons,* O., 18, 139.
41. *Théorie de la démarche,* O.D., 2, 629.
42. *Splendeurs et misères des courtisanes,* O., 16, 143.
43. *L'Envers de l'histoire contemporaine,* O., 20, 294.
44. *Voyage de Paris à Java,* O.D., 2, 576.
45. *Splendeurs et misères des courtisanes,* O., 16, 226.
46. *Théorie de la démarche,* O.D., 2, 629.
47. *Louis Lambert,* O., 31, 66.
48. *La Peau de chagrin,* O., 27, 116.
49. *Théorie de la démarche,* O.D., 2, 620–621.
50. *Louis Lambert,* O., 31, 97.
51. *Traité de la vie élégante,* O.D., 2, 168.
52. *Le Chef-d'œuvre inconnu,* O., 28, 9.
53. *Physiologie du mariage,* O., 32, 216.
54. *Le Cousin Pons,* O., 18, 132.
55. *La Bourse,* O., 1, 413.
56. *La Fille aux yeux d'or,* O., 13, 377.
57. *Physiologie du mariage,* O., 32, 152.
58. *Splendeurs et misères des courtisanes,* O., 15, 21.
59. *Ursule Mirouet,* O., 8, 151.
60. *La Fille aux yeux d'or,* O., 13, 370.
61. *Clotilde de Lusignan,* 323.
62. *Sténie,* 154.
63. *Wan-Chlore,* 146.
64. *Physiologie du mariage,* O., 32, 176.
65. *La Père Goriot,* O., 6, 358.
66. *Le Médecin de campagne,* O., 24, 234–235.
67. *La femme de trente ans,* O., 6, 162.
68. *Les Chouans,* O., 22, 305.
69. *Le Père Goriot,* O., 6, 357.
70. *Séraphita,* O., 31, 243.
71. *Séraphita,* 332–333.
72. *Séraphita,* 197.
73. *Introduction aux Études de mœurs,* par Davin.
74. *Séraphita,* O., 31, 259.
75. *Louis Lambert,* O., 31, 167.
76. *Théorie de la démarche,* O.D., 2, 625.
77. *Théorie de la démarche,* 642.
78. *Séraphita,* O., 31, 220.
79. *La Duchesse de Langeais,* O., 13, 233.
80. *Introduction aux Études de mœurs.*

81. *Du roman historique et de Fragoletta*, O.D., 1, 206.
82. *César Birotteau*, O., 14, 178.
83. *Massimilia Doni*, O., 27, 427.
84. *Sur Catherine de Médicis*, O., 30, 330.
85. *Louis Lambert*, O., 31, 167.

CHAPTER IX—NOTES

1. *Journal*, 27 février 1853, "*Œuvres*," Pléiade, II, p. 1305.
2. *Journal*, 14 avril 1839, "*Œuvres*," II, p. 1123.
3. *La Maison du berger*, "*Œuvres*," I, p. 176.
4. *Servitude et grandeur militaires*, "*Œuvres*," II, p. 664.
5. *Daphné*, "*Œuvres*," II, p. 791.
6. *Journal*, 24 avril 1856, "*Œuvres*," II, p. 1320.
7. *La Sauvage*, "*Œuvres*," I, p. 191.
8. *A Madame Dorval*, "*Œuvres*," I, p. 239.
9. *Daphné*, "*Œuvres*," II, p. 843.
10. *Journal*, 1842, "*Œuvres*," II, p. 576.
11. *Journal*, 19 décembre 1835, II, pp. 1035–1036.
12. Sur le thème du cercle chez Vigny on ne saurait passer sous silence deux études très riches en suggestions: François Germain, *L'œuvre littéraire et les images du cercle dans l'imagination de Vigny*, Revue des sciences humaines, avril-juin 1956; et Jean-Paul Weber, *Genèse de l'œuvre poétique*, Gallimard 1960, chap. 1er.

CHAPTER X—NOTES

1. *Œuvres*, éd. A. Béguin et J. Richer, Pléiade, I, p. 1121.
2. Jean Onimus, *Artémis ou le Ballet des Heures*, Mercure de France, 1er mai 1955, pp. 73–76. Voir surtout ce qui y est dit sur la circularité du temps nervalien.
3. *Œuvres*, Pléiade, I, p. 268.
4. *Œuvres*, I, p. 261.
5. Cf. Aristide Marie, *G. de Nerval*, Hachette, 1914, pp. 232–233 et G. Benoist, *G. de Nerval et J. Méry*, "*Revue d'Hist. litt.*," 1930, p. 192.
6. *Portraits et souvenirs littéraires*, p. 53.
7. *Œuvres*, Pléiade, I, p. 369.
8. *L'Imagier de Harlem*, tabl. 6, sc. II.
9. *Œuvres*, Pléiade, I, p. 373.
10. *Œuvres*, Pléiade, I, p. 715.
11. *Id.*, I, p. 733.
12. *Poésie et théâtre*, éd. H. Clouard, Divan, p. 357.
13. *Œuvres*, Pléiade, I, p. 882.
14. *Le cabaret de la mère Saguet*, etc., éd. Bachelin, Bernouard, p. 95.

15. *Œuvres*, Pléiade, I, p. 212.
16. *Voyage en Orient*, éd. G. Rouger, t. III, p. 46.
17. *Les deux Faust de Gœthe*, éd. Baldensperger, Champion, pp. 236–237.
18. *Œuvres*, Pléiade, I, p. 171.
19. *Poésie et théâtre*, p. 387.
20. *Œuvres*, Pléiade, I, p. 275.
21. *L'Artiste*, 7 avril 1844.
22. *Voyage en Orient*, t. II, p. 264.
23. *Voyage en Orient*, t. II, p. 306.
24. *Œuvres*, Pléiade, I, p. 264.
25. *Histoire du 41ᵉ fauteuil*, p. 363.
26. *Lorely*, éd. Bachelin, p. 28.
27. *L'Alchimiste*, acte IV, sc. 1ʳᵉ.
28. *Œuvres*, Pléiade, I, p. 151.
29. *Voyage en Orient*, t. II, pp. 307–309.
30. *Les deux Faust de Gœthe*, p. 236.
31. *Œuvres*, Pléiade, I, p. 171.
32. *Œuvres*, Pléiade, I, p. 368.
33. *Les deux Faust de Gœthe*, p. 228.
34. *Les deux Faust de Gœthe*, p. 233.
35. *La main enchantée*, etc., éd., J. Marsan, Champion, p. 258.
36. *Les Illuminés*, éd. A. Marie, Champion, p. 347.
37. *Les Illuminés*, p. 414.
38. *Œuvres*, Pléiade, I, p. 365.
39. *Id.*, I, p. 403.
40. *Id.*, I, p. 419.
41. *Id.*, I, p. 370.
42. *Le cabaret de la mère Saguet*, p. 57.
43. *Voyage en Orient*, t. II, p. 308.
44. *Œuvres*, Pléiade, I, p. 403.
45. *Œuvres*, I, p. 382.
46. *Id.*, I, p. 418.
47. *Id.*, I, p. 364.
48. *Les classiques du romantisme*, 1928, p. 226.
49. *Voyage en Orient*, t. I, p. 210 et t. IV, p. 195.
50. *Carnet du Voyage en Orient*, "*Revue de Litt. comp.*," 1933, 13, pp. 3 et 14.
51. *Œuvres*, Pléiade, I, p. 376.
52. *Œuvres*, I, p. 364.
53. *Carnet du Voyage en Orient*, pp. 16–17.
54. *Voyage en Orient*, t. III, p. 325.
55. *Voyage en Orient*, t. II, p. 86.
56. *Œuvres*, Pléiade, I, p. 355.
57. *Œuvres*, I, p. 371.
58. *Id.*, I, p. 376.
59. *Id.*, I, p. 321.

60. *Id.*, I, p. 385.
61. *Id.*, I, p. 370.
62. *Id.*, I, p. 407.
63. *Id.*, I, p. 379.
64. *Id.*, I, p. 33.
65. *Id.*, I, p. 392.
66. *Voyage en Orient*, t. I, p. 143.
67. *Œuvres*, Pléiade, I, p. 881.
68. *Lorely*, éd. H. Clouard, Divan, p. 25.
69. *Œuvres*, Pléiade, I, p. 291.
70. *Œuvres*, I, p. 424.
71. *Carnet du Voyage en Orient*, p. 14.
72. *Id.*, p. 17.
73. *Voyage en Orient*, t. I, p. 239.
74. *Carnet du Voyage en Orient*, p. 18.
75. *Œuvres*, Pléiade, p. 410.
76. *Voyage en Orient*, t. III, p. 258.
77. *Œuvres*, Pléiade, p. 1030.
78. *Œuvres*, p. 1034.
79. *Id.*, p. 1032.
80. *Id.*, p. 164.
81. *Id.*, p. 99.
82. *Id.*, p. 112.
83. *Id.*, p. 331.
84. *Id.*, pp. 407–408.
85. *Id.*, p. 410.

CHAPTER XI—NOTES

1. *The Pit and the Pendulum, Works of Edgar Allan Poe,* ed. E. C. Stedman and G. Woodberry, 10 vol., Chicago 1895, t. I, p. 310:
   "*I had swooned; but still will not say that all of consciousness was lost. What of it there remained, I will not attempt to define, or even to describe; yet all was not lost. In the deepest slumber—no! In delirium—no! In a swoon—no! In death—no! even in the grave all is not lost.*"
2. *William Wilson, Works,* t. II, p. 10: "*Encompassed by massy walls . . .*"
3. *Eleonora, Works,* t. I, p. 206: "*Shut up, as if for ever, within a magic prison-house of grandeur and glory . . .*"
4. *Berenice, Works,* t. I, p. 158: "*. . . a palace of imagination . . .*"
5. *William Wilson, Works,* t. II, p. 11: "*. . . a mental sorcery . . .*"
6. *Id.*, p. 10: "*The teeming brain of childhood requires no external world of incident to occupy or amuse it.*"
7. *Berenice, Works,* t. I, p. 158: "*. . . the realities of the world affect the dreamer as visions, and as visions only.*"
8. *William Wilson,* p. 11.

9. *Eleonora, Works,* t. I, p. 204:

"*No unguided footstep ever came upon that vale; for it lay far away up among a range of giant hills that hung beetling around about it, shutting out the sunlight from its sweetest recesses. No path was trodden in its vicinity; and to reach our happy home, there was need of putting back, with force, the foliage of many thousands of forest trees, and of crushing to death the glories of many millions of fragrant flowers. Thus it was that we lived all alone, knowing nothing of the world without the valley . . .*"

10. *The Island of the Fay, Works,* t. II, p. 87:

"*On all sides, save to the west, where the sun was about sinking, arose the verdant walls of the forest. The little river, which turned sharply in its course, and was thus immediately lost to sight, seemed to have no exit from its prison, but to be absorbed by the deep green foliage of the trees.*"

11. *The City in the Sea, Works,* t. X, p. 22:

> No rays from the holy heaven come down
> On the long night-time of that town;
> But light from out the lurid sea
> Streams up the turrets silently.

12. *The Domain of Arnheim, Works,* t. II, p. 107:

"*At every instant the vessel seemed imprisoned within an enchanted circle, having insuperable and impenetrable walls of foliage . . .*"

13. *The premature Burial, Works,* t. III, p. 227: "*. . . emerge from total unconsciousness into the first feeble and indefinite sense of existence.*"

14. *Lettre à George W. Eveleth,* 4 janvier 1848: "*I became insane, with long intervals of horrible sanity. During these fits of absolute unconsciousness I drank, God only knows how often or how much.*"

15. *The Pit and the Pendulum, Works,* t. I, p. 310:

"*Arousing from the most profound of slumbers we break the gossamer web of some dream. Yet in a second afterward (so frail may that web have been) we remember not that we have dreamed.*"

16. *Id.:*

"*In the return to life from a swoon there are two stages: first, that of the sense of mental or spiritual, secondly, that of the sense of physical, existence.*"

17. *Id.:* "*. . . impressions eloquent in memories of the gulf beyond.*"—La traduction est de Baudelaire.

18. *Marginalia, Works,* t. VII, p. 313: "*. . . instantaneous intuition.*"

19. *Id.,* p. 312: "*An inappreciable point of time.*"

20. *Id.,* p. 314: "*A point of blending between wakefulness and sleep.*"

21. *Id.:* "*Not that I can continue the condition—not that I can render the point more than a point—but that I can startle myself from the point into wakefulness; and thus transfer the point itself into the realm of Memory.*"

22. *Eureka, Works,* t. IX, p. 134:

"*We walk about, amid the destinies of our world-existence, encompassed by dim but ever-present Memories of a Destiny more vast—very distant in the bygone time, and infinitely awful.*

"*We live a Youth peculiarly haunted by such shadow; yet never mistaking them for dreams. As Memories we know them.*"

23. *The Narrative of Arthur Gordon Pym, Works,* t. V, p. 157:

"*I have since found that this species of partial oblivion is usually brought about by sudden transition, whether from joy to sorrow or from sorrow to joy—the degree of forgetfulness being proportioned to the degree of difference in the exchange.*"

24. *The Pit and the Pendulum, Works,* t. I, p. 311:
     "*He who has never swooned, is not he who finds strange palaces and wildly familiar faces in coals that glow; is not he who beholds floating in mid-air the sad visions that the many may not view . . .*"

25. *Berenice, Works,* t. I, p. 158:
     "*There is a remembrance of aerial forms, of spiritual and meaning eyes, of sound musical yet sad; a remembrance which will not be excluded; a memory like a shadow—vague, variable, indefinite, unsteady . . .*"

26. *William Wilson, Works,* t. II, p. 17:
     "*. . . Dim visions of my earliest infancy—wild, confused and thronging memories of a time when memory herself was yet unborn.*"

27. *The haunted Palace, Works,* t. X, p. 32:
     > *And round about his home the glory*
     > *That blushed and bloomed*
     > *Is but a dim-remembered story*
     > *Of the old time entombed.*

28. *Ligeia, Works,* t. I, p. 186:
     "*In our endeavors to recall to memory something long forgotten, we often find ourselves upon the very verge of remembrance, without being able, in the end, to remember.*"

29. *Eleonora, Works,* t. I, p. 204: "*A condition of shadow and doubt, appertaining to the present and to recollection.*"

30. *The Masque of the Red Death, Works,* t. I, p. 249:
     "*A strong and lofty wall girdled it in. This wall had gates of iron. The courtiers, having entered, brought furnaces and massy hammers, and welded the bolts. They resolved to leave means neither of ingress or egress to the sudden impulses of despair or of frenzy from within . . . Security was within. Without was the* Red Death.*"

31. *Shadow, Works,* t. I, p. 126:
     "*To our chamber there was no entrance save by a lofty door of brass; and the door . . . was fastened from within. Black draperies, likewise, in the gloomy room, shut out from our view the moon, the lurid stars, and the peopleless streets—but the boding and the memory of Evil, they would not be so excluded. There were things around us and about of which I can render no distinct account . . .*"

32. *Silence, Works,* t. I, p. 242:
     "*The waters of the river have a saffron and sickly hue; and they flow not onward to the sea, but palpitate forever and forever beneath the red eye of the sun with a tumultuous and convulsive motion.*"

33. *Id.,* p. 245: "*The waters sink to their level and remain . . .*"

34. *Dream-land, Works,* t. X, p. 20: "*The sheeted Memories of the past.*"

35. *The Conqueror Worm, Works,* t. X, p. 33: "*A circle that ever returneth in/To the self-same spot.*"

36. *The Coliseum, Works,* t. X, p. 27: "*The Memories that hang upon/and cling around as a garment.*"

37. *Ms. Found in a Bottle, Works,* t. II, p. 231:
     "*. . . There will occasionally flash across my mind a sensation of familiar things, and there is always mixed up with such indistinct shadows of recollection an unaccountable memory of old foreign chronicles and ages long ago.*"

38. *The Colloquy of Monos and Una, Works*, t. I, pp. 224–225:

"*And now from the wreck and chaos of the usual senses, there appeared to have arisen within me a sixth, all perfect. In its exercise I found a wild delight: yet a delight still physical, inasmuch as the understanding had in it no part. Motion in the animal frame had fully ceased. No muscle quivered; no nerve thrilled; no artery throbbed. But there seemed to have sprung up, in the brain, that of which no words could convey to the merely human intelligence even an indistinct conception. Let me term it a mental pendulous pulsation. It was the moral embodiment of man's abstract idea of Time . . . And this sentiment existing . . . independently of any succession of events— this idea—this sixth sense, upspringing from the ashes of the rest, was the first obvious and certain step of the intemporal soul upon the threshold of the temporal Eternity.*"

39. *Id.,* pp. 226–227:

"*A year passed. The consciousness of being had grown hourly more indistinct, and that of mere locality had in great measure usurped its position. The idea of entity was becoming merged in that of place. The narrow space immediately surrounding what had been my body was now growing to be the body itself . . .*

"*The worm had food no more. The sense of being had at length utterly departed, and there reigned in its stead—instead of all things, dominant and perpetual, the autocrats Place and Time.*"

40. *The Facts in the Case of M. Valdemar, Works,* t. II, p. 331: "*I am dead.*"

41. *The Pit and the Pendulum, Works,* t. I, p. 312:

"*Very suddenly there came back to my soul motion and sound—the tumultuous motion of the heart, and, in my ears, the sound of its beating. Then a pause in which all is blank. Then again sound, and motion, and touch—a tingling sensation pervading my frame.*"

42. *The Premature Burial, Works,* t. III, p. 227:

"*Slowly—with a tortoise gradation—approached the faint grey dawn of the psychal day. A torpid uneasiness. An apathetic endurance of dull pain. No care—no hope—no effort. Then, after a long interval, a ringing in the ears; then, after a lapse still longer, a prickling or tingling sensation in the extremities; then a seemingly eternal period of pleasurable quiescence, during which the awakening feelings are struggling into thought; then a brief re-sinking into nonentity; then a sudden recovery.*"

43. *Shadow, Works,* t. I, p. 126:

". . . *Terrible state of existence which the nervous experience when the senses are keenly living and awake, and meanwhile the powers of thought lie dormant.*"

44. *Berenice, Works,* t. I, p. 160:

". . . *Nervous intensity of interest with which, in my case, the powers of meditation . . . busied or buried themselves in the contemplation of even the most ordinary objects of the universe.*

"*To muse for long unwearied hours, with my attention riveted to some frivolous device on the margin or in the typography of a book; to become absorbed, for the better part of a summer day, in a quaint shadow falling aslant upon the tapestry or upon the floor; to lose myself, for an entire night, in watching the steady flame of a lamp, or the embers of a fire; to dream away whole days over the perfume of a flower; . . . such were a few of the most common and least pernicious vagaries induced by a condition of the mental faculties . . .*"

45. *Id.*, p. 161:

"*In my case the primary object was invariably frivolous, although assuming, through the medium of my distempered vision, a refracted and unreal importance. Few deductions, if any, were made; and those few pertinaciously returning in upon the original object as a center.*"

46. *The premature Burial, Works*, t. III, p. 227:

"*At length the slight quivering of an eyelid, and immediately thereupon, an electric shock of a terror, deadly and indefinite, which sends the blood in torrents from the temple to the heart. And now the first positive effort to think. And now the first endeavor to remember.*"

47. *The Pit and the Pendulum, Works*, t. I, p. 312:

"*Then the mere consciousness of existence without thought—a condition which lasted long. Then, very suddenly, thought, and shuddering terror, and earnest endeavor to comprehend my true state.*"

48. *The Premature Burial*, p. 224:

"*Upon awakening from slumber, I could never gain at once thorough possession of my senses, and always remained, for many minutes, in much bewilderment and perplexity;—the mental faculties in general, but the memory in especial, being in a condition of absolute abeyance.*"

49. *The Narrative of Arthur Gordon Pym, Works*, t. V, p. 29:

"*Upon awaking I felt strangely confused in mind, and some time elapsed before I could bring to recollection all the various circumstances of my situation. By degree, however, I remembered all.*"

50. *Id.*, p. 33:

"*As in a former occasion, my conceptions were in a state of the greatest indistinctness and confusion . . . For a long time I found it nearly impossible to connect any ideas; but, by very slow degrees, my thinking faculties returned, and I again called to memory the general incidents of my condition.*"

51. *The Pit and the Pendulum, Works*, t. I, p. 320:

"*I could no longer doubt the doom prepared for me by monkish ingenuity in torture.*"

52. *A Descent into the Maelström, Works*, t. II, p. 249:

"*No one ever will know what my feelings were at that moment. I shook from head to foot as if I had had the most violent fit of the ague . . . With the wind that now drove us on, we were bound for the whirl of the Ström, and nothing could save us.*"

53. *The Fall of the House of Usher, Works*, t. I, p. 138:

"'*I shall perish,*' said he, '*I* must *perish in this deplorable folly. Thus, thus, and not otherwise, shall I be lost.*'"

54. *Ms. Found in a Bottle, Works*, t. II, p. 235: "*Stupendous ramparts of ice, towering away into the desolate sky, and looking like the walls of the universe.*"

55. *Id.*: "*. . . Whirls dizzily, in immense concentric circles.*"

56. *A Descent into the Maelström, Works*, t. II, p. 254: "*Upon the interior surface of a funnel vast in circumference, prodigious in depth, and whose perfectly smooth sides might have been mistaken for ebony, but for the gleaming and ghastly radiance they shot forth, as the rays of the full moon, from a circular rift amid the clouds, streamed in a flood of golden glory along the black walls.*"

57. *The Narrative of Arthur Gordon Pym, Works*, t. V, p. 237:

"*And now I found these fancies creating their own realities, and all imagined horrors crowding upon me in fact.*"

58. *The Power of Words, Works,* t. I, p. 236:
"*Even the spiritual vision, is it not at all points arrested by the continuous golden walls of the universe?—the walls of the myriads of the shining bodies that mere number has appeared to blend into unity?*"

59. *Marginalia, Works,* t. VII, p. 345:
"*Having once passed the limits of absolutely practical admeasurement, by means of intervening objects, our ideas of distances are one: they have no variation.*"

60. *The Island of the Fay, Works,* t. II, p. 85:
"*I love to regard these (things) as themselves but the colossal members of one vast animate and sentient whole: a whole whose form (that of the sphere) is the most perfect and most inclusive of all . . .*"

61. *Id.:* "*We find cycle within cycle without end . . .*"

62. *Id.:* "*Revolve around one far-distant center, which is the Godhead.*"

63. *Eureka, Works,* t. IX, p. 46: "*Absolute Unity being taken as a centre, then the existing Universe of Stars is the result of radiation from that centre.*"

64. *Id.,* p. 63: "*The Law which we call Gravity exists on account of Matter's having been radiated, at its origin, into a limited sphere of space.*"—Et Poe ajoute en note: "*A sphere is* necessarily *limited, I prefer tautology to a chance of misconception.*"
Il semble bien que l'idée de la sphère cosmique limitée soit venue à Poe de Kant.

65. *Id.,* p. 46: "*Radiated spherically—in all directions—to immeasurable but still definite distances.*"

66. *Id.,* p. 39: "*According to a determinate law of which the complexity, even considered by itself solely, is utterly beyond the grasp of the imagination.*"

67. *Id.,* p. 136:
"*Just as it is in your power to expand or to concentrate your pleasures (the absolute amount of happiness remaining always the same), so did and does a similar capability appertain to this Divine Being, who thus passes His Eternity in perpetual variation of concentrated Self and almost Infinite Self-Diffusion.*"

68. *The Power of Words, Works,* t. I, p. 238:
"*. . . As no thought can perish, so no act is without infinite result. We moved our hands, for example, when we were dwellers of the earth, and, in so doing, we gave vibration to the atmosphere which engirdled it. This vibration was indefinitely extended, till it gave impulse to every particle of the earth's air, which thenceforward, and forever, was actuated by the one movement of the hand.*"

69. *Article sur les Contes de Hawthorne, Works,* t. VII, p. 33: "*The impressions produced (by Hawthorne's tales) were wrought in a legitimate* sphere *of action . . .*"

70. *Compte rendu du "Culprit Fay" de Rodman Drake,* éd. Harrison, t. VIII, p. 281:
"*If, indeed, there be any one circle of thought distinctly and palpably marked out from amid the jarring and tumultuous chaos of human intelligence, it is that evergreen and radiant Paradise which the true poet knows, and knows alone, as the* limited *realm of his authority—as the* circumscribed *Eden of his dreams.*"

71. *The Domain of Arnheim, Works,* t. II, p. 105: "*. . . The most objectionable phase of grandeur is that of extent; the worst phase of extent, that of distance. It is at war with the sentiment and with the sense of seclusion.*"

72. *The Philosophy of Composition, Works,* t. VI, p. 42: *". . . It has always appeared to me that a close* circumscription of space *is absolutely necessary to the effect of insulated incident."*

73. *Marginalia, Works,* t. VII, p. 210: *"The circumscription of space, in these pencilings, has in it something more of advantage than inconvenience."*

74. *The American Drama, Works,* t. VI, p. 212: *"The pleasure which we derive from any exertion of human ingenuity is in direct ratio of the approach to this species of reciprocity between cause and effect."*

75. *A Chapter of suggestions, Works,* t. VIII, p. 331: *"Let the poet press his finger steadily upon each key, keeping it down, and imagine each prolonged series of undulations . . ."*

76. *Id.,* p. 329: *"(The plot) is that from which no component atom can be removed, and in which none of the component atoms can be displaced, without ruin to the whole."*

77. *The Fall of the House of Usher, Works,* t. I, p. 134:
    "I had so worked upon my imagination as really to believe that about the whole mansion and domain there hung an atmosphere peculiar to themselves and their immediate vicinity—an atmosphere which had no affinity with the air of heaven, but which had reeked up from the decayed trees, and the grey wall, and the silent tarn . . ."

78. Leo SPITZER, *A Reinterpretation of "The Fall of the House of Usher,"* Comparative Literature, 1952, p. 360.

CHAPTER XII—NOTES

1. *Journal,* 7 novembre 1851. Inédit. Tous les passages qui suivent et qui ne sont pas référés à une édition, sont tirés des manuscrits d'Amiel à la Bibliothèque publique de Genève. Je remercie ici MM. Auguste Bouvier et Bernard Gagnebin pour la courtoisie avec laquelle ils ont mis à ma disposition ces manuscrits.—Je dois aussi remercier ici le Fonds de recherche scientifique de l'Université de Zurich, dont l'aide m'a permis de compléter ces recherches sur Amiel.

2. *Journal,* 5 juillet 1852.

3. *Lettre à François Bordier,* 28 décembre 1847; Bernard BOUVIER, *Jeunesse d'Henri-Frédéric Amiel,* 1935, p. 385.

4. *Lettre à Camilla Charbonnier,* 22 décembre 1842, *op. cit.,* p. 170.

5. *Journal,* 9 février 1869.

6. *Journal,* 26 janvier 1854.

7. *Journal,* 18 septembre 1853.

8. *Journal,* 24 avril 1854.

9. *Journal,* 14 octobre 1857.

10. *Journal,* 30 mai 1867.

11. *Journal,* 19 décembre 1877; édition Bernard BOUVIER, Stock, p. 418.

12. *Journal,* 23 novembre 1856.

13. *Journal,* 6 septembre 1851.

14. *Journal,* 18 avril 1857.

15. *Journal,* 18 octobre 1853.

16. *Journal,* 25 août 1880.

17. *Journal*, 6 septembre 1859.

18. *Journal*, 25 juin 1879.

19. *La Bulle de savon, Jour à jour*, poème XL.

20. *Journal*, 2 avril 1870.

21. *Journal*, 2 juin 1864.

22. *Maximes et directions* (carnet inédit), 5 janvier 1861.

23. *Journal*, 9 juin 1851.

24. *Journal*, 23 avril 1860.

25. *Journal*, 23 mars 1860.

26. *Journal*, 18 septembre 1853.

27. *Journal*, 5 février 1854.

28. *Journal*, 19 janvier 1860.

29. *Journal*, 14 mai 1861.

30. *Journal*, 18 septembre 1865.

31. *Journal*, 30 janvier 1854.

32. *Journal*, 12 juillet 1863.

33. *Journal*, 19 septembre 1864.

34. *Journal*, 14 juillet 1880.

35. *Cours d'anthropologie*, Aide-mémoire, 22 mars 1857.

36. *Aphorismes* (feuilles volantes), 26 octobre 1849.

37. *Journal*, 18 septembre 1862.

38. *Lettre à Jules Vuy*, Bernard BOUVIER, *Jeunesse d'Henri-Frédéric Amiel*, p. 320.

39. *Lettre à Charles Heim*, 18 avril 1847, Bernard BOUVIER, *Jeunesse d'Henri-Frédéric Amiel*, p. 345.

40. *Journal*, 30 novembre 1851, et *Grains de mil*, p. 190.

41. *Grains de mil*, p. 138.

42. *Journal*, 23 février et 3 mars 1854.

43. *Journal*, 16 octobre 1864.

44. *Journal*, 9 mai 1867.

45. *Journal*, 27 octobre 1856, éd. Bouvier, p. 116.

46. *Journal*, 23 avril 1871, éd. Bouvier, p. 283.

47. *Journal*, 27 octobre 1856, *op. cit.*

48. *Cours d'anthropologie*, 15 mars 1856.

49. *Journal*, 25 février 1871.

50. *Journal*, 19 juin 1872, éd. Bouvier, p. 295.

51. *Journal*, 6 septembre 1877.

52. *Journal*, 17 mai 1870.

53. *Journal*, 7 avril 1869.

54. *Cours d'anthropologie*, Aide-mémoire, 26 mars 1854.

55. *Délibérations sur les femmes*, éd. L. Bopp, Stock, 1954.

56. *Délibérations sur les femmes*, p. 74.

57. *Schriften*, éd. P. Kluckhohn, Bd. 2, 375: "*Im Ich—im Freiheitspunkte sind wir alle in der Tat völlig identisch—von da aus trennt sich erst jedes Individuum. Ich ist der absolute Gesamtplatz—der Zentralpunkt.*"

58. *Journal*, 19 septembre 1864.—Le livre d'Oken auquel Amiel se réfère est

Lehrbuch der Naturphilosophie, Iéna, 1809, voir surtout N°s 19, 20, 24, 25, 26, 30, 32, 101.

59. *Journal,* 1er septembre 1869.

60. *Journal,* 25 juin 1856.

61. *Journal,* 15 juin 1851.

62. *Journal,* 13 mai 1872.

63. *Journal,* couverture du 2e Cahier (1848) cité par Bouvier dans son édition du *Journal,* Introd., p. 18.

64. *Journal,* 21 septembre 1864.

65. *Grains de mil,* p. 190.

66. *Journal,* 9 août 1864.

67. *Journal,* 3 février 1862, éd. Bouvier, p. 153.

68. *Journal,* 8 mars 1868, éd. Bouvier, p. 209: "Cette faculté de métamorphose ascendante et descendante, de *déplication* et de *réimplication* a stupéfié parfois mes amis . . ."

69. *Journal,* 3 février 1862, *op. cit.*

70. *Journal,* 30 juillet 1863.

71. *Journal,* 29 novembre 1851.

72. *Journal,* 16 novembre 1852, éd. Bouvier, p. 80.

73. *Journal,* 24 mars 1853.

74. *Journal,* 31 août 1856, éd. Bouvier, p. 115.

75. *Journal,* 31 octobre 1880, éd. Bouvier, p. 491.

76. *Journal,* 8 août 1876, éd. Bouvier, p. 378.

77. *Journal,* 2 novembre 1860, *Philine,* éd. Bouvier, p. 109.

78. *Journal,* 20 novembre 1865.

79. *Journal,* 31 mai 1880, éd. Bouvier, p. 467.

80. *Lettre à Charles Heim,* 13 octobre 1845.

81. *Aphorismes* (feuilles volantes), novembre 1848.

82. *Journal,* 26 décembre 1852.

83. *Cours d'anthropologie,* chap. IV.

84. *Maximes et directions* (carnet), 28 avril 1861.

85. *Journal,* 27 novembre 1861.

86. *La Part du rêve,* p. 58.

87. *Journal,* 29 avril 1852, éd. Bouvier, p. 69.

88. *Journal,* 2 avril 1851, éd. Bouvier, p. 55.

89. *Journal,* 12 janvier 1867.

90. *Journal,* 11 janvier 1865.

91. *Journal,* 18 mars 1856.

92. *Journal,* 18 mars 1851.

93. *Journal,* 13 mars 1872.

94. *Journal,* 13 mars 1872.

95. *Journal,* 9 décembre 1859.

96. *Journal,* 20 janvier 1857.

97. *Journal,* 12 janvier 1852.

98. *Grains de mil,* pp. 112–113.

99. *Journal,* 7 janvier 1866, *Journal intime de l'année 1866,* p. 47.
100. *Journal,* 19 mars 1868, éd. Bouvier, p. 211.
101. *Journal,* 30 avril 1851.
102. *Journal,* 23 janvier 1867.
103. *Grains de mil,* p. 160.
104. *Journal,* 4 août 1872.
105. *Journal,* 12 octobre 1853.
106. *Journal,* 12 juillet 1854.
107. *Journal,* 30 mai 1852.
108. *Journal,* 3 juillet 1865.
109. *Journal,* 26 juin 1872.
110. *Journal,* 7 août 1863, éd. Bouvier, p. 165.
111. *Journal,* 1er avril 1851.
112. *Journal,* 5 mai 1867.
113. *Journal,* 29 juin 1867.
114. *Journal,* 6 janvier 1862.
115. *Journal,* 6 janvier 1862.
116. *Journal,* 2 septembre 1863, éd. Bouvier, p. 166.
117. *Journal,* 1er juillet 1860.
118. *Journal,* 31 mars 1874.
119. *Journal,* 26 août 1880.
120. *Journal,* 25 mars 1870.
121. *Journal,* 28 novembre 1861.
122. *Journal,* 26 juillet 1856.
123. *Journal,* 26 mars 1856.
124. *Journal,* 27 mai 1866, *Journal intime de l'année 1866,* p. 297.
125. *Journal,* 12 mai 1860.
126. *Journal,* 16 octobre 1873.
127. *Journal,* 6 février 1867.
128. *Journal,* 26 septembre 1866, *Journal intime de l'année 1866,* p. 464.
129. *Journal,* 11 août 1853.
130. *Journal,* 22 janvier 1866, *Journal intime de l'année 1866,* p. 89.
131. *Journal,* 18 novembre 1872.
132. *Journal,* 21 novembre 1864.
133. *Journal,* 23 août 1863.
134. *Journal,* 5 juillet 1862.
135. *Journal,* 6 avril 1851.
136. *Journal,* 21 octobre 1873.
137. *Journal,* 28 novembre 1872, éd. Bouvier, p. 304.
138. *Journal,* 27 novembre 1861.
139. *Journal,* 26 mai 1857.
140. *Journal,* 16 novembre 1864, éd. Bouvier, p. 175.
141. *Journal,* 21 janvier 1866, éd. Bouvier, p. 188.
142. BRUNSCHVICG, *Le Progrès de la conscience dans la philosophie occidentale,* 2

vol., 1927, t. II, p. 658: "L'éternité à laquelle Amiel aboutit est bien plutôt, pour reprendre les expressions de M. Bergson, une éternité de mort qu'une éternité de vie."

143. *Journal*, 10 janvier 1881.

144. *Journal*, 7 avril 1867.

145. Passage non daté situé à la fin du tome I de l'édition Scherer.

146. *Journal*, 28 novembre 1872, éd. Bouvier, p. 304.

147. *Journal*, 26 septembre 1860; *Philine*, p. 82.

148. *Journal*, 2 octobre 1865.

149. *Lettre à Félix Bovet*, 30 décembre 1868, et *Journal*, 23 mai 1875.

150. *Journal*, 21 novembre 1869.

151. *Journal*, 12 février 1871.

152. *Journal*, 5 janvier 1877, éd. Bouvier, p. 390.

153. *Journal*, 15 mars 1853.—Le thème sera constamment repris et associé au conte de Poe, *le Puits et le Pendule*. Cf., par exemple, *Journal* du 15 février 1863: "L'isolement, la maladie et la décrépitude resserrent leur cercle fatal, et comme dans *le Puits et le Pendule* de Poe, au centre du cercle est le gouffre où il faut inévitablement se jeter . . ."

154. *Journal*, 20 juillet 1876.

155. *Journal*, 12 juillet 1876, éd. Bouvier, p. 371.

CHAPTER XIII—NOTES

1. Erich AUERBACH, *Mimesis, The Representation of Reality in Western Literature*, Princeton, 1953, pp. 482–491.

2. *Madame Bovary*, édition définitive, Conard, p. 91.

3. *Madame Bovary, ébauches et fragments inédits*, Conard, 2 vol. t. I, p. 193.

4. *Œuvres de jeunesse*, Conard, t. II, p. 95.

5. *Œuvres de jeunesse*, p. 192.

6. *Corr.*, Conard, t. II, p. 41.

7. *Corr.*, t. IV, p. 252.

8. *Trois contes*, Conard, p. 48.

9. *Trois contes*, p. 108.

10. *Madame Bovary, ébauches et fragments*, t. I, p. 268.

11. Cf. *La Distance intérieure*, pp. 320–323.

12. Ceci rappelle le titre du livre déjà cité de Marjorie HOPE NICHOLSON, *The Breaking of the circle*, Northwestern U., 1950.

13. *Madame Bovary*, éd. déf., p. 73.

14. *Madame Bovary*, nouvelle version, éd. Pommier-Leleu, Corti, 1949, p. 50.

15. *Madame Bovary, ébauches et fragments*, t. I, p. 253.

16. *Madame Bovary*, éd. déf., p. 81.

17. *Madame Bovary, ébauches et fragments*, t. I, p. 256.

18. *Corr.*, t. III, p. 308.

19. *Madame Bovary, ébauches et fragments*, t. I, p. 433.

20. *Œuvres de jeunesse*, t. I, p. 27.

21. *Tentation de saint Antoine*, Conard, p. 414.
22. *La Tentation de saint Antoine*, p. 333.
23. *Id.*, p. 418.
24. *Corr.*, t. II, p. 371.
25. *Corr.*, supplément, t. I, p. 100.
26. *Œuvres de jeunesse*, t. I, p. 528.
27. *La Tentation de saint Antoine*, p. 255.
28. *La Tentation de saint Antoine*, p. 255.
29. E. W. FISCHER, *Études sur Flaubert inédit*, Leipzig, 1908, p. 128.
30. *Corr.*, t. II, p. 373.
31. *Corr.*, t. III, p. 139.
32. *Id.*, t. III, p. 289.
33. Maxime DU CAMP, *Souvenirs littéraires*, Hachette, 1906, t. I, p. 316.
34. *La Tentation de saint Antoine*, p. 250.
35. *Corr.*, t. IV, p. 180.
36. *Madame Bovary*, éd. déf., p. 432.
37. *Par les champs et par les grèves*, Conard, p. 103.
38. *Œuvres de jeunesse*, t. III, p. 57.
39. *Madame Bovary, ébauches et fragments*, t. II, p. 256.
40. *Madame Bovary, ébauches et fragments*, p. 108.
41. *Id.*, p. 272.
42. *Corr.*, t. III, p. 27.
43. *Madame Bovary, ébauches et fragments*, t. I, p. 488.
44. Charles DU BOS, *Approximations*, t. I, p. 178.
45. *Corr.*, t. VIII, p. 224.
46. *La Tentation de saint Antoine*, p. 603.
47. *La Tentation de saint Antoine*, p. 523.
48. *Id.*, p. 600.
49. *L'Éducation sentimentale*, Conard, p. 168.
50. *L'Éducation sentimentale*, p. 229.
51. *Id.*, p. 269.
52. Jean-Pierre RICHARD, *Littérature et Sensation*, Seuil, 1954. C'est la plus belle étude sur Flaubert depuis Du Bos.
53. *L'Éducation sentimentale*, p. 78.
54. Région merveilleusement explorée par Leo Spitzer dans *Milieu and Ambiance*, Philosophy and Phenomenological Research, décembre 1942.
55. *L'Éducation sentimetnale*, p. 97.

CHAPTER XIV—NOTES

1. *Introduction aux Histoires extraordinaires*, Calmann-Lévy, p. 31.
2. *Œuvres*, Pléiade, II, p. 164.
3. *Œuvres*, Pléiade, II, p. 164.
4. II, p. 164.

5. II, p. 331.
6. I, p. 413.
7. II, p. 331.
8. I, p. 38.
9. I, p. 132.
10. I, p. 22.
11. I, p. 249.
12. I, p. 144.
13. I, p. 31.
14. I, p. 132.
15. I, p. 38.
16. I, p. 23.
17. I, p. 430.
18. I, p. 51.
19. I, p. 409.
20. I, p. 42.
21. I, p. 124.
22. I, p. 429.
23. I, p. 61.
24. *Introduction aux Histoires extraordinaires*, p. 27.
25. I, p. 35.
26. I, p. 307.
27. I, p. 49.
28. II, p. 487.
29. I, p. 427.
30. II, p. 488.
31. I, p. 306.
32. II, p. 633.
33. II, p. 634.
34. I, p. 305.
35. I, p. 307.
36. *Introduction aux Histoires extraordinaires*, p. 31.
37. I, p. 305.
38. I, p. 306.
39. II, p. 663.
40. I, p. 262.
41. I, p. 243.
42. I, p. 640.
43. I, p. 23.
44. I, p. 26.
45. II, p. 633.
46. II, p. 68.
47. I, p. 389.
48. II, p. 255.
49. II, p. 642.

50. I, p. 60.
51. I, p. 378.
52. I, p. 100.
53. I, p. 363.
54. I, p. 161.
55. I, p. 144.
56. I, p. 294.
57. I, p. 346.
58. I, p. 265.
59. II, p. 367.
60. II, p. 627.
61. I, p. 379.
62. I, p. 171.
63. I, p. 355.
64. I, p. 390.
65. I, p. 44.
66. I, p. 304.
67. II, p. 691.
68. I, p. 145.
69. I, p. 145.
70. I, p. 357.
71. I, p. 194.
72. I, p. 412.
73. I, p. 160.
74. I, p. 87.
75. I, p. 92.
76. I, p. 362.
77. I, p. 175.
78. I, p. 85.
79. I, p. 400.
80. II, p. 98.
81. I, p. 33.
82. II, p. 98.
83. II, p. 163.
84. I, p. 305.
85. I, p. 638.
86. II, p. 163.
87. II, p. 332.
88. II, p. 647.
89. I, p. 42.
90. I, p. 41.
91. I, p. 382.
92. II, pp. 332–333.
93. II, p. 638.
94. II, p. 492.

95. I, p. 255.
96. I, p. 81.
97. I, p. 467.
98. II, p. 384.
99. Cf. *Blackwood,* mars 1845, vol. LVII, Introduction aux *Suspiria de Profundis.*
100. II, p. 327.

CHAPTER XV—NOTES

1. *Œuvres, complètes,* éd. H. Mondor et Jean Aubry, Pléiade, p. 394.
2. P. 392.
3. P. 396.
4. P. 352.
5. P. 545.
6. *Tribulat Bonhomet, Œuvres,* Mercure, t. III, p. 118.
7. P. 334.
8. P. 393.
9. P. 396.
10. P. 615.
11. P. 434.
12. P. 329.
13. *Fragment d'Igitur, Les Lettres,* 1948, p. 24.
14. P. 380.
15. P. 73.
16. P. 437.
17. P. 857.
18. P. 647.
19. P. 852.

CHAPTER XVI—NOTES

1. *Lettre à Henry James Junior,* novembre 1813, *The Letters of Henry James,* éd. Percy Lubbock, New York, 1920, t. II, p. 347:
   "I have to the last point the instinct and the sense for fusions and inter-relations, for framing and encircling . . ."
2. *Lettre à Grace Norton,* 28 juillet 1883, *op. cit.,* t. I, p. 100: *"Consciousness is an illimitable power . . ."*
3. *Partial Portraits,* MacMillan, p. 388: *"Experience is never limited and it is never complete; it is an immense sensibility, a kind of huge spider-web of the finest silken threads suspended in the chamber of consciousness and catching every air-borne particle in its tissue."*
4. *Partial Portraits,* p. 207: *". . . Life is, immensely, a matter of surface . . ."*
5. *The Ambassadors,* Preface, *Novels and Tales,* New York edition, t. XXI, p. xix: *". . . The terrible fluidity of self-revelation . . ."*

6. *A small Boy and Others*, Macmillan, 1913, p. 73: "*My brother professed amazement, and even occasionally impatience, at my reach of reminiscence . . .*"

7. *A small Boy and Others*, pp. 2–3: "*(I found) discrimination among the parts of my subject again and again difficult—so inseparably and beautifully they seemed to hang together . . . This meant that aspects began to multiply and images to swarm . . . To knock at the door of the past was in a word to see it open to me quite wide . . .*"

8. *Id.*, p. 242: "*I lose myself, of a truth, under the whole pressure of the spring of memory . . .*"

9. *Essays in London and elsewhere*, New York, 1893, p. 300: "*. . . We are weaving our work together, and it goes on for ever, and it's all one mighty loom . . . And the tissue grows and grows, and we weave into it all our lights and our darkness, all our quarrels and reconciliations, all our stupidities and our strivings, all the friction of our intercourse, and all the elements of our fate. The tangle may seem great at times, but it is all an immeasurable pattern, a spreading many-coloured figure.*"

10. *The Awkward Age*, Preface, *Novels and Tales*, t. IX, p. VIII: "*Though the relations of a human figure or a social occurrence are what make such objects interesting, they also make them, to the same tune, difficult to isolate, to surround with the sharp black line, to frame in the square, the circle, the charming oval, that helps any arrangement of objects to become a picture.*"

11. *Roderick Hudson*, Preface, *Novels and Tales*, t. I, p. VIII: "*A young embroiderer of the canvas of life soon began to work* in terror, fairly, of the vast expanse of that surface, *of the boundless number of its distinct perforations for the needle, and of the tendency inherent in his many-coloured flowers and figures to cover and consume as many as possible of the little holes.*"

12. *Roderick Hudson*, p. VII: "*Therefore it is that experience has to organise for convenience and cheer, some system of observation—for fear, in the admirable immensity, of losing its way.*"

13. *Id.*, p. VIII: "*Really, universally, relations stop nowhere, and the exquisite problem of the artist is eternally but to draw, by a geometry of his own, the circle within which they shall happily* appear *to do so.*"

14. *Lettre à Grace Norton*, 28 juillet 1883: "*. . . Something that holds one in one's place, makes it a standpoint in the universe . . .*"

15. *Notes on Novelists*, New York, 1914, p. 395: "*The first thing we do is to cast about for some centre in our field.*"

16. *The Portrait of a Lady*, Preface, *Novels and Tales*, t. III, p. XV: "*Place the centre of the subject in the young woman's own consciousness,*" I said to myself, "*and you get as interesting and as beautiful a difficulty as you could wish.*"

17. *The Spoils of Poynton*, Preface, *Novels and Tales*, t. X, p. XII: "*The real centre, as I say, the citadel of the interest, with the fight waged round it, would have been the felt beauty and value of the prize of battle, the Things, always the splendid Things, placed in the* middle light . . ."

18. *The Spoils of Poynton*, p. XVI: "*My problem has decently to be met—that of establishing for the other persons the vividness of their appearance of comparative stupidity, that of exposing them to the full thick wash of the penumbra surrounding the central light . . .*"

19. *The Ivory Tower*, *Novels and Tales*, t. XXV, p. 340: "*It isn't centrally a drama of fools or vulgarians; it's only circumferentially and surroundedly so.*"

20. *The Ivory Tower*, p. 109: *"That such an hour had its meaning, and that the meaning might be great for him, this of course surged softly in, more and more, from every point of the circle that held him."*

21. *The Wings of the Dove*, Scribner, 1902, t. I, p. 29: *"The sense was constant for her that their relation was as if afloat, like some island of the south, in a great warm sea that made, for every conceivable chance, a margin, an outer sphere of general emotion; and the effect of the occurrence of anything in particular was to make the sea submerge the island, the margin flood the text. The great wave now for a moment swept over."*

22. *Roderick Hudson*, Preface, p. xvi: *"(The novel) remains in equilibrium by having found its centre, the point of command of all the rest. From this centre the subject has been treated, from this centre the interest has spread, and so, whatever else it may do or may not do, the thing has acknowledged* a principle of composition . . ."

23. *A Small Boy and Others*, p. 73: *"The ragbag of memory hung on its nail in my closet, though I learnt with time to control the habit of bringing it forth."*

24. *The Aspern Papers*, Preface: *"I delight in a palpable imaginable* visitable *past—in the nearer distances and the clearer mysteries, the marks and signs of a world we may reach over to as by making a long arm we grasp an object at the other end of our own table."*

25. *The Sense of the Past*, Collins, 1917, p. 47: *". . . To remount the stream of time, really to bathe in its upper and more natural waters . . ."*

26. *The Sense of the Past*, p. 47: *". . . Oddly indifferent to the actual and the possible."*

27. *Id.: "It was when life was framed in death that the picture was really hung up."*

28. *Lettre à Grace Norton*, 5 mars 1907, *Letters*, t. II, p. 69: *"I don't know, and how should I? much about you in detail—but I think I have a kind of instinct of how the sidebrush of the things that I do get in a general way a reverberation of, touches and affects you, and as in one way or another there seems to have been plenty of the stress and strain and pain of life on the circumference (and even some of it at the centre, as it were) of your circle I've not been without feeling (and responding to,) I boldly say, some of your, vibrations."*

29. *The Golden Bowl*, Preface, *Novels and Tales*, t. XXIII, p. v: *"I have already betrayed my preference . . . for 'seeing my story,' through the opportunity and the sensibility of some more or less detached, some not strictly involved, though thoroughly interested and intelligent, witness or reporter, some person who contributes to the case mainly a certain amount of criticism and interpretation of it, . . . a convenient substitute or apologist for the creative power otherwise so veiled and disembodied."*

30. *The Golden Bowl*, t. XXIV, pp. 2–3: *"She had walked round and round it— that was what she felt; she had carried on her existence in the space left her for circulation, a space that sometimes seemed ample and sometimes narrow; looking up all the while at the fair structure that spread itself so amply and rose so high, but never quite making out as yet where she might have entered had she wished."*

31. *The Sacred Fount*, Macmillan, p. 101: *"This was the light in which Mrs. Server, walking alone now, apparently, in the grey wood and pausing at sight of me, showed herself in her clear dress at the end of a vista. It was exactly as if she had been there by the operation of my intelligence . . ."*

32. *The Sacred Fount*, p. 131: *"The perfection of that, enjoyed as we enjoyed it, all made a margin, a series of concentric circles of rose-colour (shimmering away into the pleasant vague of everything else that didn't matter), for the salient little figure of Mrs. Server, still the controlling image for me, the real principle of composition, in this affluence of fine things."*

33. *The Reverberator*, Preface, *Novels and Tales*, t. XIII, p. VII: *". . . The planned rotation of aspects . . ."*

34. *The Portrait of a Lady*, Preface, p. X: *"The house of fiction has in short not one window, but a million . . . At each of them stands a figure . . ."*

35. *The Ivory Tower*, p. 148.

36. *The Awkward Age*, Preface, p. XVI: *". . . I drew on a sheet . . . the neat figure of a circle consisting of a number of small rounds disposed at equal distance about a central object. The central object was my situation, my subject in itself, to which the thing would owe its title, and the small rounds represented so many distinct lamps, as I liked to call them, the function of each of which would be to light with all due intensity one of its aspects."*

CHAPTER XVII—NOTES

1. Paul CLAUDEL et André GIDE, *Correspondance*, p. 91.

2. *Art poétique*, p. 95.

3. *Id.*, p. 105.

4. *Id.*, p. 111.

5. *Id.*, p. 87.

6. *Id.*, p. 70.

7. *Mémoires improvisés*, p. 195.

8. *Cantique des Cantiques*, p. 212.

9. *Mémoires improvisés*, p. 195.

10. *L'Évangile d'Isaïe*, p. 219.

11. *Figures et paraboles*, p. 134.

12. *Art poétique*, p. 95.

13. *Figures et paraboles*, p. 120.

14. *Id.*

15. *L'Épée et le Miroir*, p. 44.

16. *Cantique des Cantiques*, p. 319.

17. *Art poétique*, p. 106.

18. *Présence et Prophétie*, p. 84.

19. *Art poétique*, p. 106.

20. *Cantique des Cantiques*, p. 186.

21. *Théâtre*, I, p. 120.

22. *Mémoires improvisés*, p. 337.

23. *L'Oiseau noir dans le soleil levant*, p. 213.

24. *Le soulier de satin*, II, p. 224.

25. *Cinq grandes odes*, p. 141.

26. *Discours et remerciements*, p. 119.

27. *Le soulier de satin*, II, p. 224.

28. *Cantique des Cantiques*, p. 401.

29. *Cinq grandes odes*, p .48.

30. *Correspondance avec Jacques Rivière*, p. 61.

31. *Art poétique*, p. 130.

32. *Id.*, p. 100.

33. *Correspondance avec Jacques Rivière*, p. 61.

34. *Art poétique*, p. 81.

35. *Paul Claudel interroge l'Apocalypse*, p. 267.

36. *Art poétique*, p. 95.

37. *Mémoires improvisés*, p. 195.

38. *L'Épée et le Miroir*, p. 192.

39. *Conversations dans le Loir-et-Cher*, p. 115.

40. *Cantiques des Cantiques*, p. 339.

41. *Id.*, p. 283.

42. *Art poétique*, p. 112.

43. *Cantique des Cantiques*, p. 348.

44. *Mémoires improvisés*, p. 38.

45. *Cinq grandes odes*, p. 105.

46. *Ode jubilaire . . .*, p. 11.

47. *Discours et remerciements*, p. 12.

48. *Positions et proposiitons*, I, p. 165.

49. *Connaissance de l'Est*, p. 77.

50. *L'Annonce faite à Marie*, p. 205.

51. *Art poétique*, pp. 9–11.

52. *Connaissance de l'Est*, p. 228.

53. *Trois figures saintes*, p. 25.

54. *Art poétique*, p. 48.

55. *L'Épée et le Miroir*, p. 192.

56. *Mémoires improvisés*, p. 131.

57. *Art poétique*, p. 181.

58. *Id.*, p. 80.

59. *Id.*, p. 52.

60. *Mémoires improvisés*, p. 128.

61. *Cantique des Cantiques*, p. 299.

62. *Un poète regarde la Croix*, p. 12.

63. *Trois figures saintes*, p. 27.

64. *Cantique des Cantiques*, p. 88.

65. *Discours et remerciements*, p. 61.

66. *Conversations dans le Loir-et-Cher*, p. 163.

67. *Mémoires improvisés*, p. 132.

68. *Positions et propositions*, II, p. 9.

69. *Cantate à trois voix*, p. 23.

70. *L'Annonce faite à Marie*, p. 198.

71. *Cantique des Cantiques*, p. 150.

72. *Id.*, p. 391.

73. *Paul Claudel interroge l'Apocalypse,* p. 140.
74. *Cantique des Cantiques,* p. 407.
75. *L'Épée et le Miroir,* p. 43.
76. *Trois figures saintes,* p. 57.
77. *Id.,* p. 126.
78. *Mémoires improvisés,* p. 274.
79. *Trois figures saintes,* p. 115.
80. *Discours et remerciements,* p. 147.
81. *Paul Claudel interroge l'Apocalypse,* p. 10.
82. *Cantique des Cantiques,* p. 317.
83. *Connaissance de l'Est,* p. 104.
84. *Théâtre,* III, p. 144.
85. *Théâtre,* IV, p. 228.
86. *Paul Claudel interroge l'Apocalypse,* p. 146.
87. *Emmaüs,* p. 138.
88. *Les aventures de Sophie,* p. 187.
89. *Art poétique,* p. 146.
90. *Id.,* p. 145.
91. *Id.,* p. 192.

CHAPTER XVIII—NOTES

1.   *Kinderseelen, die noch niemals sangen,—*
        die nur leis in immer weitern Ringen
        zu dem Leben ziehn . . .
Frühe Gedichte, Gesammelte Werke, Inselverlag, Leipzig, 1927, I, p. 264.

2.   *Leben hat Sinn nur verbunden mit vielen*
        Kreisen des weithin wachsenden Raumes . . .
Das Buch der Bilder, Gesammelte Werke, 2, 164.

3.   *Ich lebe mein Leben in wachsenden Ringen*
        die sich über die Dinge ziehn.
Das Stunden-Buch, Gesammelte Werke, 2, 175.

4. *Lettre à Catherine Pozzi,* 7 juillet 1924.

5. *Lettre à Antoinette de Bonstetten,* 1924.

6. *Lettre à Clara Rilke,* 17 décembre 1906: ". . . *da doch meine Welt mit Euch erst so recht ins Namenlose gewachsen ist; damals von jenem kleinen verschneiten Hause, darin Ruth geboren wurde, zu wachsen begann und seither wächst und wächst, von diesem Mittelpunkte fort, auf den ich meine Aufmerksamkeit nicht beschränken kann, solange die Peripherie vorrückt auf allen Seiten, ins Unendliche hinein.*"

7.   *Und selbst im Schlaf. Nichts bindet uns genug.*
        Nachgiebige Mitte in mir, Kern voll Schwäche . . .
Narziss, Gesammelte Werke, 3, 415.

8.   *Seltsam,*
        alles, was sich bezog, so lose im Raume
        flattern zu sehen.
Duineser Elegien 1, Gesammelte Werke, 3, 262.

9. *Lettre à Lou Andreas-Salomé*, 8 août 1903: *"Das Ding ist bestimmt, das Kunst-Ding muss noch bestimmter sein; von allem Zufall fortgenommen, jeder Unklarheit entrückt, der Zeit enthoben und dem Raum gegeben, es ist dauernd geworden, fähig zur Ewigkeit."*

10. *Lettre à Catherine Pozzi*, 21 août 1924.

11. *"Wie gross auch die Bewegung eines Bildwerkes sein mag,*
    sie muss und sei es aus unendlichen Weiten, sei es aus
    der Tiefe des Himmels, sie muss zu ihm zurückkehren,
    der grosse Kreis muss sich schliessen, der Kreis der
    Einsamkeit, in der ein Kunst-Ding seine Tage verbringt."
    Auguste Rodin, Gesammelte Werke, 4, 320–321.

12. *Les Roses, Poèmes français*, Lausanne 1944, p. 143.

13. *Lettre à Clara Rilke*, 19 octobre 1907: *". . . Wir haben im Grunde nur dazu-sein, aber schlicht, aber inständig, wie die Erde da ist, den Jahreszeiten zustimmend, hell und dunkel und ganz im Raum . . ."*

14. *Lettre à un travailleur.*

15. *"Gegengewicht,*
    in dem ich mich rhythmisch ereigne."
    Die Sonette an Orpheus, Gesammelte Werke, 3, 341.

16. *Lettre à Lou Andreas-Salomé*, 8 août 1903: *"Er wollte, dass sie sei, und sah seine Aufgabe darin, Dinge (denn Dinge dauerten) in die weniger bedrohte, ruhigere und ewigere Welt des Raumes zu passen; und et wandte an sein Werk unbewusst alle Gesetze der Anpassung an, so dass es organisch sich entfaltete und lebensähig wurde."*

17. "In flickering intervals of light and darkness," *The Family Reunion, The Complete Poems and Plays*, Harcourt, New York, 1952, p. 250.

18. *Only a flicker*
    Over the strained time-ridden faces
    Distracted from distraction by distraction
    Filled with fancies and empty of meaning
    Tumid apathy with no concentration
    Men and bits of paper, whirled by the cold wind
    That blows before and after time . . .
    Burnt Norton, The Complete Poems and Plays, p. 120.

19. *In and out, in an endless drift*
    Of shrieking forms in a circular dessert . . .
    The Family Reunion, The Complete Poems and Plays, p. 277.

20. *The sudden solitude in a crowded desert*
    In a thick smoke, many creatures moving
    Without direction, for no direction
    Leads anywhere but round and round in that vapour . . .
    The Family Reunion, The Complete Poems and Plays, p. 250.

21. *"The leap of one fish, at a particular place and time, the scent of one flower, an old woman on a German mountain path, six ruffians seen through an open window playing cards at night at a small French railway junction . . ."—The Use of Poetry and the Use of Criticism*, Faber, London, 1933, p. 148.

22. *"A sudden illumination"—The Complete Poems and Plays*, p. 133.

23. *"There is a first, or an early moment which is unique, of shock and surprise, even of terror (Ego dominus tuus): a moment which can never be for gotten . . ."—Dante*, Faber, London, 1929, p. 33.

24. "Partial ecstasy."—Burnt Norton, *The Complete Poems and Plays*, p. 119.

25.   *Because I do not hope to know again*
        The infirm glory of the positive hour . . .
Ash-Wednesday, *The Complete Poems and Plays*, p. 60.

26.   *Not the intense moment*
        Isolated, with no before and after,
        But a lifetime burning in every moment . . .
East Coker, *The Complete Poems and Plays*, p. 129.

27. "How can we be concerned with the past and not with the future? or with the future and not with the past?"—*The Complete Poems and Plays*, p. 259.

28. "In my beginning is my end . . . In my end is my beginning."—East Coker, *The Complete Poems and Plays*, pp. 123 and 129.

29. "And the way up is the way down, the way forward is the way back."—*The Dry Salvages*, *The Complete Poems and Plays*, p. 133.

30.   *O perpetual revolution of configured stars,*
        O perpetual recurrence of determined seasons . . .
Chorus from "The Rock."

31.   *"At the still point of the turning world."*
Burnt Norton, *The Complete Poems and Plays*, pp. 118 and 120.

32.   *And all shall be well and*
        All manner of thing shall be well
        When the tongues of flame are in-folded
        Into the crowned knot of fire
        And the fire and the rose are one.
Little Gidding, *The Complete Poems and Plays*, p. 145.

33.   *Against the World the unstilled world still whirled*
        About the centre of the silent word.
Ash-Wednesday.

34.   *. . . that the wheel may turn and still*
        Be forever still.
Murder in the Cathedral.

35.   *"It is out of time that my decision is taken."*
Murder in the Cathedral.

36.   *"At the still point of the turning world." Op. cit.*

37. *The Complete Poems and Plays*, p. 64.

38. *Ibid.*, p. 119.

39. *Ibid.*, p. 145.

40.   *Queda curvo el firmamento,*
        Compacto azul, sobre el día.
        Es el redondeamiento
        Del esplendor: mediodía.
        Todo es cúpula . . .

41. *Cántico*, Mexico, 1945, p. 189.
        Y a los rayos del sol,
        Evidentes, se ciñe
        La ciudad esencial.
    P. 124.

42.   *Todo es cúpula. Reposa,*
        Central sin querer, la rosa,
        A un sol en cenit sujeta.
    P. 189.

43.
>Con su creación el aire
>Me cerca. Divino cerco!
>A una creación continua
>—Soy del aire—me someto.

P. 383.

44.
>Con la luz me perfecciono.
>Yo soy merced a la hermosa
>Revelación: este Globo.
>Se redondea una gana
>Sin ocasos . . .

P. 393.

45.
>Era yo,
>Centro en aquel instante
>De tanto alrededor,
>Quien lo veía todo
>Completo para un dios.

P. 375.

46.
>"Oh concentración prodigiosa!"

P. 274.

47.
>. . . el presente ocupa y fija el centro
>De tanta inmensidad así concreta.

P. 133.

THE METAMORPHOSES
OF THE CIRCLE

BY GEORGES POULET
translated from the French by Carley Dawson
and Elliott Coleman in collaboration with the author

designer:	Edward King
typesetter:	The Maple Press Company
typefaces:	Baskerville
printer:	The Maple Press Company
paper:	Mohawk Tosca Book
binder:	The Maple Press Company
cover material:	Columbia Fictionette Natural Finish